14 Secrets to Developing the Dog You Want

Kyra Sundance

A Fireside Book
Published by Simon & Schuster
New York London Toronto Sydney

Fireside
A Division of Simon & Schuster, Inc.
1230 Avenue of the Americas
New York, NY 10020

First Fireside hardcover edition March 2009

For information about special discounts for bulk purchases, please contact Simon & Schuster Special Sales at 1-800-456-6798 or business@simonandschuster.com.

Designed by Ruth Lee-Mui

Manufactured in the United States of America

10 9 8 7 6 5 4 3 2 1

Library of Congress Cataloging-in-Publication Data

Sundance, Kyra.
The dog rules: 14 secrets to developing the dog you want/Kyra Sundance.
p. cm.
Includes bibliographical references.
1. Dogs—Training. 2. Human-animal relationships.
I. Title.
SF431.S864 2009
636.7'0887—dc22 2008020829

ISBN-13: 978-1-4165-8866-5
ISBN-10: 1-4165-8865-5

To all the great dogs out there who just need a chance to shine

WHETHER HE'S YOUNG OR OLD, ATHLETIC OR LAZY,
QUICK-WITTED OR DUMB AS A ROCK—
HE'S YOUR DOG AND HIS SUCCESS
NEED ONLY BE MEASURED IN YOUR EYES.

I HOPE THIS BOOK INSPIRES YOU TO
"DO MORE WITH YOUR DOG!"

—KYRA SUNDANCE

Acknowledgments

This book is the fruit of my experiences and of the education and support I have received from many people, and it is important to me that I give credit to those who have had a role in its creation, in my dog training career, and in my life.

First among them are the dog sports trainers and coaches who have mentored and guided me. Shirley Indelicato is an AKC Obedience judge and a rare breed of trainer who acknowledges that there is more than one correct way to train a dog. Jimmy Rice, my hunting coach, taught me to "man-up." Carole Kelly, fellow member of my High Desert Obedience Club, always encouraged me to follow my gut in doing what is in the best interest of my dog. Both Kate Moureaux and Terry Simons are world-class agility instructors whose insight and demeanor have made them a pleasure to learn from. Lou Mack, former head trainer of the Purina Incredible Dog Team, gave me my first Frisbee, as well as advice on "looking cool" during a show. (Hey, I learn from the best!) Nichole Royer introduced me to the exhilarating sport of dogsledding.

Lana Maeder (of Busy Bee Dogs) is a fellow performer who will talk endlessly with me about dogs, props, routines, and the challenges of live shows. Claire Doré is a movie-animal trainer and a great friend. She and her smart dogs have helped with several of my projects. Rob Bloch (Critters of the Cinema) and Gloria Winship (Animal Actors) have put their trust in me as a movie-dog trainer. Alex Rothacker (TOPS Canine Officer Training Programs) has shown me that even big, tough police dog trainers can turn to mush with the love of a dog. Thanks to Bill Langworthy, a producer with Animal Planet's *Pet Star*

TV show, who gave me and many other pet owners the chance to show off our animals' unique talents.

Nannette Klatt and her guide dog Flame are an inspiration in their commitment to each other, and have been kind enough to allow me to share their story in this book. I wish Nannette well with her new guide dog breeding facility. And thanks to the other animal trainers who allowed me to share their stories in this book: Priscilla Valentine (Valentine's Performing Pigs); John Baldwin, chimpanzee trainer; Adam Berman (Le PAWS movie-dog agency); David Hartwig and his performing dog Skidboot; Karen Quest from the Bermuda Animal Extravaganza Circus; Kay Rosaire and her animals and trainers from Big Cat Habitat and Gulf Coast Sanctuary; Kathy Sdao (Bright Spot Dog Training); and His Majesty Mohammed VI, King of Morocco.

Thanks to Vicki Ruiz and Joan Valdez, whose commitment to responsible breeding resulted in my wonderful Weimaraner puppy. Dave Gantenbein, DVM (Antelope Valley Animal Hospital), and wife, Janice, have gone beyond the call of duty, both as friends and in providing veterinary care for my pets. They have more than once made house calls or opened up the hospital after hours for my dog.

Cesar Millan, the Dog Whisperer, who is as personable and talented as you'd expect from seeing him on his TV show, gives us a great example of "calm assertive energy," which comes from a place of kindness and not harshness.

Thanks to my editor, Sulay Hernandez, and all the folks at Simon & Schuster who trusted in my vision and allowed me the freedom to write the book I always wanted to write.

I wish to thank my father, Ted Horn (now deceased), and my mother, Heidi Horn, for having taught me the virtues of a good work ethic and self-reliance. Thanks to my brother, Deric Horn, for procreating, so that I can get away with merely offering a "granddog."

My deep and sincere thanks to Chalcy, who has, with little more than the occasional nudge in my back with her toy Bumper, allowed me to stare for countless hours at this silly screen instead of doing much more important things, like lizard chasing, cat harassing, and Bumper throwing.

And most of all, I need to thank my wonderful husband, Randy Banis, who never bargained for all this dog craziness when he married me. (He's really more of a cat person.) Much of what I know about a great relationship with my dog I have learned from Randy. I couldn't imagine a better husband. Thank you.

Contents

ONE CAN MAKE A DIFFERENCE
ONE
www.purinaone.com

Introduction

There are rules! There are actual rules! Whether you're frustrated trying to get through to your dog, or whether you're training competition-level precision, there are definable rules that will get you to your goal. And they work!

The Dog Rules does not suppress behavior and teach subservience. *The Dog Rules* develops joyful relationships with dogs who balance enthusiasm and self-control. It fosters confident, happy dogs who are motivated to do the right thing rather than fearful of making a mistake. It inspires dogs to listen to us and work with us as a team, trusting in our leadership and recognizing the need to respond appropriately.

Too often, dog owners live in a war zone of battling bad behavior after bad behavior. The training we do to correct each behavioral issue is like laying an individual brick of a structure. But bricks are laid upon a foundation, and if the foundation is weak, the entire structure will be weak. By cultivating a foundation of a loving, trusting, and respectful relationship, we develop our dog's motivation to be our willing partner. This is the solid foundation upon which real training can stand.

The Rules Empower You with a Clear Strategy

When we become frustrated and angry with our dog, it's not because our dog is being bad. And it's not because our dog is being stubborn, and it's not because our dog is being stupid. Frustration and anger happen when we don't know what to do—when we've tried everything we can think of, and none of it has worked. We feel mired in despair and guilt. This is an awful feeling for a dog owner.

But we don't have to go down that path of frustration and anger. When we have rules, we have a strategy to follow and the conviction to follow it. *The Dog Rules* empowers you with this strategy and the tools and knowledge to implement it.

At the end of a class sit-stay exercise, I correct one of my students who had just rewarded his dog *after* the dog had gotten up from his stay. "Do you realize you've just rewarded your dog for standing up?" I asked. "Giving him the treat after he's gotten up will cause him to think that standing up during a sit-stay will get him a treat. The rule is: Reward your dog *while* he's in the correct position."

"Oh!" said my student in surprise. "Of course! That makes perfect sense. I wish somebody had told me that years ago!"

That epiphany changed everything for this student. How many times had he rewarded his dog for the wrong thing? What was the dog doing at the exact moment the student had given the reward? Once the student understood the rule, he knew how to reward his dog correctly not just during a sit-stay, but in every situation. Understand the rule set, and details will take care of themselves.

The Dog Rules uses tried-and-true behavior modification concepts that don't involve intimidation or escalating corrections. With principles such as *"Focus on the solution, not the problem," "One command, one consequence,"* and *"Praise, touch, treat—in that order,"* you'll have the rule set to navigate any training challenge.

The Dog Rules answers questions such as

- Why should we always reward our dog with praise, touch, treat—in that order?
- How do we focus on the solution rather than the problem?
- How are "horse whisperers" able to achieve with gentleness what traditional trainers were able to achieve only with force? And how do we use these same methods with our dog?
- What motivates police dogs and Search & Rescue dogs to work enthusiastically and without treats?
- How do we teach our dog to manage his frustration?

- When should we use our dog's name ("Buster, heel") and when should we not ("Stay")?
- What does a dog's blink, yawn, or lip lick tell us?
- How do we "hypnotize" a dog with our eyes?

A Whole Dog Approach

Traditional animal training uses sterile operant conditioning principles of reward and punishment. In this type of training the animal is not working for the trainer, but rather he is working for himself. The animal works to gain pleasure and works to avoid pain. This is a one-sided relationship where the trainer invites no input from the animal and makes no compromises.

But successful dog trainers today recognize that our dogs have the capacity for communication, affection, and regard, and treating them like a rat in a Skinner box is short-changing them. *The Dog Rules* looks beyond sterile training methods that manipulate a dog solely through reward and punishment, and instead takes a "whole-dog" approach that recognizes the broad spectrum of your relationship with your dog. At the core of the whole-dog approach are the five pillars of the successful dog/owner relationship.

- Encourage trust
- Instill a desire to please
- Teach behavior
- Expect respect
- Build the bond

When we train the whole dog, we look at training not as something that happens during a specified session, or when a particular problem arises, but rather as something that occurs with every interaction with your dog—every look, every communication, and every consequence.

A whole dog approach thrives on mutual communication, and your dog is encouraged to express his intentions and desires to you in appropriate ways, such as by ringing a bell on the doorknob when he wants to go out, or bringing you his leash when he wants a walk. We empower our dog to think and to make choices—choices based on his understanding the consequences of his actions. We put our dog on the path to becoming confident, communicative, and eager to please.

Your Dog Doesn't Need *More* Training. Your Dog Needs *Better* Training.

Have you ever had a coach or a teacher try to teach you something that you weren't getting? And they kept repeating the same instruction to you over and over? You didn't need *more* instruction. You needed *better* instruction.

If you're having the same problem with your dog over and over, then the training method you're using isn't working. It sounds obvious, but it is a trap that all too many trainers fall into. Spending more time training with a flawed method isn't going to get the results you want. *The Dog Rules* isn't about doing more training with your dog. *The Dog Rules* is about doing better training.

Developing the Dog You Want

I take my Weimaraner Chalcy with me wherever I go, and I spend a lot of time talking to her and interacting with her. This has contributed to our extremely close relationship. But it has also resulted in her becoming extremely fixated on me, following me from room to room, choosing my company over that of other people or dogs. Over the years, I've had various people try to tell me that Chalcy is *too* fixated on me and that I should fix this "problem" in my dog. My response is always the same: "I realize that this is not the dog *you* want, but this is the dog *I* want."

The Dog Rules isn't going to define ideal dog behavior. It's not going to tell you that your dog shouldn't sleep on your bed, or shouldn't jump on you when you come home, or shouldn't pull on his leash. How you want your dog molded is up to you—*The Dog Rules* will show you how to do it.

How I Use the Rules

"Are you her other half?" an audience member asks my husband after Chalcy and I finish our Stunt Dog show. Randy answers with a grin, "I'm her other third!"

I am a professional Stunt Dog Trainer and performer, a movie-dog trainer, and a dog sports competitor. But most of all I am best friend and partner to my joy, to my dog.

Chalcy is my once-in-a-lifetime dog; those of you fortunate enough to have had one know what I'm talking about. She and I have that rare connection which allows us to function almost effortlessly as a team.

I began training Chalcy when she was only eight weeks old, and we soon became heavily engaged in dog sport competition, training in Obedience, Agility, Hunting, Retrieving, Versatility, Tracking, Dog Sledding, Dock Diving, Flyball, Dog Dancing, and Disc Dog. Chalcy earned many competition titles and competed at the elite level to earn nationwide ranking in several of the sports.

We weren't so focused on competition, however, that we didn't take time for silly dog tricks! Chalcy learned over one hundred tricks, including answering the phone, tidying up toys into her toy box, turning off the light, bringing me a soda from the fridge, playing basketball, rolling on a barrel, jumping rope, covering her eyes with her paw, and getting the mail from the mailbox. I put these training techniques on paper and wrote the industry-standard dog-tricks book, *101 Dog Tricks: Step-by-Step Activities to Engage, Challenge, and Bond with Your Dog.*

With Chalcy's athleticism and my gymnastics background, we collaborated on a precision acrobatics routine that I termed "dogrobatics." Relying heavily upon teamwork and trust, we execute passes of synchronized tumbling stunts and body vaults. Chalcy jumps over me as I do a dive roll, or through my legs as they extend in a handstand. Chalcy and I went on to become one of the nation's premier professional Stunt Dog Teams, performing this high-energy routine at professional sporting event halftime shows for the NBA, MLB, and AFL.

We've performed on some of the world's premier stages. We were honored to star in a command performance for the king of Morocco at his royal palace in Marrakech. We starred in Disney's *Underdog* stage show production in Hollywood. We performed on *The Tonight Show, Ellen, Entertainment Tonight, FOX News Live, Best Damn Sports Show Period, Animal Planet,* and *MTV.*

But Chalcy is first and foremost a family member and my best friend. We train and perform together not for the money or the acclaim, but for the joy of working together. The compliment I receive most frequently, and the one I cherish the most, is when people say, "It's obvious what a close bond you have with each other."

Chalcy's admirable work ethic is not something that has been achieved merely with treats. It is truly a testament to her commitment to our relationship, and something that touches my heart deeply.

This is the type of motivation we want. *The Dog Rules* is the path to progressing to the highest levels of training, and the path to developing a reliable canine partner who is a true member of your family.

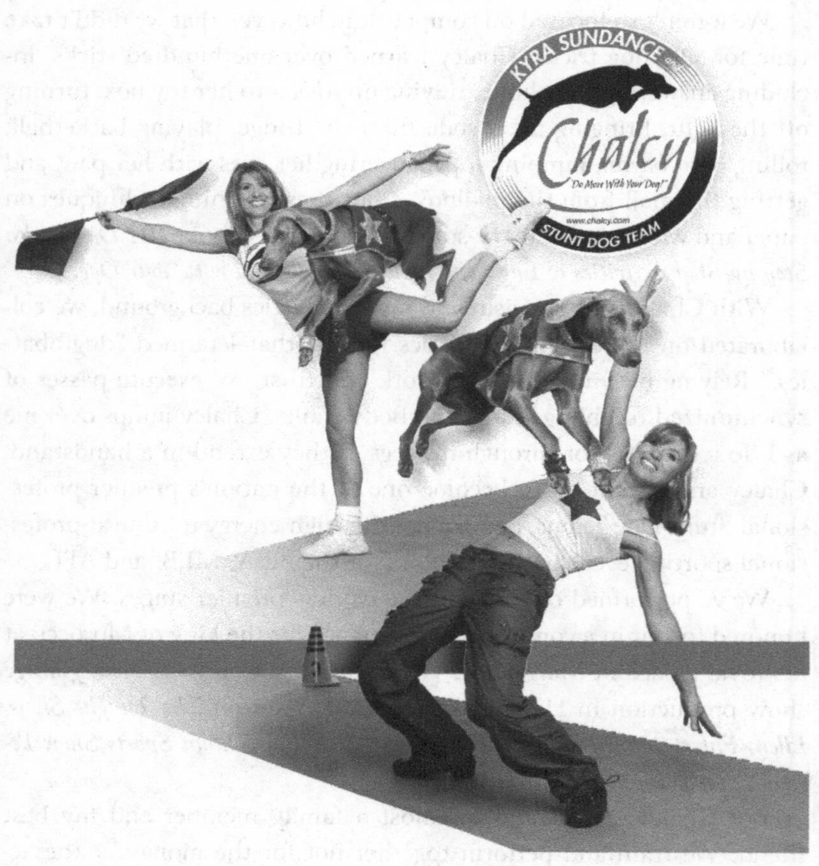

You Owe These Things to Your Dog

Our dogs play a significant role in our lives, whether as working dogs or as companions. We've taken them into our households, and we are responsible for fulfilling their needs. For all the joy and companionship your dog gives you, you owe your dog the following:

- Adequate food and medical care
- A life that goes beyond mere survival
- Grooming, ear and teeth cleaning, nail trimming, skin and coat conditioning
- Exercise—not only the option for exercise, but also the encouragement
- Twenty minutes of your undivided attention each day
- Three enrichment activities a day (a walk, a game of fetch, a training session, a car ride)
- Exposure to the world beyond your fence
- Socialization with people and dogs outside your family
- The right to give and receive unconditional love
- Training, so that your dog does not become a prisoner of his own misbehavior
- Fresh air and green grass
- Respect for your dog's needs and wants
- Responsible breeding, or none at all
- Time and space all his own
- The freedom to be foolish and silly, and to make you laugh
- The right to earn your trust and to be trusted in return
- Forgiveness
- The right to die with dignity
- The honor of being remembered well

Your Dog Owes These Things to You

You provide your dog with a lot: good food, a nice home, medical attention, and safety and security. It's not asking too much to require the following from him:

- Come when called.
- Obey house rules.
- Respect me and my family members.
- Don't eat my shoes. (Seriously, you owe me that much!)

Enjoy the Journey

A great relationship with your dog does not necessarily begin when you first bring home a puppy, or when you first sign up for a training class or first discipline your dog. A great relationship begins the day you make up your mind to establish a conscious and consistent pattern of relating to your dog in a meaningful partnership based upon trust, communication, and respect.

Great dog/owner relationships are not the result of ambivalent pats on the head, nor even of loving cuddles on the couch. Great relationships are built through work, collaboration, challenge, inspiration, exhilaration in goals met, and consolation in goals missed. They are built through shared experiences, communication, and reliably meeting each other's needs.

Some of this book's readers are pet owners, some are beginners in dog sports, and some are advanced competitors and trainers. Some use their dog as a working partner or service animal, and others merely take pleasure in their dog's companionship.

However your dog fits into your life, there are probably ways you can do more with him—teach him a new sport, find an activity you can enjoy together, work with him, engage him, challenge him, strive for common goals, take him places with you, spend more time with him, and bond more deeply with him. These are the ways great relationships are built.

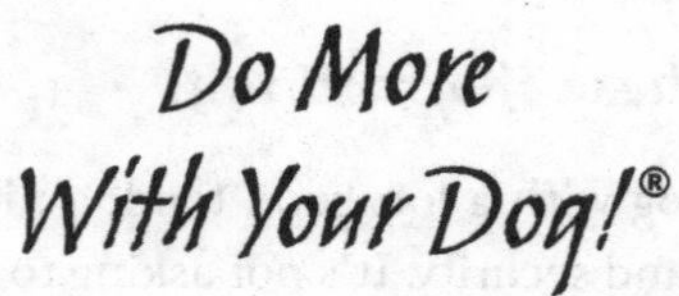

Encourage Trust

Chalcy is an experienced circus dog, and frankly she is less wary of bears and elephants than she is of our cat. So being hired to perform in an "animal extravaganza" circus in Bermuda gave me no particular concern. Little did I know that this circus would test my dog's trust in me to its limit.

When I arrived for rehearsal I was shown to my dressing room by the circus promoter who, in a thick Bermudian accent, informed me that I would be sharing with grizzly bears and "de caw-gahl fa Sa'fasisco who be flyin' in fa de show." Wait . . . did he say call girl? Did he say grizzly bears?

I took Chalcy to the circus tent, where I was bewildered by her fearful behavior. She didn't want to enter the tent, and she startled at every little motion or noise. I carefully guided Chalcy around the tent, attempting to reassure her.

After an hour of largely unsuccessful desensitization, I spoke with the other animal trainers, who unanimously agreed that it was the pungent scent of the tigers from their morning rehearsal that was causing Chalcy's fear. Apparently it is a scent that evokes intense fear in all animals. The monkeys, I was told, would refuse to perform unless considerable care was taken to change the sawdust and keep them away from the tiger area. Great.

I had hoped to keep the tigers hidden from Chalcy, but on the first

show day, minutes before our act, the inevitable happened: Chalcy saw the tigers staging outside the tent.

Desensitization had not worked, avoidance had not worked. The only tool I had left was trust. "Heel!" I said authoritatively. Chalcy skitted to the side, not taking her eyes off the tigers. Once more, "Chalcy,

heel!" and I drew my left wrist to my side, stepping forward with my left foot. Chalcy instinctively stepped alongside me and walked by my side. Chalcy responded, trusting in my leadership as she had always done before, and performed as I asked her to.

It was only through years of developed trust that Chalcy was able to overcome an intense instinctive fear and have confidence in my judgment and ability to keep her safe.

At the end of the circus run I had my picture taken with Chalcy, one of the tigers, and the "caw-gahl." (Who, by the way, turned out to be not a call girl, but rather a trick-roping cowgirl. Who knew!) I laugh at the picture because I am hugging Chalcy—and she is obeying me—yet leaning as far as possible *away* from the tiger. Gotta love her!

The foundation of our relationship with a dog, as with a human being, is based on trust. When your dog trusts you, he believes in your strength and truthfulness and feels safe in following your direction. He believes you know, and will do, what is best for him. Chalcy trusted in my ability to keep her safe and my commitment to doing so, even in the face of an instinctive predator. Without trust, your dog may feel the need to override your decisions and make his own choices.

When we create physical pain in the relationship we lose our dog's trust. Love and fear are opposites, and if your dog fears you, he cannot love and trust you without reservation. Although aversive techniques and fear tactics have traditionally been used in dog training, we have to acknowledge their negative effects on our overall relationship with our dog.

When I misbehaved as a kid, my German-born mother would hold up the wooden cooking spoon and say, "Don't make me use the *Kochlöffel*!" Although that punishment was often threatened, I was probably only ever spanked with the spoon a few times in my life. But to this day I have an aversion to all wooden spoons. This exemplifies the strong impact and long-lasting effects an aversive technique can have.

Some dog trainers advocate teaching a dog to stop jumping on you by grabbing his front paws during a jump and squeezing them to cause a bit of pain. It works. The dog certainly won't want to give you the opportunity to touch his paws again. But the next time you try to trim his nails, he won't want to give you his paw. And when he has a pricker in his foot, he won't want to give you his paw. He no longer trusts you. Was this quick-fix for jumping worth the injury to your relationship? Do you want a dog behaving out of fear, or a dog working for you out of pleasure?

To encourage your dog's trust, do what is in the best interests of your dog, yourself, and your pack. Be dependable, honest, and fair, so that your dog may have confidence in your judgment and abilities. Be consistent and firm in your rules, yet kind and instructional in enforcing them, and not punitive.

Rule 1: Be Honest

"Hey, Buster, if you come over here, I'll give you a cookie! See, good cookie, yum yum! Ha! Fooled you! Now we're going to trim your nails!"

"Go get the stick, Lucy, go get it! Ha! Dumb dog, made you look!"

"Stop being dramatic, Bear, I'm not leaving you. I'm just going out to check the mail. Yeah, that's right . . . I'll be riiiiiiight back." Slam! *Va-rooom, screech.*

Sure, it's sometimes easier to trick our dog into doing what we want, but building trust isn't easy, and dishonesty will surely not get you there. Any of you who have bipedal children may have been tempted at some point to tell your kid that the TV is broken tonight, or the toy store is closed, or the cookie jar is empty. In the short run it's easy, it's quick, it avoids a tantrum. But in the long run it's doing nothing to foster that child's trust. A history of dishonesty will make you less trustworthy in your dog's eyes as well.

THE RULE

The secret to demonstrating your honesty to your dog is in your sincerity (you don't try to fool him), in your predictability, and in your intention to help him be successful. Doing the honest thing is not necessarily the easiest thing.

Be Sincere

A distinguishing feature of human intelligence is the ability to understand the goals and intentions of others. We do not merely imitate another's actions, but can adjust how we imitate them according to the circumstances. Fourteen-month-old human babies, for example, will imitate an adult turning on a light with her forehead only if they see the adult doing it with her hands free. If the adult is clutching a blanket, infants will use their hands to turn on the light, presumably because they can reason that the adult resorted to using her forehead only because her hands were full.

Dogs also seem to possess this ability to understand the intentions of others. In an experiment similar to the human baby–light switch one, a trained dog demonstrated in front of other dogs how she could push a horizontal wooden rod with her paw to get a treat. A dog would generally use its mouth for this task, but most of the dogs who watched the demonstration imitated the trained dog and used their paws. In a second experiment, the trained dog held a ball in her mouth while she demonstrated pushing the rod with her paw. This time most of the dogs who viewed the demonstration used their mouths! The dogs reasoned that the demonstrator dog had used her paw only because she was unable to use her mouth.[1]

Chimpanzees do not use this **selective imitation** but merely mimic, or "ape," an action. Remarkably, dogs *are* able, just like human babies, to actually think about your intention and draw inferences about what you are thinking. Dogs can seemingly put themselves inside the head of another being to make relatively complex decisions.

It is likely that your dog doesn't see your actions as a bunch of coincidences, but is able to put complex actions together to understand your intentions. Your dog is likely able to gauge your sincerity.

To gain your dog's trust, be sincere and predictable and not dishonest or deceitful. Your intentions should be clear and your implied promises kept. Calling your dog while pinching your fingers together and then not giving him the treat you had implied is not an honest trade. I'm not saying you *have* to give your dog a treat for coming, but rather that if you promise it, you need to keep your promise. Your dog should be able to predict the consequence of his action. There are times when your dog will be required to obey a command without a treat, and that's fine—just don't lie to him.

I am honest with my dog, and when I call her to hop in the truck for a ride to the park, she trusts my word. That's because I've never lied to her—I never say we're going to the park when I'm taking her to the vet.

I'm not advocating that you always have to communicate the WHOLE truth to your dog. If you're leaving for work, say a goodbye. Short and sweet is fine, and even recommended, but don't be deceptive and just slip out behind his back. And if you're taking your dog to the vet, don't tell him you're going to the park, but rather don't tell him anything at all.

Perhaps you've been dishonest with your dog in the past by tricking him into the bathtub, and now when you call him he doesn't want to come. A bath is one of those cases where you don't want to *lie* to your dog, but neither do you have to be totally forthcoming. The best way to handle a bath is to go and get your dog rather than call him to you. Be matter-of-fact, and the fewer words used, the better.

Set Your Dog Up for Success

One of the most common infractions of our rule of being honest with our dog is in setting the dog up to make a mistake and then punishing him for it—we leave a sandwich on the coffee table and then punish our dog for taking it. In doing this, you are not trying to help your dog; you are trying to punish your dog. This mind-set of waiting until your dog has done an offending behavior and then punishing him for it is detrimental to the trust you are trying to establish. It may be easier and quicker to smack your dog once for jumping on you, rather than coach him fifty times to sit politely, but smacking him is not doing what's best for him—it's doing what's easiest for you.

Think of it this way: If your spouse is trying to lose weight, do you leave bonbons lying around the house and then criticize him or her for succumbing to the temptation? Wouldn't it be better to set out delicious healthy snacks and praise your spouse for his or her good choices? By doing so, we help our spouse to succeed. We encourage our spouse to trust that our intentions for him or her are good. This not only creates a closer relationship, but is also the more effective way to achieve the goal.

Setting a dog up for failure can manifest as not letting your dog out often enough and then punishing him for pottying in the house, or leaving ballpoint pens lying around when you know he can't resist chewing them.

Practice success, not failure, to create a confident dog who habitually does the right thing. If your intention is truly to help your dog be successful, then your actions should support that goal. Set your dog up to get it right so that you can praise and reward him. Take your dog out more often to potty, so that he is able to hold it until the next opportunity, and praise him for pottying in the correct spot. Or give your dog a "leave it" command, then praise him for ignoring the pens on the table.

World-renowned psychologist B. F. Skinner proved through his experiments that an animal rewarded for good behavior will learn much more rapidly and retain what he learns far more effectively than an animal punished for bad behavior. A dog learns from successes, not failures. Don't set your dog up for a task that is beyond his capabilities or knowledge, as it is a prescription for failure. Instead, lower the criteria for success and coach him toward the goal.

"Spin," cues Peter, a student of mine, and his Boston terrier named Beans happily spins. "Roll over," Peter continues. "Now curtsy, shake, paw, beg, jump . . . jump . . . Beannnnns! No! Geez!" After receiving

no reward for the last two minutes of work, Beans has lost interest and stopped working. This unfortunate outcome was bound to happen, as Peter had set his dog up for failure.

Peter asked Beans for trick after trick, not stopping until his dog missed one, at which time the dog was reprimanded. It was a no-win situation for our Boston, Beans.

I advised Peter to set his dog up for success by setting a goal before he gave his first cue to Beans. Peter decided, "I want Beans to perform three behaviors in a row." This way, Peter (and Beans) could feel successful at meeting a goal, instead of disappointed when the streak of successes ended. If Beans performed the three behaviors, Peter would praise and treat her. If meeting the goal was consistently too difficult, Peter would know he had set too high a goal for where they were in their training.

Do Things the Easy Way

When Chalcy was little, she was always sneaking into the open kitchen trash can. I'd gotten to the point where every time Chalcy was out of my sight for a minute or two, I'd be paranoid she was in the trash again. This was a huge source of frustration and anxiety for Randy and me. And then . . . we bought a new trash can with a better lid. Problem solved. Anxiety gone.

I think at first I was determined that we had a right to have an open trash can, and that Chalcy must be disciplined to leave it alone. But I've since changed my mind. Leaving that open trash can within her reach was as bad as leaving bonbons out for a dieting spouse. It was setting Chalcy up for failure. Dogs *do* need to be disciplined to follow house rules, but seriously, choose your battles. Sometimes, for the goal of a more harmonious relationship, you need to just do things the easy way. Get a better trash can.

Another way to choose the easy way is by giving your dog a "welcome-home cookie" every time he either comes home voluntarily or comes when you call him. It's sure nicer to have a habit of willing compliance than a fight with this command.

Your Dog's Right to Dignity

Every dog has a right to his dignity and a right to be treated respectfully—not mocked, ridiculed, or humiliated. Don't push a dog's face in the spot where he pottied in the house, and don't leave him in a soiled crate. A dog does not make the correlation between his elimination and the punishment if time has elapsed. More important, this just isn't appropriate punishment. Don't compromise trust by shaming your dog.

It was a television first. In a grand spectacular, fifty-one dogs representing all the states and District of Columbia gathered to compete for the coveted crown in FOX's Emmy-nominated "Miss Dog Beauty Pageant." Bitches of all breeds came together in dog-eat-dog competition in the categories of beauty, talent, poise, and (you guessed it) evening wear.

Chalcy (Miss California) was one of ten finalists selected in prejudging. These ten would demonstrate their talent on television, and would be outfitted in custom couture gowns and jewels. The dogs had multiple fittings for their original ensembles with doggy couture designer Sharon Day. The first thing Sharon told the dog owners and camera crew was, "Don't laugh at the dogs when we put the dresses on them. They'll know they are being mocked, and they'll look embarrassed on the runway."

So when Chalcy had her first fitting, I told her, "Aww, look how pretty you look! What a pretty dress!" And you know, she stood up a little straighter and grinned!

Appreciate Your Dog's Personality

At the end of a performance I'll often spend a few minutes talking to people in the audience. Kids will excitedly tell me, "Chalcy is the best dog in the world!"

"No," I'll tell them, "YOUR dog is the best dog in the world. And that's because he's YOUR dog."

When we bring a dog into our household, we attempt to train him and mold him into what we want him to be. Perhaps you wanted a duplicate of your childhood dog—loyal, calm, intelligent, loving. And perhaps what you got was a clumsy, overexuberant Lab, or a terrier with the tenacity of a bird pulling on an earthworm. We don't always get what we want. Sometimes we have to accept and love a dog for what he is, despite the fact that his personality may not fit our mold of the perfect pet. Some behaviors are too entrenched, too instinctive to train away. Don't begrudge your dog for who he is. You'd be doing your dog and yourself a disservice if you didn't recognize your dog's unique and undeniable character, and accept and learn to love his personality.

Whether he's young or old, athletic or lazy, quick-witted or dumb as a rock—he's YOUR dog and his success need only be measured in YOUR eyes.

The Domestic Dog as a Human Creation

On the subject of honesty, let's make an honest appraisal of the genetics and capabilities of the domestic dog.

You've probably heard the comparisons that are made between the domestic dog and his wolf ancestors. It's true that many dog behaviors are rooted in ancestorial instinct, and we can learn a lot about dogs' behavior by viewing it in this light.

Dogs, however, are not wolves. They really aren't. Although dogs did descend from wolves, the fact is, we have so modified the genetics and disposition of the domestic dog that dogs today are significantly different from their wolf ancestors, not only in appearance but in how they relate to humans and interpret human behavior. Dogs have been under domestication for something on the order of a hundred thousand years—longer by far than any other domestic species. And during this time, their evolution has largely been influenced by humans.

The majority of the artificial-selection regimes used in breeding dogs have been intended to make the dogs more useful to humans—as hunters, herders, protectors, and draft and sled animals. Dogs have been bred for their willingness to work for humans, and their ability to do so. They have also been bred for relatively intense social interaction with humans—the ability to take direction well, understand us, be willing to please, and integrate well into our households. Through this selective breeding, dogs developed a special predisposition for interacting and communicating with humans. Dogs are actually genetically designed to have relationships with humans.

How different are dogs from wolves? What if dogs and wolves were raised by humans and similarly socialized? Would a hundred thousand years of selective breeding make a difference in their willingness to take human guidance? This question was answered in a study published in 2003, in which a human pointed to one of two upturned pails and allowed a dog to choose one or the other (only one contained food). Dogs readily trusted the human guidance, going to the pail that was indicated. Human-raised arctic wolves given the same test, however, paid no heed to the human guidance.[2]

This genetically determined ability of dogs to comprehend and fol-

low human signals allows us remarkable options for communicating with our dogs.

Work with Your Dog's Genetics

Each dog breed has unique mental and physical traits, as each was designed for a particular purpose. Specific abilities and limitations were bred into each breed. Dogs meant to pull wagons were bred calm, steady, and strong. Those meant to herd sheep have good vision and are quick and athletic.

The characteristics bred into your dog influence his reaction to training and his ability to do what you ask. Knowledge of your dog's breed can help you tailor a training program to take advantage of his skills and primary motivations.

Herding dogs (border collies, Australian shepherds, corgis, Shelties, German shepherd dogs, and others) were bred to control the movement of other animals, and instinct often prompts them to herd members of their human family, especially the children. Herding dogs are people-focused, and they take instruction readily. They are intelligent and quick to learn, and they often excel in competitive dog sports. They are intensely prey driven and often value a Frisbee reward over food. They are very visual and will stare intently at a moving object.

Working dogs (Rottweilers, Doberman pinschers, Great Pyrenees, Alaskan malamutes, Great Danes, Newfoundlands, boxers, and others) were bred to perform a specific job, such as guarding property, pulling sleds, and performing water rescues. They are generally large and strong, and they can be assertive, stubborn, and independent.

Sporting dogs (including pointers, retrievers, setters, spaniels, and Weimaraners) were bred to run, swim, and find and retrieve birds for their hunting masters by scent (notice the long noses). Sporting dogs can be easily distracted by smells, but they enjoy games that use their noses such as searching out hidden treats around the house. Sporting dogs are bred to have "soft mouths," and they don't generally bite often; however, the most dog bites in America actually come from cocker spaniels, possibly due to an inherited condition called "rage syndrome." Sporting dogs have high logic intelligence. They are intensely motivated by food and by moving objects for chasing, such as Frisbees.

Hounds are hunters. Scent hounds (such as beagles, basset hounds, and bloodhounds) follow their noses, while sight hounds (greyhounds and Salukis) use their vision and stamina to run down quarry. Sight hounds love to chase moving things, and the famous Ashley Whippet was the first superstar disc dog champion in the 1970s. Both types of hounds can be very single-minded; nothing matters except finding their prey—hence the term "hounding" someone. Because hounds can be easily distracted, training in an empty environment to start is best.

Terriers (including fox terriers, Airedales, Parson Russell terriers, and American Staffordshire terriers) are intense hunters. Named after Terra (Earth), most were designed to hunt vermin, and they love a game of tug as a reward, as it imitates the shaking of a small prey animal. Sometimes called "terrors," they are feisty and energetic, and they typically have little tolerance for other animals. Terriers love training that is fun and not overly harsh. Some, such as cairn terriers, Westies (West Highland white terriers), and miniature schnauzers, are enthusiastic barkers. Bullseye, the Target dog, is a bull terrier.

Most of the **toy** breeds were bred as companion dogs. Many toys, like the miniature pinscher, are tough as nails and require as much training as a larger dog. Enthusiastic barkers include Yorkies (Yorkshire terriers), Chihuahuas, toy poodles, and Pekingese. Toy poodles are traditional circus dogs and most toys take to training quickly and enthusiastically.

Do some breed research to find out what your dog's breed was originally designed to do; this will help you better understand your dog. If you have a mixed-breed dog, you'll have to guess his breed makeup based upon his physical characteristics and character traits. If you are curious enough, recent mapping of the dog genome has now made possible tests that determine your mutt's breed heritage.[3]

SUMMARY

- Be sincere. Don't be deceptive with your dog, either in words or in actions.
- Be predictable. Your dog should be able to predict the consequence of his action.
- Set your dog up for success, not failure. Help him achieve a goal, rather than punish him for not achieving it.
- Your dog has a right to dignity. Don't mock him and don't use humiliating tactics as punishment.
- Appreciate your dog's unique capabilities and personality. He's YOUR dog and his success need only be measured in YOUR eyes.
- Dogs are genetically predisposed to interaction and communication with humans.
- Understand your dog's breed characteristics and how they affect his drives and motivations.

Rule 2: Be Fair

"You bad dog! You pulled up all of my gardenias! How could you!"

"I can't believe you killed one of our chickens! You're headed right back to the pound!"

"Phew! You stink! How could you roll in stinky stuff when you *know* I have visitors coming tonight!"

It's easy to feel justified in scolding your dog for something he should have known better than to do. But in all fairness, are you certain your dog understood that his behavior was against the rules? I mean, are you really certain?

Dogs are honest. They will give you what you want within the limitations of their physical and mental capabilities, and of their training. Accepting this is the first step in knowing what is fair to ask of your dog.

Earning the trust of your dog is not about being nice to him all the time. It's about being fair and predictable. With training, you and your dog will establish paths of communication so that you can both become clear on expectations and consequences.

THE RULE

The secret to treating your dog fairly is in having rules that are specific, clear, and achievable, and consequences that are fair and predictable.

Fair Rules Are Specific, Clear, and Achievable

Rules of conduct are inherent in dog-pack culture. Dog packs have rules governing the order in which dogs eat, the manner in which they greet one another, and the other ways in which they interact with one another. Our human pack has comparable household rules as well.

Having rules helps lessen the frustration for both you and your dog, as you are both clear on expectations and consequences. When your dog understands and follows your rules, he is able to become a bigger part of your life by being allowed freedoms and interactions he couldn't otherwise have.

In order for a household rule to be fair, it has to be specific, clear, and achievable.

Rules Must Be Specific

Is your dog allowed to dig? Is he allowed to dig in one spot but not another? Is he allowed to jump on you? Is he allowed to jump on your spouse?

It is easiest for your dog to have rules that are as basic as possible, such as: No jumping on anybody, ever. But so long as you are consistent, and you make the distinctions clear to him, your dog can learn different rules for different situations. A service dog knows he is free to play when he is off duty, but goes into working mode when his cape is on. A hunting dog is taught to pursue birds when in the field, but not when in the obedience ring. Your dog may be allowed to jump on you, but not on guests.

Rules Must Be Clear

In order for a rule to be fair, your dog must have a clear idea of expectations. He needs to be taught, through reinforcement and correction, which behaviors are allowed and which disallowed, and in which circumstances. In order to communicate these expectations to your dog, you must first have them clear in your own mind. Take some time to plan out your rules, and involve your entire family so that you are all giving a consistent message.

A clear rule is a consistent rule. It's not fair to your dog to let him on the couch sometimes and scold him other times, giving him different messages on different days. If you don't want your dog on the couch, then he should never be allowed on the couch. Likewise, if you don't want your dog to jump on you when you are dressed for work, then he should not be allowed to jump on you when you are wearing jeans.

Show your dog that your rules are predictable, and that the consequences for his behavior are predictable as well.

Rules Must Be Achievable

Although *you* may think it's entirely reasonable for your dog to ignore the squirrel running across the fence top, your dog may not see it that way.

A fair rule is realistically achievable. You wouldn't expect a six-month-old puppy to sit still while you watch an entire TV show, any more than you'd expect a kid to not wake up the household on Christmas morning. Give your dog goals he can achieve MOST of the time. Once his success rate increases, then you can challenge him with more difficult rules.

Start with a Small Number of Rules

We mostly all want the same things from our dogs: We want them to be happy when we're happy, still when we're still. We want them to stay out of the road, not pee on the carpet, don't bark, don't bite, don't pull, don't roll in stinky stuff, don't chase the cat, don't beg at the table, don't sniff inappropriately, lie down, leave it, get out of there, and cut that out. . . . That's a lot of rules!

Think about the MOST important rules you need your dog to follow, perhaps three to five of them, and write them down. This will help you to keep them in the forefront of your mind and to react quickly when they come into play. It's better to train a few rules consistently than a lot of rules loosely. Here are some suggested rules:

- No jumping on any people, ever.
- No chewing on anything other than your own toys.

- No getting on the furniture.
- No touching the kitchen trash can.
- No entering the kitchen at all.
- Do not go through doorways ahead of me.
- No jumping into or out of the car until instructed.
- Sit before receiving your dinner.

Your Dog Should Obey All Family Members

Chalcy is required to obey my commands every time, and obey Randy's commands every time. She can choose to obey or not obey others' commands at her discretion, but she may not allow another person's command to override my own. If I've put her in a sit-stay and someone else commands her to "come" or to "lie down," Chalcy will disregard that person's command so as not to break my command. That is the rule set we have established. It's a good idea to train your dog to obey at least all the adult and teenage members in your household, so that they can control him should the situation require.

In your dog's mind, your family is a pack unit and everyone in your family has a certain place in the hierarchy within the pack. In most families, one or both of the parents are considered the pack leaders and the dog is subordinate to them. But when small children are involved, dogs almost always consider the children equal to them or lower in the pack hierarchy. Because the dog considers the child an equal or a subordinate, he may refuse to obey the child's commands or may even "accidentally" bump into the child and knock her down.

Accustom your smaller children to dog-training techniques by standing next to them as they give a command, and allow them to reward your dog if he obeys. If your dog does not obey, immediately step in and enforce the command, so that your dog learns to obey your children.

Although it is important that every household member know and adhere to the rules, I recommend that one family member be in charge of enforcing the rules. Otherwise it is likely that no one will end up disciplining the dog.

Enforce Fairly

Being fair has a lot to do with not getting mad at your dog and not letting your emotion alter your response. Fairness is not angry and is not punitive. Teach your dog the house rules by lovingly praising him for appropriate behavior, and firmly but gently disciplining him for infractions.

> Monica teaches weekly competitive obedience training classes in her backyard, and she cuts her students little more slack than she does their dogs. When Cowboy started having aggression problems in class, growling at other dogs, Monica decided to fight back and made a plan with his owner, Jean. The next time Cowboy growled, Jean quietly and immediately tied him to a tree and left. She walked right out of the backyard and behind the house, out of Cowboy's view.
>
> Poor Cowboy didn't know what was happening. He whined, licked his lips, barked, paced, and kept his eyes fixed on the gate through which his owner had left. After a few minutes Jean returned, untied Cowboy without comment, and continued the lesson. The next week, Cowboy growled again, and Jean escalated the consequences. This time Jean tied Cowboy to a tree, exited into the driveway, started up her van, and left! Now, she only went to the end of the block and sat there for ten minutes, but I couldn't help feeling sorry for Cowboy when Jean told me this story. The poor guy must have thought his owner tied him to a tree and abandoned him!

Jean had rationalized that this was not a cruel punishment, as the dog was not being physically hurt. But to my mind, the mental anguish inflicted on the dog outweighed his crime. It was like saying, "If you do that one more time, Mommy is going to drive off and never come back!"

Your dog relies upon you for everything. It's not fair to wield more power than necessary. In Cowboy's case, a fairer consequence might have been a stinging finger flick on his rump to jolt him out of his mind-set, or a withdrawal of his owner's attention by means of a time-out for him in his kennel.

Don't mess with your dog's mind—enforce fair consequences for his behavior.

Reward Fairly

If you want your dog to trust you, you have to play by the rules. Fairness is predictability, and your dog will be much more likely to work for you if he trusts that he will be paid as expected. In your relationship with your dog, you've established a currency, a history of work as it is connected with rewards. When he gets the newspaper in the morning, he gets a cookie. If he comes to you when called, he is rewarded with a game of fetch. When your dog obeys your command, give him the reward he was expecting.

Be fair to your dog's needs. If you've been away all day, don't you think it's fair that your dog gets your attention when you return? If he has been cooped up for a long time, isn't it fair that he gets to go for a walk, even when your favorite TV show is on? The fact that you are tired, or have had a bad day, does not relieve you of your responsibility to give your dog his nightly walk or training session.

A great dog/owner relationship is a balance of give and take. It is giving loving attention and enrichment, and also enforcing structure and rules. Knowing that you are being fair to your dog's needs will make you feel more confident and resolute when enforcing your rules.

SUMMARY

- A fair rule is specific, clear, and achievable.
- Have specific discriminating factors for your rule that your dog is capable of deciphering. (Is he allowed to jump on you but not on your spouse?)
- Be clear in your own mind as to what the rule is. Be consistent with your rule. (Don't allow your dog on the couch sometimes and scold him other times.)
- Give your dog achievable goals he can succeed at MOST of the time.
- Start with a small number of rules and write them down. Enforce the rules consistently.

- **Train your dog to obey all members of your family. Have one person in the household primarily responsible for enforcing the rules.**
- **Enforce fairly; don't wield more power than necessary. Don't mess with your dog's mind. (Don't tie him to a tree and abandon him.)**
- **Reward fairly; pay your dog for his work. Knowing that you are being fair with regard to your dog's needs will make you feel more resolute when enforcing your rules.**

Rule 3: Be Consistent

"Mommy, Mommy, can I have this candy?"
"No, honey, come on now, put it back."
"But Mommy, Mommy, I WANT it!"
"I said no, now put it back."
"But . . . I . . . WAAAAANT IT!"
"FINE! If it will make you be quiet, then take it!"

Oooh, that was so not good. I cringe in the supermarket as I watch this scenario play out. The child just learned a valuable lesson—that "no" doesn't really mean "no." Instead it means that he needs to whine a little longer to get what he wants.

Throughout this book I stress the importance of consistency. Making the commitment to consistency is the single most influential factor in gaining desired and reliable behavior from your dog.

THE RULE

Consistency is strength (as it will not be budged) and consistency is dependability, both of which encourage trust. The secret to being consistent with your dog is to be clear yourself about what you want, to ask for it in a consistent way, and to not go back on your decisions. Do what you say you are going to do and use good judgment.

Be Consistent in Your Requests

Don't Go Back on Your Decisions

Consistency means not going back on your decisions—not giving in to the child's whining after you've already told him "no." Being consistent with your rules makes the rules easier for your dog to figure out, and thereby reduces anxiety associated with confusion.

But what should you do if you change your mind? What if you told your dog "no," he can't have the ball, and then you decide you want to throw it for him after all? You can't go back on your decision, since that would let him think he wore you down. Instead, ask your dog for a behavior, such as a sit. If he performs it, you can *reward* him by throwing the ball. This way he gets rewarded not for nagging you about the ball, but rather for obeying your command.

Know What Correct Behavior Looks Like

If you don't know what correct behavior looks like, neither will your dog. What do mean when you tell him to "stay"? If your dog moves two feet, is that acceptable? If he changes position from sitting to lying down, is that what is meant by "stay"? When you tell your dog to "stay" at the front door, is he allowed to move once you've crossed the threshold, or is he to wait until he receives a release command from you?

There is no right or wrong answer to these questions, so long as you have a clear understanding of what you are asking for. Whatever you decide the meaning of the word is, stick to that—don't be wishy-washy. **A great dog trainer is not determined by what rules he makes, but rather by how consistently he trains those rules.**

Use Consistent Cues

The average dog understands 165 words—make the most of them by standardizing your cues. Is the cue "down," or is it "lie down"? When your dog jumps on you, is the cue "off," or are you also saying "down"? Is it "quiet," or is it "no barking"? It may be helpful to make a list of all of your verbal cues, in order to help you use them consistently.

Don't assume your dog understands the same meaning of the word when it is spoken in a different tone. Baby-talking "no, no, pupsy-wupsy" can sound more like praise than a reprimand, even though the word "no" was used. A single command can sound very different when given in a different voice: "Kiva, staaaaay. Stay!" Enunciate your verbal cues clearly and consistently.

Separate Your Emotional State from Training

It's all too common in dog training to let our emotions and frustrations get the better of us. It can seem as though our dog is *deliberately* trying to annoy us, or *deliberately* pretending to be stupid, in that same exasperating way that a teenager does when being taught the mind-boggling concept of separating the laundry.

But with your dog, it's probably not the case that he is pushing your buttons intentionally. He just needs to be shown, in a consistent manner, over and over and over. I've taught enough dogs that this phase doesn't get to me anymore. I know it's going to take a hundred repetitions, and I proceed, in an almost mechanical way, to do the same thing over and over. The dog will learn eventually. They all do.

Professional animal trainers distinguish themselves from pet owners by their ability to separate their own emotional states from the actions they take and the sounds they make. They use their voices to make sounds that elicit a desired response, rather than sounds that represent their emotions. It's not just *what* you say, but *how* you say it.

Go into the training session with this attitude and don't allow your emotions and frustrations to get the better of you. If you feel yourself getting angry or frustrated, the best thing you can do is walk away. Frustrations taken out on your dog during one episode can set training back considerably.

Be a Dependable Dog Owner

People who consistently and reliably meet their dogs' needs develop dogs who trust them. These dogs are happier and more confident, and they exhibit less problem behavior because they're free from worry about not getting fed today, being left outdoors during a scary thunderstorm, or waiting too many hours in a crate. A puppy who knows he can rely upon a dependable owner to respond to his signs to go out to potty will become happy and eager to communicate. If his owner is unresponsive, the puppy will learn that his owner is not there for him, and he'll learn to go on the floor.

Being dependable is doing what you say you are going to do, and being dependable is using good judgment. Your dog needs to believe you are smart and strong and capable in order for him to follow your guidance. If you coach your dog to trust you and jump into your arms—you'd better not drop him! Trust builds slowly but can break down in an instant.

Alex Rothacker, owner of the TOPS police dog training facility in Grayslake, Illinois, recounts a recent event in which one of his canine graduates trusted his human partner with his life.

Quanto, a German shepherd dog, had been on the police force three years. One afternoon, his police officer handler stopped to remove a deer carcass from the road. The squad car's automatic door lock malfunctioned, and upon his return the officer discovered that Quanto was missing. On one side of the road was a parking structure, and on the other was a forest. The officer turned toward the forest and shouted several commands of "Quanto, come!" Quanto, however, was not in the forest. He was on the third floor of the parking garage. He trusted his partner's judgment . . . and jumped.

Fortunately, Quanto survived the jump, but he required surgery and rehab for the trauma to his front legs. Quanto returned to limited work a year later, and he continues to live and work with his partner. The two are working every day to rebuild the trust in their relationship.

Persevere

I didn't set out to become a marathon runner, but somehow my jog around the block turned into longer and more frequent runs, and eventually I was competing in twenty-six-mile races. The thing I love about marathons is that they represent a remarkable feat that can realistically be achieved by most people. Completing a marathon is the result of consistency in training and of perseverance.

Woody Allen once said, "Eighty percent of success is just showing up." A big part of dog training is just showing up—putting in the time. When you are teaching a new behavior, it may seem as though your dog is not getting the concept. Don't stress it. Go through the same repetitions day after day, keeping an even temper and a consistent training method. Then one day you'll see a light bulb go off in his head—the Eureka! moment. That's the moment that truly bonds you with your dog.

The difference between successful dog trainers and unsuccessful dog trainers is often, simply, perseverance.

SUMMARY

- **Don't go back on your decisions. If you change your mind, don't reward your dog's pushy behavior. Instead, ask your dog for a new behavior and reward that.**
- **Know in your own head what correct behavior looks like, so that you can know if your dog has achieved it or not.**
- **Give consistent cues. Write down all your cue words. Enunciate cues clearly and consistently.**
- **Separate your emotional state from training. Use your voice consistently, and don't let frustration enter it.**
- **Be dependable—do what you say you are going to do and use good judgment. If you tell your dog to jump into your arms, you'd better not drop him.**
- **A big part of dog training is simply perseverance.**

Instill a Desire to Please

Workers in neighboring offices smile but no longer do double takes as Chalcy and I arrive at work each day, I with my backpack and Chalcy carrying my purse. Up the stairs we go, across the ramp, and through our office door, where Chalcy prances past the lobby and into my office. She dances in happy circles while waiting for me to thank her for her indispensable help and give her a treat from the tin on my desk. It's part of our routine, and one of the many ways each day in which Chalcy proves herself a "good girl" and earns my praise or other reward.

There are two ways to get animals (or people, for that matter) to do something. You can get them to WANT to do it, or you can get them to FEAR *not* doing it. Both ways are effective, but the first is active and the second is passive. When a dog is continually motivated by fear of punishment, he will try to fly under the radar as much as possible. He won't want to draw attention to anything he is doing or not doing.

A dog motivated by a potential reward, on the other hand, will go out of his way to offer behaviors in order to earn the reward. This is the type of motivation we want. This motivation creates a more willing, happy, and cooperative partner in your dog, and a dog who actively looks for ways to be a "good dog."

We instill this desire to please in our dog by rewarding good behavior, building his desire for a reward, and cultivating his desire for our attention which we can use as a reward.

- We focus on the positive and help our dog to be successful instead of punishing him for misdeeds.
- We build his natural drive to an intense level in order to gain the highest level of motivation for performance.
- We develop his desire for our attention in order to have a thing of great value that we can give as a reward or remove as a consequence for inappropriate behavior.

Rule 4: Motivate with Positive Reinforcement

I sometimes hear a complaint from pet dog owners that their dog is "too wild" in the house, and has therefore been banished to the backyard. What message is this giving to the dog? It's telling him that he is an outcast. It is not instructive and it is doing nothing to solve the problem.

The Cockney flower girl in *My Fair Lady* could never have learned to behave properly as a lady while spending her time on the streets of London. Her transformation occurred only when Henry Higgins gave her instruction and integrated her into high society. She observed the fancy ladies in her new social circle, and she attempted to mimic their behavior in order to fit in. People behave like the people they hang out with. And, to some extent, the same is true for our dogs.

We can effect a positive change in our dog's behavior by making him feel proud of his good behavior and ability to fit into our pack. Dogs desire a sense of communal belonging within our family in an instinctual way similar to their desire to belong to a dog pack. A dog desires to please his pack leader in order to remain in good standing within the pack. This is a great attribute of dogs, and we want to take advantage of it. The more integrated into your household your dog feels, the more predictable his behavior will be, and the more likely he will be to follow your household rules. After all, who would be more likely to break our laws—a person who sees himself as a respected and upstanding member of the community, or a person who sees himself as an outcast, shunned by society? We want to bring that feeling of self-esteem and belonging into our dog's world, in order to inspire him to please us.

THE RULE

We build a dog's motivation to please by rewarding his good behavior. We focus on solutions rather than problems. We help the dog develop a pattern of success, which increases his motivation to perform.

The Dog's Hierarchy of Needs

Human needs can be depicted in the form of a pyramid. Only when the needs at the foundation of the pyramid have been met can the human being focus on the next tier. For example, an employee probably won't be too concerned with developing great new ideas for his company if his office is really cold, or the coffeemaker is broken, or his chair has an annoying squeak. His energy is going to be focused on getting warmer, or getting some coffee, or covertly switching chairs with his coworker. Only when his basic comfort needs have been met can he focus on higher levels of need, such as the need to feel accomplished or successful or secure in his job.

This pyramid represents psychologist Abraham Maslow's "hierarchy of needs." At the base of the pyramid we find our most basic needs: breathing, food, water, sex, sleep, homeostasis, and excretion. Only when these needs have been met can we focus on the next level of need, which is our need for safety and security.

Dogs are highly intelligent pack animals, like humans, and presumably they have a similar hierarchy of needs. Most dogs, we hope, have at least these two most basic levels of need fulfilled.

The third level of need can be described for a dog as his need to feel he is part of a pack. The dog needs to interact daily with the family, understand his place in the pack's hierarchy, and sleep, travel, and eat with the pack. Now, I'm not advocating that your dog sleep in your

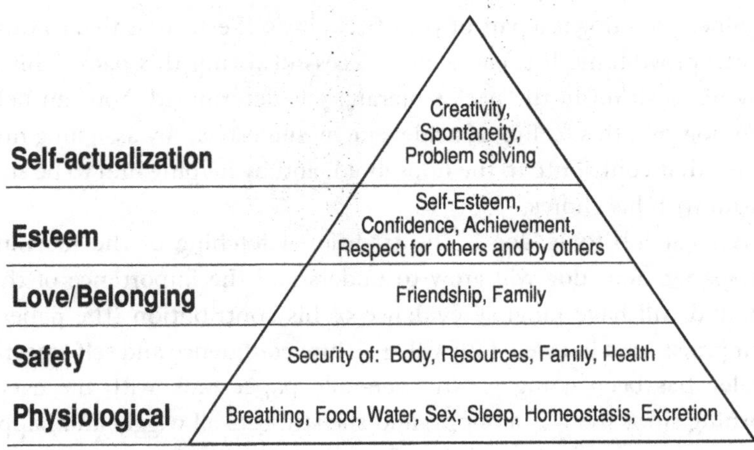

bed and have a plate at the dinner table, but I do think it's important that he be a part of the rituals of eating, sleeping, and playing. His food is prepared and served by your hands, and his bed and belongings are washed and maintained in a way that makes him feel loved and cared for.

Lucky dogs feel loved and included, and can progress to the fourth level of need: the need for esteem and self-worth.

Your Dog's Need for Self-Esteem

So how does a dog achieve self-esteem? With successful completion of challenges.

When my mother visits, I attempt to entertain her by having Chalcy do dog tricks. "Oh, Kyra," she always frets, "don't make her work all the time! Just let her lie on the couch and be a dog."

"But, Mom," I say, "she *wants* to do things! She *likes* it when I ask her to do something and then tell her she's a good girl."

Dogs don't want to lie on the couch all day. Dogs want to be challenged and to have goals to strive for. They want to be taught things, and to struggle with physical and mental contests, and to taste sweet success! A dog is much happier searching out veggies you've hidden around the room, or rolling a treat ball full of kibble, than just being given a handful of food.

Since your dog is a part of your pack, his self-esteem is tied to ways he can prove himself capable and successful within this pack. This is how his position in the pack's hierarchy is determined. You can help your dog gain this feeling of achievement and esteem by assigning him chores that contribute to the household, and by helping him to be successful with his chores.

A great job for a dog is the traditional fetching of the morning newspaper. Your dog will grow to understand the importance of this job, and will have tangible evidence of his contribution (the paper). Your praise for a job well done will give him confidence and self-esteem. Chalcy has been going on the one-mile paper walk with me every morning since she was a puppy, and she still gets all wiggly and happy when she runs into the house and up the stairs to shove it at Randy. She strangely gets more pleasure from showing it to him than in getting her treat for it. Since Randy does 90 percent of the newspaper reading (the comics count for 10 percent, right?), she senses that the paper is of greater value to him than to me.

Other useful jobs could include having your dog get your slippers in the evening. Unfortunately, my "fetch shoe" command is probably not specific enough, as I'll often get a boot the first time, and maybe a nice pump the second time. If I'm lucky, I'll even get one right shoe and one left. (I suppose I should pick up my bedroom more often.)

"Tidy up your toys into your toy box" is a great one—a really great one, actually. Maybe we'll start next on "tidy Randy's laundry into the hamper"!

Chalcy often helps me carry other items besides my purse. Her favorite is helping Randy and me carry groceries in from the truck. Randy and I will load up with eight bags each of groceries, and Chalcy will race up with her one box of rice or cereal and be as proud as if she'd just moved a mountain. (Of course, I praise her as if she's done so!)

The best challenges you can give to your dog are training and learning challenges. Help your dog achieve regular successes to keep him motivated. Watch him, increase the challenge as he becomes proficient, let him regress temporarily when he struggles. Participating in challenges together will strengthen your bond as you work collaboratively and celebrate your shared successes.

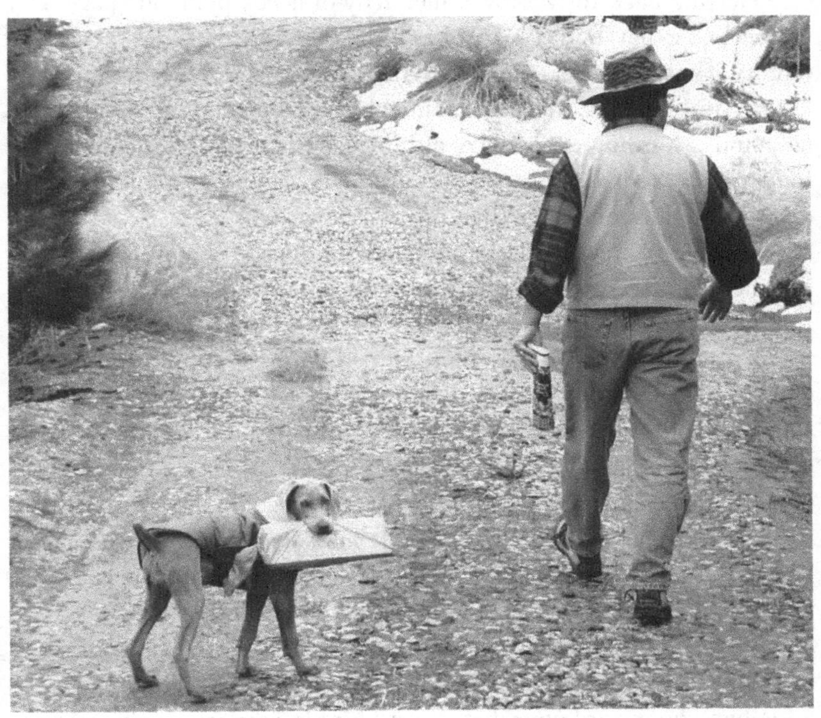

Praise, Touch, Treat—in That Order

In obedience class, twelve dogs are lined up and told to lie down. "Stay" is commanded in unison by their trainers, who then turn silently in formation and file out of the training yard and out of sight. The dogs hold their stays. They hold them for five minutes. They hold them despite my calling the kitty cat across the lawn, despite my tossing a tennis ball, and despite my tempting them with a meatball in front of their noses. (Wicked, aren't I?) When the timer rings, the trainers file silently back into the yard and take their places to the right of their dogs. In calm voices they praise their dogs, and then gently pet their heads. As the dog's pleasure increases, tails begin to wag harder. The dogs continue to hold their stays, knowing the food treat will come next.

Referring back to Maslow's hierarchy-of-needs pyramid (page 41), we recognize that food is a most basic and therefore most desirable commodity. Thus, food treats rank extremely high as a reward for dogs.

Physical touch is, for most mammals including dogs, also a pleasurable and rewarding experience, although not usually to the degree of food treats. Verbal praise and attention is also pleasurable for your dog, but to a lesser degree than touch and treats.

This value of rewards is instinctive. Our dogs can, however, be conditioned to place higher value on the lesser rewards in the same way that we condition children to do this.

As a toddler, a child may be rewarded with candy or a toy. As the child grows older, he learns to feel rewarded with less tangible things, such as a gold star on a paper, or the promise of a big reward upon the achievement of a long-term goal. This progression shows a maturation of self beyond purely instinctual drives. That gold star on the child's paper in itself has no inherent worth. It gains its potency because it has been pleasantly associated with praise, or maybe even a special treat from the parents. In the same way, we can condition our dog to associate our touch or praise with a food treat, increasing the value of these less inherently gratifying rewards.

When you reward your dog, reward him in escalating value of gratification. First give verbal praise, then a pat or scratch, then the food reward. Not only will this serve to keep your dog in a calm state of mind, but your verbal praise will become pleasantly associated with your touch, and your touch will become associated with the food reward. Your verbal praise and your touch thereby become more desirable and potent rewards.

Positive Reinforcement Training Gets Results

In the familiar cliché, there are two ways to get a cart horse to pull: lure him forward with a carrot or smack him from behind with a stick. In the first scenario he is moved by a desire for a reward or pleasure, and in the second he is moved by a desire to avoid or end the pain. In both cases you are **reinforcing** (or making more likely to happen) the behavior you want. But the carrot is much more effective in motivating an animal and instilling in him a desire to please. The carrot also leads to higher retainment of a behavior. The carrot is the rewarding of good behavior, or **positive reinforcement**.

Positive reinforcement training methods strengthen and enhance the relationship between you and your dog as you work collaboratively toward a shared goal in an encouraging, stress-free, and fear-free environment. The dog participates in the learning process with a positive attitude, and actually enjoys working and interacting with the trainer.

Positive reinforcement is used to train animals for performances at theme parks, on TV, and in movies, and it is the predominant training method used in all dog sports. Dog tricks are taught almost exclusively with positive reinforcement, as the dog becomes motivated to experiment and actively offer new behaviors—what is called "throwing behaviors at the trainer."

In positive reinforcement, a reward (most often a treat) is given while, or immediately after, the dog performs a desired behavior, making it more likely that he will repeat that behavior. In high-drive sports the reward may be simply the opportunity to engage in the sport. In herding or lure-coursing, for example, treats are not given as a reward. For following the trainer's rules, the dog is rewarded with the opportunity to engage in this desirable sport.

A motivator, or reward, can come in different forms—a food morsel, a favorite toy, a play session, or praise and affection. In teaching a new behavior, food is commonly used because it is a high-value reward that is easy to administer. Food is enjoyed by virtually all dogs, is quick to dispense and to be swallowed, and is a clear way to signal a correct response. Toys are great motivators after behaviors are well learned, but during the beginning stages of learning, a toy can actually be a distraction as it takes time for you to get it back and get your dog to regain focus. Praise is great, but it's just not that high-value for most dogs. Use a small but tasty food treat to reward desired behavior.

For tasty dog treats, microwave hot dog slices on a paper-towel-covered plate for three minutes.

Positive Reinforcement is used not only to teach new behaviors, but also to encourage good existing behavior. When your dog is off-leash at the park, reward him with a treat or a ball when he periodically comes back to check in with you. He will learn to check in with you more often.

How to Teach with Positive Reinforcement

Positive reinforcement is the easiest, most effective way to teach a behavior. You get your dog to do a behavior, you give him a treat, and he learns to repeat the behavior. "Rule 7: Cue, Action, Reward" will describe in detail the methods of getting that behavior in the first place.

TEACH A TRICK! CARRY MY PURSE

Use positive reinforcement to get your little helper to carry your purse or bag as you walk. Start by knotting the straps of your purse so that your dog won't become entangled. Put a handful of treats inside the purse and close it. Hand your purse to your dog and have him "take it" (this skill needs to be taught separately). Walk a few steps while telling him to "carry" and patting your leg to indicate that he should come with you. If he drops the purse, do not pick it up but rather point to it and instruct him again to "take it." Your dog should only be allowed to release the purse to your hand and should not merely drop it on the floor. After he has carried the purse for a few steps, praise your dog as you take the purse and give him a treat from inside. When he realizes that treats are inside the purse, he will be less likely to abandon it if he gets bored. Retrieving breeds take to this trick most readily, as they naturally enjoy walking around with things in their mouths.

Be Careful of What You Are Rewarding

Once you are aware of the concept of positive reinforcement, you may be surprised to find it at the root of some behavior problems. If you give your dog a scrap when he begs at the dinner table, you are effectively using positive reinforcement to teach him to continue this undesirable behavior. If you throw your dog's ball in response to his pestering you with it, you are encouraging this pushy behavior. Be careful of what you are rewarding.

Positive Reinforcement Implies a Choice

The basis of positive reinforcement is encouraging your dog to do things in anticipation of a reward. The dog does the behavior because he WANTS to, not because he HAS to. When a dog learns to do something solely in pursuit of a reward, it means he can choose to do or not do the behavior with the only consequence being the potential forfeit of the reward. A dog trained solely with positive reinforcement might at times feel he can just blow you off.

A fellow dog trainer is extremely successful in the obedience competition ring, achieving scores approaching the perfect 200. After her training session in the park, she puts an electronic collar on her dog to let him run free for a while.

"Why do you need the collar?" I ask.

"Because without it, he sometimes won't come back when I call him."

Really?!? This highly trained obedience dog won't obey a command? The dog had been trained using purely positive reinforcement methods, and if the lure of a squirrel was stronger than his desire for a treat, he chose to disregard his owner's command.

In teaching a new behavior, we want our dog to do it because he WANTS to. We want to make him think it's HIS idea, just as we do with kids. Once the dog has learned the behavior, however, enforcement is another issue. Life is not only about what pleases your dog, and positive reinforcement has to be mediated with discipline. For some commands it is much more important that your dog obey, whether he wants to or not. I'll discuss proper enforcement of commands in the chapter "Rule 8: One Command, One Consequence."

Focus on the Solution, Not the Problem

It is unfortunately the case that dogs get many more instructions that tell them DON'T DO THIS rather than DO THIS. We tell our dogs, "Don't jump on me," "Don't lie on the couch," and "Don't chew my shoe," when it would be more effective to tell them what to DO.

Teaching our dog to DO something gives him the opportunity to be rewarded instead of punished. Achieving these successes increases his confidence and motivation to please. In this way we make a habit of focusing on solutions rather than problems.

Instead of saying "don't jump on me" when you first come home, rechannel your dog's excitement by teaching him to "go find your toy." Instead of "don't lie on the couch," teach him "lie on your dog bed." When you catch him chewing on your shoe, tell him "no," take it away, and then give him something appropriate to chew on. He just wants to chew, and if he gets reprimanded for chewing one thing, and praised for chewing another, he'll take the praise!

Wheeee! Chalcy races so fast over the teeter-totter that she flies off the end before it has even fallen to the ground! Wheeee!

Those familiar with the sport of dog agility are no doubt cringing right now. This is an immediate failure in competition. There are three "contact obstacles" that the dog has to scale: the teeter-totter, the A-frame climb, and the dogwalk (a balance beam with a ramp at each end). The bottom portion of these obstacles is painted yellow; it constitutes the "contact zone." The dog is required to touch at least one paw in the contact zone as he descends. This is for control and safety reasons, so you don't get dogs, for example, launching off the teeter-totter.

"Well, if you don't want her launching off the middle of the teeter-totter, what do you want her to do instead?" The question came from my coach, Kate Moureaux, a national and world dog agility champion. "I want her to stop at the bottom of the plank," I answered. Kate placed a small plastic disc at the base of the teeter-totter, and placed a treat on it. Each time Chalcy summited the teeter-totter I

would direct her attention to the treat by saying "touch!" She would lower her center of gravity and crawl down the plank to get the treat.

Thus, by focusing on the solution rather than the problem, Kate and I taught Chalcy to DO a behavior (crouching at the bottom of the incline) rather than NOT DO a behavior (launching off the middle of the teeter-totter).

The best solutions are the ones that do two things: they offer the dog a bigger reward for the new behavior than for the undesired behavior; and they use a new behavior that is impossible to do at the same time as the undesired behavior. The dog can't both touch a target at the bottom of the teeter-totter and also jump off the middle of it at the same time.

This method of using positive reinforcement to replace unwanted behavior with a new behavior is termed **differential reinforcement of incompatible behaviors** (DRI). The dog is trained to DO a new behavior that replaces the unwanted behavior. The new behavior is specifically selected as one that cannot be done at the same time as the undesirable behavior. It is "incompatible" with the undesired behavior.

A classic example of DRI is the zookeeper who wanted to stop the cranes from landing on his head when he came into their enclosure at feeding time. He used DRI to train them to do a new behavior that was incompatible with landing on his head. He set a mat on the ground and gave a food reward to the birds when they landed on the mat. Since the birds couldn't land both on his head and on the mat at the same time, he had effectively stopped them from landing on his head. Brilliant!

When you ask yourself, "How do I stop my dog from jumping on me?" the DRI method prompts the follow-up question "What do I want my dog to do instead?" It focuses on training a preferred behavior that can be rewarded, rather than on punishing the undesirable one. "I want my dog to sit on the doormat instead of jumping on me."

This approach gives the owner a definable action to train, and gives the dog a definable action to perform. First, at a calmer moment, teach your dog to sit on the doormat. Give him a unique cue, such as "welcome spot." Next, leave your house (with treats in your pocket) and then reenter and immediately tell your dog to sit on his "welcome spot." Reward him while he is in the correct position, sitting on the doormat. Stash some treats in your garage or car, so that when you come home you can immediately tell your dog to sit on his "welcome spot" and reward him there. You can even run over to the mat with him, as it will be hard for him to go far from you at this exciting time.

Thinking in terms of DRI solutions takes a little practice. Here are some examples of how they can be used:

- **Problem:** Jumping on visitors at the door
  Solution: Teach your dog that sitting when the doorbell rings earns him a reward.

- **Problem:** Dinner table begging
  Solution: Reward your dog for lying down on a nearby dog bed.

- **Problem:** Aggressive behavior
  Solution: Reinforce calm behavior. Aggressive behavior and calm behavior are incompatible. If calm behavior receives more reinforcement than aggressive behavior, it will increase. Keep in mind that reinforcement means not only food, but also your touch, praise, and even attention.

- **Problem:** Excessive barking
  Solution: "Down" can be a DRI for unwanted barking, as most dogs will cease barking when lying down.

Counterconditioning

Emotions are so instinctual that it is really worthless to tell someone not to have a particular emotion. If you go in for a job interview and a friend coaches you, "Don't act afraid, don't say something stupid," that's not going to be particularly helpful. More helpful advice would be "Act confident, say something smart." Okay. Now I know what my goal is. Now I know what I'm supposed to do.

Instead of telling your dog "don't be afraid," find a way to replace his fear with a more positive emotion.

Charlie is scared of vacuum cleaners. Always has been, as far as his owner, Ryan, can remember. The vacuum doesn't even have to be turned on—the mere sight or sound of it rolling out of the closet is enough to send Charlie running for the bathtub (his all-purpose safe spot).

With the help of a trainer, Ryan embarks on a plan to turn the object of his dog's fear into an object that his dog loves to see. Out of sight of his dog, Ryan sets the vacuum in a corner of the room. He leashes Charlie and brings him calmly into the room, keeping constant focus on his dog. The moment Ryan sees Charlie's eyes fall on the vacuum, he says "good boy!" and gives him a big chunk of hamburger.

Over the days and weeks that follow, Ryan continues to give treats to Charlie for looking at the vacuum, discovering it, touching it, watching it roll, and finally being there when it is turned on. Before long, Charlie's new favorite game is to run around the house and look for where Ryan has hidden the vacuum—and you should see Charlie's tail wagging in anticipation of his treat for finding it!

Ryan effectively changed his dog's behavior toward the vacuum cleaner from one of fear to one of enthusiasm. Ryan didn't trivialize his dog's fears and demand that the dog overcome them, nor did he validate them. He acknowledged them and sought to change the association of the feared item with something more pleasant. Instead of telling his dog "don't be afraid of the scary vacuum," he told his dog to "find the magical treat vacuum!"

This is the process of **counterconditioning**, the pairing of a stimulus that evokes one response with a stimulus that evokes an opposite response. The goal is to replace the fear of the vacuum cleaner, for example, with the pleasure elicited by the food. Counterconditioning must be done gradually, however. If the process were rushed, the treat could take on the fear association instead. The dog should be worked subthreshold (at the level that does not set off the fear) and gradually worked closer and closer to the triggering object. It is very nuanced, and it can take a long time, but it certainly works when done correctly.

It is vital to pair the stimuli incredibly consistently. The dog needs to get the treat just about every single time he sees the vacuum. If he gets the treat only 70 percent of the time, the process probably won't work.

Instilling confidence in your dog not only serves to give you a more pleasant roommate, but it is also key to any performance training or competitive sport. If your dog is fearful on an agility obstacle or in a particular environment, your goal should be to make the fearful thing become a wonderful thing.

If your dog is fearful of the loud bang of the teeter-totter, instead of coddling him through it, try a different approach. Make the bang an indicator of positive reinforcement. Teach your dog to bang a mini teeter board, and give him a treat when he does. The noise of the bang will soon become an exciting indicator of a treat to come.

The Power of the Treat

Chalcy and I had just finished performing our Stunt Dog Show at a school assembly and the principal was escorting us back through the quad when a boy ran up and shot a question at me: "What's the most important thing in dog training?"

In retrospect, I probably should have answered something about patience, or discipline, or hard work. But the question came so fast that I answered the first thing that popped into my head: "Food!"

I won't lie, all those wonderful tricks that Chalcy does—rolling on a barrel, playing basketball, getting the mail from a mailbox—they were all taught with food. That's not to say that Chalcy values food treats over all else, as she would certainly rather play a roughhousing game of keep-away than get a piece of hot dog, but food is a very immediate and definitive way to mark a correct behavior, and therefore a favorite among dog trainers.

In popular dog-training vernacular, a treat is called a "cookie": "Do you want a cookie?"

What's in It for Me?

"Shouldn't my dog want to please me without a reward?" Dogs do, in general, want to please their owners—but learning is hard! A reward sure makes work more enticing—whether it be a half hour of TV or a nice liver treat! You'd have to admit that as much loyalty as you may have toward your employer, if he stops paying you, it won't be long before you'll stop working for him.

Dogs are all about "what's in it for me?" and "what do I have to do to get it?" It's not a bad quality, and it doesn't mean they love you any less if they want to be paid for their work. In fact, I remember myself as a shiftless teenager, carefully evaluating the list of chores against their posted renumeration. What was the best value here? What was the easiest chore for the most money? I think my mother quickly saw the flaw in her system when I started watering the plants twice a day (a dollar each time!) and would only empty the dishwasher (fifty cents) but not fill it, as filling paid the same but was harder ("grosser" was probably the term I used).

Just because I wanted to get as much pay for as few chores as possible didn't mean I loved or respected my parents any less. If my parents had insisted it was my responsibility to do the chores without pay, I would still have done them. But instead of doing them eagerly and happily, I would have done them slowly and unhappily and with frequent tortured sighs.

It's the same with our dogs. Training and getting willing compliance are easier with treats. And when you pay your dog for 50 percent of the things you ask him to do, he will usually be pretty willing to perform the other 50 percent without treats. You want to make sure that you are not paying your dog for *every single thing* you ask him to do, or he will come to expect this payment and will refuse to do even 1 percent of things without a treat. If you can easily get a behavior without a treat, don't use a treat.

Give 'Em the Good Stuff!

Novice dog trainers are notoriously stingy with treats. They offer praise, kibble, or veggies as a reward, opting for healthier or more convenient alternatives. Honestly, high-value treats make a world of difference in your dog's motivation, especially in the early stages of learning a new behavior. Keep your dog extra-motivated by using "people food" treats such as hot dogs, string cheese, pizza crusts, noodles, meatballs, chicken, steak—whatever gets his mouth watering!

Do I Have to Carry Around Treats for the Rest of My Life?

Before worrying about emptying our pockets of treats, we need to make the behavior an automatic response. If you tell your dog to "sit" five hundred times, and he sits, it becomes an automatic response. It is at this point that you can start weaning your dog off his expectation of a reward. Rather than weaning completely off treats, however, use them as sporadic rewards.

Excited verbal praise definitely helps in training, but mostly when paired with a treat. Praise alone just isn't a big-enough payoff. Think about it: How different would your behavior be if your boss said "If you work overtime, I'll give you a bonus" versus "If you work overtime, I'll give you my sincere thanks"?

No matter how good of a relationship you have with your dog, treats are always going to be a huge part of motivating him. It makes the difference between his happily and eagerly performing, and reluctantly and slowly complying.

Schedules of Reinforcement

How often should you give your dog a reward? Should you give a treat EVERY time he does the behavior, or just sometimes?

During the initial process of learning, your dog's motivation will be highest if you give a treat every single time, for every single behavior. Once a behavior is well established, you can require several repetitions from your dog before rewarding. When you do reward, it is advantageous to do so on a variable (versus fixed) schedule.

Rewarding your dog on a **fixed-ratio** or **fixed-interval** schedule (meaning the dog is rewarded after every X number of behaviors, or after every X number of minutes) results in poor, run-stop-run patterns of response. If you reward your dog for every third behavior, he will come to recognize the pattern and perform reluctantly, perking up only for the third iteration. He knows he won't be getting a reward for the first and second behaviors, and thus he has little incentive to perform.

In contrast, **variable-ratio** and **variable-interval** schedules of reinforcement produce steady and high rates of response. In a variable schedule, there is no pattern to the reward. Because of the unpredictability of variable schedules, dogs are more likely to maintain motivation. Slot machines are an example of variable schedules of reinforcement. We keep repeating the behavior (putting in a coin) because we never know if the *next* time might yield the big payoff.

Jackpot

It's a good idea to vary not only the schedule of reinforcement, but also the type and amount of the reward. We all know the lure of a jackpot—having won it once, we will sit at the slot machine all night in hopes of being rewarded again with that elusive prize. The jackpot theory, when applied to dog training, can be a more effective motivator than consistent rewards.

Here's how to use it: Ask your dog to perform some behaviors he is working on. If he does them fairly well, give him no reward or a small reward. When he performs a behavior very well or better than he has in the past—jackpot! Give him a whole handful of treats! Wow, will that make an impression on him! He will continue trying extra hard in the hope of hitting that jackpot again.

I'll discuss using prey-drive motivators in the next chapter, but a session of tug, if your dog enjoys that, is another great jackpot reward. Keep the tug toy in your back pocket and whip it out when your dog does something really good. Search & Rescue dogs are rewarded with a game of tug when they find their quarry.

Using several different types of treats during a training session can also keep your dog motivated—a goldfish cracker for a mediocre effort, a hot dog for a good effort. It takes more than a little coordination, but you can hold several low-value treats in one hand and several high-value treats in the other, so that you can be ready with either reward.

Upping the Ante

The purpose of a treat is to reward a good effort. In kindergarten, a child gets a gold star for printing her name. In first grade, she gets a gold star only if she prints it neatly, and in second grade, cursive is required for that same reward. What may have earned your dog a treat in the past may no longer be enough to earn a treat today. We call this "**upping the ante**," as it is refining the rudimentary behavior into a more extreme version. When first teaching your dog to "shake a paw," reward him for barely lifting his paw, or for simply batting your hand. Once he has the hang of this, withhold the treat until he lifts his paw higher, or holds it up longer. The rule of thumb is that every time your dog is achieving a step with about 75 percent success, you should up the ante and require a higher skill to earn the treat.

Regression Is a Part of Progression

The key to keeping your dog motivated is to keep him challenged and achieving regular successes. This requires constant alternation between upping the ante by asking for a more difficult behavior, and **regressing** by asking for an easier behavior.

Try not to let your dog be wrong more than two or three times in a row, or he could become discouraged and reluctant to perform. If your dog is struggling, temporarily lower the criteria for success. Go back to an easier step where he can be successful for a while.

"We want the dogs to fly" was the call that came into Critters of the Cinema owner Rob Bloch. "An airplane?" asked Rob. "No, no, no," answered the production assistant. "We want them flying . . . you know . . . through the air."

After thirty years in the animal-actors business, Rob was used to this. "No problem. We'll get right on it."

Over the next couple of days, Rob and I set about teaching pit bull mix Edie to "fly." We set up two sturdy wooden platforms about a foot apart. I would hold Edie at one end, and Rob would call her from the other end. Edie, with all her dog exuberance, would race across the platforms to Rob. We then spread the platforms a little wider apart, making a two-foot gap, and I called Edie back across to me. Taking our time, we slowly increased the gap until she was confidently jumping four feet. When we tried a five-foot gap, Edie stopped at the edge, unsure. We immediately pushed the platforms back to an achievable three feet. Edie was back on track. We again worked our way up, and she again had periods of regression. We never pushed her to do a jump she wasn't comfortable with. We helped her be successful by setting up trials that were just a little challenging for her.

The shoot turned out to be an ad for the Diesel jeans "Live Fast" campaign, where (with the help of a little Hollywood magic) the models are pictured running down the street with Edie and Chalcy flying behind them on leashes. The director had required only a four-foot jump—which is why we trained for five!

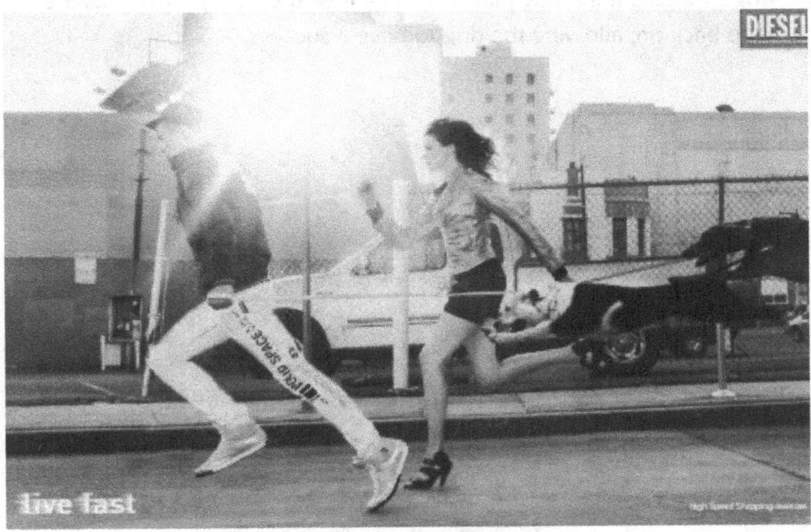

The process of learning a behavior is not linear. Your dog will go through numerous spurts of learning and regression. Don't be reluctant to go back a step—it's usually needed for only a short while, and it will give your dog confidence to move forward.

No matter what the issue, never push ahead in the training process if you reach a point where your dog is not confident. Instead, back up a few steps to where your dog showed the greatest degree of confidence and build his skills from there.

TEACH A TRICK! COVER YOUR EYES

One of the cuter dog tricks is teaching a dog to cover his eyes by hooking his paw over his muzzle. The first step in teaching this trick is to stick a sticky note or piece of tape to his muzzle and encourage him to "get it!" One swipe at his face is usually enough to dislodge the tape, at which point he gets a treat. As your dog improves, fade out the tape and instead just tap his muzzle at the spot where you normally put the tape. Trainers usually go through many periods of regression back to the tape. The trainer will cue "Cover" and tap the dog's muzzle. If the dog fails twice in a row, then the trainer puts the tape back on, allowing the dog to have a success.

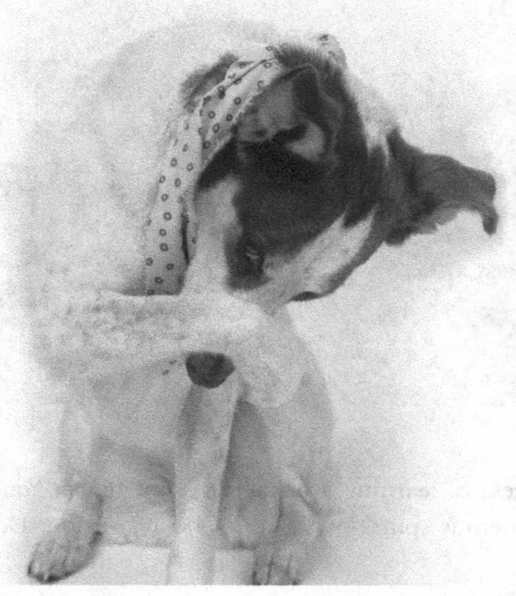

Your Dog Will Look Forward to Training Sessions!

You want your dog to be motivated to train, looking forward to your training session as a highlight of his day. Follow these rules to keep your dog highly motivated.

Blur the Line between Play and Work

If you feel as if you are engaged in a "training session," then so does your dog. If you're not having fun, then your dog is probably not, either. Don't plod through an uninspiring training session or your dog will associate training—and you—with boredom.

MOTIVATE your dog! Blur the line between play and work by playing when you train and training when you play. Is your dog ball- or Frisbee-crazy? Incorporate a toy reward after a great performance. Play a few minutes after every training session, to further blur the line between play and work.

Praise a Job Well Done

In everyday tasks, build your dog's motivation to perform by praising a job well done. Be sincere with your praise, and read the newspaper he fetched, put on the slippers, and thank your dog for putting away his toys.

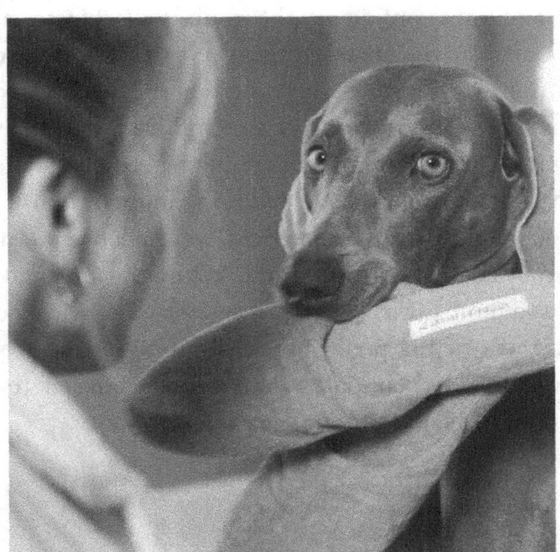

Remember, Training Comes before Playtime

Be careful not to make the mistake of letting your dog run around the park before his training session, to "get his zoomies out." This may be fine if you are training passive behaviors, such as "stays" and heeling, as the dog will be a little tired and less likely to put up a fuss. I don't, however, recommend opening a session with playtime if you are teaching active behaviors such as a sport, or tricks, or teaching new skills. Having a romp before a training session is like having recess before studies. When the bell rings and you have to go into the school building, you are going from something fun to something less fun, and you have little motivation. Instead, in the half hour or hour before your training session, make sure your dog is bored. Keep him in his crate, or in the house, or not with you. Then when you take him out for training, he'll be excited and eager to work. This is especially true in dog sport competitions, as you want your dog superenthusiastic to be working.

Train, Don't Practice

Practice is the continual repetition of the same skill with no increased expectation of performance (such as having your dog run a set of weave poles identically, over and over). Your dog soon becomes frustrated and bored, and loses confidence; the result is a lackluster performance. Trainers often make the mistake during repetitive practice of giving the most attention to their dog when the dog messes up—pops a weave pole, for example. This only serves to reinforce the incorrect behavior.

You're not teaching anything by doing repetitive practice. Your dog is not getting better if you're not requiring more of him.

When we train (instead of practice), we challenge our dog's current performance with higher expectations. We up the ante and ask more of him (such as a more difficult angle of entry to the weave poles) and we reward increases in his performance. Training engages the dog and makes him think. It habituates him to push himself toward higher goals. Training is the path to improved performance.

Determine the Right Number and Length of Training Sessions

"How many times a day should I train?" "For how long?" The answer to both of these questions, of course, is "It depends."

Puppies ideally should have several three-to-five-minute sessions throughout the day. Do just a few repetitions of each of their behaviors, and keep it fun. For now, the most important thing is to develop a relationship and a love of training.

Movie animal trainers prepping a dog for a specific scene will work the animal five times a day, for ten to fifteen minutes each session.

Basic obedience training (heeling, recall, sits, downs, stays) can easily go for one-hour sessions, as it is not as brain-intensive as some other types of training.

When training high-drive activities such as herding, agility, and search and rescue, you want to only allow the session to continue as long as the dog remains very enthusiastic. You want to keep that drive high by making your dog crave the activity. Hunting dogs are commonly put immediately into their kennel after a training session so that they will sit and think about how much fun it was, building their craving for next time!

Trick training is very brain-intensive. You're asking your dog to problem solve, experiment, offer new behaviors, and pay close attention to what he has done to earn a reward. It's very mentally tiring for a dog. In a usual one-hour training session with Chalcy, I'll start with behaviors she knows and is confident with. We then move into athletic tricks while her energy and motivation are high. At this point Chalcy has had success with the first part of her training session and is feeling confident. This is the perfect time to practice new behaviors. We spend just a few minutes on each new behavior. This is a very collaborative time, during which I give her a lot of feedback, a lot of treats, and a lot of excited praise.

Next comes brain work: problem solving. This utilizes skills Chalcy knows well as a vehicle for challenging her brain. Double commands are one type of brain-work exercise. I'll tell Chalcy to "target-sit" and she will run to a cone, and once there, sit. Or I'll have her hold a baton in her mouth while she does a second behavior. Much of this brain work has no real application—I just like to make her think!

We'll end our session with something fun, yet still educational. For Chalcy it's usually prey-drive games. Even playtime has rules, however, and I'll require her to "down" before a Frisbee throw, or "go hide" behind a tree before a bumper throw.

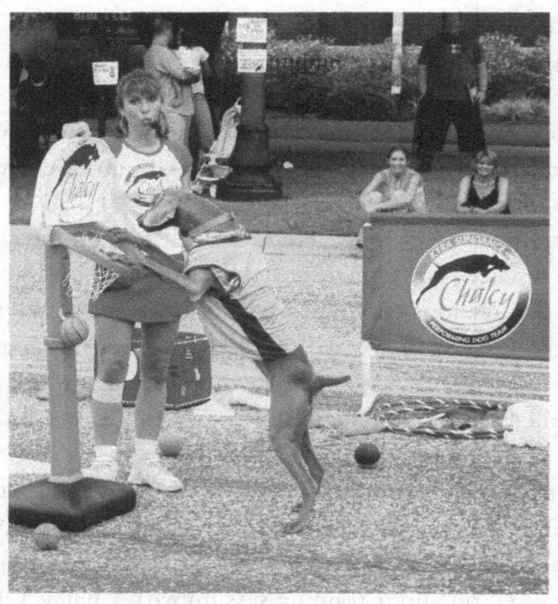

Have a Goal for Each Session

I would caution you against imposing time requirements on your training sessions. For one, you want to quit with your dog wanting more, so if he's having an off day or a really killer day, you may want to shorten or lengthen your session.

But mostly I would caution about wasting time with unstructured dillydallying and setup. This is detrimental to your training, as it teaches your dog that he can turn his attention on and off of you. Training with other people can be detrimental as well, as it encourages trainers to talk among themselves rather than focus on their dogs. During a session, you and your dog should be focused on each other constantly. Have a plan, have a set list, and keep it moving. If your dog needs a break, or you do, put your dog in a down-stay rather than have him wander aimlessly. This way he will look forward to going back to work.

My good friend Lana Maeder is a top stunt dog show performer and former disc dogger, having earned nationwide ranking in the competitive sport of canine flying disc. She structures her training sessions to work each of her dogs in two five-to-ten-minute sessions a day. Like me, she rarely practices tricks that the dogs have already mastered. She instead keeps them challenged with new behaviors. She'll jump right in with a new behavior at the start of her session, "when their minds are fresh." She does not put time criteria on her training sessions, but rather goal criteria. Before she starts, she'll define her goal: "My dog needs to jump rope six consecutive jumps." If her dog achieves it on the first try, then he gets his reward and the exercise is over! Woo-hoo! If not, she and the dog keep working on it until he gets six jumps. Through this method, the dog benefits from giving his best effort right away. Very smart, Lana!

TEACH A TRICK! JUMP ROPE!

Step one in teaching your dog to jump rope is to teach him to jump in place. While your dog is in a playful mood, hold a toy or food high in the air and tease him with it. Tell him to "jump" and encourage him by jumping along with him. Reward even small jumps at first. Remember, your job as a trainer is to MOTIVATE! Use your most excited "happy voice" to get him amped. Some dogs—terriers, Australian shepherds, and whippets, to name a few—are naturally bouncier than others. Other dogs may need much more encouragement to put forth the effort.

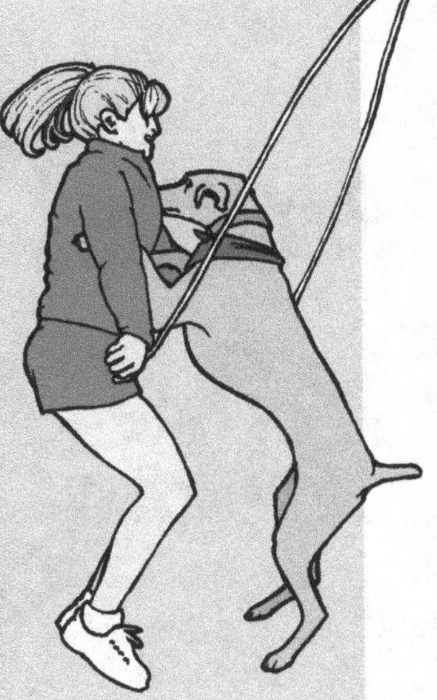

Reward Moments, Not Only Complete Behaviors

Even if you are training a longer behavior, reward your dog at any point during that behavior when he excelled. If you are training a difficult weave-pole entry, reward your dog the moment he does the successful entry, instead of waiting until he has completed the entire set of poles. You want to really reinforce that specific challenging behavior. Otherwise your dog will just think he got his reward for once again running the weave poles. Rewarding the exact moment helps your dog understand which specific action he performed so well. This also builds excitement for your dog, as he never knows when and where he will get the next reward.

Don't be predictable with your rewards—look for opportunities to reward a great moment. This is especially important if your dog has been struggling and suddenly has a breakthrough moment.

Quit with Him Wanting More

Randy and I often go on off-roading excursions in our Land Rover. Randy usually has a full itinerary of things he wants to see and do on each day,

making the most of the trip. What invariably happens is, after a wonderful, enjoyable day, he decides to take one last detour and we blow a tire, or have mechanical problems, or get stuck in the sand. For the next two hours I'll be freezing cold, using the stupid shovel to dig out the stupid tires that got stuck in the stupid sand. I'm not having fun anymore, and I have no desire to go on another trip anytime soon. This scenario has actually happened so many times that I've coined a phrase for it: "You always do one thing too many!"

When training your dog, quit while both of you are having a good time, and before your dog gets bored or tired. Quit with him wanting more so that he looks forward to the next session. Don't do one thing too many!

End on a High Note

Practicing new tricks is mentally tiring for your dog. To keep him motivated and excited about training, always end on a note of success, even if you have to go back to an easier behavior to achieve this. I won't end a training session with a missed Frisbee catch. Instead, I'll toss an easy one to Chalcy so we can end successfully. If we're working on a new behavior that is frustrating, we won't end there. I'll ask her for a few easy behaviors and praise her excitedly for them, and end the session then.

SUMMARY

- **Build your dog's confidence and motivation by giving him challenging chores that he can be successful at.**
- **Praise, touch, treat—in that order.**
- **Motivate through positive reinforcement to strengthen your relationship with your dog and make him a willing partner in the learning process.**
- **Positive-reinforcement needs to be mediated with discipline.**
- **Focus on the solution, not the problem. Help your dog develop a pattern of success, which will increase his motivation to perform. Think "What do I want my dog to do instead?" (e.g., sit on a mat instead of**

jumping on you) or "How do I want my dog to feel instead?" (e.g., excited to see the vacuum cleaner).

- Use tasty treats. Give them for every behavior during initial learning, and on a variable schedule once the behavior is mastered. Give a treat "jackpot" for very good efforts.
- Up the ante. Once your dog is achieving a 75 percent success rate, require more of him to get the same reward.
- Let your dog regress to an easier behavior rather than have him be unsuccessful more than two or three times in a row.
- Have your dog look forward to training sessions. Play when you train; praise a job well done; train before playtime; challenge your dog rather than practice repetitively; have a goal for each session; reward stellar moments and not just end behaviors; quit with him wanting more; end on a high note.

Rule 5: Fuel the Drive

Part of my training gear is a wide elastic band below my right knee which holds a canvas dog disc. After a sequence of fast-paced acrobatic stunts I reach down and fling the disc for Chalcy to lunge at and pull from the air. That's her reward.

Treats are a powerful primary reinforcer, but in many dogs there is an even stronger reinforcer: the opportunity to engage in a **prey-drive** activity. There is a kind of intensity you get in using a toy reward with a highly prey-driven dog that you can't get with food. The dog will do just about *anything* to get that toy! This can produce highly reliable behavior because the dog's desire to satisfy the drive is so compelling to him.

The fastest dogs with the most drive and endurance are those working for toys rather than food. Schutzhund, Police K-9, tracking, Search & Rescue, and bomb and narcotics detection dogs work relentlessly in order to get their Kong or jute stick reward upon finding their target object. Disc dogs are so high-drive that they often will reject treats in favor of chasing more discs. Flyball trainers have long known about the power of toys to get their dogs amped, and tug-toy rewards have become very popular among competitive agility and performance dog trainers. Nowadays, trainers in every dog sport are using toys to motivate their dogs' best possible performances.

Although more innately present in some breeds, intense prey drive can be developed in most dogs through drive exercises.

THE RULE

A highly prey-driven dog working for a toy reward will have the highest level of motivation to perform. Prey drive can be developed in any dog through drive exercises.

What Is Prey Drive?

A drive is an internal mechanism that pushes an animal into taking action. Dogs have a number of basic drives that evolved in the species to aid survival. Dogs needed to have the drive to chase, capture, and kill prey. This is their **prey drive**.

Prey drive (also known as predator drive) follows a predictable sequence: the search, the eye stalk, the chase, the grab bite, and the kill bite. In wolves the prey drive is complete and balanced. However, in different dog breeds certain of the five steps have been amplified or reduced by human-controlled selective breeding. The search aspect of the prey drive, for example, is very much amplified in tracking and detection dogs, such as bloodhounds and beagles. The eye stalk is a strong component in herding dogs, who are said to be able to "hypnotize" a herd animal with their stare. The chase drive is seen most clearly in racing dogs and lure-coursing dogs, while the grab bite and kill bite are strong in the terriers, who were bred to kill vermin.

Although prey drive is a hunting instinct, prey-drive behavior and play are closely related. As trainers we use prey-drive instincts in a play capacity, where the dog in prey mode is bouncy, with ears up, tail up, and excited about chasing his ball. The dog is not growling, but rather sometimes emitting high-pitched playful barks that are actually prey-flushing barks (barks intended to stimulate the prey to get moving so the dog can chase it). Engaging in prey-drive activities is great fun for a dog, and it stimulates and satisfies this drive.

If you have a highly prey-driven dog . . . consider yourself lucky. No, really, I'm serious! Prey-driven dogs can admittedly be a challenge to live with. They are high-energy, they can turn into freaks at a moment's notice, and they *never* tire of the game before you do. But the prey drive can be used as a superpowerful motivator to entice optimal performance from your dog. Dogs with well developed prey drive can be a pleasure to train; they have exceptional endurance, enthusiasm, and motivation for performance activities. Prey drive, not food rewards, is the motivation for dogs to perform activities such as disc dog, dock diving, hunting, herding, lure coursing, and go-to-ground.

How to Use Prey Drive as a Motivator

Enunciated by experimental psychologist David Premack, **Premack's principle** is a principle of operant conditioning that basically states, "If you do something I want, then you'll get to do something *you* want" (e.g., play with the toy). All mothers have used this technique, saying things like "Do your homework and you'll get to watch TV." Building your dog's desire for the toy gives you a highly desirable reward with which you can tempt your dog.

> **Police dog trainer Alex Rothacker explains how, when training dogs for search and rescue work, the trainer who acts as the quarry holds a jute stick or Kong tug toy. The quarry lays a track by walking through a field, or around the block. Alex puts the dog on a lead and prompts him to smell a "scent pad" at the beginning of the track which indicates the scent the dog is to follow. The dog's drive to track his quarry is obvious—he pulls on his harness, and he whines or quivers with excitement as he closes in. His tail flags side to side, indicating he is on the scent. When he finds the trainer (quarry) at the end of the track, the trainer pulls out a jute stick and rewards the dog with a rambunctious game of tug. In effect, the dog tracks the scent trail with the goal of finding his jute stick at the end.**

Developing a prey-drive reinforcer takes time and work on your part. You don't just hand the toy to your dog as you would a treat. You

have to really get into it—play a good game of tug, throw a good Frisbee toss, run with him, challenge him. A toy play session reward generally lasts from ten seconds to a few minutes, and is generally saved for the end of a series of exercises, rather than used after every single exercise.

The most common drive toys are ones that are used in a game of tug and ones that are used as retrieves, and there are advantages to each. A game of tug serves two purposes (besides being rewarding for your dog). It serves to keep your dog close to you, which is necessary at the end of an agility or flyball run to keep him from running zoomies all over the park. And it is a bonding activity, as it is something that your dog cannot play alone, but rather must engage in with you.

The advantage of a retrieval toy such as a Frisbee or ball is that it allows you to reward your dog from a distance. This is important in agility, as you want to encourage your dog to range out and not always hang next to your ankles. If you send your dog "away" to "tunnel," you can throw the reward at the end of the tunnel. This encourages speed from your dog, as he'll want to reach the end of the tunnel as quickly as possible to get his toy at the other end.

A toy motivator can be used in conjunction with food rewards. You can routinely reward your dog from your bait bag and then jackpot him with the toy at the end of a training segment or when he does something especially great. You can increase the toy's value by first throwing it, and then exchanging it for a treat when your dog brings it back.

A toy is also a great way to rev your dog up before an activity. At an agility start line, have someone hold your dog back while you stand beyond the first several obstacles and wave his toy at him. Release the dog at the height of his frenzy and watch his drive and speed explode!

There is always the need to balance drive with control, and that pendulum is constantly shifting. Toys build drive. They get your dog amped, and fast, and intense, and motivated to work. But they also get your dog vibrating with such excitement that he has a hard time sitting still. If he can see the toy, he may get so preoccupied with it that he can't focus. Keep your toy hidden under your shirt while you train, and whip it out when you wish to reward your dog. When you train control exercises, such as stays, it's better to reward with just food. Food is also better when training new behaviors, as it is quick and easy to dispense.

Bringing Out the Prey Drive

If your dog is tennis ball crazy, chasing balls and relentlessly hunting for them when they roll out of sight, he is high-drive. The same goes for chasing Frisbees, rabbits, lizards, gophers, or flashlight circles. But *all* dogs have some degree of prey-drive instinct. A trainer who complains, "My dog doesn't like toys" just hasn't worked enough at it. The challenge for trainers is to build drive to a usable level through games that encourage an obsessive expression of prey behaviors, primarily through games of tug, Frisbee, or ball.

Drive benefits from frequent stimulation. The more you engage in prey play with your dog, the more he'll desire it. Over time your dog will get very excited at the sight of the toy, and will be more determined to get it. Now you've got a prey-drive toy as a reinforcer!

Trainers usually have one special toy that is reserved for training. Your power as a trainer comes from the fact that you control access to this toy. Don't leave it accessible to your dog during the day. The toy is to be played with only with you, and on your terms. When you decide the game is over, say "mine" and take the toy and put it in the closet.

Choosing the Right Toy

Finding the right toy is critical, as many dogs will play tug or catch or fetch only with the right toy used at the correct point in their training development. Many trainers have supposed that their dog lacks drive, when in reality the dog simply needs different toys or a different form of engagement from his trainer.

Buy a bunch of different toys and let your dog choose the one he likes. Sporting breeds have some kind of inbred obsession with cylindrical rubber hunting bumpers, while Labs adore balls, and herding breeds go bonkers over Frisbees. Police dogs and Schutzhund dogs respond to a jute stick, which is a stuffed tube with a handle on one end used for tugging.

If your dog is an avid retriever but doesn't show the same enthusiasm for playing tug, there are toys that are designed for both—that is, first you throw, and then you tug—such as a ball or Kong on a rope, or rope-and-canvas discs. Tennis balls shouldn't be used, as their texture actually acts like sandpaper, wearing down your dog's teeth. Likewise, hard plastic discs aren't appropriate for games of tug.

When you are trying out new toys with your dog, do so outdoors, when your dog is excited. Trying to train prey drive in your living room is fighting an uphill battle.

Tug

Using a tug toy as a reward has become widely popular in recent years in amped-up dog sports such as agility, flyball, dock diving, Schutzhund, and even in the more controlled sport of obedience. In agility it has become popular to use specially designed "tug leashes," because toys are not allowed at the finish line, but leashes are.

> **Some prey-driven dogs are rewarded with a jute, some with a ball, some with a Frisbee, and one with . . . Well, I'll let Terry explain.**
>
> **"Reveille goes crazy for the broom as a reward."**
>
> **I'm confused. "What, like a regular broom? What does she do with it?" Crazy border collie!**
>
> **"Yeah," answers Terry. "There's an old broom lying out in the agility yard. When we finish a run, she grabs the bristles and shakes it around and we play tug. I've tried to give her food as a reward, but she's so intense that she doesn't want the food. She just wants the broom!"**
>
> **Terry Simons, prominent dog agility trainer, is host of the AKC International Agility Invitational for Animal Planet. He does the play-by-play you see on TV, calling the action of the nation's top competitions. Terry gets top performance from all of his agility dogs not with treats, but with tug toy motivators.**

Although it's easiest to bring out the prey drive in a puppy versus an older dog who has never built the drive, it is possible with all dogs. If your dog is a puppy, or hasn't had much opportunity to develop his drive, start with an appropriate drive-building toy that is long and whippy and easy to manipulate. Since your dog will be biting the toy, it should be of a thin, easy-to-grab material. Good drive-building toys are

- Toys with fleece tops and hanging leather pieces
- Leather puppy rags—chamois or jute material, at least eighteen inches long
- Long fleece toys with pieces hanging from them, such as snake or octopus shapes (these may come with squeakers, which can help to entice some dogs)
- Fleece or real fur toys with a pouch for food inside (food is

sometimes a distraction, but it can help build interest with a dog who isn't responding to the toy alone)

Build your dog's interest in the toy by making playful gestures with it, tossing it in the air to yourself or playing monkey-in-the-middle with another person. If you put an apparent value on the toy and make it appear interesting to you, it should become interesting to your dog.

Move the toy on the ground in an erratic fashion, but always away from your dog. If your dog is hesitant, let the toy rest on the ground, but occasionally have it skitter away in fear if your dog approaches. Your toy should imitate a real prey animal that doesn't want to be caught. Keep the toy just out of your dog's reach, building prey drive to the maximum. When he chases with great enthusiasm, let him catch it. The victory is much sweeter for your dog if he believes he has earned it. If you "feed" the toy to him, he won't want it nearly as much.

Play a little tug once your dog catches it, to teach him to hold on to his prey. Move the toy relatively smoothly side to side (not a backward/forward tug), with an occasional careful jerk. Just remember that if the toy ever falls out of his mouth, it goes back to being live prey that tries to run away from your dog.

Frisbee / Flying Disc

Lou Mack, legendary disc dog competitor and former head trainer of the Purina Incredible Dog Team, knows how to find a Frisbee dog. He has a pack of them that he tours with, performing at fairs and halftime shows. In his travels he'll often check out the local animal shelters, always searching for the next super-high-drive disc dog to augment his show. His tactic? He just wiggles a Frisbee past the rows of kennels in the shelter. "Some dogs couldn't care less," he says, "and some get all excited. Every once in a while, though, there is one that just goes berserk! That's what I look for!"

A flying disc is inherently intriguing to a dog, as it flies away from him, birdlike, just out of his reach. There is more human skill required with this toy than with a tug toy, which is why you should be practicing three times as many throws as your dog practices catches.

Start with a flexible or canvas disc that is easy on your dog's mouth, such as an Aerobie Dogobie or a Soft Bite floppy disc. Play tug-of-war and retrieval games until your dog is comfortable with the disc in his mouth. Many competitive disc dog trainers familiarize their dogs with the plastic disc by using it as a feeding dish, creating a positive association with the sight, smell, and feel of it.

When your dog is in a playful mood, spin the upside-down disc in circles with your finger. When he shows interest, throw a "roller"—rolling the disc along its edge like a wheel. Your dog can actually seize the disc while it is rolling, without the added difficulty of catching it in the air.

To throw a disc in the air, hold it parallel to the ground, with your fingers curled under the inside edge, your index finger slightly extended. With shoulders perpendicular to your target, pull the disc across your body. Snap your elbow and wrist just before you release the disc.

If your dog catches it, or attempts to catch it, praise him lavishly and repeat the exercise. If he simply watches it and lets it fall to the ground, go back to building drive and desire by regressing to where your dog is once again successful. Build confidence with success.

Once your dog is chasing the disc, encourage him to bring it back to you by clapping your hands and calling to him. If he tries to play keep-away, use two identical discs and enthusiastically present the second disc while showing no interest in the disc your dog is holding in his mouth. Throw the second disc the moment the first one is dropped, so your dog thinks that he is causing you to throw the second disc by dropping the first. With the hard-core keep-away artist, you must be prepared to walk away from the game after only one toss.

When you finally have your dog catching and returning the disc with the expectation of getting another one thrown, you have successfully converted prey to play.

Dogs can get hurt doing sports, so do your part and think about potential dangers and how to avoid them. Here are some safety tips:

- Dogs under fourteen months should not be jumping for the disc, and all dogs should be checked by a veterinarian to ensure soundness.
- Use a flying disc specifically designed for a dog, such as the Hyperflite or the Frisbee Fastback soft plastic disc. Hard plastic toy discs could injure your dog's mouth and teeth.
- Don't throw directly at your dog, as you could hit him.
- Throw the disc in a low, flat trajectory. Dogs should jump in such a way that they land with four paws on the ground, rather than vertically, which can stress their spine and rear knees.
- Beginners always throw slicers, discs that tilt during flight and slice down at an almost vertical angle. To correct this, throw with "hyzer" by tilting the outside edge of the disc toward the ground at a 45-degree angle.

Ball

I was about the third or fourth week into teaching a dog-tricks class when I brought a bucket of tennis balls to teach the dogs to fetch. After instructing the class, I went from student to student, giving individual help. Out of the corner of my eye I saw a Sheltie going bonkers for the tennis ball. He was racing after it and barking excitedly if his owner didn't throw it fast enough.

"What happened to Dakota?" I asked incredulously. This little dog had spent the first few weeks of class completely disengaged, refusing to take a treat or participate in the class. "Oh," said Dakota's owner, "it's just the tennis ball. He goes crazy for them. We play ball every day."

I showed Dakota's owner how to use the tennis ball as a motivator and reward for behavior. The next week, Dakota was a completely different dog participating eagerly in class! Instead of a treat as a lure, the owner used a tennis ball. And instead of a treat as a reward, she used a tennis ball. And when she wanted Dakota's attention, she brought out the . . . Well, you know the rest!

TEACH A TRICK! FETCH

Teach your dog to fetch by cutting a slit in a tennis ball with a box cutter. Let your dog watch as you drop some kibble inside. Then toss the ball for him and encourage him to "get it." He will soon figure out that he can't get the kibble out himself, but if he brings it back to you, you can squeeze it open and let the kibble drop out.

Once your dog is enamoured with the game of fetch, double the fun by adding a tug element. Drill a hole in the ball and guide a rope through it and secure it with a knot. Soon your dog will eagerly fetch the new toy and tug it like crazy to win it. Now you can hurl this exciting toy as a reward for stellar performance.

SUMMARY

- Prey drive produces the highest form of motivation in a dog, but it needs to be developed through drive exercises.
- Use a prey-drive object as a jackpot reward, or to rev up your dog before an activity.
- The more your dog engages in prey play, the more drive he'll build.
- Designate a special motivator toy, and do not allow your dog free access to it.
- Try different toys until you find the right one: flying disc, tug, bumper, ball, Kong on a rope, jute stick, etc.
- Begin to develop prey drive with an appropriate drive-building toy. Make the toy behave like a live prey animal.

Rule 6: Attention Is a Reward

6 THE RULE

Recognize your attention toward your dog as the powerful reward that it is. Cultivate your dog's desire for your attention and you've got something of great value that you can use to influence his behavior. Use it as a payoff for your dog's good behavior or learned behavior, and withdraw it as a consequence for his inappropriate behavior.

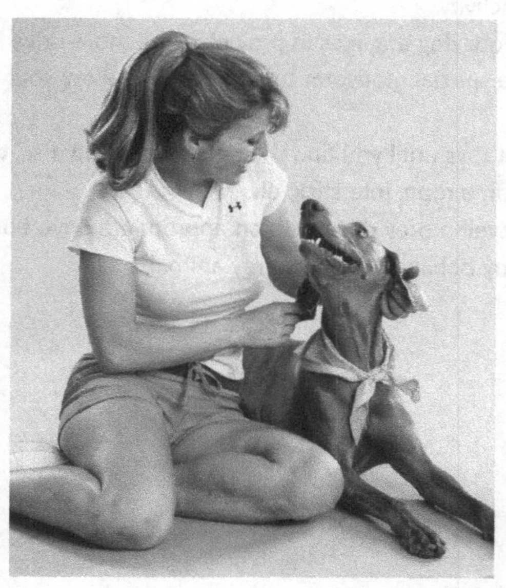

Despite the resulting paw prints all over your clothes, you'll surely admit that one of the most wonderful qualities of our dogs is their exuberant yearning for—and appreciation of—our attention.

The more your dog values your attention, the more he will strive to please you in order to retain your attention.

Make Your Dog Value Your Attention

Be a Fun Person to Be Around!

Here's my favorite piece of advice for dog owners: "Be a fun person to be around!" The more fun you are, the more your dog is going to value your attention, and the more powerful this reinforcer will become.

When your dog is nearby, make an effort to be the center of a "radius of fun," where life is enjoyable and exciting. Have treats, throw balls, pull your dog's tail, hide from her, chase her, make funny noises, wrestle, tug, hide things, laugh, and smile—make your radius of fun the best place in the world.

If you want a dog who is enthusiastic and attentive to you, then you have to be attentive to him. Don't chat with your friends while your dog meanders during a training session. If your dog is not directly engaging with you, his focus and work ethic will be compromised, and he will develop a pattern of inattention and sniffing that is hard to break.

Make Time for Three Enrichment Activities a Day

Why do you think so many pets are overweight? It's probably because we feel guilty about not giving them enough quality time, and so we give them food to compensate. And why do you think so many dogs are lacking in discipline? Probably for the same reason. We spend too little quality time with them, and then we feel guilty when the time in which we do focus on them is spent in discipline. We want to be nice to them, and therefore we let them get away with inappropriate behavior.

So what's the solution? The solution is to give that dedicated time and enrichment to your dog. Knowing that you are being fair to your dog by satisfying his needs will make you feel more confident and resolute when enforcing your rules.

Dogs need quality time and interaction with us; they crave attention and things to keep their minds busy. A great dog owner is involved in activities with his or her dog, engages the dog's mind, exposes him to new things, teaches him to make good choices, and gives him emotional support and confidence. If you don't make the effort to engage your dog's mind, then he will become more independent of you and likely find other, less constructive ways to entertain himself.

Your goal should be to engage in three enrichment activities with your dog every day. An enrichment activity can be a walk, a game of fetch, a training session, a trip to the mall, a game of "find the hidden veggies," a car ride, a roughhousing play session, a grooming session, a play date with another dog, or a chore such as getting the morning newspaper. Make the most of this time with your dog by really being present in the moment. Don't talk on the phone, don't listen to the radio, don't converse with your spouse. Give your dog your undivided attention.

Ideally, one of the daily enrichment activities should be a **side-by-side** team-building activity, such as a walk or an excursion. The second enrichment activity should be an **eye-to-eye** activity, in which you interact with your dog while the two of you look into each other's eyes. Training a trick is a perfect eye-to-eye activity as it encourages eye contact communication. And I like the third activity to be something playful—maybe a good game of chase, or tug, or "got your tail," or hide-and-seek.

I have a dry-erase board on the inside of my closet door, to help keep me true to this promise to my dog. Every evening I write on the board the three enrichment activities I did with Chalcy that day. As I go through my day, I am more likely to take time for Chalcy, as I know I will be holding myself accountable to my promise at night.

What Are You Rewarding?

Now that you are such a fun person to be around and your dog craves your attention, you can bestow or withhold it in order to gain his cooperation. Good, well-behaved dogs should get attention, while naughty dogs should not. Notice that I *didn't* say "Good dogs should get GOOD attention, and naughty dogs should get BAD attention." Whether it is positive or negative, any attention can be rewarding to your dog, and it is therefore best to respond to inappropriate behavior with the least attention possible.

Extinction: Stop Reinforcing Unwanted Behavior

I grit my teeth and continue working in my office, trying to ignore Chalcy in the lobby as she brazenly pushes a box off our bookshelf with her paw, and then turns to look back at me defiantly. My staff snicker. I ignore them. And her. Chalcy moves to the next cubbyhole in the bookshelf and knocks a second box over with her paw. She looks. They snicker. I ignore.

Chalcy has always come to work with me, and as a puppy she would roust me every hour or so to take her for a walk. I would try to stall for a few minutes as I finished that last e-mail, or made that last phone call, placating her with "just a minute" or "almost finished, honey." She would become progressively more demanding and would pester me by pulling things, jumping on the door, bringing me things she found in the lunchroom trash can, nudging my arm, or loudly scratching at the grating on her kennel.

Apparently the tactic she found most effective in getting me out of my chair was knocking software boxes off the bookshelf that divided our lobby. The structure served as a room divider, with open cubbies that allowed one to see through to the other side. In each cubby I had artfully placed a software box, highlighting the tools of our Internet business. Chalcy would deliberately and systematically push each from its cubby, knocking it to the floor. She knew it aggravated me. Each push was followed by a stare back into my office.

Whether it resulted in a walk or a reprimand, it almost always resulted in my getting out of my chair, Chalcy had discovered. So over

the years she had successfully trained me. Her bad behavior resulted in a response from me, so she continued to engage in it. I blame myself, of course, as a good trainer knows that "it's always the trainer's fault."

This story does have a happy ending. One day, much to the disappointment of my snickering staff, I decided to change this behavior in Chalcy. I gritted my teeth and refused to reward this undesired behavior with any attention. I gave no more reinforcement to the unwanted behavior of knocking over boxes. This behavior, however, didn't just disappear overnight, as it had been reinforced over several years, and was well ingrained in her head. The behavior had to go through an **extinction** process.

When you stop rewarding a behavior that had previously been rewarded, and thereby teach your dog to stop engaging in it, you extinguish the behavior. If you stop giving your dog scraps from the table, he will eventually stop begging at the table. Simple enough?

I'm not telling you anything you don't already know (although I *did* use a fancy name for it!). I just want to draw your attention to behaviors your dog may be doing in response to inadvertent reinforcement from you. Is your dog (or possibly *my* dog) being rewarded for knocking over software boxes by getting attention or a walk? When your dog jumps on you, do you pet him? When he scratches at the door, do you let him out? When he acts shy or fearful, do you coddle him? If you coddle him then, you are rewarding a fear behavior, contributing to its continuation.

If you want these behaviors to stop, simply stop rewarding them with your attention and they will become extinguished. Although there are other methods of curbing a previously rewarded behavior, such as reprimanding your dog for engaging in it, extinction is the easiest and clearest method. You need not do anything more than refrain from rewarding the unwanted behavior. Are you ready to give it a try?

All right, without laying blame, we'll just admit that mistakes have been made. For whatever reason, your dog has picked up some bad habits and has continued to practice them because he has been rewarded for them in the past. Well, today is a new day and you've decided this behavior will no longer be rewarded. Your dog will receive no more scraps from your table, and my dog will receive no more walks for knocking over software boxes. Strap yourself in—we are about to embark on the process of behavior extinction!

During the process of extinction, the unwanted behavior will often get worse before it gets better, in a flurry of attempts known as an **extinction burst**. The dog will not immediately give up the behavior once he has stopped being rewarded for it, but rather he will try the behavior again and again, harder, faster, more emphatically, in a burst of activity. It's like the final tantrum before the child gives up. Or, in Chalcy's case, it was a tantrum of knocking over every single software box on the shelf, and then stomping on them for good measure.

An example of an extinction burst that most of us can relate to is the common reaction to a broken crosswalk button. You cross streets every day; you press the crosswalk button and are rewarded with the little "walk" icon that allows you to cross. One day, you push the button and nothing happens. Do you think, "Hmm, this button must be broken, I'll have to cross at the next block," or do you continue to push the button again and again, and harder and faster? Yes? *That's* the extinction burst that happens right before you give up.

At the start of the extinction process with your dog, the unwanted behavior subsides gradually, and then has one last sharp spike, where the dog performs the behavior very strongly. This extinction-burst spike usually occurs right before the dog finally gives up. Hang in there! If at all possible, ignore your dog's misbehavior during this extinction burst, as giving attention to it will likely cause the behavior to get even worse.

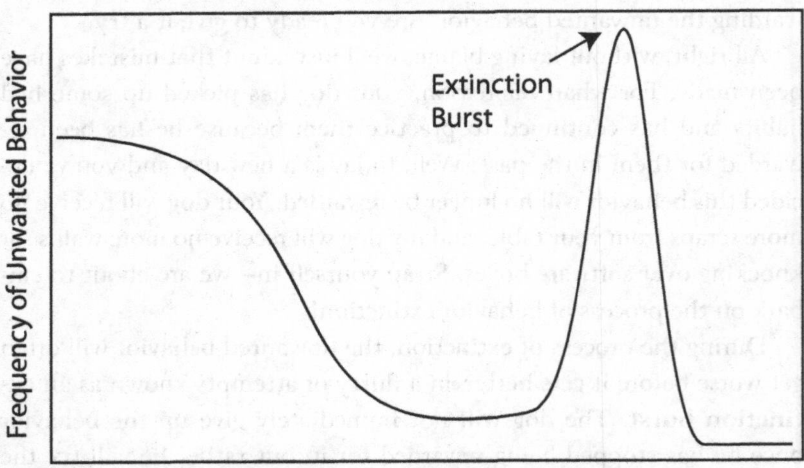

A variable schedule of reinforcement (see page 54) makes a behavior harder to extinguish. If your dog is accustomed to being rewarded sporadically for a behavior, he is not likely to stop the first few times his action fails to generate a reward. If you've rewarded your dog *every*

single time he has begged, and then you stop, he'll actually give up more easily than if you had rewarded him only intermittently. If the behavior is re-rewarded after it has been extinguished, it will pop back into existence much more quickly than it took for the dog to learn it the first time.

Internal Reinforcers and Punishers

Trainers unfortunately cannot control all **reinforcers** (things that cause a behavior to increase) and **punishers** (things that cause a behavior to decrease). There are a number of environmental factors over which we have no control that affect the dog's behavior. Some of these come from the dog's internal environment—his own reactions. Relief from stress, pain, or boredom are common reinforcers, and some "self-reinforcing" behaviors are actually maintained due to this reinforcement. A dog may bark because barking relieves boredom, chase a cat because it's fun, or chase his own tail to relieve stress. Extinction won't work if the behavior you are trying to extinguish is self-rewarding. You can ignore a dog chewing a bone all you want, but because the act of chewing the bone is, in and of itself, rewarding to the dog, your lack of reinforcement will not affect the continuation of the behavior. Your best bet in reducing self-reinforcing behaviors is to break the cycle by using DRI (see page 49) to teach your dog to choose a different behavior that is even more rewarding. Instead of his chasing the cat, get him obsessed with chasing a ball that you throw.

Teach Your Dog to Manage His Frustration

I can remember many a homework lesson from my dad, skiing lesson from my mom, and backflip-off-the-diving-board lesson from my brother that ended with me crying, or hitting, or slamming my door. I *wanted* to learn, I wasn't getting it fast enough, and I got frustrated.

Your dog can also get frustrated during the learning process. Nothing worthwhile comes out of a dog's frustration, so we want to manage the learning process so that it never gets to that point. We want to teach our dog to manage his frustration.

Your dog, Buddy, is jumping with excitement, trying to get you to throw his ball. He pokes at you, paws at you, jumps on you, barks at you—"Throw it! Throw it!" You tell him, "Sit! Sit!" Buddy is overexcited, and he becomes frustrated at not getting his reward. Frustration leads to aggression, and Buddy bites you.

Let's play this out again using what is called the "least-reinforcing scenario." Buddy is poking and pawing at you. You are trying to get him to sit, but he isn't understanding. He becomes frustrated and barks at you. You put your arms at your sides, stand still, and look away from him a few seconds until he calms down. The cycle is disrupted, and Buddy waits for your attention to return to him. You then praise him, rewarding him for his calm attention. Now, calmer, he has an easier time understanding your command. Once he sits, you reward him by throwing the ball.

You've quickly and effectively broken the escalating cycle of excitement and frustration, and have taught Buddy to control his frustration and give you renewed attention to learn.

If a dog is giving an incorrect behavior, he obviously will not be rewarded. Not getting his reward can cause frustration, and frustration can sometimes lead to aggression. In order to avoid perpetuating the mistake-frustration-aggression sequence, we need to either reduce frustration or teach the dog to react to frustration in an acceptable manner. The LRS technique (described below) achieves both of these goals.[1]

- LRS reduces the dog's frustration.
- LRS teaches the dog to react to frustration in an acceptable manner.

The Least-Reinforcing Scenario Technique

If a trainer requests a particular behavior and the dog responds with an incorrect behavior, any response—positive or negative—from the trainer can fuel the incorrect behavior. If the dog's behavior provokes no trainer response, however, it will typically die away. This nonresponse from the trainer is termed the **least-reinforcing scenario**, or **LRS**.

Following an incorrect behavior, the trainer executes an LRS by simply standing still, looking away, and doing nothing for a few seconds, making it least likely that he is delivering any reinforcer to his dog. The trainer does not ignore his dog, as this could make his dog think that the trainer didn't see his behavior, and thus could cause the dog to continue trying to show the behavior to the trainer. Instead, the trainer monitors the dog's behavior while taking care not to show a response.

In the example above, when Buddy gave an incorrect behavior (barking), the trainer put his arms at his sides and looked away. This served two purposes: It gave no reinforcement (neither positive nor negative attention) to Buddy, and it signaled Buddy to give calm attention to his trainer. Over time, the dog learns that when his owner does an LRS, it is actually an opportunity for him to earn a reward by giving calm attention.

- LRS gives no reinforcement of the unwanted behavior.
- LRS signals the dog to give us calm attention.

Training using LRS follows this progression:

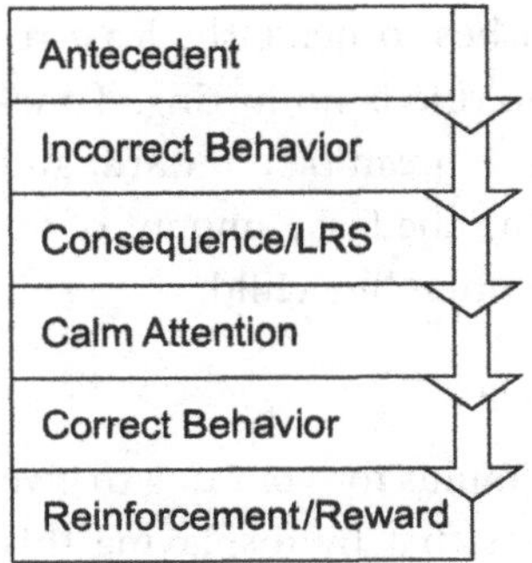

In the example with Buddy, the LRS progression looks like this:

Antecedent	You tell Buddy to "sit."
Incorrect Behavior	Buddy barks at you instead.
Consequence/LRS	You turn away from Buddy for a few seconds.
Calm Attention	Buddy stops barking and looks calmly at you.
Correct Behavior	You tell Buddy to "sit" and he sits.
Reinforcement/Reward	You throw Buddy's ball as a reward.

No Reinforcement of Unwanted Behavior

LRS is sometimes misinterpreted as "doing nothing in response to bad behavior." It is important to make two distinctions. First, we need to distinguish between **bad** behavior and **incorrect** or **inappropriate** behavior. Bad behavior is the dog doing something naughty that he either knows he is not supposed to do, or is being trained not to do. Rooting in the kitchen trash is bad behavior, and should be corrected with a sharp "no!" Incorrect or inappropriate behavior is a behavior that may be either correct or neutral in some situations, but is not the desired behavior in this particular situation. Such behavior would include Buddy's barking in the example above. This is not bad behavior, but is also not behavior that will result in a reward.

The other distinction to be made is that between "doing nothing" and responding with "the least response necessary." If a child hits his brother and the parent doesn't impose a consequence, that would be "doing nothing." If, however, the parent wishes to make the least response necessary, he might say, "Johnny, the rule is no hitting. Time-out." No discussion, no argument. All attention can be a reward, and by responding in this way the parent is giving the least amount of attention—either positive or negative—to the offending child.

Reward Calm Attention

An LRS is not a punishment, but rather a stimulus for your dog to give you calm, attentive behavior. The dog learns that by displaying this calm, attentive behavior he will be either rewarded or given the opportunity to perform another behavior that will result in a reward. Rather than becoming frustrated because "mistakes" are not rewarded, your dog learns to manage his frustration and react in a nonaggressive way. Your dog is never forced into a situation, nor is he ever punished.

Do you remember the teacher in school who tried to get the class to settle down by standing silently in front of the room? "I'm just going to stand here until every last student is quiet," she'd say. That tactic didn't work very well, did it? As long as you weren't the *very* last one talking, you could pretty much stretch out your conversation a few more minutes. This teacher was using LRS on her class—

but why wasn't it working? It wasn't working because we had no reward to entice us to give her calm attention. The consequence for finally settling down was that we had to start our lessons—not much of a reward!

Rewarding your dog's calm attention is key. Make a habit of requiring a moment of calm attention before giving routine rewards, such as at the front door before you take your dog for a walk, or at the food dish at chow time. Wait for your dog to be still and hold eye contact with you for a second or two, or longer if he is able, then immediately tell him "good" and give him his reward. This will help teach your dog self-control, and let him know that calm, attentive behavior is rewarded.

Withdraw Your Attention, Stop Problem Behavior

Part of training your dog is teaching him things you want him to do, and part is teaching him which things you don't want him to do. Traditional animal-training methods rely on pleasure and pain consequences. Inflicting pain, however, works against the close, trusting relationship we are trying to build with our dog. Instead, we have another tool in our tool kit: withdrawing our attention. You can remove your attention as a consequence for bad behavior.

We use this strategy with our kids all the time. When kids misbehave, we may remove our attention or take other pleasurable things away from them. You may tell a child, "If you don't stop hitting your sister, I'll take away your video game." By taking away or threatening to take away something pleasant (his video game) as a consequence, you teach the child to stop hitting his sister.

With a child, we can explain the cause and effect of this type of punishment—that he is losing his video game privileges because he broke a rule. It certainly would make our job easier if we could explain things to our dog the same way. But, of course, we can't convey long-term consequences to a dog; that is why consequences have to be immediate.

With a dog, we have only a handful of immediate pleasurable things we can take away. The most common of them are our attention and the dog's play environment.

I play-wrestle with Chalcy as a puppy, and she gets a little too excited and bites my ear. "Ouch! That hurt, I'm not playing with you anymore," I pout as I cross my arms and turn my back on her.

Puppy Chalcy immediately quiets down and peers apprehensively at me.

In this example I withdrew my participation in the play session as a consequence for her hard bite. She learned not to bite me hard in the future.

Here are some more ways to use attention withdrawal to stop problem behavior:

- Your dog jumps on you and you walk away from him. You are removing something that your dog finds pleasant: your attention. Your dog will learn not to jump on you in order to avoid losing your attention.
- You are playing ball and your dog decides to play keep-away. You walk away, again removing the pleasant condition of your attention and the play session. Your dog learns not to play keep-away.
- Your dog plays roughly with another, more timid dog, so you leash him and remove his opportunity to play. Your dog learns not to play roughly in future.

Again, be aware of your own actions, as unfortunately it is also possible to teach incorrect behavior with this method. If you call your dog to "come," and when he does come you leash him and take him from the park, you have just removed his play session as a consequence of his coming when called. Your dog will be less likely to respond to the recall the next time. Instead, go and get your dog when you are ready to leave.

Remember the anecdote under Rule 2, where Cowboy was tied to a tree as a consequence for his growling in class? His owner was attempting to use attention withdrawal to stop this problem behavior. There were a couple of things, however, which made his owner's execution of this technique ineffective. First, her withdrawal of attention lasted way too long. After the first minute, the dog is no longer making the association between what he did and the consequence of his action. Second, the consequence was so traumatic for the dog that his anxiety overshadowed any learning that could have helped him associate the action and the consequence. The moment his owner walked out the gate, his entire attention turned to the anxiety at hand: "Oh my gosh! Where's my owner? What's happening?"

How could this have been better executed? When the dog growls, the owner puts him in a crate or ties him to a tree and turns her back on him. That way, the dog's thoughts are of "Hey, what happened? Why is everybody ignoring me? I want to go back to our class!" Also, when the consequences are short, the owner can execute more of them during the one-hour class period. Growl; crate. Growl; crate. Growl; crate. "Oh . . . I get it!"

SUMMARY

- Be a fun person to be around so that your dog values your attention.
- Engage in three enrichment activities with your dog every day: a side-by-side activity, an eye-to-eye activity, and a play activity.
- Give attention only to behavior you wish to reinforce. Giving any attention to bad behavior could inadvertently reinforce it.
- Use extinction to stop a behavior that had previously been rewarded (such as knocking software boxes off the shelf).
- Use the least-reinforcing scenario (LRS) when your dog gives an inappropriate response:
  - Put your arms at your sides and look away for three seconds.
  - Reward your dog for his calm attention. (Reward with a treat or a new opportunity to perform a behavior and earn a reward.)
- Require a few seconds of calm attention before routine rewards.
- Withdraw your attention as a consequence for bad behavior. (When your dog jumps on you, turn your back and walk away.)

Teach Behavior

In the spring of 2007 I received an extraordinary phone call. It was Morocco's chief ambassador requesting Chalcy and me for a command performance at the pleasure of His Majesty the King. Cool!

Our stunt dog show at the royal palace garden in Marrakech honored the crown prince, Moulay Al Hassan, on his birthday. The audience was delighted by Chalcy's antics, which transcended our English/French language barrier.

After the show the king played with Chalcy, attempting to push the right buttons to get her to perform. *"Aboie!"* he commanded. *"Aboie!"*

Chalcy, being entirely unfamiliar with this word, looked intently into his eyes. She observed his hands and body language. She looked around at his immediate surroundings for a ball or a bar jump or a hula hoop . . . something that would give her a clue as to what he was trying to communicate. *"Aboie!"* again. She began to try things: Did you want this basketball? No? Do you want me to sit? To shake hands? How about a bark? "Woof!"

This overjoyed the king. *"Elle me comprend!* She understands French!"

The typical untrained dog has little ability to communicate with humans. Not only does the dog not have the training to understand and obey commands, but, in a larger sense, he isn't even speaking the same language as we are. If an untrained dog had been given an unfamiliar command by the king, the dog would probably have ignored the king and just sniffed the grass. Chalcy, however, because of her training, not only had the desire to understand the king's command, but also had some pretty good assumptions as to how to do it.

Teaching behaviors to your dog does more than teach individual words; it serves as a vehicle for establishing communication pathways. It offers us an opportunity to better understand how our dog thinks, and to have our dog better understand our cues, as well as to understand people and the human world in general.

Without training, a dog is ignorant of your expectations and becomes a prisoner of his misbehavior—unable to accompany you to friends' houses, and to shopping malls, and on off-leash walks—because he does not have the manners and responsiveness necessary to participate in these activities.

With training, your dog can be integrated into your life in so many more ways! He can walk nicely alongside you as you stroll in outdoor malls, lie next to you in a café, behave himself in other people's houses, and play happily at the park, coming back to you when called. He understands your communications and responds readily. He makes you feel proud rather than embarrassed.

Training offers us a way to bond with our dog as we strive toward common goals and delight in our successes. The trust and cooperative spirit developed through this process will last a lifetime.

A trained dog is the result of two things: your lovingly teaching him behaviors through consistent and patient repetition, and your providing him with a predictable and fair discipline structure.

Rule 7: Cue, Action, Reward

Chalcy and I were being filmed for the reality show *Off the Leash,* which documented the start-up of the Hollywood animal talent agency Le PAWS. In this episode, talent scout Adam Berman came to watch Chalcy and me perform our stunt dog show at a baseball game. After our show, we sat in the stands together as Adam courted us for his agency. The show's producer thought it would be cute to have Adam ask Chalcy if she wanted to sign with Le PAWS, and to have Chalcy bark as an affirmative response. (What, you didn't think reality TV was *real*, did you?)

I showed Adam the hand signal cue for a bark, and gave him a piece of hot dog. "Let Chalcy know you have the hot dog," I instructed, "so she'll work for you."

Roll cameras, and action! Adam hands Chalcy the hot dog, which she swallows instantly. "Chalcy, how would you like to sign with Le PAWS agency?" Adam asks, and gives the hand signal. No bark.

"Dude, Adam!" I laugh. "You paid her before she did the work. She's not going to work for you now, you've got nothin'!"

Teaching a behavior consists of three parts: the verbal or physical **cue**, the **action**, and the **reward**.

These components have to be executed in order—you cue your dog to bark, he performs that action, and then you give him the reward. Later, when you are watching TV and your dog wants your attention, he may do a spontaneous bark in front of you. This is cute, and nice, but it does not earn a treat because you had not asked for (or cued) the behavior. Your dog should not get a treat anytime he wants one simply by barking at you. Because if he did, he would be the trainer, and you would be the one jumping through hoops on *his* cue! First comes the cue, and then the action.

And the action happens before the reward. Do not give the reward before the dog has performed the action (as Adam did), as this is bribery, and it doesn't work.

THE RULE

The basis of teaching any cued behavior is the sequential and proper execution of the cue, action, and reward. The key is to get as many successful repetitions of the behavior as possible (there are multiple ways to elicit it), and to mark the success with precise timing and while the dog is in the correct position.

Timing and Reward Markers

Imagine you are searching for something and being guided by feedback of "hot" or "cold." But now imagine that this feedback is being delayed before you hear it. You may actually be receiving "cold" feedback as you approach the object, or vice versa. Not only are you not finding the object, but you are getting frustrated at the inconsistency of the feedback. Imagine how much easier this task would be if you received feedback with correct timing.

In dog training, the consequence for a behavior has to be immediate in order for the dog to be able to link it clearly to the behavior. With humans, we can explain the connection between the consequence and the behavior, even if the two are separated in time. We can reward a child with ice cream for having been brave at the doctor's office, or we can ground a teenager for having earned a bad grade. With dogs, as with very young children, we can't explain the connection between the behavior and the consequence. It is therefore imperative that you mark (with a word, treat, or clicker) the exact moment that your dog performed correctly. Don't reward five seconds later, as you may be rewarding a completely different behavior. **I can't stress this enough—precise timing is crucial to training.**

Reward Your Dog While He's in the Correct Position

Let's say you tell your dog to "sit," and he does. You fish for a treat in your pocket, and he stands up to receive it. What did you just reward? You rewarded him for standing up! The treat should have been given while the dog was in the proper position—sitting.

When I taught Chalcy to crouch down at the bottom of the agility teeter-totter, I gave her the reward while she was posed in the correct position at the bottom of the plank. When you teach a dog to heel, you give him the treat as he is walking in the correct position with his shoulder lined up with your leg. When you teach your dog to "shake a paw," you give him the reward while his paw is in your hand, not after he has put it down.

Why Do We Need a Reward Marker?

Around the turn of the twentieth century, Russian physiologist Ivan Pavlov performed experiments in which he rang a bell just before presenting food to a dog. After a while the dog began to salivate merely at the sound of the bell. This is now termed **classical conditioning**. An existing behavior (salivating for food) is associated with a new stimulus (the ringing of a bell). The bell is not inherently pleasurable to the dog, but it becomes *associated* with a pleasurable thing.

The food, because it is something that the animal likes naturally, is a **primary positive reinforcer.** The bell is something the animal learns to like through association, and is therefore a **secondary positive reinforcer.** Animal trainers use a specific secondary positive reinforcer (like a bell) to let the animal know that food will be forthcoming shortly.

Why do trainers do this? As discussed, it is imperative to reward the dog at the exact moment he performs correctly. But sometimes this is logistically impossible—if your dog is not close to you, for example, or is being asked to do several behaviors in a row. If your dog is learning to jump through a hoop, you won't be able to toss a treat in his mouth at the exact second his body intersects the hoop. However, you *can* generate a specific sound at that exact moment to let your dog know that that was the moment he earned the reward, which will be forthcoming momentarily. In animal training, this unique sound is known as a **reward marker**.

Marine mammal trainers use a whistle as a reward marker, horse trainers use a tongue pop, other trainers may use a tone, a finger snap, or simply a distinct word such as "good!" or "yes!" The most common reward marker among dog trainers is a handheld gadget called a "clicker," a thumb-sized box with a metal tongue that makes a *click-click* sound when pressed.

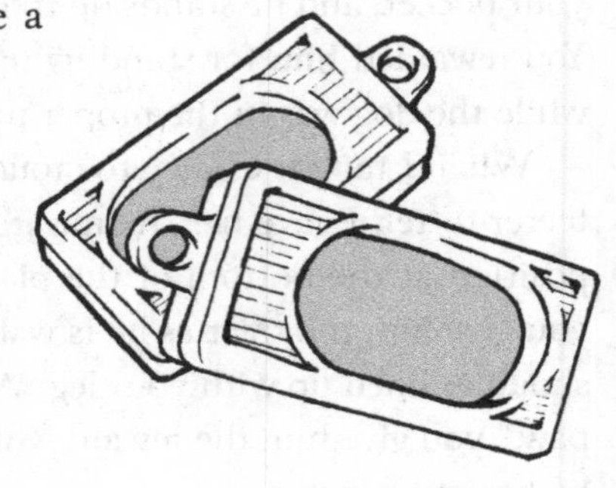

Clickers have gained steadily in popularity in the dog training community, spanning all skill levels and many different dog sports. Traditionally used in zoos in the training of exotic animals, and in training animal actors for movies and TV, training with a clicker benefits from the fact that it can be standardized across all the trainers working with the animals.

Bridge the Gap

The reward marker is also sometimes known as a **bridge**, because it bridges the time between when the dog performs the correct behavior and when he gets his reward. You can use this bridge concept during daily life with your dog. If your dog does something that you wish to reward, but you don't have a treat with you, mark that instant by saying "good boy!" and then bridge the time until he gets his reward by saying "get your cookie, get your cookie" as you run with him to the cookie jar. (It's good to have "cookie" jars in key rooms so that you can be ready to reward your dog at a moment's notice.)

In obedience competition the handler is not allowed to carry treats inside the ring; that is why competitors prepare by training with their treat bag off their body. When their dog performs well, they'll say,

"Good job! Get your cookie, get your cookie!" And then the two of them will run back to the trainer's bag to get a treat. That way, when the dog is in the competition ring he will still think he has a chance of getting a treat, even if he knows his handler has none on his or her person.

Getting Started with Reward-Marker Training

Ready to give it a try? You can choose a unique word or other sound to be your reward marker, but for the purpose of example, I'll assume it is a clicker.

Your first step is to "charge up the clicker" by building the association between the clicker sound and the food reward. This is easily done by occasionally giving a click and then immediately giving a treat to your dog. It doesn't take long before that click sound makes his head spin toward you—which indicates that he has formed the association. Within a few minutes (and maybe twenty clicks), you can be ready to start training.

There are only three rules in using a reward marker:

1. Click to mark any behavior you wish to encourage.
2. Click the INSTANT the correct behavior happens (while the dog is in the correct position).
3. Follow each click with a treat (no multiple clicks).

TEACH A TRICK! SIT

Use a clicker to teach your dog to sit. The first task is to get him into the sit position, so that you can click it and reward it. There are several ways you can get him into the position; they will be explained later in this chapter. You can lure him into position by moving a treat backward above his head; you can wait for him to get tired and sit on his own; or you can press on his hindquarters. The basic premise is that you need to get the behavior so that you can reward it. As soon as his rear drops to the floor, click and follow quickly with a treat. It will be easy for your dog to make the association between the instant he feels the cold linoleum on his rear and the clicking sound, and he will know exactly what he is being rewarded for. For the first dozen times, while your dog is figuring out what you want, it is unnecessary to give the verbal cue of "sit," as it's not really helping anything, and could even betray frustration through your tone of voice. Once your dog seems to catch on, however, follow the sequence of cue, action, reward.

TEACH A TRICK! WALK ON A LOOSE LEASH

Perhaps you wish to teach your dog to stop pulling on his leash. He pulls and pulls, and then the instant the leash goes slack, you click. He immediately turns around to receive his treat. The precise timing of the click let him know the exact moment he earned the reward. If you had tried to reward your dog without the use of a clicker, you would have had to call his name to get him to turn around, and then he wouldn't have known exactly how he had earned the treat. Had he earned it for turning his head toward you? Had he gotten it because you said his name? He likely would have forgotten about the slack leash.

Clickers are helpful in creating a training environment that is more sterile, less cluttered with your voice and emotion. Once your dog has been trained via a reward-marker system, he has learned the rule set and will generalize easily between different reward-marker sounds. If you forget your clicker one day, you can substitute a tongue pop or verbal "good" marker.

Why Can't I Just Use My Voice Instead of a Clicker?

One of the hardest parts of clicker training is . . . actually using the clicker! You've got the clicker in one hand, the treats in the other hand, the leash in another hand. . . . "Wait! I'm out of hands!" Why in the world, then, would a trainer choose a handheld gadget over simply marking the event with a tongue pop, or "good!" or "yes!"?

The main advantages of the clicker tool are that it is precise, it is consistent, and it is devoid of emotion.

Precision Timing: The clicker sound is short, crisp, and distinct, and can mark a very precise moment in time. If you choose a verbal event marker, make it short and crisp. Novice trainers seem to have a quicker reaction time using a handheld device than using their voice.

Consistent Sound: Not only will different trainers vocalize a verbal marker differently, but even one trainer will vocalize differently depending upon his or her mood. Clickers always, always, always sound the same.

Absence of Emotion: Dogs are very sensitive to our mood. A clicker separates the marker from any frustration or anger or other emotion in your voice. If you know yourself to be a person who lets his emotion show in his voice (which 90 percent of people do), then a clicker is a good solution. It allows the dog to focus on what *he's* doing, rather than worrying about how your mood is changing. Don't underestimate the importance of this point—it's one of the main advantages of the clicker.

The Importance of Your Voice in Training

With most trainers, the clicker is used primarily in teaching the initial stages of a new behavior or in fine-tuning precise ones. The clicker is usually phased out once the dog responds to a cue. The sterility of the clicker is one of its advantages, but for advanced trainers it can also be one of its disadvantages. If you can keep your temper and not let frustration enter your voice, using verbal feedback will enhance your communication pathways as you train.

> **When I show up to perform at an event, I'm invariably greeted with "Hey! The dog lady's here!" I might have taken issue with this term, except that I've heard a similar greeting used for "the pig lady." So I suppose I could have it worse.**
>
> **The pig lady is the world's premier pig trainer and performer. Pris-**

cilla Valentine trained her troupe of swine to play basketball, to skateboard, and to jump through a paper-covered hoop.

I asked Pris if she was a clicker-trainer. "Well, like all of us professional trainers, I have a clicker, and I've used a clicker, but it's just one of the tools in my tool kit." Pris described the limitations with a clicker: "I can't indicate degrees of success. With my voice, sometimes I'll say 'good' and sometimes I'll say 'great job!' And when my pig does it better than she's ever done it before, I'll say 'FAN-TASTIC!' With a clicker, it's always just a click."

Out of curiosity, I asked Pris what a good job looked like compared to a fantastic job. "Snort pushes a lawn mower," she explained. "And if she doesn't put her snout right in the middle, it will tip over when she pushes it. So the closer she gets to the center, the more excited my praise for her is."

Teaching your dog to read your feedback can be a wonderful tool in building more intense communication between the two of you. Be careful not to treat training too clinically. The clicker is best used as a part of your training scheme, in conjunction with methods that emphasize more of an emotional connection. Enjoy your dog!

Learning Occurs with Repeated Successes

A dog's brain learns through repetition (as does our brain). Every time an experience is reinforced, the brain strengthens that chemical connection. The stronger the connection, the less conscious thought is required to accomplish the task. This ability of the brain to rewire itself through experience is called "brain plasticity."

When I first took up the sport of disc dog (Frisbee) with Chalcy, I had to learn to throw a steady, on-target disc. I threw disc after disc at a ribbon tied on a chain-link fence. I'd vary my technique slightly with every throw: a little more wrist, more hyzer (tilt), less shoulder, etc. And with each attempt, my brain evaluated the outcome as compared to the one I was trying to achieve: too far right, too wobbly, too high, perfect! After many repetitions my brain started to process the odds—determining which variations led to more successful throws.

The difference between my repetitions, in learning to throw a disc, and my dog's, in learning a new behavior, is that in throwing a disc I knew what the goal was. I had a model in my head of what the perfect throw looked like, and I was comparing each attempt to that model. My dog, on the other hand, does not know what the correct behavior looks like. It is therefore critically important that I immediately and clearly let her know if each attempt was a success (click) or nonsuccess (no click).

The dog only learns from successful attempts, so we need to get as many successful attempts as possible in the early stages of teaching a new behavior. This often means stacking the deck in the dog's favor. Make it as easy as you can for your dog to do the behavior correctly. Have him fetch an object that is only two feet away, and reward that. And reward it again, and again. Giving lots and lots of tiny, soft treats is the key to quick training. Novice trainers tend to ask too much from their dog before giving a reward. If you make the challenge too difficult for your dog, you won't have as many opportunities to reward, and that brain pathway won't be built as quickly. Remember, you want your dog to be successful with 75 percent of his attempts before you up the ante and require a more difficult behavior.

Reward Success, Ignore the Rest

Because we want to encourage our dog to keep trying, we don't want to make him feel reprimanded in any way while learning a new behavior. We reward his successes and basically ignore all other unsuccessful attempts.

The No-Reward Marker

In most of your training, you reward the correct behavior and ignore the incorrect behavior, and your dog eventually figures out the correct behavior. Sometimes, however, your dog can get stuck repeating an incorrect behavior, and it is helpful to let him know that he is on a path that will not yield a reward, and he needs to try a new path.

Pointing out too many of your dog's incorrect behaviors can be discouraging for him, but there are times when you can speed learning by giving information on both right and wrong actions. If you were learning to drive a car, for example, you'd want your instructor not only to tell you the right things you did, but also point out the wrong things.

A **no-reward marker**, or NRM, is a way to tell your dog that he's on the wrong track—to tell him to try something different. If, for example, you are trying to get your dog to touch a bell with his nose, and he keeps pawing at it instead, you can let him know that that behavior earns "no reward."

It's a delicate balance, though. How many of us made it through driving lessons with our parents without at least a few tears shed? Tears emerged when we felt we were trying our best and were being criticized excessively. (Parents can be so dramatic!) By the time tears are being shed, learning has stopped altogether.

So what we want to do is convey the "information" of a wrong action without the condemnation. The word "no" is a condemnation. It's a condemnation because you probably use it for times when your dog is naughty, and it's a condemnation because it's hard to keep the word neutral, devoid of negativity when you are frustrated.

When a dog is learning a new behavior, you want to keep his enthusiasm high or he could shut down for fear of being wrong. If your dog is giving you an incorrect behavior, it is probably not intentional. Instead of "no," many trainers use a more lighthearted "whoops!"

Chalcy competes in the Utility Obedience ring, which is the highest level of competition exercises, and the realm of precision-trained dogs performing intense mental challenges. One of the exercises is called "scent discrimination." A cluster of dumbbells is laid out by the judge's hand in the middle of the ring. The dog is sent across the ring to the cluster, where he must find by scent the one dumbbell that has been touched by his handler. Boy, does this exercise trip up a lot of dogs!

Dogs get tripped up not because they have a hard time distinguishing one scent from another, as the average dog can easily find a noodle in a haystack. Dogs get tripped up due to a lack in self-confidence.

No one seems to know what it is about the scent-discrimination exercise that makes dogs so sensitive, but it's a well-known problem. Dogs may go through years of training this exercise, often doing quite well, and then periodically go through months where they will run off if they think they are wrong, or will pick up one dumbbell and look to their handler's face for approval, dropping it if they don't see the approval. Sometimes they will pick up the correct dumbbell and start to bring it back to their handler, and then compulsively go back to the pile again and again to double-check that they got the right one.

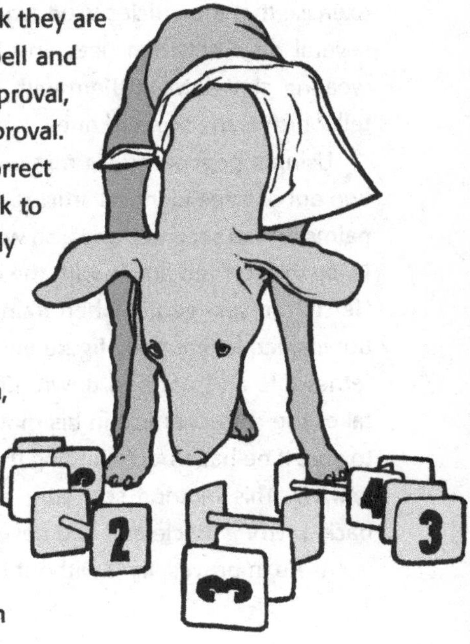

As in all obedience competition, the handler may not speak, or move even slightly, until the exercise is finished. Dogs rely upon our feedback, and often they have self-doubt if they don't get it. If they have been trained with

only positive feedback, they might interpret their handler's lack of feedback in the ring as negative feedback.

Which is why the majority of trainers use both positive and negative feedback in training. The trainer will use a particular sound to *gently* indicate a wrong choice. This word is often "whoops!" or "try again!" or "keep looking!"

NRMs can actually build confidence for a dog who worries a lot about being wrong.

Some dogs will take an NRM neutrally, simply as information offered. Others will view it as a mild punisher. Keep the NRM very neutral, and use it more for when your dog is stuck rather than for every single time he makes a mistake (which can be frustrating for him).

TEACH A TRICK! SCENT DISCRIMINATION

Many dogs can learn the basic scent discrimination skill in a few weeks. Metal and leather dumbbells are used in competition, but you can use wooden dowels or even tennis balls. It is vital to this exercise that the articles used are free of your scent. Air them out for several days between uses and handle them with tongs or while wearing gloves. Mark them with unique identifiers so that you can tell which is the scented one!

Using a pegboard or a mat with holes poked through, tie down two out of three identical articles. Scent the third by rubbing it in your palms for ten seconds, and also with a little of the treat you are using. Place the scented article with the other two, and instruct your dog to "fetch." Be very gentle when training scent work. Avoid saying "no," but instead let your dog figure out on his own that only one article is retrievable and not tied down. Click or praise him the moment he takes the correct article in his mouth, and reward him for bringing it to you. If he has trouble finding the free one, encourage him to keep looking. This method sets your dog up for success—he can't bring back a wrong article and you never have to tell him he is wrong.

As he improves, try it without the tie-down mat. If your dog picks

up a wrong article, either ignore it or tell him "whoops!" Do not accept a wrong article if he brings it to you, but rather keep your hands at your sides and encourage him to keep looking.

The Cue Is the First Hint

When your dog is first learning a behavior, he needs a lot of help from you to understand what he needs to do to earn the reward. You need to help guide him into the correct position. As he gets better, he needs less and less help, until finally all he needs is simply the verbal cue or hand signal to understand your request.

A key technique of dog training is to give help, or hints, to your dog in progressively greater amounts. Your dog wants the treat as quickly as possible, so he is going to learn to anticipate what you want him to do.

If you are teaching your dog to "shake a paw," for example, you would first say the verbal cue; that's hint number one. Then you give him hint number two: a slight tap on his wrist. Then hint number three: gently lifting his wrist. As he catches on, he will anticipate each step, and will learn to do the behavior merely at your wrist tap, as he remembers that the tap always precedes the lifting of his paw. And later he will do the behavior already at your verbal cue, as he remembers the verbal cue always precedes the wrist tap.

If your dog knows the verbal cue for "shake a paw," but does not yet know the hand signal, ask for the behavior by first giving the less-known hint of the hand signal, followed by the better-known hint of the verbal cue. Your dog will learn that the word "shake" always follows this particular hand signal, and he will then learn to do the behavior upon the hand signal alone.

When to Use Your Dog's Name

Hearing his name should elicit a positive feeling in your dog. He should respond to it with enthusiasm, never hesitancy or fear. Whenever possible, use your dog's name positively, rather than in conjunction with reprimands, warnings, or punishment.

- Use your dog's name only in a pleasant situation. When your dog is in a stressful situation, or is scared or aggressive, don't use his name.
- If your dog does something naughty, just say "no!" or "cut it out!" without using his name.
- Using your dog's name implies she should perform an action. Use your dog's name when you want her to DO something ("Chalcy, come" or "Chalcy, heel"), but not when you want her to refrain from doing something ("stay" or "leave it").

Five Ways to Elicit a Behavior

We know that learning occurs through achieving successes. We get our dog to perform a behavior, and then we reward it. The trick is often in figuring out how to *get* him to do the behavior in the first place!

There are five ways to elicit a behavior: through modeling, mimicking, luring, capturing, and shaping. Not all methods of getting the behavior are created equal, and none is right for every trainer, every dog, and every situation. These are the tools we have in our tool kit, but sometimes the best solution is to use a combination of methods.

Modeling

The first and probably the most obvious method of eliciting a behavior is **modeling**, which entails physically guiding or manipulating the dog into position. An example of modeling would be pushing down on a dog's rear to get him to sit. Trainers commonly use modeling in teaching agility weave poles by leading the dog on his leash through the poles, and in teaching heeling by leading the dog by his leash.

You would generally model only the core part of a dog's body, and do so to produce large behaviors such as sit, down, beg, or bow. Beware of physically manipulating your dog's head or tail, as this could make him fearful and unable to learn.

It is tempting to manipulate your dog's body physically because it is faster and more precise than other methods; however, this can actually delay the learning process. By manipulating your dog, you are encouraging him to relinquish initiative and allow himself to be led. He is not required to engage his brain and is not learning the motor skills necessary to position his body by himself.

When modeling, use the least amount of pressure needed at every stage of learning. You want to use your touch as a hint, or reminder, and let your dog come up with the behavior on his own.

Molding is the same as **modeling**, except that it involves using a prop to compel the behavior, as in teaching heeling by walking alongside a wall, or using guide wires to teach weave poles, or teaching your dog to cover his eyes with his paw by using a sticky note on his muzzle.

Stanley Steemer carpet cleaner ran a TV ad that garnered a lot of attention and was widely viewed on YouTube. In the commercial, a lady watches in horror as her yellow Lab scoots his butt across her white living room carpet. Hmm, I wonder how they trained that?

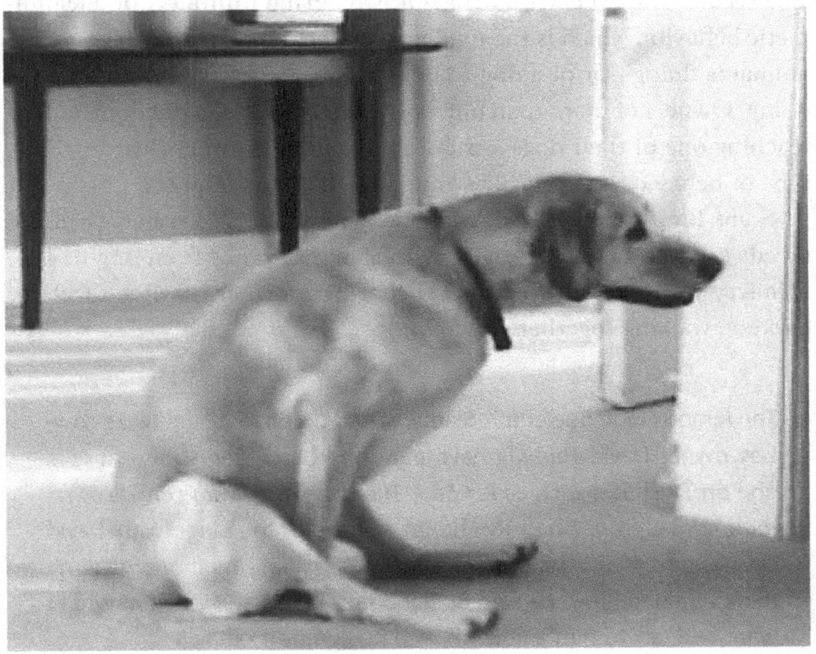

Longtime friend and elite movie-dog trainer Claire Doré had that task! Claire used a molding technique with Sutton, training five times a day for two weeks in preparation for the shoot. Sutton, by the way, is the handsome yellow Lab demonstrating some of the tricks in my book *101 Dog Tricks.*

To train this behavior, Claire put a piece of tape on Sutton's rear. As he was unable to get it off in any other way, he sat and wiggled a bit. Claire clicked and treated! It took about six days before he caught on that the scoot was the desired behavior, and not the sit. Claire then withheld the reward, upping the ante until he had scooted a little longer and a little farther.

Just in case you want to teach this trick, Claire says the verbal cue is "scoot your butt" and her signal is a hokey-pokey-style wiggle of her rear. Just in case . . .

Using Mimicry

The second way to elicit a behavior is by using **mimicry**, or allelomimetic behavior, which is the tendency of an animal to do what another animal is doing—or of a dog to do what the trainer or another dog is doing. Owners of more than one dog will testify to the phenomenon of teaching one of their dogs a trick, and having the others learn it. This type of behavior is especially strong in half-grown puppies.

Some breeds are easier to train using mimicry than others (herding breeds seem to take to it easiest), and success varies from dog to dog. Mimicry works best with natural behaviors, such as howling together, barking, walking together, or fetching.

The famous blue heeler mix Skidboot and his plain-talkin' Texas cowboy owner David Hartwig have performed trick dog shows at fairs and on TV shows such as *Pet Star, The Late Show with David Letterman,* and *Oprah.* I had the honor of sharing the stage with David several times, and asked him about his training methods. "I don't think I trained him," he said of Skidboot. "I kind of show him what I want and talk to him a little bit, and he figures it out."

David said he taught Skidboot to crawl by crawling himself. He taught him to spin by spinning, to shake hands by extending his, and to hold real still by standing frozen himself. It's worth a try!

Luring

Whenever possible, it is preferable to **lure** your dog to position his body himself rather than to physically model him into position. With luring you encourage your dog to follow a treat to get himself in the correct position. The most common way to teach a sit is by holding a treat in front of the dog's nose and then moving it back over his head. As the dog's head follows the food, his rear will generally drop to the floor. The instant this happens, reward him with the treat.

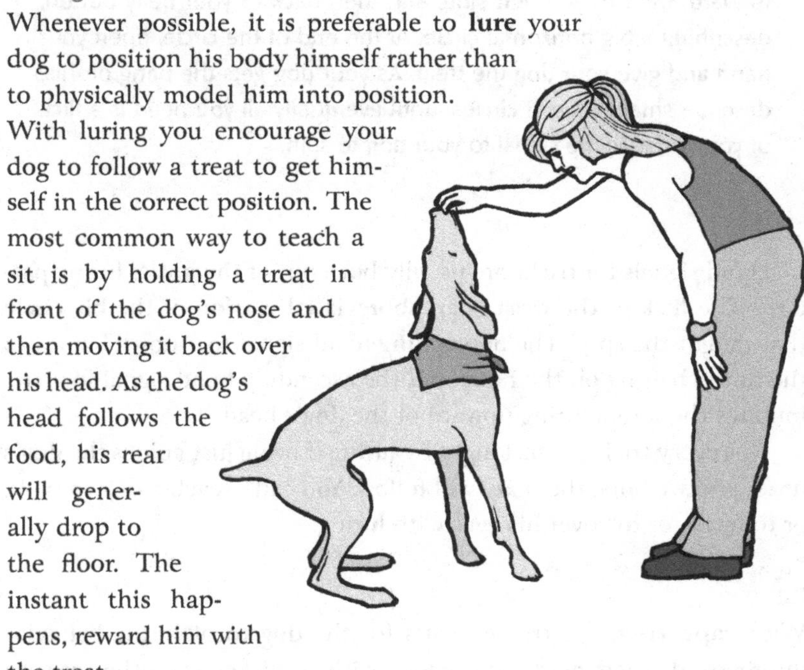

Clickers are superfluous with luring, as the treat can be delivered at the instant the behavior happens, and the clicker imparts no additional information.

Luring is fast, flexible, and precise. This method is easy to learn for both the dog and the trainer. Many dog tricks are taught by luring. Teach a rollover by starting with your dog in a down, and then moving the lure from his nose to his shoulder blade, causing him to flop onto his side. Keep moving the lure toward his backbone to get him to roll the rest of the way over. Voilà!

TEACH A TRICK! SPIN

To teach a spin, hold a treat in your right hand near your belly button. Lure your dog in a circle by moving your hand to your right, then forward, then to your left side, and then back to your belly button, describing a big horizontal circle. At the end of the circle, open your hand and give your dog the treat. As your dog gets the hang of this, describe smaller, faster circles, until eventually all you need is a flick of your wrist as the signal to your dog to spin.

Hand signals for tricks are usually born out of the initial luring pattern. The flick of the wrist is an abbreviated version of the big circle that taught the spin. The descending hand signal for "down" imitates the initial baiting on the floor, and the ascending hand signal for "sit" imitates the initial luring upward of the dog's head.

Not every trick can be taught by luring. Luring just guides the dog's head, and we hope the body will follow. You can't teach a dog to bark, or to fetch, or to cover his eyes with luring.

Capturing

With **capturing**, the trainer waits for the dog to offer the behavior unprovoked, then marks the event with a clicker (or other reward marker). If you want to teach your dog to bow, for example, watch him and wait for him to do so naturally, as when he wakes from a nap and stretches. At that second, click the behavior and give him a treat. Over time he'll figure out that every time he bows, you give him a treat. Once he is offering this behavior, you can start to associate it with a verbal cue.

Capturing is limited to naturally occurring behaviors—you probably won't capture your dog playing the piano, going through weave poles, or tidying up his toys! Capturing is also limited to behaviors that occur with enough frequency that the dog can figure out a pattern to the click. This is a slow process, and one that requires you to be ready with a clicker and treats at all times.

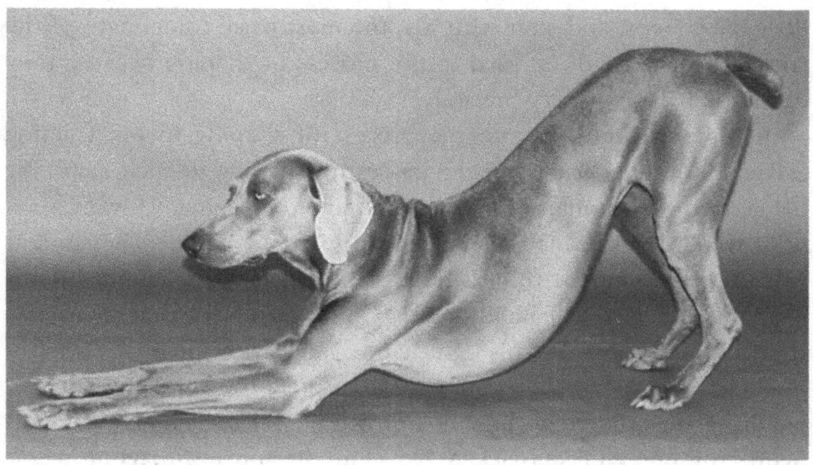

A few movie-dog trainers have successfully used the capturing method to train dogs to yawn on cue. The only way to teach a yawn is for a patient, patient trainer to wait for the dog to yawn and to capture it. Some trainers have told me they try to elicit the yawn using mimicry and yawning themselves, but the evidence is a little sketchy as to whether this helps. Other trainers have fallen asleep in the process.

Shaping

Suppose you are waiting to capture a behavior and it never happens. Suppose it's a behavior that you can't teach with luring, modeling, or mimicry—perhaps a behavior such as teaching your dog to roll a soccer ball into a net. When none of the other methods will work, you can always rely upon shaping.

Shaping is the process of building a new behavior by gradually rewarding approximations of the behavior, requiring the dog to come closer and closer to the goal. The general rule is that you reinforce any behavior that is a closer approximation of the target behavior than the behavior you last reinforced. Shaping is similar to capturing in that you don't elicit the behavior by luring or touching the dog. You just stand back and wait to capture any behavior that looks like it is going in the right direction, and reward that. You break a behavior down into little baby steps, and start with just the most basic component of the trick. Clickers are often used in the process of shaping because they can mark behaviors very precisely.

In order to demonstrate the process of shaping in my training classes, I'll use a clicker and the process of shaping to elicit a specific behavior from a student. I'll first determine the behavior I want, such as "I want him to touch his belly with his right hand." The student will then try random things: he'll lift a leg, make a sound, lift his left hand, lift his right hand—*click!* "Ooh! Let me try that again," he thinks. The student lifts his right hand again—*click!* He lifts it again—*click!* He lifts it again . . . nothing. I have upped the ante, and am now requiring the student to lift his arm further for a click. The student figures this out, and gets clicked. Now I up the ante again, requiring his elbow to bend. Now I require it closer to his belly, and now touching his belly. This is the process of shaping, and it has taken the student just two minutes to progress through approximations and achieve the goal behavior.

When using shaping, the trainer needs to be able to break a behavior into small-enough increments so that the dog remains consistently successful and does not become frustrated. The trainer needs good observational skills and a quick reaction time. Sometimes during this process, the trainer isn't immediately sure if the behavior offered by the dog is going in the right direction or not. Is an arm raised above the head better than an arm pointed downward? You don't have a lot of time to think about this, you have to react immediately, with a click or no click. You have to read your dog. Is he getting frustrated? Do you need to go back to rewarding him for a lesser approximation in order to keep him motivated?

TEACH A TRICK! SOCCER

Teach your dog to roll a soccer ball by using the shaping method. Use a large ball, because the dog is less likely to pick it up in his mouth. Set the ball in front of your dog and watch him. Start shaping the

behavior by clicking and treating any interest your dog shows in the ball. Then up the ante and wait for him to sniff or touch the ball, and click that. If he sends the ball rolling with his nose, even by accident, click it and give him a big jackpot treat! As he becomes better, you can require longer-distance rolls, or rolls in a certain direction, as criteria for the click.

Once a dog learns the shaping process, this technique becomes a powerful tool. Your dog will understand the concept of successive approximations toward a goal and will learn to exaggerate his behaviors more quickly. A dog who has been trained heavily with shaping techniques is apt to be very active in experimenting and offering new behaviors.

Kathy Sdao had the enviable experience of working with marine mammals in Hawaii as part of her graduate school research. Although incredibly smart, these animals pose challenges in training due to obvious factors such as their size, habitat, and limited hearing and seeing of land-based cues. The signals from the trainers have to be easily visible. Kathy demonstrates one of the signals during an Iron Dogs seminar at which we are both instructors. Her left arm stretches to the side, and her hand is brought rigidly to her chest (fetch). Then her right arm extends to the side and does three flutters (ball). Verbs are always on the left side of the trainer's body, and nouns on the right.

When Kathy turned her skills later in life to dog training, she began using the shaping techniques she had learned in her marine mammal training on her dog, encouraging him to offer different behaviors, or "throw behaviors at the trainer."

Kathy tells a funny story of her dog Nick, who loves apples so much that he often stands under her backyard apple tree scavenging the fruit. Intermittently, due to the wind or something, an apple will drop from the tree. Nick, having been heavily trained with the shaping technique, apparently surmised that he must have done something to earn this reward, so he started offering behaviors to the tree! A bow, a bark, a scratch—trying to once again hit on the behavior that would result in a reward from the tree.

Building on Multiple Behaviors

Chaining

This is the really fun part! Once your dog has learned individual behaviors, you can **chain** them together into one continuous behavior with a single cue. "Tidy up your toys," for example, chains the behaviors of "pull on a rope" (to open the toy box lid), "fetch," "drop it," and "close the lid" to produce the impressive trick of your dog putting away all of his toys!

TEACH A TRICK! TIDY UP YOUR TOYS

First, teach each of the components separately. Teach "pull on a rope" with a game of tug, and then transfer that behavior to having your dog pull on the rope attached to the toy box lid to open it.

Teach your dog to drop the toy into the toy box by having him fetch his toy and then holding a treat right over the toy box, so that when he opens his mouth to get the treat, the toy falls inside.

Finally, teach him to close the lid by holding the lid slightly open and holding a treat high above the lid. When your dog steps on the lid as he tries to reach the treat, he will end up pushing the lid shut.

Now practice the behaviors in sequence. Start by saying the cue word for the chain, "tidy up," and then cue the first behavior, "open." Always give the chain cue first, before the cue for the first behavior. Initially this chain cue is just the first hint to your dog, but eventually you will fade the cues for the individual behaviors and your dog will perform the entire chain sequence merely at your cue of "Tidy up!" Now that's a trick!

Back-Chaining

Back-chaining is combining the individual behaviors in reverse—training the last behavior in a chain first, then adding the next-to-last behavior, then the behavior before that, and so on.

When you have a movie-animal trainer as your owner, you learn a few tricks. Claire Doré's dog Dana, a sweet, sensitive Aussie mix, was taught every trick in the book.

You may have seen Dana in an adorable Motel 6 commercial which advertises that motels in the chain accept pets. Dana lies down on a blanket, grabs the corner of the blanket with her mouth, and rolls over, thereby rolling herself up nice and cozy. Claire taught her this impressive trick through back-chaining.

Claire first taught Dana the last behavior in the sequence, a roll-over. Then Claire had Dana take the blanket in her mouth before rolling over. Working her way back, she then had Dana lie down on the blanket, take it, and roll over. Finally she positioned Dana at the other side of the room and had her come, lie down, take it, and roll over. Sweet!

Adduction, or A + B = C

Sometimes the most original tricks are born of accidents. Claire had told Dana to lie down. Then she told Dana to back up. Taking this

literally, Dana attempted to do both. This resulted in her shuffling backward in a sort of bow position. Hey, you're moonwalking!

This procedure is called "adduction." You train behavior A and put it on cue, then train behavior B and put it on cue, then give both cues together to get behavior C on the first try.

A "crawl" can be taught using adduction, by alternating commands of "down" and "come." Once your dog gets the hang of it, use the new cue word as a hint before you use the other two cues: "crawl, down, come." This way, as your dog wants to get the treat sooner, he'll start to anticipate that "down" and "come" always come after "crawl," and he'll start the behavior already on the word "crawl." At that time you can fade the other two cue words.

SUMMARY

- Cue, action, reward—this sequence constitutes a cued behavior.
- Precise timing of a reward marker or treat is the key to teaching a behavior.
- Reward your dog while he's in the correct position.
- To use a reward marker:
  - Mark any behavior you wish to encourage
  - Mark the INSTANT the correct behavior happens
  - Follow each mark with a treat (no multiple marks)
- Learning occurs through successes. Get as many successful repetitions of the behavior as possible.
- Sometimes use a no-reward marker (NRM) such as "Whoops!" to let your dog know to try something different.
- Give hints to your dog in progressively greater amounts (first the cue for "shake", then a wrist tap, then a wrist lift).
- Use your dog's name positively, and when associated with action.
- There are five ways to elicit a behavior:
  - Modeling (using physical manipulation)
  - Mimicry (using the dog's tendency to copy)
  - Luring (having the dog follow a treat)

- Capturing (waiting until your dog does it naturally)
- Shaping (rewarding approximations)

- Build more complex behaviors by building on easier ones:
  - Chaining ("tidy up your toys")
  - Back-chaining ("roll yourself up in a blanket")
  - Adduction (A + B = C, "moonwalk" or "crawl")

Rule 8: One Command, One Consequence

In a pet store, I overhear the dog-training class in progress behind me. The instructor has brought in her own dog, presumably to demonstrate what a well-trained dog can do. "Down, Shakespeare," she says sweetly. No response from the dog. "Down, Shakey! Down. Lie down. Shakey, down!" And then: "Very good! Here's your cookie!" This last part was the part that made me swallow my gum.

Shakespeare should have earned a cookie if he had gone down on the first command, but not on the fifth. In fact, there never should have been a fifth command.

When you give a command, there should be only one acceptable outcome. One command (two, max!) should equal one response. Repeated commands are nothing but nagging and serve only to condition your dog to treat your first several commands as merely a bluff. Repetition depicts you as begging your dog for compliance, which is not the position you want to be in. When a command is given, your dog needs to give the correct response—whether your dog does it of his own choice, or whether you have to enforce the command.

The easy part of loving your dog is showing him affection. But another way we show love to our dog is with discipline. Discipline is not punishment; it is not punitive or retaliatory. Discipline is calm, fair, and predictable, and it actually relieves your dog of the stress associated with confusion. It provides a structure to allow your dog to make choices and understand the consequences of those choices. It shows him how to be a "good dog."

Discipline teaches your dog the skills which allow him to be more integrated into your daily life. Discipline gives your dog a more fulfilling life as a true member of your family, rather than merely a pet.

THE RULE

A part of loving your dog is disciplining him so that he does not become a prisoner of his own misbehavior. Discipline prepares him with the skills and manners to have additional freedoms and to be integrated into more areas of your life. Discipline is not punishment, and is not hurtful; it is the compassionate enforcement of fair rules. Discipline is a clear and consistent structure for you and your dog to understand expectations and consequences.

Commands Are Not Compromises

Half-enforced commands are not commands, but rather suggestions. And suggestions only have to be obeyed by your dog when he feels like it. Suggestions, when not obeyed by your dog, weaken your authority.

Commands are requirements. If you're not in the mood to enforce a command, it's better to not give it at all than to give it and allow it to go unobeyed.

Command versus Cue

A **command** is different from the dozens of words and phrases your dog may otherwise understand, such as "bath," "chow time," "wanna go for a walk?" "good boy," and "where's Mr. Monkey?" A command is also different from a verbal **cue** used for dog tricks, such as "shake hands," "rollover," or "bark." The difference lies in the requirement of compliance.

A verbal cue is merely an opportunity for your dog to earn a reward. The dog WANTS to do the behavior indicated by your cue, in the hope or anticipation of getting a reward. The consequences for his not taking advantage of a cue are generally merely the loss of the potential reward. Cues are used in the early stages of learning, and also with unimportant behaviors and while playing games. If you cue your dog to "roll over" and he doesn't do it, he has missed his opportunity for a reward. That's all. You wouldn't generally force him to comply. Cues are said in a happy tone and with treats implied for performance.

A command is also a signal to do something, but a command requires compliance regardless of a reward. Disobeying a command could be a safety issue to a person or to your dog—think how important it is that your dog come upon your command if he is headed into traffic, or that he "leave it" if he is about to eat a pill he has found on the floor during a therapy visit to a hospital.

A command is used only after the behavior is well trained and understood by the dog. A command is said in a firm (but not necessarily stern) voice, while you are looking directly at your dog. You generally want your body posture to convey authority, so stand upright and square, with your arms at your sides. Don't lean over your dog, pat your legs, or clap your hands.

Daily life with your dog should have a mixture of both cue-based reward opportunities and required commands. You don't want to overly control your dog, but give him some opportunities to make choices. With a child, we might say "If you finish your broccoli, you'll get ice cream for dessert." If the child makes the choice to not eat the broccoli and forgo the dessert, we have to be okay with that. He's experimenting and testing and learning. There are other times, however, when noncompliance is not an option. "Wash your hands before dinner," for example. The child's hands WILL be washed, whether he does it himself or whether you walk him to the sink and do it with him. This is a sanitation and safety command, and there is no room for bargaining.

Whether it is a command or a cue, you don't want to say it more than once or your dog might become accustomed to not performing the behavior until the second or third time you've asked. With a cue, say it once, and then either reward your dog for doing it right or don't reward if he didn't attempt the behavior. If he didn't attempt the behavior, wait at least ten seconds before trying it again, as a sort of ten-second penalty delay in your dog's quest to get his reward. With a command, say it once, and then reward your dog if he responds correctly or enforce your command if he does not.

Enforce the Command If Your Dog Doesn't Do It on His Own

Back to the dog trainer in the pet store. Instead of giving her dog five commands, and rewarding the dog for finally obeying, what should she have done? The rule is: Give only one command and allow only one consequence to that command. The consequence to the "down" command is for the dog to lie down. If the dog chooses to do this on his own, then "good boy!" and possibly a treat. If the dog chooses NOT to lie down on his own, then he is still going to end up lying down. He's going to end up lying down because you're going to enforce your command.

Enforce your command by using pressure with the flat of your hand against your dog's shoulder blade to gently offset him and bring him to the down position. Once he's down, release the pressure and praise your dog—yes, praise him! (No treat, though, as he gets a treat only for lying down on his own.)

Let me explain why you would praise your dog even though you had to physically pressure him into position. There are two things going on here. There is the choice your dog made to not obey your command. That's a bad thing. Then there is the state of compliance, in which he did what you asked him to do—lie down. That's a good thing.

The bad thing (your dog's choice to not obey) becomes associated with the unpleasant consequence of being pressured into position. Mind you, the pressure on his shoulder is not intended to be painful or rough; it is unpleasant merely in that it is a form of pressure, and a requirement for your dog to do something he had not wished to do.

As soon as your dog entered the state of compliance by lying down, then he was doing a good thing. The unpleasant pressure on his shoulder was released, and he was rewarded with praise.

In this way, your dog associates his choice to not obey your command with the unpleasant pressure. The unpleasantness lasts only as long as the period when your dog is in noncompliance. Once your dog enters the state of compliance (being in the down position after hearing the "down" command), this state becomes associated with praise.

Many trainers, both novice and experienced, forget to give this very important praise portion of the equation. If the praise were omitted, the dog would learn to associate the word "down" with just unpleasant pressure. We instead want to create a dog who enthusiastically complies because he is eager for the reward.

Give One Command at a Time

> **"Hunter, wait . . . heel! Hunter, no! Off! Cut it out. Heel! Hunter, no! Leave it. What are you doing? Come! Hunter, get in the truck. Come!"**

Yikes! That dog was given a dozen commands on the short trip between his outdoor kennel and the truck. In his excited state he is having trouble concentrating anyway, and the constant stream of different words sounds like chatter to him, rather than a command.

Slow down and concentrate on one command at a time. Remember: One command, one consequence. Make sure the first consequence is carried out before you give the next command.

Treats Are Rewards, Not Bribes

We've all done it in a moment of weakness—held up a treat to entice our dog to come, or to get off our bed, or to drop the shoe he is holding in his mouth. But let's not kid ourselves, this is a bribe.

Tempting your dog with a treat to get him to comply is a bribe, and a bribe depicts you as weak. It means you are giving all the power to your dog, as he gets to make the choice as to whether or not he wants to take the deal—the behavior for the food you hold in your hand. If you habitually bribe your dog, then when you ask him to do something without holding up a treat, he won't be inclined to do it.

It's a better habit to keep the treat hidden in your pocket, and REWARD your dog for complying quickly and willingly. This way, your dog is more apt to follow your commands consistently, as he never knows when one of them might possibly result in a treat.

A Command Is Not an Endless Loop

Lana Maeder of Busy Bee Dogs performs live trick dog shows at fairs and events. In her show, each of her dogs plays a character based on the dog's own personality. Sydney plays the princess; Rio, the clown; Slyder, the athlete; and little Chiquita is the clever one. As trainers, we love the clever dogs. And as performers, we are tormented by the clever dogs.

During her act, Lana cues one dog at a time to join her onstage while the others wait in open crates off-stage, supervised by Lana's assistant. Lana and I had the pleasure of performing in the same lineup at a Bark at the Park dog fair, and after her second set of the day Lana came into the greenroom frustrated. Clever Chiquita had missed several cues to come onstage for her routines.

"Um, Lana?" I ventured. "Do you know what's going on with Chiquita and your assistant off-stage?" Lana didn't know. I explained what I had seen. It seems that clever Chiquita had learned to take advantage of the assistant. Chiquita was repeatedly coming out of her crate, as she had discovered that the assistant would reward her with a treat every time she was sent back in. The assistant was

unwittingly retraining Lana's dog, and causing the dog to focus more on this little game they were playing than on her cues for the show.

After learning this, Lana put a stop to the game immediately. Once the dog is in the crate, she explained to her assistant, the dog is required to remain in the crate until cued to come out. There are to be no rewards for disobedience.

The assistant and Chiquita were caught in an endless loop of command, obey, reward, disobey. Dogs will learn this scam very quickly if you let them. The rule is: One command, one consequence. The dog should not be given multiple commands (nor given multiple rewards) for one behavior.

So what should the assistant have done? She should have sent Chiquita into the crate, and possibly given her a treat for compliance the first time. When Chiquita then came out of the crate uninvited, this should have been viewed as disobeying the command. Chiquita should have been sent back to her crate or physically returned to her crate with no reward. Again and again, if necessary. This concept should be nothing new to parents who use a time-out chair and have to put the child back into place repeatedly, while giving no reinforcement. (Remember, any form of attention can reinforce the behavior, so we want to give the behavior the least attention possible.)

Pressure and Release

The old-time cowboys of the American West needed to break large numbers of semiferal horses to saddle in a short period of time, and the economics of doing so led to the development of some harsh training methods. The Natural Horsemanship movement specifically set out to replace those methods with more humane ones. Often called "horse whisperers," practitioners cultivate a connection with the animal and achieve the same results with a softer, easier training method. **Natural Horsemanship** is based upon working with the horse's natural instincts, using behavioral reinforcement in a humane way to create a calmer, happier, and more willing partner in the horse. It holds at its core the operant conditioning principle of pressure and release.

If the trainer uses his fingers to apply pressure to the horse's side—starting with gentle pressure and moving to stronger pressure if the horse does not respond—the horse will naturally learn that if he moves away from the pressure, the pressure is released. This is the basis for teaching the horse that if the rider applies pressure with his right heel, the horse needs to move left in order to make the pressure stop. The horse thereby discovers for himself the "window" he can navigate into to cause the release.

When I discussed enforcing the "down" command by pressing the dog's shoulder to guide him into position, I talked about putting **pressure** on the dog, and **releasing** the pressure when the dog lay down. The concept of **pressure and release** is at the core of all animal training, although most trainers don't even realize they are using it.

Rather than reprimand the dog for doing the wrong thing, when we use **pressure-and-release training** we encourage the dog to find for himself the right thing—the "easier window." We make the right thing easy to do and the wrong thing hard to do. In this way we do not battle our dog, and we do not give harsh corrections. Instead, our power comes from our steadfastness in maintaining pressure (active or passive) until the dog moves himself into compliance.

Heeling is traditionally taught through pressure and release. "Bonded heeling" is taught with a short leash, which the trainer basically grips to the seam of his pants. The dog feels collar pressure when he walks anywhere except in correct heel position. When he comes in line by his trainer's left leg, he causes the pressure to be released. Thus, he finds for himself the correct action—the "safe window" by his trainer's left leg.

When I teach a dog to go through an agility tunnel, I'll hold the dog at one end of the straight tunnel and ask the owner to call the dog from the opposite end. Dogs are reluctant to go inside the tunnel at first, and they try to go around the tunnel to get to their owner. Without forcing the dog, I gently but repeatedly block him from moving to the side of the tunnel. The only time I don't block him is when he moves toward the tunnel entrance. I don't push the dog into the tunnel, but rather let him find for himself the "easier window."

Learning Comes with the Release

The most important thing to understand when using pressure-and-release training is that learning occurs with the release, rather than with the pressure. The release is what lets the dog know he has done something right.

When we use a reward marker such as a clicker in training, the precise timing of the click is what lets the dog know what he has done to earn the reward.

In pressure-and-release training, timing is just as crucial, as the release acts as the reward marker. We release the pressure at the instant that the animal performs correctly. To teach a horse to "give to the bit," the trainer applies a light, steady pull on the rein. When the horse "gives," the trainer releases the pressure on the bit. The horse is learning from the release of pressure, not from the pressure itself.

Maintain Pressure Until the Dog Complies

The pressure is the cue, or the command. We want to hold to "One command, one consequence," so once the command is given (once the pressure is started), the pressure is maintained until the dog complies. Releasing the pressure before gaining compliance would only teach the dog that he should resist complying.

A friend of mine owns a pack of Alaskan malamutes that she runs on a dogsled team. As this is a dog-aggressive breed, my friend occasionally has to break up fights among her pack, after which she demands a down-stay from all her dogs. When her young, strong male lead dog refused to lie down after one fight, she attempted to gain his compliance by pressing downward on his shoulder. A low rumbling growl advised her that this tactic could take a very bad turn, so she instead attached a leash to the dog and applied a steady downward pressure on the leash with her foot. It took forty-five minutes, but her persistence paid off when the dog finally submitted and released himself from the pressure by lying down. Over time, this dog learned to submit earlier and earlier, as his defiance never paid off.

Meet Resistance with Equal Resistance

Throughout my college years, I worked as a windsurfing instructor—for UCLA and at Club Med. Somewhat surprisingly, I found that the female students learned this sport quicker than the male students. And here's why.

During their beach lesson, I would explain to the students how to stand on their board and gently pull the uphaul rope to lift the sail out of the water. The sail is very heavy at first when it is submerged, but as it starts to lift, water slides off and it becomes lighter and lighter.

Adrenaline would be high when my students then entered the water with their rigs. The men would invariably grab that uphaul and use their big, strong muscles to yank the sail out of the water—at which point it would snap up, throwing them off balance and sending them splashing backward into the ocean.

Windsurfing requires a delicate counterbalancing of the sail, by putting pressure on the sail with your body weight. The women didn't have the big muscles that the men did, and couldn't yank the sail up the same way. Instead, they were more graceful and controlled, making minute adjustments as the sail rose incrementally. They were constantly negotiating, and always meeting resistance with equal resistance. This proved to be the more successful tactic.

Pressure-and-release training is a dance. It requires you to constantly read your dog, using just enough pressure to compel him, yet not so much as to stress him. As he moves toward compliance, you move toward release.

If your dog wants to investigate a telephone pole during his walk, don't allow him to pull you over there, as you don't want to teach him that he gets what he wants by being insistent. The moment your dog starts to pull, stop walking. Meet his resistance with equal resistance. As your dog eases up, you ease up, and he can then walk (without pulling) to the telephone pole. Teach your dog that he gets release when he is soft and never when he's hard.

After your dog has started to learn the pressure cue, you should be able to anticipate his commitment to doing the behavior. You can feel it coming—you can tell when his mind is committed to performing the behavior. Now beat him to the release—release the pressure in that instant before he has even performed the behavior. By doing so you are conditioning your dog to respond to lighter and more subtle suggestions. Your pressure signal becomes softer and shorter, and the dog becomes softer and more responsive.

Dogs' sensitivity can be accentuated by your softness. It's a circle in which one begets the other. It's just a matter of your being soft enough and receptive enough to pick up on their response. How soft can you be and how quiet in your request can you be and still be heard by your dog?

Degrees of Pressure: Passive to Active

There is a range of pressure we can use, from passive to active. The pressure should never escalate to a high level, however, as we don't want our dog to think of it as punishment. We just want to make it harder for him to do the wrong thing, and easier for him to do the right thing. By consistently rewarding the dog with a release, he will grow to understand that there is always an "easier window," and he will seek it out sooner.

Always start with minimal pressure and use the least amount of pressure necessary to gain compliance. The first gesture of pressure is your dog's first hint; it should be barely detectable, optimally only a thought. If your dog doesn't catch that hint, then you gradually increase the pressure to give him a bigger hint. And then, when your dog does comply, it is your turn to give, and you must do so immediately.

When a trainer wants a horse to move its head, the first hint he gives the horse is by pushing his hands toward the horse, but not touching him. If the horse does not move, the trainer gives a bigger hint by gently tapping him, and then by using stronger finger pressure until the horse responds. As soon as the horse responds by moving its head, the trainer releases the pressure immediately and backs off.

There are many ways of putting pressure on an animal, and many of them, such as swinging a rope near a horse, involve no physical contact at all. "Dog whisperers" such as the famous Cesar Millan get their mystical reputation from their ability to control a pack of dogs without verbal or physical cues. They control through looks, stature, and subtle gestures. Eye contact is a form of pressure (which is why you shouldn't try to stare down a wild animal or volatile dog). Stepping toward the dog and invading his space is pressure (which is why unfamiliar dogs approach each other in a curve, rather than straight on).

A dog whisperer can put pressure on a dog to lie down by lowering his head and staring intensely from under his brow at the dog. If the dog still doesn't lie down, the dog whisperer can increase the pressure by walking toward the dog, invading his space. A step or two is usually enough to do the trick, but if not, the next step would be to physically pressure the dog's shoulder down.

The Five Steps of Pressure and Release

There are five consecutive steps to pressure and release training:

ASK	Apply steady pressure, active or passive.
↓	
ANTICIPATE	Anticipate the animal's compliance, so that you can be ready with a quick release.
↓	
GET	Get the response.
↓	
RELEASE	Release the pressure instantly.
↓	
REWARD	The release is the reward, but a treat after the release speeds up learning.

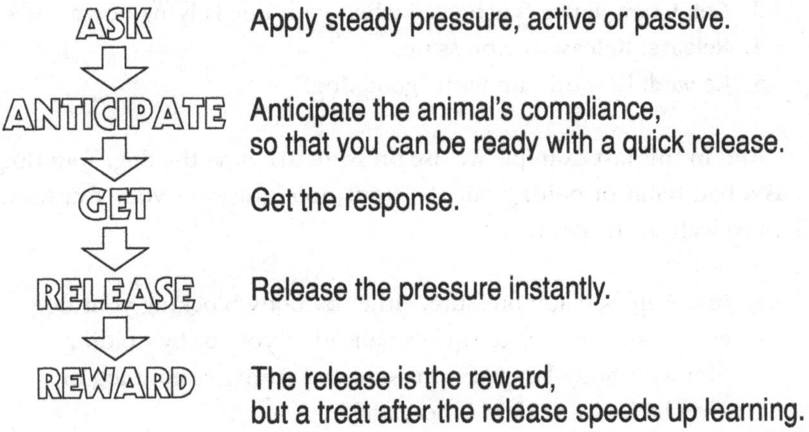

We can use pressure-and-release training to **teach**, **enforce**, and **control**. In this first example, we will use pressure-and-release tactics to ***teach*** the dog a behavior. Your dog is pulling on his leash and you want to teach him to walk by your side.

1. **Ask:** Apply pressure on his collar toward you.
2. **Anticipate:** Watch your dog and learn the signs that precede his compliance. Be ready to release the instant he complies.
3. **Get:** Your dog maneuvers himself to your side.
4. **Release:** Let the leash go slack, releasing the pressure.
5. **Reward:** Say "good dog" right when you release.

In this next example, we use pressure and release to *enforce* a command that the dog understands but has chosen not to obey. You tell your dog to "lie down," and he doesn't. Since the rule is "One command, one consequence," you will not repeat the command, but will now enforce it.

1. **Ask:** Put pressure with the flat of your hand on your dog's shoulder blade, pressuring him sideways and down.
2. **Anticipate:** Anticipate his going down once he is committed to the action (usually when he is about halfway down). Don't keep pushing him once he is committed to the action.
3. **Get:** Compliance is achieved when your dog is lying down.
4. **Release:** Release the pressure.
5. **Reward:** Reward him with "good dog."

And in this last example we use pressure to *control* the dog. Your dog has a bad habit of bolting out the front door ahead of you. You want him to wait at the door.

1. **Ask:** Apply steady pressure, either by body-blocking your dog every time he tries to squeeze ahead of you, or by holding him with body-language pressure and stern eye contact, or even by leashing him, if necessary.
2. **Anticipate:** Constantly evaluate the degree of pressure needed to hold your dog, and apply the least amount of pressure necessary. Don't hold your arms out if a stare will do the job.
3. **Get:** Compliance is achieved when you exit the door and your dog waits inside.

4. **Release:** Release the pressure by telling him "okay" and softening your body language and eye contact.
5. **Reward:** The release of pressure is the reward.

Once you understand the concept of pressure and release, notice how it is being used to reinforce behaviors in your dog's daily life. Perhaps your child is pulling your dog's tail until he nips her, causing her to release it. Your dog will learn to bite your child to cause her to release her pressure.

Noncompliance Is Not an Option

Sitting on the tailgate of my truck, Chalcy and I wait our turn in the hunting competition, in which sporting breeds compete to find and point planted birds in a marked area of the desert chaparral. I watch a fellow hunter return with his dog from a romp in the field. He has no leash, no electronic collar, no treats in his pocket . . . and his young dog is heeling by his side.

> As the hunter approaches, I compliment him on his well-trained dog. "Oh," he stammers, "he's not really obedience-trained. He's just a huntin' dog."
>
> How do hunters have this kind of control over these intense dogs? Through pressure and release. They use their body language, eye contact, and growly voices to apply pressure to their dog until the dog falls into line, at which time the unpleasant pressure is released. "Get over here!" they command in a low, growly voice. "Heel!" When the dog falls into line, they release the pressure and acknowledge the compliance with a softer "good dog."

Contrast this anecdote with the strictly positive-reinforcement obedience competitor I described under Rule 4 who had to put an electronic collar on her dog in the park because her control over him was reliant upon the presence of treats in her pocket. With pressure and release, noncompliance is not an option for your dog.

Corrections

We use the release of pressure to mark the instant our dog did the RIGHT thing. But there are other times when we need to mark the instant our dog did the WRONG thing. For these instances, we use a **correction.**

If your dog has his head buried in your trash can, you could enact a correction by sneaking up behind him and startling him with a loud shaker-can (a soda can containing a few pennies). That would instruct your dog that being in the trash is a wrong behavior.

Ideally, a correction does two things: it communicates to the dog that he did something wrong, and it gets the dog to do the correct behavior. This is considered instructive, hence the euphemism "correction." The startling effect of the shaker-can lets the dog know that he is doing something wrong, and it also causes him to instinctively back out of the trash, which is the correct behavior we desire.

This shaker-can correction is an example of an **avoidance correction**, in which we teach the dog to have an aversion to something (the trash can). More often, though, a correction is used when the dog understands a command and refuses to comply. Be aware that noncompliance is not always a refusal to comply. Before blaming your dog, first determine whether he truly knows what you want, and whether he is stressed, fearful, or confused. We correct a dog for a refusal to comply only when we are sure that the dog understood the command and chose to not obey it—if you told your dog to "sit," for example, and he didn't. You could then enforce your command with a correction of a finger flick on his rear. The sting lets him know he did something wrong, and because it was inflicted downward on his rear, it instructs him to put his rear down.

Why does the finger flick have to sting? Why can't we just gently press his rear down? During the learning process we *do* just gently press his rear down. But if the dog is willfully not complying, there has to be an element of agitation as a penalty. The idea is that if you tell your dog once, and he obeys, then he is rewarded. If you have to tell him a second time (by way of a correction), it's not going to be as pleasant. In this way, the dog is given a motive to obey the first command.

In pressure-and-release training we increase pressure gradually and can gauge the dog's reaction along the way. A correction, however, is a single action of midlevel agitation. It is far better to use too little agitation than too much, as you can do irreparable damage to your relationship with your dog by causing him fear with too strong a correction. Dog training can be a frustrating endeavor, and your frustration and anger, when paired with physical corrections, can escalate to inappropriate and unfair amounts of force. Don't give corrections when you are angry. Instead, kennel your dog and walk away.

A Correction Must Be Immediate

We use a reward marker to mark the exact moment our dog did something right. And we use the release of pressure to mark the exact moment our dog did something right. With a correction, the timing also has to coincide with the exact moment of the action, so that the dog knows which action caused the consequence. We use a correction to mark the exact moment our dog does something wrong.

If you were to catch your dog chewing on the table leg and then collar-correct him when he came to you, your dog would make an association between the thing he was currently doing when you collar-corrected him (such as coming to you). By timing incorrectly, you'd have taught your dog to not come to you!

Follow Up a Correction with Praise

When we put pressure on our dog's shoulder to guide him into a down position, we released and praised him the moment he achieved the correct position, so that the scenario of his being down after hearing the word "down" would be a pleasant one.

When your dog obeys an instructional correction, praise him to reinforce the desired behavior. If you finger-flick his rear to get him to sit, praise him as soon as he sits. That way the finger flick is associated with his choice to not comply, but your praise is associated with his compliance. Don't hold a grudge—once your dog has made up for the mistake, let it go.

Verbal Correction

The verbal correction (the word "no") can become a powerful directive that your dog will respect. Here are the basic rules for developing your verbal correction:

1. First give the verbal correction, "no," and then give the leash correction a half-second later. That way the word "no" gains the aversive association of the leash-pop.
2. Say "no" in a firm but steady voice. If you habitually raise your voice when you say it, then your dog won't give it much mind when you say it in a normal voice.

Startling Correction

There are times when your dog is not paying attention, or is headed off in a direction you don't want him to go. A tap on his side or a sharp "hey!" can be used as a correction to redirect his attention, like saying, "Hey! Focus back on me!"

Motivating Correction / Discouraging Correction

Stationary exercises such as sits, downs, and stays require a dog to come out of drive mode and remain calm. Other exercises, such as competition heeling, require a dog to stay in drive—to be up and actively performing. Some corrections can *take drive out* of a dog while others can *add drive* to a dog.

When a dog breaks a stationary exercise it is often a result of his having too much drive, possibly due to distractions. To take drive out of this dog, the trainer should say "no" and give one sharp leash correction. This is usually enough to get the dog to settle down and comply.

It may seem like a contradiction to say that a correction can *add drive* to a dog, but in fact that's exactly what can happen when the correction is done properly. This type of correction is sometimes known as a **motivating correction.** To add drive, give three low-level corrections very quickly. Pop! Pop! Pop! "No! No! No!" This sort of turns the dog's nerves on and gets him excited, and thus causes him to quickly move into compliance. It is important that these corrections are not hard corrections; if they are too hard we can lose drive.

I rarely use physical corrections with Chalcy, as after years of training together she has become very responsive to my voice alone. A motivating correction for her is simply "heyheyhey!"

Avoidance Correction

One of the hazards of living in California's Mojave Desert region is the rattlesnakes. This is why Chalcy, at two years of age, was put through a snake-avoidance training clinic.

I passed my unsuspecting dog over to a clinic handler, as the dog owner is excluded from the process so as not to build unintended associations between the owner and aversive consequences of the snake. Chalcy was fitted with an electronic collar (also called a "shock collar"). The handler led Chalcy nonchalantly toward a live, but muzzled, rattlesnake. The instant Chalcy's eyes fixed on the snake she was zapped by the collar–*youch!*

Chalcy was taken to another part of the desert lot and led upwind

toward a ventilated upturned bucket with a rattling snake inside. As soon as Chalcy's interest was piqued by the rattling, odoriferous bucket—*zap!*

The third and final station was a fenced corridor. The handler entered with Chalcy at one end, a muzzled snake lay curled in the middle, and I stood at the other end. Chalcy wanted desperately to come to me, but wouldn't pass by the snake to do so. She had passed the test.

Three years later I took Chalcy back for a refresher course at a new location. I parked and opened the door for her, but she vehemently refused to come out of the truck. I assumed she detected the snake scent and remembered her lesson, and so I closed the door and took her home.*

When applied correctly, avoidance corrections are the most effective way to teach a dog to stay away from something. The rattlesnake shock-collar experience was strong enough that I will probably never need to teach that lesson again. However, too many corrections of this kind can cause generalized fear in a dog, so you want to use them only in limited scenarios, for critical lessons. Because we don't want to use the corrections often, we want to make them count when we do. Do it once and make it strong enough to deter future behavior, so that hopefully that lesson will never have to be relearned.

What Constitutes an Aversive?

Different dogs require different amounts of an aversive. It's your job as a trainer to know your dog, and to use an appropriate deterrent.

An aversive can be anything your dog finds unpleasant:

stern eye contact
verbal correction ("no")

* Don't try to administer snake-avoidance training on your own. Precise timing is crucial, and a good clinic leader can read dogs very well. As an added precaution, you may wish to consider having your dog vaccinated against snake venom. The past few years have seen great success with new snakebite vaccines for dogs. If a snakebite occurs, the vaccine can slow the reaction to the venom, buying you a little more time to rush your dog to the vet.

spray bottle
shaker-can
citronella collar
tap on the nose
finger flick on the rump
collar correction

SUMMARY

- Discipline is not punishment; it is the compassionate enforcement of fair rules and a structure for understanding expectations and consequences.
- Commands are not compromises. Do not vary your criteria for acceptable behavior.
- Give only one command at a time, give each command only once, and make sure it is complied with. If you're not in the mood to enforce the command, then don't give it in the first place.
- Treats are rewards, not bribes. Keep the treat hidden in your pocket.
- Don't get caught in an endless loop of repeatedly rewarding your dog for the same command (as Chiquita was rewarded in coming out of her kennel).
- When enforcing a command, release the pressure once your dog is in the correct position, and praise him.
- We can use pressure-and-release training to teach, enforce, and control. The five steps of this technique are:
  - Ask (apply steady pressure, active or passive)
  - Anticipate (compliance, so you can be ready with a quick release)
  - Get (the response)
  - Release (the pressure instantly)
  - Reward (the release is the reward, but additional praise or a treat after the release is even better)
- The release is the reward, and it requires the same precise timing that is necessary with other reward markers.
- Start with the minimal amount of pressure and gradually increase the pressure. Once pressure is started, do not release until you get compliance.

- **A correction does two things: it communicates to the dog that he did something wrong, and it guides the dog to do the correct behavior.**
- **Precise timing of a correction is essential for it to be instructional.**
- **Follow up a correction with praise once your dog is in the correct position.**

Rule 9: The Seven Tenets of "Come"

Chalcy has gotten very "stage-wise" over the years, and has learned that she can take advantage of the times I talk to the audience to slowly make her way to the edge of the stage, mugging people for a petting or a piece of their sandwich.

As I was striking the set after my show, two women approached me and accused me of zapping Chalcy with a shock collar during our show. "What? No!!! I don't shock her! What gave you that idea?"

"We saw you," they said. "Every time Chalcy went to the edge of the stage, you hit a button behind your ear and she came bolting back."

I removed the gadget from behind my ear and showed it to them. It's a wireless headset, and the button they saw me hit was the mute button. As I talk to my audience, between sentences I'll briefly hit the mute button and command, "come." Chalcy always responds immediately and emphatically to this command. So emphatically, I guess, that it looks like she is being shocked!

You give a lot to your dog and your dog owes you the obedience of coming when called. Immediately. Every time. Without exception.

Why the strictness with this command? Because this command could save your dog's life. Picture your dog having bolted out the door and into the road. A car is speeding directly at him. You call "come" and your dog chooses, as he has so many times before, to ignore you.

This scenario could have had a happier ending if you had worked with your dog to get him to reliably obey your command. Cars aren't the only threat to your dog; there are snakes, aggressive dogs, cliffs, manholes, electric fences, cats, motorcycles, hot barbecues, lawn mowers, coyotes, skunks, and countless other potential dangers that your dog needs to be called away from.

I don't think anyone will argue with the importance and convenience of having a reliable "come," so we'll move on to the question of how to achieve it.

Just as we want this command to be obeyed every time, we have to be equally consistent with our rules in training it. Learn them, love them, live them—they are the seven tenets of "Come."

THE RULE

"Come" should be obeyed by your dog immediately, every time. Use the command consistently, reward it consistently, and enforce it consistently. Associate positive, and never negative, outcomes with your dog obeying this command.

Tenet 1: "Come" for Good Things, and Not for Bad

We want to condition our dogs to come automatically when called. If we call our dog to us a hundred times, and our dog reacts to this call by coming a hundred times, the response becomes an automatic or conditioned response. The hundred-and-first time we call, our dog's muscle memory will kick in even before he weighs his options.

Therefore, we don't want our dog to have to evaluate his options when he's called. And he WILL stop to evaluate his options if his past experiences in coming when called haven't always been positive ones. If you sometimes call your dog for a bath, or call him to go to the vet, or call him to punish him, he may not be so eager to come to you the next time you call!

Coming to you should always be a positive experience for your dog. Only call your dog to "come" for good things—a walk, chow time, a treat, a play session—or at least for neutral things, so that the command becomes associated with a positive outcome.

If, on the other hand, you need to give your dog a bath or take him to the vet or need him for some other unpleasant chore, go and get him instead of calling him to you.

Tenet 2: Mean It When You Say It

There are times you wish to merely rein in your dog, and there are times when you need a full, immediate recall. Make it easy for your dog to understand your commands by using your terms consistently. The "come" command is the word to use for a serious recall.

Look directly into your dog's eyes and use a serious tone of voice with this command—authoritative and straightforward, with no lilt at the end: "Come."

The word "come" should be used only in cases where a mandatory, immediate recall is required. In all other cases, just call your dog's name or use "c'mon, boy," "here," "let's go," or similar verbiage.

Tenet 3: "Come" Is Rewarded When It Is Obeyed

When your dog obeys your "come" command, it's one of the best things he can do! Reward him every time—with a treat, a little bit of play, a belly rub or petting, or genuine praise. This simple step is often neglected by dog owners, but it makes a world of difference to your dog. He CHOSE to obey your command over other enticing options, and your appreciation and rewarding of his good deed is important to him.

Precede routine daily rewards with a "come" command; prepare your dog's dinner and call him to "come" when it's ready. If you happen to have a treat or kitchen scrap you want to give to your dog, call him to "come" before giving it to him. When you are ready to play some fetch, call him to "come" and reward him with a play session.

Tenet 4: "Come" Results in Discipline When It Is Not Obeyed

If coming when called is the best thing your dog can do, then NOT coming when called is the worst. Not obeying a "come" command is a serious infraction and should be treated as such.

When Chalcy was nine months old, we had a milestone event that forever changed her response to my "come" command. Randy and I had been working outside, while Chalcy poked around nearby.

As I looked up from my hot, sweaty work this summer day I saw no sign of her. I called to her. No response. I called several more times before spotting her up on the hillside. I was pretty sure she saw me before jogging off the hillside, AWAY from me. She reappeared higher up, on a neighbor's front lawn, cavorting with their beagle!

I cupped my hands around my mouth and called as loudly as I could, "Chalcy, come!" But Chalcy paid no mind. She was deliberately blowing me off. Aargh!

I set out up the hillside after her. A half hour later when I finally reached her, I took her by the collar and told her sternly that she needs to "come when I say come," a sentiment that I reiterated a dozen more times during our long walk back, ensuring she understood what she was being reprimanded for.

Chalcy was all too glad to have her "walk of shame" end when I finally released my hold on her collar and put her in her kennel. After twenty minutes for her in time-out, I attached a long line to her collar and we practiced several iterations of "come" in the yard. Chalcy obeyed each command, and I praised her sincerely for each. When it was over, all was forgiven.

From that day forward Chalcy came immediately, almost without fail, every time I called. Without raising my voice at her or hurting her, I had conveyed my displeasure with stern eye contact, body language, and tone of voice.

You may be wondering why I called "come" multiple times, when we know the rule is "One command, one consequence." In this case, I had no way to enforce the command, so I used the repeated calling as a form of consistent pressure that didn't let up until the command was eventually complied with.

Now, here's the difficult thing: Since you need to reward your dog for coming to you, and discipline him for not coming to you, what if he only *sort of* obeys you, taking his own sweet time to come? You can't discipline him, as it could make him hesitant to come to you the next time you call. But neither should you reward him, since he basically blew you off until he decided he was ready to come. This is where you really have to read your dog and give him just the right amount of praise and chastisement to motivate him to do better next time. It's sort of like visiting your dentist. He doesn't reprimand you TOO much about not flossing, or you might *never* come back. Yet he wants to chastise you a little, so that you'll do better in the future in order to avoid another reprimand.

Tenet 5: "Come" Is Enforced—EVERY Time

During an outing at the lake I watch a man call to his Lab from his beach chair. "Charlie, come!" Charlie's attention is on a stick that is bobbing lightly at the edge of the water. "Charlie, come!" Still Charlie does not come. "Charlie. Charlie! Come! Oh, forget it." And the man lazily resigns himself to the situation, subsiding into his beach chair.

Charlie had no intention of coming. After all, why should he? He had long since learned that "come" was not a command, but rather a suggestion that could be ignored without consequence. If he waited long enough, his owner would tire or become bored with calling him and would eventually stop.

Although you may not be superstrict with all household rules (slipping an occasional table scrap to your dog or letting him hog two-thirds of your bed), the command "come" needs to be strictly enforced. If you expect your dog to come every time he is called, then you need to enforce this rule every time it is issued.

Every time you enforce or don't enforce a command, give in or administer discipline, your dog is processing the odds and taking them into consideration for the next time. If your dog has been made to come every single time the command was given, he will learn that the odds are drastically against his ever getting away with disobeying this command.

Once you command "come," your dog needs to come, whether voluntarily or involuntarily. If your dog comes voluntarily, he will be rewarded; if he doesn't come voluntarily, he will still be made to come, but will not be rewarded. Your dog is no dummy; he will learn that he might as well get the reward if he is going to have to come either way.

If you find yourself in a situation where you know you will not be able to enforce the command, then you should avoid giving the command at all, as every time your command is neither complied with nor enforced, your dog is learning that obedience to your command is optional. Some trainers recommend only giving the "come" command in controlled situations, such as when your dog is on a long line, in order to guarantee a way to enforce it. I tend to place less importance on physical control in guaranteeing enforcement; rather I define success in enforcement as not giving up until the dog has been brought to the location where the command was first issued.

Let's imagine you command "come" and your dog dances around and runs away from you. At this point, the worst thing you could do would be to give up, resigned that he'll come home when he gets hungry. Your whole job now is to keep calling, harassing, dogging, and putting pressure on your dog until he comes. You need to be the winner—to not give up before he does. The purpose of this exercise is not to punish your dog, but to show that he WILL be obeying this command, every time.

Tenet 6: Plant Your Feet

One of dogs' favorite games is keep-away. Dogs love to brandish a prized toy, or a bone, or your shoe, while you chase around after them. It's all too easy to get sucked into this game when your dog is not obeying your "come" command. Some trainers teach "come" by running away from the dog, engaging his prey drive to chase them. Although that is somewhat effective, we don't want to confuse "come" with a game that your dog has the option of playing or not playing. When "come" is a command, it removes his options.

Plant your feet at the spot where you gave the command. Stand upright and tall with your arms at your sides to convey authority and seriousness, and look directly at your dog, drawing him in with your eyes. Do not bend over or lean forward, as that is a weaker stance, and can look like a play stance. Do not lunge at your dog, as it is likely you will miss and he will think it a fun game. He needs to come to you, not you to him.

If you must go and get him, walk deliberately and authoritatively. When you get hold of him, walk him back to the spot where you were when you originally gave the command. From that spot, tell him "come" again, and pull him toward you and then praise him. Remember, we only want the unpleasant pressure to be associated with the dog's choice to disobey a command. As soon as the dog comes into compliance (by being near you) we release the pressure and offer praise.

Tenet 7: "Come" and Release

Too often, "come" is used at the end of a play session: "Come and put your leash on," "Come inside the house," "Come away from the rabbit." This can develop a negative connotation of the word for your dog.

Teach your dog that "come" doesn't necessarily mean the end to playtime. While playing at the park, call your dog to "come," quickly praise him or give him a treat, and then release him. He will be much more likely to come in the future if it often just means quickly checking in with you.

Troubleshooting

Q: I called my dog to "come" and he didn't come. What do I do?

A: Don't give up. Keep commanding him and putting pressure on him, or walk deliberately to him and bring him back to the spot where you initially gave the command.

Q: My dog comes, but she stops about five feet away from me. How close does she need to come?

A: You make the rules—decide in your own mind how close is satisfactory. In dog sport competition it is common that a dog needs to come close enough so the owner is able to touch the dog's head without moving his feet.

SUMMARY

Tenet 1: "Come" for good things, and not for bad

Tenet 2: Mean It When You Say It

Tenet 3: "Come" is rewarded when it is obeyed

Tenet 4: "Come" results in discipline when it is not obeyed

Tenet 5: "Come" is enforced—EVERY time

Tenet 6: Plant your feet

Tenet 7: "Come" and release

Expect Respect

I first met Nannette Klatt when I almost tripped over Flame, her Doberman pinscher guide dog, in a restaurant (entirely my fault). Nannette is an attractive woman in her midthirties with stunning pale green eyes. Ironically, those beautiful green eyes can hardly see. Nannette describes her type of vision loss as being similar to what a sighted person looking through a straw would see; her vision is limited to a very narrow spot. So Flame does the seeing for her. By means of a harness, Flame pilots Nannette through stores and across streets. Flame literally has Nannette's life in her keeping. Flame works diligently for her master, not for treats, and not from force, but out of respect.

The first time Flame and Nannette met, Flame was brought into a room where Nannette was seated. The person does not go to the dog, but rather the dog goes to the person. Right off the bat, this sets the tone for their relationship and establishes Nannette in the leadership position. Nannette does not bend over and coo at the dog, but behaves like a strong and capable leader, inclining the dog to feel secure in her presence.

After their introduction comes their "bonding ceremony": a bath. The dog demonstrates trust in her new master by allowing herself to be put into this vulnerable position.

Master and dog spend every minute of the next twenty-eight days side by side, living and working together at the guide dog training facility. During this time, the dog is expected to show a high level of respect for her new master. Flame must not put her paws on her master's lap, jump on her, get up on the furniture, or sleep on her master's bed as Nannette's leadership position must not be compromised.

The guide dog trainer told Nannette that it would take one year for her to bond with her dog, after which she would be closer to her guide dog than to her husband and her kids. The trainer was correct. I ask Nannette to what she attributes that closeness, and she has a hard time putting it into words. Physical proximity, dependence upon each other, mutual trust in each other's judgment, and mutual respect are key themes.

In order for a dog to respect his owner, he must have confidence in his owner's ability to be a strong, capable, and effective leader. When a dog has confidence in his leader, he will follow his leader's direction. In order for your dog to respect you, he must trust that you know what you are doing, that you are able to carry out your plan, and that you are strong enough to keep order in the pack and kibble in the bowls. When your dog respects you, he will be motivated to please you, as pleasing you solidifies his good standing within the pack.

Your dog, like any animal, has his own well-being as his priority and wants to associate himself with a leader who is going to help him be successful. I once worked under a boss who was very nice to me and brought me cupcakes on holidays. And I actually switched positions within the company so that I could work under a different boss—one whom I respected as a smart guy who made good decisions and who was on his way up in the company. This was the guy who was going to best use my talents and lead me to success. This was the guy I was motivated to work for. This was the guy I wanted as my leader. You win friends with cupcakes, but you earn respect by being a good leader.

It's not uncommon for a dog to obey 80 percent of the time and still not respect his owner. When dogs who lack respect for their owners are asked to do something they don't want to do, and the owner tries to enforce compliance, these dogs often become aggressive. Their owners find themselves scratching their heads wondering what went wrong. What went wrong, of course, was a lack of respect for a leader. A dog with solid leadership guidance is not going to be aggressive with his leader or even in the presence of his leader.

Earn your dog's respect by acting like a leader and by controlling your pack's resources.

Your dog should respect you, cooperate, and try to do what you ask. Think of it as not just "good behavior," but "expected behavior." Expect effort, expect compliance, and expect respect.

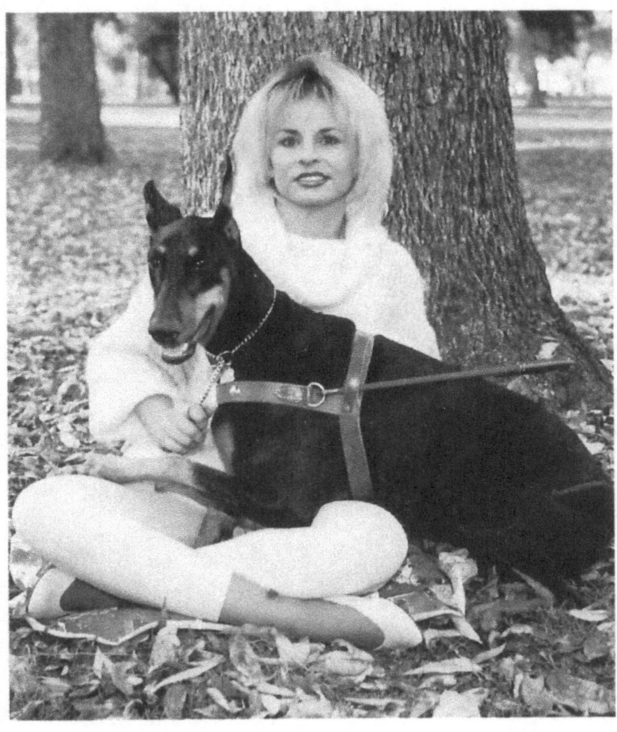

Rule 10: Benevolent Leadership

As a studio-animal trainer I'm never sure what surprises each job will hold. I've trained chihuahuas and Great Danes, and worked with rookies as well as celebrities like Bullseye the Target dog.

Job details are often sparse, and for one particular print shoot Chalcy was hired to "sit with talent." Not very exciting, but I agreed to take the job.

It was an outdoor shoot at the historic Greystone mansion in Beverly Hills (as seen in the *Dynasty* movie and in Luke and Laura's wedding on *General Hospital*). Chalcy was being fitted with a collar in Wardrobe, when up walked a stunning woman in a gorgeous silvery St. John Knits gown—"the talent," I presumed. She strode slowly and confidently toward me, her head high and her shoulders back. "Hi," she said. "I'm Angie."

There was something about Angelina Jolie that immediately changed the dynamic of the setting. The crew were transformed from a bustling group of self-important individuals into a subservient and attentive pack. Without her saying a word, it was obvious she was in charge. It was obvious to the crew, and, I noticed, it was obvious to the dogs. Chalcy was now standing still, tail upright but motionless, ears relaxed, and nose slightly down. Angelina projected a confident, calm energy that resonated with the dogs.

The shoot resulted in beautiful photos, and also a few extra bucks when Randy later told his friends that for five dollars they could "kiss the dog that kissed Angelina Jolie." What a bunch of dogs!

Dogs instinctively respond to leadership. In wolf packs it is the leader, or alpha wolf, who decides the actions of the pack, such as who eats first, where to hunt, and who is allowed to mate. The pack relies upon a leader to maintain organization and peace, for without a clear leader, members of the pack will jostle for position and fight among themselves.

Establishing yourself as leader is not about getting your dog to cower or kowtow. It is about getting your dog to listen to and respect you, to function as a well-adjusted member of the family, and to behave calmly and confidently in any situation because he trusts in his leader—you—to take care of him.

The vast majority of alpha dogs lead their packs benevolently. There is not often the need for physical domination, as they lead through subtle psychological control, such as confident posture, withering glances, staring, stalking, dogging (persistently hassling), barking, or growling. Day-to-day interactions within the pack are largely ritualistic displays of deferential and cooperative behaviors.

Leadership is a mental quality whereby you project confidence, and set and enforce rules and boundaries without intimidation. You let your dog know how to treat you with respect.

Act like a leader—don't beg, don't cajole, don't force. Just lead, and expect your dog to follow.

THE RULE

Dogs instinctively understand hierarchy and respond readily to leadership. Earn your dog's respect by showing yourself to be a benevolent leader. Inspire confidence in your strength and ability by projecting an "alpha attitude."

Dogs Respond Readily to Leadership

How often have you looked at someone else's child and thought, "That child is controlling the household" or "That child is spoiled rotten." You've probably followed the thought with "That child needs discipline and boundaries!" The house this type of child lives in is most likely an aggravated household. It does not function like the well-oiled machine of a harmonious household because roles are not clear and there is no hierarchy of leadership. It is unclear who is making the decisions, and when decisions are made, they are not always upheld. Favors are won through nagging, tantrums, hitting, and persistent rebellion. These methods are no more fun for the child than they are for the parent. The child has learned, through the positive reinforcement of getting what he wants, that being pushy and demanding is the way to behave within his pack. Imagine how much happier the child would be under the security of the clear and benevolent leadership of his caretakers. Let's think of our dogs in the same way.

Dogs are geared, through their evolution by way of selective breeding, to respond to human authority and leadership. In a multidog household, it is not unnatural that the human be the leader of the pack—in fact, dogs are predisposed to this condition. Without you as the clear leader in a multidog household, it is likely you'll have fighting among your pack.

Pack and Rank Drives

Dogs are highly social animals who naturally want to be part of a pack, and who seek out the companionship and social acceptance that the pack offers. As with all drives, dogs vary as to their degree of **pack drive**. A social dog who can't stand to be left out of anything the humans are doing would be high in pack drive. At the extreme would be the dog who manifests separation anxiety, becoming highly anxious when left alone. He may bark and whine and engage in destructive or obsessive behavior, even if the owner just goes into another room and closes the door.

A dog with low pack drive is independent and aloof, even with his own family. A dog with very low pack drive does not desire to bond as closely with his human partner and will be more difficult to motivate in training. Pack drive varies by breed, as this quality was emphasized or deemphasized in breeding depending upon the job of the breed.

"If you took him home tonight it would take him about a week to adjust, and then he'd be like, 'Oh, okay, I live with you now.' " My friend Nichole says this of her huge Alaskan malamute, Kwest.

"Doesn't that kinda . . . hurt your feelings?" I ask incredulously. After all, Nichole raised Kwest from a puppy. She trained with him daily, and had put several competition and show titles on him.

"No," she answers, "I don't take it personally. It's the breed. Malamutes have low pack drives. Sled dogs were bred to be independent, to make decisions on their own. If the sled driver tells them to go left, and they smell an ice hole danger to the left, they have to have the confidence to disobey their driver."

At the other end of the spectrum would be my childhood Weimaraner, Kuno, who had a strong pack drive. My mother and father performed an experiment on her once, by each taking a separate path at a fork in the forest road. Poor Kuno did not like that one bit!

She raced from one to the other trying desperately to keep the pack connected, even as they grew ever farther apart.

It's easier to manage the behavior of a high-pack-drive dog like Kuno, because the dog doesn't want to offend you and get kicked out of the pack.

More independent, aloof dogs like Kwest tend to be higher in rank drive and harder to control. The dog figures we're all here to please him, rather than the other way around.

Rank drive is the drive for dominance within the pack—the desire to improve social standing, to become the leader. A low-rank-drive dog is content to remain in a submissive or a midlevel position within in the pack. A high-rank-drive dog may fight to the death to assume the alpha position among the dogs in the household, but may readily accept human leadership and be completely respectful of humans. Other high-rank-drive dogs will challenge human rank often. There is a wide range here, from a mildly rank-driven dog who has a cocky attitude to a dog who won't hesitate to bite his owner.

It is dogs' natures to challenge—to see what they can get away with—and you need to teach them that challenging you will not be a successful tactic. A dog's misbehavior, however, is not always a challenge to your leadership. In many cases our wayward pet dogs are more unruly than status-seeking. In the absence of structure and consistent rules, they've learned annoying, attention-getting behaviors. Some are pushy, like children who test their parents' limits to see what behavior they can get away with. If, however, your dog nips when you try to take a toy from him, ignores your request to get off the couch, yanks ahead on walks, or generally challenges your authority, then he probably thinks he is the alpha of your pack. He needs to be taught a new, well-defined pecking order—and a new, lower place in the family hierarchy. He needs YOU to become his leader.

"Alpha" Is an Attitude

"Alpha" is an attitude—a position not achieved by force, but rather earned through confident, consistent behavior. A general doesn't enter a room and throw his weight around. He simply appears, and everyone starts saluting. And it wasn't Angelina Jolie's celebrity that let the dogs know she was in charge. It was her attitude. The mark of a true leader is the ability to control without force.

In life, people know how they ought to be treated, and they project that energy to others around them. People are generally treated the way they are asking or allowing themselves to be treated.

Think about how you are allowing yourself to be treated by your dog. Is it the way you want to be treated and feel you deserve to be treated? Are you allowing your dog to blow you off, to take advantage of you, to disrespect you? There may be times when you feel you deserve more respect—like when he doesn't come when called, or when he growls at you when you try to order him off your bed. When we concentrate on projecting an alpha attitude, we let others know the level of respect with which we expect to be treated.

Let your dog know that it is not okay for him to ignore you, or growl at you, or snap at your hand. Let him know in the same way your grandmother may have let you know to stop playing with your food at the table, or to stop fidgeting in church—with body language, stern eye contact, and a sharp "psssst!"

Projecting an alpha attitude is a learned skill. What if it's not in your nature to stand up for yourself, to take charge, to be assertive, to speak authoritatively and confidently? Well, perhaps that's why you have a dog in your life—to give you the opportunity to practice the attitudes and behaviors that are lacking in your life. It's a pretty empowering thought. Our dogs don't know our lifetime personality history, and we can pretend to be anyone we want! With your dog, behave like the person you wish you were. If you BEHAVE like that person, you ARE that person.

Leaders Project Authority

So how do we project that leadership authority that inspires respect? Walk tall and confident, arms at your sides. Look directly into your dog's eyes when giving a command and hold the stare longer, until your dog averts his eyes. Issue commands, not questions. Your tone of voice when issuing a command should be calm and authoritative, rather than harsh or loud, and certainly not pleading or nagging. Say it once, and mean it.

Don't stop doing something (cutting his nails, brushing his teeth) merely because your dog wants you to stop. Don't coddle a shy dog. Lead by example, with confidence.

Think: "He who moves the other's feet is higher in rank." Don't move out of your dog's way; have him move out of yours.

Don't bend over your dog, or move toward him—he should be coming to you. If you have several dogs in your household, watch them come down stairs or go through doorways. It is usually the dominant one who goes first, while the others defer. Don't allow your dog to bolt down the stairs, almost tripping you as he rushes by. That's not respectful, and not how you need to be treated. Stop, face your dog square on, and demand that he get back up the stairs behind you.

It's not necessary to assert your leader status at *all* times, as even alpha dogs sometimes show their bellies or allow their bone to be swiped. But if you feel your leadership position in jeopardy, use your alpha attitude to win it back.

Leaders Set and Enforce House Rules

Beginners often ask rather than tell their dogs to do something, pleading with their dog to mind. Don't be suckered into a subservient role with your dog. Don't be that parent who tolerates hitting from a toddler while pleading with the child to be nice. It's your job to define acceptable behavior and consistently enforce it.

Do not allow your dog to force his will on you. Do not allow your dog to change your mind. Do not give in to your dog's nagging or pushy behavior.

Once your dog is showing you due respect, you may relax your rules and allow your dog to jump on you, or sleep on your bed, but these behaviors should be on your terms, and with your permission only.

"Omega" Is Also an Attitude

One of Chalcy's jobs in our office is to greet the delivery people at the door and take their packages, which she runs back to my office in

exchange for a treat. She looks forward to these deliveries, and is quite . . . exuberant . . . when she runs to greet the delivery person.

The attitude projected by the delivery person directly affects the response they get from Chalcy. When the FedEx guy walks in, he acts like he owns the place and pays little attention to Chalcy. She responds with calm subservience. She circles his legs, *waiting* for the package, not *taking* the package.

The lady from the payroll company, however, displays quite a different attitude. Despite my best attempts to introduce her to Chalcy, she remains very afraid of Chalcy, as she is of dogs in general. She

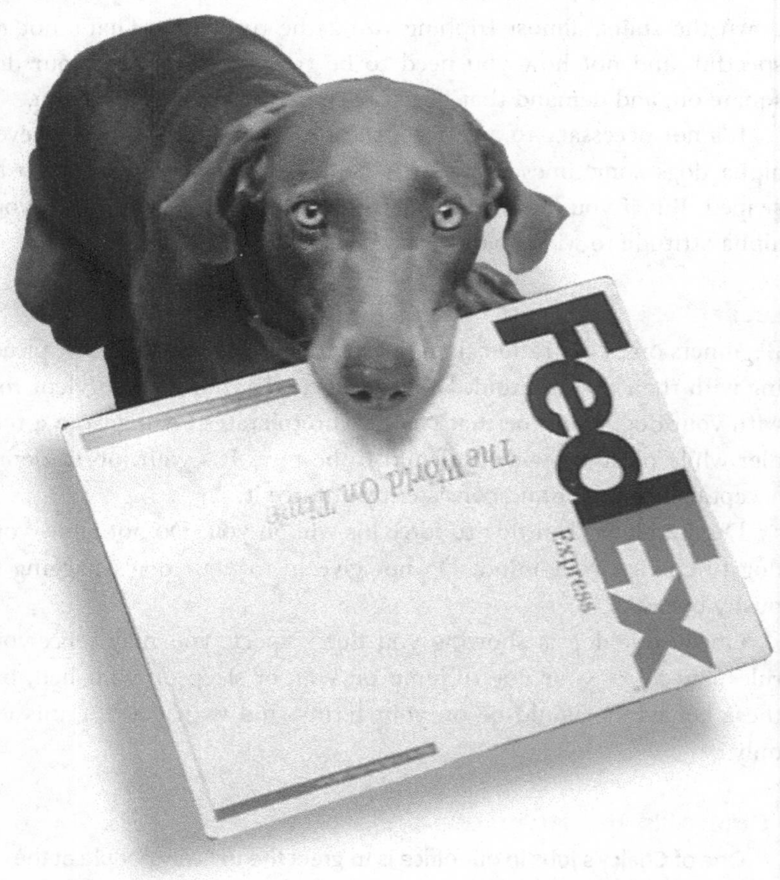

arrives at our office wearing a baseball cap pulled low over her eyes, and she peeks in the glass front door, her body crouched and tense. She taps the door with her keys in an effort to attract the attention of the closest employee who can come outside and accept her delivery. Boy, does this set Chalcy off! Chalcy senses suspicion, anxiety, and sneakiness, and she charges the door, barking and lunging.

The omega dog is the opposite of the alpha—it is the low dog on the totem pole. This is the dog who gives up food and sleeping places and freely allows the other dogs to grab his toys. He is reluctant to make eye contact, or will be the first to break a stare. The omega dog gives the most attention and affection to the other dogs, especially to the alpha dog.

You don't want to be the omega. Don't act like one.

If There's Any Growling to Be Done, I'll Do It Myself

I listen to a dog trainer describe the first time her dog growled at her when she attempted to take his bone. The trainer recounts how she addressed this resource-guarding problem using a method called "swapping," in which she gave her dog a higher-value toy in exchange for his current toy. This didn't work so well, as her dog sometimes refused to make the trade.

Next, the trainer tried offering the dog a really good food treat in exchange for the object in his mouth. This worked! The trainer practices this trading exercise several times each day, always ending with her giving the toy back to the dog.

One day her dog got hold of her shoe, and the trainer instructed the dog to "give." Well, the perceptive dog realized she had no treat in hand, and refused to give over the shoe! Blast! So the trainer recounted how she handled this problem by turning her back on her dog and walking away, in hopes that her dog would drop the shoe from lack of interest.

"Are you kidding me?" I think. "When I tell my dog to drop my shoe, she better damn well drop it. No trades, no treats. I'm the boss, it's mine, now drop it."

It is never acceptable for your dog to growl at you, at your family, or at anyone else in your presence. As leader of your pack, YOU decide when and at whom to growl, not your dog.

If your dog attempts to growl at somebody, put him in his place with "cut it out!" and step between him and the person. You lead the pack, you stand in front, and your dog stays behind you.

Rest assured, by the way, that should you ever be in real danger, your dog's instincts will take over and he will still go after a burglar, regardless of how many times you've stopped him from growling.

How Your Attitude Is Affecting Your Dog's Behavior

Dogs are very good at observing changes in our demeanor and are constantly reading our signals and reflecting our energy back to us. They feel what we feel; when we convey nervous energy, they become nervous. When we are anxious, they become anxious; when we are sad, they are sad; when we laugh, they laugh. Their reflection of our energy can be so subtle that we fail to see ourselves in their behavior, and may even be unaware of the feelings we are holding. Dog behavior, particularly problem or idiosyncratic behavior, can sometimes be an expression of the feelings of the dog's owner, possibly feelings of which the owner is unaware.

In a study by researchers at Tufts University School of Veterinary Medicine, personality tests were given to owners of dogs with aggression and behavioral problems (dominance-related aggression, fear aggression, and separation anxiety).[1] These owners scored less favorably than the control group in two areas. They scored lower in "dominance," indicating that they had an unassuming, overly compliant, and unforceful nature. This may mean they were more likely to permit their dogs to engage in aggressive displays, and less likely to encourage independent behavior in their dogs, which could foster overdependence.

They also scored lower in "capacity for status," indicating that they were less secure and less motivated, and that they inspired less confidence. This may have led to their having less confident dogs who were more apt to have behavioral problems. The findings indicate that more confident, independent-minded persons are less likely to have dogs with aggression or behavioral problems.

Other studies have found similar correlations between specific owner personality traits and dogs with behavioral problems. Owners of aggressive English cocker spaniels tended to be "tense, emotionally less stable, shy, and undisciplined."[2] Owners of dominant-aggressive dogs were more likely to display anthropomorphic involvement with their dogs, and owners with high anxiety had dogs who became overexcited and engaged in displacement activities.[3]

I'm not suggesting that you are the cause of all your dog's behavioral problems, but when you encounter a problem, it's worth giving some thought to how your behavior and energy may be contributing to your dog's issues.

Getting the Bluff In

Before each show, the grizzly bears at the Bermuda circus are brought to their staging area and lined up side by side on a bench for grooming.

As a child, trainer Derrick Rosaire Jr. worked alongside his father and their bear, Gentle Ben. Now Derrick's two adult sons train alongside him.

Sitting on the bench, one of the bears slowly leans to the side and pokes his nose into the other bear's neck. *Whack!* "Knock it off!" comes the gruff reprimand from the trainer, accompanied by a whack from his bully stick. The offending bear gives an insolent grunt and a shake of his head, but returns to his face-front correct position.

I'll admit, I half expected the bear to take young Fred's head off with one swipe of his paw. Grizzlies are strong and unpredictable and quick to get into fights with one another. The fact that they could be trained and disciplined by humans astounds me.

The bears are coaxed onto their hind legs, lined up single file, and led in this manner from their staging area to the circus tent. This is more than mere showmanship. Bears on their hind legs have less strength and opportunity to break out of formation.

In the ring, the mighty bears delight the audience as they maneuver their humongous bodies to jump hurdles on their hind legs, roll on a barrel, and even ride a bicycle. Performing a trick earns them a green pepper or other veggie, or perhaps a hot dog or Teddy Graham cracker (their favorite treat).

Although the bears are taught tricks by means of positive reinforcement, a Teddy Graham is not enough to keep a bear under control when he challenges another bear or his trainer. How is it, then, that Derrick Jr. and his sons can cause these animals to mind with a mere stick and gruff voice?

The answer is that they "got their bluff in" when the bears were young. When the bears were small, the trainers asserted their dominance. Not necessarily by physical means, but they were bigger and louder than the cubs, and the cubs understood the trainers' higher rank. As the bears grew, this pattern was maintained, and they continued to acquiesce to their trainers' dominance. Through this method, the trainers never had to have a confrontation with the animals.

Likewise with our dogs, it is far easier to have them acknowledge our leadership position from the start, rather than to have to take that position back after they've come to think of themselves as alpha. It's tempting to be a little too lenient with a new dog, especially a rescued dog whom we feel sorry for. But you would be doing yourself and your dog a favor by starting off from day one with clear hierarchy roles.

Don't Even Think About It!

I think our legal system is to blame. Some people seem to be under the impression that their dog is innocent until proven guilty. They know their dog is going to do something naughty . . . they warn their dog . . . they stand there and watch it happen . . . and THEN they correct their dog.

Not me. My dog knows that I can read her mind, and I correct her for even THINKING about it. A kid would argue with you if you tried this logic, but a dog seems to understand the correlation between the thought in his head and the consequence.

You can often see your dog's brain working, and know what his intentions are. Stop the thought in your dog before it becomes an action. If you see him headed down a bad path, correct him before he has a chance to do the wrong thing. If he starts to show his teeth, discipline him before he bites, so as not to let him have the experience of biting someone. The more he does the bad thing, the more it becomes a part of him.

Conversely, you can reward your dog for thinking about doing the *right* thing. If your dog is in a sit-stay, for example, and you see that he is valiantly resisting the temptation of a squirrel running by, you can reward him for the good choice he made in his head.

No Excuses

Dogs don't make excuses. Dog make choices. People, on the other hand, make excuses.

I see this all the time in beginning obedience classes. "My dog only bit your dog because your dog started it," "My dog is not paying attention to me because there are kids over there," and on and on. They have all kinds of excuses for their dogs' aggression or distraction or disobedience.

The bottom line is, I don't want to go to work every day either, but I have to. And there are times when your dog has to do things he doesn't want to do as well. Don't make excuses for his bad behavior. Fix it. Train, don't complain.

Every dog has challenges in his background, and has difficulties with certain situations. Don't enable him. Don't make excuses for him. Expect more of him, and hold him to these higher standards.

SUMMARY

- **It is your job as the leader to define acceptable behavior and consistently enforce it.**
- **"Alpha" is an attitude. Let your dog know the level of respect with which you expect to be treated.**
- **Project authority with body language and the consistent enforcement of fair rules.**
- **It is never acceptable for your dog to growl at you, at your family, or at anyone else in your presence.**
- **Give thought as to how your behavior and energy may be contributing to your dog's behavioral issues.**
- **Start a dog off acknowledging your leadership position, so that you don't have to take that position back later.**
- **Don't wait for your dog to do something wrong. Stop him while he is just thinking about it.**
- **Don't make excuses for your dog's bad behavior. Expect more of him.**

Rule 11: No Free Meals

Chalcy and I performed in a "Wonder Dogs" segment on the television show *Soap Talk* along with friends David Hartwig and Skidboot. Backstage, host Lisa Rinna asked David about his training technique. David answered in his customary Texas cowboy drawl, "Well, I shoe horses for a living. I work, I get paid. I don't work, I don't get paid. That's what life's all about. That's what I teach to Skidboot."

Dog owners don't often realize the power they hold by controlling their dog's resources, but this is the easiest and most effective tool you have to gain your dog's respect and compliance.

The beauty of controlling resources is that you have the power without ever asserting it. With our dog, simply by asking for a few things in exchange for resources, we gain the upper hand. It's as simple as asking your dog to "sit" as a sign of respect or deference before receiving his meal. In the most gentle and least confrontational way possible, we let him know that we hold the power and we make the rules. Not he.

We have all the power we need—we just have to understand how to use it. Food is power, attention is power, access is power.

THE RULE

In order for your dog to respect you as a leader, he must believe that you are in control of the resources. He must look to you as the sole or primary source for food, access, attention, comfort, and play. He must look to you as his provider and protector.

Leverage Your Resources

As babies, we had our needs provided for and were not expected to reciprocate. It wasn't long, however, before the harsh reality of the world set in, and we began to learn the give-and-take of a symbiotic relationship. Hands had to be washed before we received a cookie; rooms needed to be tidied before playtime; tables needed to be set before dinner.

Alas, the days of the free meal were over.

When we require a child to say "please" before receiving a toy, it is to build a conditioned habit of give-and-take. This prepares the child for working to earn rewards in the future—by studying to earn grades, working at a job to earn money, and being considerate to one's friends and one's spouse to earn the reciprocal consideration. This same concept of reciprocation will benefit your dog.

We want to condition our dog to give in order to get. Don't give valued resources, such as food, toys, play, walks, and petting, away for free. Leverage them as rewards for good behavior and obedience to commands. Ask your dog to "sit" before receiving his dinner. Ask him to "come" to receive a petting, or to "stay" at the door before being allowed to go out.

If your dog is pushy, withhold the resource—do not reward him with attention or with whatever it is that he wants. If your dog tries to push ahead of you out the door, do not reward him by allowing him to do so. Teach your dog that YOU control access.

As dramatized in the film *The Miracle Worker*, Anne Sullivan turned life around for an unruly, spoiled, blind and deaf child by the name of Helen Keller.

Having made no headway with the strong-willed child during her first week as Helen's teacher, Anne saw the need to gain the upper hand. She did not want to crush the girl's spirit by using force, so instead she took control by taking control of all the resources.

Anne removed Helen from her indulgent parents and set up a secluded, sparse cottage in which they would both live. Out of her home environment, Helen had no way of getting things on her own. She had to depend on her teacher–for everything. The child was required to work for every single thing she got. If she wanted to go outside, she had to button her own boots first. If she wanted to eat, she had to sit and use utensils, rather than grab food off the plates of others. There were no more free meals.

This forced Helen to yield to her teacher's authority rather than to continue to do as she pleased.

Leaders control the lives of pack members in fair, firm, and consistent ways in order to gain the respect that a pack leader must have. If you find your dog routinely ignoring house rules and generally showing disrespect, you need to control more of his resources. Following are some ways to leverage resources in order to gain respect as your pack's leader.

Control All Food Resources

You might be wondering what finally happened with my parents' experiment in taking two diverging paths in the forest. Here's the end to that story.

Kuno tried valiantly to keep the pack connected, by running back and forth between my parents. As they grew farther and farther apart, it became evident that she would have to make a choice or risk losing them both.

It was a tough call.

My father spent the most time with Kuno, and took her on daily walks in the forest.

But my mother fed her.

She chose my mother.

The title of this chapter can be taken just as literally as it can figuratively. Your dog's most valuable resource is food. When you control the food, you control the dog. Possibly the single most important way to cultivate your dog's respect for you is to not free-feed (meaning don't leave a bowl of food out all day for your dog to take at will). Food is power and it must come from YOU.

Mealtime is a ritual in pack cohesion and confirmation of dominance hierarchy. As a mealtime ritual, before setting down the food bowl, instruct your dog to "sit." Say it only once, and give him his meal only after he has done so. If he does not display these correct doggy manners, put the bowl out of his reach and walk away, and then try again later.

Here are some more ways to control the food resource:

- Don't let anyone other than yourself give food or treats to your dog, as this would give away some of your power.
- Don't let your dog grab food from you. "Givies" are allowed, not "takies."

- Eat your meals first, before your dog gets his.
- Don't feed your dog from the table or allow him to beg. Don't share your food with him until you are done eating.
- Occasionally take your dog's food bowl while he is eating. Start this exercise when he is young by briefly taking his bowl and then returning it to him. You can even return it to him with a little extra treat in it, to reward him for his cooperation. Do not return it if he is growling at you; return it only when he is passive.

Control Sleeping Areas

- Leaders get the best resting areas. If your dog is on the couch when you walk in, you can sometimes order him off, just to assert your position.
- Dogs are not allowed on your bed. If you really want your dog to sleep on your bed, make sure he knows it is by your permission, and not by his right.

Control Your Space

- Other than in play, dogs should not put their paws on your lap or jump on you, as this is dominating behavior.
- Stay at a higher elevation than your dog. Don't sit down to pet or play on the floor with your dog. Pet and praise from a level above your dog's head.

Control Access to Areas

- Before you put your dog's leash on him to go for a walk, ask him to "sit." You control access to the outside.
- The leader goes first down narrow hallways, up and down stairs, and through doorways.
- Don't allow your dog to pull you on his walk. YOU determine where and how fast to walk. Do the opposite of what your dog wants, to show you are in command; if he wants to go left, you go right.
- If your dog wanders off, hide from him. He should be afraid of losing YOU, not the other way around.

Control the Attention Given to Your Dog

Affection is a reward to dogs, and it should be earned in the same way as any other reward. I'm not saying that your dog has to fetch your slippers to earn each hug, but have him do *something*, just for the idea of doing *something*. You can still give your dog a hug whenever you want; just ask him to do something first. Your dog will enjoy the affection even more, having earned it as a reward.

- Have your dog "come" or "sit" or do a trick before you reward him with a petting session.
- If your dog prods you for attention, ignore him. The idea is to convey that YOU decide when to begin and stop petting.
- When greeting, give attention and petting to your dog only when he sits.

Control the Games

- Don't be bullied into playing tug or throwing a ball by your dog's pushing it at you. The leader decides when a game starts and when it stops.
- When you decide the game is over, take the toy and say "mine" and put it away in the closet. You control access to the toy.
- When playing fetch with your dog, ask him to "sit" or "down" or "stay" before throwing the ball.
- Stop playing before your dog loses interest, so it is you ending the game first.
- If your dog has dominance issues, don't play tug with him or he may see his winning as further proof of his dominance. Instead, play a less aggressive game such as fetch or hide-and-seek with a prized toy.

SUMMARY

- **The leader of a pack is the one in control of the resources. Be the primary source for food, access, attention, comfort, and play for your dog. Be his provider and protector.**

- Don't give free praise or treats to your dog. Having to earn his reward will cause him to respect you as his leader.
- Control all food resources. Don't free-feed. Don't allow other people to feed your dog.
- Control sleeping areas, your space, and access to areas.
- Your attention is a resource and should not be given away for free. Have your dog do a "come" or "sit" or perform a trick to earn a petting session.
- Control the games—you decide when they start and stop. Say "mine" and put the toy in the closet when you are done playing.

Build the Bond

Disney shows are highly scripted, and Disney's *Underdog* stage show starring Chalcy and me was no different. We performed five shows a day (six on weekends) for five weeks straight. Every show was the same—the same script, the same routine, the same witty banter with the MC. Early on in the show's run, a problem developed in our last skit.

"Chalcy wants to run an obstacle course, just like Underdog!" was the start of the last skit. As scripted, Chalcy would run all the way through the course but fail to jump through the last hoop for the grand finale. "Aww," I would say, cueing Chalcy to put her paws on my arm and bow her head between them, "you messed up!" Then a doorbell would sound and Chalcy would run to her mailbox and retrieve a package containing an Underdog superhero cape! Chalcy would don the cape and attempt the obstacle course again, this time making it through the grand finale with flying colors. Yay!

That's the way the routine was *supposed* to go.

When we performed it live, however, the doorbell would sound, but Chalcy wouldn't move. "Get the mail!" I would coax. She would turn her head to "blink" the mailbox, purposely not looking at it. I would try again, wiggling the little string on the mailbox door. "Get it . . . right there . . . get the mail. . . ." It was torture.

I recognized Chalcy's blinking of the mailbox as a sign of stress. In my competitive hunting experience I had seen dogs sometimes blink

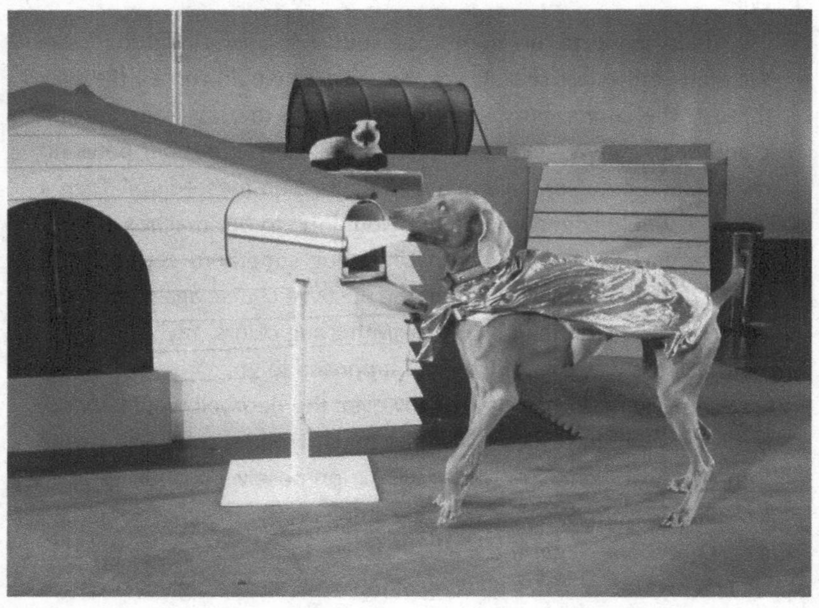

birds. It happens early in their training. At first they discover the grand fun of locating the birds and pouncing into the brush after them. Then they start to be disciplined to "hold point." For a usually brief time the dog can be confused. This confusion leads him to blink the bird, or pretend he doesn't see it, in order to avoid the stress of not knowing the correct thing to do.

At this point in the Underdog story I've given you enough information to figure out our problem. If you've already solved it, you're smarter than I, for I hadn't yet put two and two together. Read on for the next piece of the puzzle.

Chalcy is trained to miss that last, grand finale hoop jump by watching my body language. Well, in one show we miscommunicated, and she took the grand finale jump on the first pass. "Oh!" said I and the MC, not sure what to do. "Uh . . . yay . . . uh . . . she made it." And then *ding-dong* went the doorbell. "Chalcy, what's in the mail?" To my surprise, she happily ran over to the mailbox and fetched the superhero cape!

This was the clue that finally made sense of her behavior.

Because she had accidentally completed the grand finale on the first pass, I'd skipped the bowing-of-her-head behavior and my coinciding line, "Aww, you messed up!" It was that sentence that was causing her to blink the mailbox! My tone of voice led her to believe she had done something wrong, making her self-conscious and reluctant to do the next behavior. She, like other eager-to-please dogs, would rather do nothing than do something wrong.

After changing the script to give that one line to the MC, Chalcy hit her mark on every show thereafter!

I repeat this story occasionally to dog trainers, and many of them pipe up halfway through: "She's blowing you off," "Don't let her get away with that," "She's being dominant." Few of them stop to wonder, "What was Chalcy feeling to make her behave in this way?"

We're very keen on making our dog suit our needs, but relationships are seldom one-sided. It's not likely your dog will make an effort for you if you don't make the same for him.

The dog/human bond is at the center of your dog's well-being. If you take the time, practice communication, share experiences, and practice forgiveness, the bond that develops will result in a more loving, confident, and willing partner in your dog. When you create and maintain a good bond with your dog, you make him a true member of your family.

Rule 12: Communicate

John Baldwin has been a professional animal trainer and performer for the past twenty-five years. His experience has made him an expert in the field, and he has shared his knowledge in lectures to university faculties. John believes intelligent animals such as chimpanzees and dogs can tune in to human thoughts almost like they are seeing an image in our heads.

As a performer with a chimpanzee act, John always dressed his chimps for their stage shows in little pants, dresses, and shoes. As the mischievous animals sat on their high stools, they sometimes fussed and pulled off their restraining clothing, especially their shoes. Once one started, the others saw it as permission that they too could undress. John hated this.

John reiterated to me how, during one show, as he was speaking to his audience, a thought came into his head that his chimps hadn't taken off their shoes in several months. When he turned around to start his next routine, he saw that the chimp had taken off its shoes!

John explained his belief that humans form mental images of thoughts, and these images can be read by chimps and other intelligent species such as dogs. We convey these images in our head through our energy, which encompasses a variety of forms of nonlanguage communication. Dogs are very tuned in to these subtle clues that humans give.

Even when you're silent, your body is sending signals. These signals consist of a combination of looks, vocalizations, gestures, posture, breathing, and smells, including hormones and pheromones that each person gives off, which communicates your state of mind and intention. We communicate to our dogs all the time, whether or not we realize it. Our dogs know when we are sick, sad, angry, or scared. Our words can say one thing, but our body language will reveal our true feelings. By tuning in to our own as well as our dog's communication signals, we open up a whole new world of communication with our dog.

THE RULE

Whether we realize it or not, we communicate with our dogs more through energy than through words. We can learn to project our energy in a way our dog can understand, informing him of our state of mind and intention. We can also learn to read our dog's energy and better understand his intention and anticipate his behavior.

Communicate with Your Body Language

The greatest animal trainers understand the power of communicating with their energy rather than their voice. Horse whisperers have long believed in the effect on their animals of their own energy. A so-called dog whisperer can walk into a group of dogs and be given a respect space, while another person may walk in and have the dogs jump all over him. The dogs are responding to the different energies of the two people. Dogs sense if a person is confident, or if he is insecure and nervous, and they respond accordingly.

Through selective breeding, dogs have evolved to be excellent interpreters of human signals. They easily perceive tiny details—a quick signal, a slight change in our behavior, the expression in our eyes, the rhythm of our breathing. And dogs, not distracted by the meaning of words coming out of someone's mouth, are often a better judge of the person's intention than even we are!

We sometimes rely too much on our language as a way to communicate with our dogs, at the expense of more intuitive methods of communication. My hunting coach once threatened to duct-tape my mouth shut. A half century of working with hunting dogs had taught him that verbal communication did more to hinder than to help my dog by breaking her focus and making her less confident in her mission. "She can read your energy," Jimmy told me. "You don't have to communicate with words."

If you can start to notice in your own body how you are emitting energy, you can then present a more intentional energy in order to communicate a message to your dog. You can communicate leadership, or pressure, or encouragement, or relaxation.

Your Dog Will Do What You Expect Him to Do

In her younger days, before her vision deteriorated to the extent it has now, Nannette was an avid horsewoman. She worked with children with cerebral palsy, using riding as a form of therapy for them. "There is something about the horse's body that the children could feel straight through them," Nannette explains. "Being led by a guide dog is like that—the dog's harness is like a horse's reins. I can listen to my dog and feel her intentions through the harness. And when she tells me something, such as that it's okay to step out into the street, I trust her. I *have to* trust her. I have to show her I have absolute confidence in her. I have to give myself over to her. If I don't, if I hesitate at the curb, if I doubt her, then she'll hesitate. She'll start to doubt herself too. She'll do what I expect her to do."

When you let your dog off leash, do you expect him to run away? Do you tense up and spread out your arms in an attempt to contain him? Does he run away? Or, expecting him to follow your lead, do you casually unclip his leash and keep walking confidently?

When you're in competition, do you expect your dog to break his stay? Do you know he's going to do it, and predict it happening, and then watch it happen?

When your dog approaches another dog, do you expect him to bite? Does he?

Do you know your dog is afraid of men, and expect to see him react with fear when a man approaches? Does he react that way?

Many people don't understand this concept, but to a large extent, your expectations are conveyed in the energy you present. Your dog will do what you expect him to do. Our dog knows when we have fear for him or doubts in him, which is why he does the thing we are expecting him to do.

We have a picture in our head, seeing our dog do something, and then he does it. When you are able to control that picture, you create the change in the dog through simple and subtle communications. We have to tell ourselves that our dog will do the right thing, and we have to believe it. To borrow a concept from the best-selling book *The Secret,* by Rhonda Byrne, your thoughts will bring about the reality.

Nerves Travel Down the Leash

I recently had the pleasure of judging the dog-tricks competition at the one-hundredth-episode celebration event on *The Dog Whisperer*. Owner after owner became flustered onstage when demonstrating his dog's trick, expressing the sentiment, "My dog does this trick at home all the time, I don't know what's up with him today!" What was up, I'm sure, was that the owner's tension caused by performing on a televised stage was influencing the dog's behavior.

Even our subtle stress behaviors affect the stress levels of our dog. That "nerves travel down the leash" is a common warning from trainers in all areas of dog sports, and one that has proven validity. We know that dogs can sense our anxiety, as there are actual hormonal correlations between owners' stress hormones and their dogs' anxiety (cortisol levels).[1]

Verbal abuse or even the withdrawal of affection by a dog's owner can have a significant impact on the dog's internal stress levels. If you know yourself to have a tendency to react negatively in stressful situations, try to avoid being in these situations with your dog, or attempt to consciously regulate your own behavior during stressful periods. Learn instead how to provide emotional support for your dog by playing with him or petting him.

Jacobson's Organ

If you feel on the roof of your dog's mouth, behind his front teeth, you'll feel a lump. This is the *Jacobson's organ,* or *vomeronasal organ* (VNO), a pair of fluid-filled sacs filled with receptor cells.

The organ is receptive to substances that have large molecules usually lacking detectable odor, such as pheromones (body scents, or chemicals we emit in response to our emotional state). Dogs use this organ to gather information about another dog's social status and reproductive state. This also gives dogs their ability to "smell fear."

Dogs access the organ by licking or snapping the air, drawing molecules into their mouths.

All mammals have a Jacobson's organ, but it is more limited in function in humans than in dogs. In a study, human volunteers were surprisingly accurate when asked to identify "happy smells" and "scared smells" (with three-quarters of the women and half the men able to identify the one "scared smell" out of six).[2]

It's a common myth around the dog obedience competition ring that you should suck on a peppermint candy before taking your turn in the ring, as the mint supposedly masks your "fear scent." Other than anecdotal indication, I've found no evidence that this works. Bummer.

Do Dogs Read Our Minds?

In the 1960s, Cleve Baxter, founder of the FBI's polygraph unit, discovered that a polygraph instrument attached to a plant leaf registered a change in electrical resistance when the plant was mentally threatened by a human. This led to his theory of "primary perception"—that plants and animals perceive human thoughts and emotions. This theory has little support in the modern scientific community, and we now recognize that a dog is not literally a mind reader, but rather an excellent interpreter of our signals.

> **Chalcy and I filmed a segment for the Korean TV show *Woong Ja,* which follows the wacky adventures of two Korean men and their spaniel. (I can't say I fully get it, but it's a whole phenomenon in Korea.)**
>
> **Woong Ja's owner/costar and I took turns learning each other's cues and giving commands to each other's dogs. Both dogs responded well to the commands, which is amazing, as I imagine my Korean must have been at least as bad as Woong Ja's owner's English. I'm sure the dogs were responding not so much to the verbal cue as to the fact that they had overheard their owner instructing the other person on how to say the cue. When the stranger said something to the dog, the dog's first guess was the command he had recently overheard from his owner. Dogs pick up much more than we give them credit for!**

Studying an animal and making consistent efforts to read its communications—and teach it yours—builds a common language of understanding.

Dogs as Associative Learners

Chalcy recognizes Randy's Land Rover coming home several minutes before I do. At our office she recognizes the cadence of his cowboy boots as he approaches, and she runs to greet him at the door. Dogs are among the world's best associative learners, expertly connecting clues and associating them with events. **Associative learning** has to do with correlating things, and making associations between things happening. The dog thinks: "When my owner picks up his keys, it means he is going to leave. Why? Because I've seen these two things together many times." A dog makes all sorts of associations to your actions, including your subtle body language cues.

Dogs Read Our Body Language

Dogs are hugely attuned to subtle changes in our physiology, breathing, and smell. In expert-level Master Hunter competition, the handler controls the dog almost solely with his eyes and body language. In expert-level Utility Obedience competition, the handler may be disqualified for as little as clearing his throat, smiling, or even raising his eyebrows, as the judge recognizes that these may be subtle, intentional communications to the dog.

Dogs follow these body signals more readily than they follow verbal cues, and when presented with conflicting information (you say "sit" but do the hand signal for "down"), they will almost always follow your hand signal.

Terry Simons once had me run an entire agility session without giving any verbal commands to Chalcy. It surprised me how well she read my body language, and how superfluous my verbal commands were.

There are three main rules to using your body language in agility: First, point your shoulders in the direction you want your dog to go. Second, use the arm closest to your dog to signal him. Third, use an imaginary leash in that hand; raise your arm to shoulder level to cast your dog out, giving him lots of leash, and pull your arm down to-

ward your leg to draw him in closer on a short leash. (And rule four, of course, is to try not to trip over your own feet.)

The Clever Hans Effect

In the late 1800s, a German mathematics teacher named Wilhelm von Osten set out to prove that humanity had underestimated the intelligence of animals by tutoring a horse named Hans in math. Hans learned to use his hoof to tap out solutions to math problems. A question of "1 + 2" produced a tap-tap-tap from Hans.

Some people remained skeptical, and an investigation was conducted. The investigator noticed that each questioner's breathing, posture, and facial expression changed involuntarily each time the hoof tapped, showing ever-so-slight increases in tension. Once the "correct" tap was made, that subtle underlying tension suddenly disappeared from the person's face, and Hans apparently took this as the cue to stop tapping. Remarkably, even when the questioner tried not to signal with his body language, he was still doing it.

It has since been found that many animals are sensitive to such subtle cues from humans, especially from their owners. Today, the term "Clever Hans effect" is used to describe the influence of questioners' subtle and unintentional cues upon their subjects, both human and animal. For this reason, modern science employs the double-blind method, where researchers and subjects are unaware of many details of the experiment until after the results are recorded. For instance, when drug-sniffing dogs undergo training, the people present do not know which containers have drugs in them; otherwise their body language might unintentionally betray the location and render the exercise useless.

Dogs, as well as horses like Hans, are so perceptive of our signals that they can learn to read our every twitch, blink, breath, and contraction of our pupils. Whether you realize it or not, your dog is constantly reading your energy. If you want to affect a change in his behavior, then you need to consciously change your demeanor.

The Eye-to-Eye Bond

Dogs can read our faces, and they pay most attention to one particular part: our eyes. A seemingly simple cognitive task like following the gaze of a human is easily taken for granted, but this skill is more developed in dogs than in wolves and even in nonhuman primates. "Looking" behavior has an important function in initiating and maintaining communication, and the readiness of dogs to look in our eyes has led to complex forms of dog/human communication.

When chimpanzees are presented with two identical upturned cups, with food hidden under only one, the chimps don't seem to understand when a human experimenter signals the correct cup by looking directly at it.

Dogs, however, perform exceptionally well at this test, and are easily able to select the correct cup when a human does no more than track his or her eyeballs to it.[3] This skill in reading our eyes seems to be genetically determined, as even puppies with little human exposure are very good at interpreting human "looking" behavior.

Eye contact is one of the predominant ways dogs communicate within packs, but unfortunately humans tend to feel uncomfortable with a long stare into another's eyes. Dogs seek out this eye contact, and making the really deep connection with your dog requires eye-to-eye communication. Make a conscious effort to look into your dog's eyes, especially while communicating.

TEACH A TRICK! WATCH ME

When you have your dog's eyes, you have his attention. Encourage your dog to look into your eyes by holding a treat in front of your face and coaching your dog to "watch . . . watch. . . ." Once he holds eye contact for a second or two, give him the treat. As he improves, have him hold that stare for longer periods of time, and then fade out the treat in front of your face so that he learns "watch" as a cue to stare into your eyes. Aside from having this behavior on cue, you are also building a habit and comfort level for him to look into your eyes.

Hunting is a sport of control, and my hunting coach Jimmy Rice is the epitome of calm, assertive energy.

"Eye contact with a dog is the most important thing," says Jimmy. "Your eyes click onto each other's and it's like you hypnotize them. You and the dog have become one. When the dog is looking into your eyes, he's taking direction from you."

"When a dog won't look you in the eyes," continues Jimmy, "it means he doesn't want to take your direction. It could be that he's hardheaded, or it could be that he's under stress and blinking you. In either case, nothing good can come out of training at that point, so I usually end the session."

Trainers in obedience and retrieving competitions know that maintaining soft eye contact is a way to "draw the dog in" and is used when the dog is doing a recall or a bird retrieve.

Control the Energy You Project

To clearly project the energy you wish to convey to your dog, you must first have it clear in your head. Know what it is that you are trying to convey. Instead of nebulous words, try forming a mental picture of what you want before attempting to convey it to your dog.

Here are some observations and suggestions about body language communications:

- Put "pressure" on a dog with hard eye contact, invasion of space, and strong body posture. Use your energy to get your dog to back up, to stay, or to lie down.
- Hunters and agility competitors know that dogs usually pull toward their owners, so they control the direction of the dog by pivoting their body. Orient your shoulders in the direction you want your dog to go.
- All dog sport competitors have to struggle with their breathing patterns, as this is something dogs are really hip to. Deep, centered breaths communicate to a dog that everything is okay. By contrast, holding your breath because you're worried that your dog is going to mess up is likely the thing that will cause him to mess up.

- To communicate a warning, lower your chin and roll your eyes upward to look at your dog with slightly hooded eyes.
- Soft eyes and slow, gentle movement will soothe an anxious dog.
- Smiling may be interpreted by unfamiliar dogs as an aggressive baring of teeth, so it is best to keep your lips closed when confronting them.

Communicate Vocally

We humans tend to put almost exclusive importance on language as a form of communication—with other humans, and also with animals, divine beings, broken vending machines, televised sports, trains that run on time when we are not, and uncooperative hairdos.

We inflict an injustice on our dogs when we try communicate to them predominantly with words—words they often don't understand. We can all laugh at the sitcom scenario in which a person tries to communicate with someone speaking a foreign language. The actor says the word or phrase, and upon realizing his message has not been understood, he says it louder and louder, or slower and slooooower, as if this will help get its meaning across, which, of course, it doesn't.

Dogs instinctively understand our emotional state as communicated through our emotional-content vocalizations. Help your dog out by using vocal strategies which are intuitively understood by him.

Happy

Your dog will know you're pleased with him when you use your high-pitched "happy voice." Dogs instinctively associate high-pitched noises with reward or excitement. A high-pitched, singsongy vocalization means that an animal is nonthreatening, peaceful, or empathetic. Think of a dog who whines when it sees its owner or a mother cooing to her infant.

If you're not in touch with your happy voice, you'll need to practice. The phrase or word should rise in pitch at the end: "Good boy!" in a singsongy tone. It will help to smile while you say it.

Authoritative

While humans generally associate a loud voice with command, dogs associate a loud voice with defending territory, sounding an alarm, or expressing great excitement. A dog in control is usually silent. When you get frustrated and yell at your dog, he may see you as excited and not in control.

Low sounds convey authority, so use them to communicate insistence. Use a low-pitched, commanding, matter-of-fact tone that falls at the end: "Lie down."

Do not repeat a command—say it once and mean it. If you have to say it a second time, it should be with a more adamant energy, and in a lower tone. You will be more respected and your dog will learn to listen to you better.

Want to really insist on a command? Use your "growly voice." You'll definitely need to practice this one, and preferably out of earshot of your dog so that you don't scare him. Practicing in your car during your commute is pretty safe, or if you supervise others at your work, maybe practice on them: "Work faster!" (No, just kidding, please don't do that!)

It's easiest to learn a growly voice by vocalizing loudly, and once you get the growl, you'll learn to do it at a lower volume. Use a loud but low voice. The purr of a growl should come through the call, so much so that it hurts your throat if you do it too much.

A friend once referred to it as my "Wicked Witch of the West" voice because I can switch on a dime from my happy voice to my growly voice, as if I had just turned from the good witch into the wicked witch. The more dichotomous you can make those two voices, the better.

Disapproving

Have a specific word for when your dog is naughty, like when he pokes around in the trash or chews on your shoe. Don't whine, don't fuss; simply use a stern "no!" The sharpness of that one word will startle your dog and become an aversive. Increase the power of the word by accompanying it with other aversives, such as stern eye contact or a pointed finger.

Dog trainers sometimes use a staccato growly sound that sounds like "a-a-a-a-a." This can be used in place of "no!" and is an aversive sound in its own right because it is accompanied by the low-pitched growl.

Vocal Patterns of Professional Trainers

Sound patterns used by animal trainers of various languages have overwhelmingly consistent patterns. In a research study of 104 animal handlers and sixteen different languages, it was found that short, rapidly repeated notes ("tut-tut!") were used to speed animals up, while single continuous notes ("whoooooa") were used to slow them down or stop them.[4] The kinds of sounds used by trainers varied—claps, whistles, smooches, clicks, and words in their own languages—but the pattern of sound was always the same.

Jockeys, rodeo riders, and horse trainers of all languages used repeated clicking and smooching noises to get their horses to go faster. Sheepdog handlers used short, repeated whistles to get their dogs moving. Sled dog racers used "hike! hike! hike!" or "hyah! hyah!" to speed up their dogs. Dog agility handlers speed their dogs through weave poles with "go! go! go!" or "weave, weave, weave!" We clap repeatedly to get puppies to come to us, as it gets them moving.

To slow their animals down, handlers used a single continuous note: "whooooa," "eaaaasy," "steaaady," or "huuush" (which is used by North African camel trainers). Sheepdog handlers use a long, continuous whistle to slow their dogs, and hunting dog handlers use a long continuous whistle to get their dogs to pause hunting.

If an animal is moving quickly, however, a short blast is used to stop him in his tracks. This startling effect is different from the soothing, continuous note to slow an animal down. When Chalcy tears off after a rabbit, I'll use a loud "hey!" to jolt her mind-set and cause her to stop in midchase.

Whistle Training

When I was a kid, I begged my mom to buy me a dog whistle that I found on the shelves at the grocery store. I took it home and tried it out on my ten-year-old Weimaraner, and I was totally disappointed when she did no more than perk her ears at my tweet-tweeting in her face. I'm not sure, but I guess I thought I would blow it and she would obey all my commands. (Sorry about that, Kuno!)

Whistles are used in dog training in place of our voice when the dog is working at a distance. Even dogs who have never been whistle-trained seem to respond to the sound.

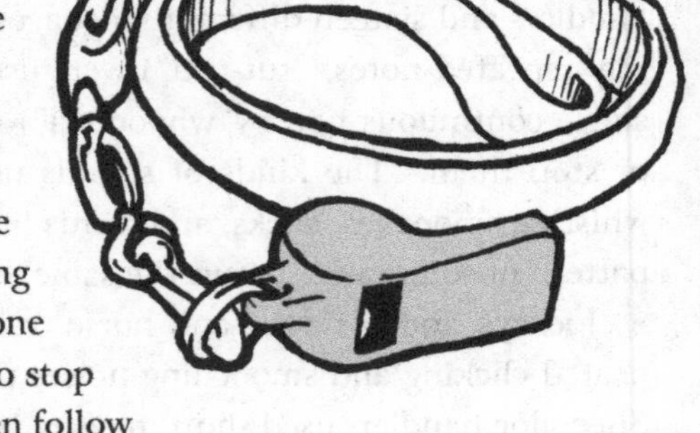

The general rule in whistle training is to use one single note to discourage a dog's activity, and to use repeated staccato notes to encourage activity. When a dog is hunting in the field, trainers will use one long whistle to get their dog to stop hunting and look at them, then follow with a rolling series of double tweets—"tweet-tweet, tweet-tweet, tweet-tweet, tweet-tweet"—to jolt the dog into action and get him to "come."

Here are some common dog-whistle commands. Notice the similarity between the hunting and herding conventions.

Hunting

Stop hunting and look at the trainer	One long, steady whistle
Sitting the dog at a distance	One long whistle with your hand raised and open
Come	Rolling series of double tweets—"tweet-tweet, tweet-tweet, tweet-tweet"—and arms stretched out to the sides (also used: three tweets)
To redirect the dog	"Pip-pip" (sharp and crisp) and the new direction indicated with your hand
Go from start line	One whistle blast

Herding

Stop / Lie down	One long, steady whistle
Come	"Tweet-tweet-tweet" (rising at the end of each tweet)
Walk up / Move toward the livestock	"Pip-pip" (sharp and crisp)

How Dogs Perceive the World

How Dogs See

People often refer to dogs as being "color-blind," but this is a bit misleading, as it implies that dogs see the world in shades of gray. Dogs instead have been shown to be "color-limited."

While normal humans see the rainbow of colors described by ROYGBIV (red, orange, yellow, green, blue, indigo, violet), dogs see only RYYYBIV (red, yellow, yellow, yellow, blue, indigo, violet). To dogs, the colors orange, yellow, and green all look alike, but look different from red and different from the various blues and purples. Dogs are very good at telling different shades of blue, indigo, and violet apart. Finally, blue-green looks white to dogs.

How do we know this? Volunteer dogs were set in front of three computer-controlled light panels and taught to "find the one that's different." In each test, two panels displayed the same color, while the third was different.[5]

The simple explanation for the differences in color vision is this: The retinas of humans have three types of color receptors, called "cones." Each cone type is particularly sensitive to light of a narrow limit within the ROYGBIV range. In dogs (and in "green-blind" humans), there are only two types of cones, and thus the perceived color range is more limited.

How can we put this information to use as dog trainers? To better understand the difference between ROYGBIV and RYYYBIV, consider what a dog would see in each of the following color combinations.

- Safety-orange hunting vest in a green/brown landscape: No obvious color difference for dogs

- Yellow tennis ball in the green grass: No obvious color difference for dogs
- Purple print on a blue dress: equally visible for humans and dogs
- Agility obstacles, commonly painted blue with a yellow contact zone: equally visible for humans and dogs

Besides color, dogs see in other ways that are different from the way we see. Dogs excel in night vision and in the detection of moving objects, and they have better peripheral vision than we do. Dogs can perceive a faster flicker rate than humans. Analog television is broadcast at a rate of thirty frames per second, and we perceive the succession of frames as a continuous scene. Dogs, however, may see it as a rapidly flickering image.

Dogs have less depth perception than we do, and their ability to see detail is roughly six times poorer than that of the average human.

But just to throw a wrench into things, it has now been found that different dog breeds have different types of retina and see the world in very different ways. Some breeds have a "visual streak"—a high-density line of vision cells that runs across the retina. A dog with a visual streak sees a clear, narrow strip going right around 240 degrees. Anything above or below that strip is blurred.

Other dog breeds have something called an "area centralis," which has the high-density vision cells arranged in a spot. They can see the middle of a scene quite clearly, but the sides are blurred.[6]

Breeds with a visual streak can see prey items better, and are the breeds most likely to hunt and chase, whereas dogs with an area centralis can see in much higher definition, and can see more nuances of their owners' expressions.

So how do you tell what kind of retina your dog has? It's directly related to the length of his nose. Long-nosed dogs have a visual streak. Short-nosed dogs have an area centralis.

How Scents Affect Dogs' Behavior and Memories

"Odors have a powerful influence on both the behavior and the physiology of the dog," says Bruce Fogle, DVM, author of *The Dog's Mind.* "Smell memories last for life and affect almost all canine behavior."

With one-third of a dog's brain set aside for scent detection, a dog's most highly developed sense is his sense of smell.

Dogs can sniff out termites, bombs, gas leaks in underground pipelines, and cancer from people's breath, skin, or urine samples. Service dogs can alert a person when his or her insulin level drops or when the person is about to have a seizure. Dogs can track a person's scent trail over multiple surfaces, even after several days. In one experiment, a line of twelve men followed in one another's footprints before veering off to hide. The dog was easily able to track his owner, who was the first man in the line of twelve.

Sniffing (rapid, short inhales and exhales) is used to help a dog rapidly identify a scent. When a dog sniffs, he is not pulling air into his lungs, but rather into his nasal passages, allowing scent molecules to accumulate in a special nasal pocket instead of being washed out upon exhalation. Rapid, short sniffing occurs during close inspection of an object, while long sniffing is used to detect more distant objects.

The sense of smell is closely linked to the subconscious. The olfactory nerves are intimately connected to the primitive region of the brain known as the limbic system, a group of structures concerned with emotionally significant events and the association of memories with smells. A large part of a dog's brain is devoted to remembering and interpreting scents. Dogs have the ability to tap into this scent-storage bank throughout their lives. The **Proust effect** describes the phenomenon of memory recall in response to a specific smell. Whole memories, complete with all associated emotions, can be evoked by smell.

Your dog values your scent. It's a familiar smell that conveys comfort and safety. That's why experts recommend leaving an article of your worn clothing with your dog when you have to leave him at the vet or a boarding kennel.

Your dog has your scent filed in his memory, along with the smells of all the other people he's been introduced to. Your dog will remember some people with affection, others with fear and loathing—and his **scent memory** will be triggered every time he meets them.

Even after obedience training, police dog trainer Alex Rothacker decided Bosco, a Doberman pinscher, was too aggressive to be suitable as a protection dog. When a man named Willie came to Alex's facility looking to buy a dog, Alex pointed him toward a row of kennels, warning him not to tease the Dobie. Ten minutes later Alex was startled by a commotion and found Willie agitating Bosco through the fence. Bosco was lunging and barking at the man.

Alex ended up keeping Bosco and training him as a trick dog. Three years later, Alex and Bosco performed their trick dog show at an outdoor street fair attended by two thousand people. At one point in the show, Bosco lifted his nose high in the air, sniffing, and started to growl. *"Pfui, Teufel!"* Alex admonished the dog.

As their show came to an end, Alex spotted a man three hundred feet away atop a light post stand, waving, and calling to him. It was Willie.

Remarkably, Bosco had singled out this man's raft (debris from dead or dying skin cells) amid all the people and all the smells at the fair. And even more remarkably, he remembered!

Aromatherapy

A dog's sensitivity to scents can possibly be used to calm him down, in a kind of canine aromatherapy. Chamomile and peppermint are thought to quiet nervous anxiety, and researchers in Northern Ireland have found that dogs riding in a car filled with the odor of lavender spent more time sitting quietly, less time racing from window to window and yapping in the driver's ear.

There are also odors that dogs dislike. Among these are citrus smells, such as lemon, lime, and orange, and spicy smells like red pepper. Dogs especially dislike the smell of citronella, which is why it's often used in sprays to keep dogs away from certain areas, or in spray collars to stop dogs from barking.

How Dogs Communicate

Dogs don't have the thousands of words that we have to describe feelings, but they do have their eyes, their ears, their nose, their body posture, and their tail carriage.

A dog's thoughts can be represented by a mental image. That image is reflected in his eyes, his movement, and his vocalizations. He is thinking the message, feeling the message. It is up to us to be perceptive enough to receive that message.

Much of dog training is reading the dog and working with what you see. When you start watching your dog, you'll discover he talks as much as we do. Notice subtle movements, shifts in attitude, or changes in behavior, and respond to those cues to encourage him to continue attempting to communicate. Every dog is different, and understanding the subtleties of each relationship is something that comes only with dedicated effort.

I had been sitting for several hours in a gun safety classroom course with Chalcy at my feet, when I quietly excused myself and slipped out the side door with her. Later, the kid who had been sitting next to me asked where I went. "Chalcy had to go potty," I explained. He nodded. A minute later, he turned back to me. "How did you know she had to go?"

"I, uh, I just knew, I guess." The truth was, I wasn't sure *how* I knew. How had Chalcy communicated to me that she had to go potty? She had been sleeping at my feet, and she got up, turned in a circle, and lay back down. But she had done this several times during the day. What was different about this time? I thought again. This time, she got up, lay back down, and then looked into my eyes with a certain look—nose a little lowered, ears down, and eyes peering up at me. She held my gaze a bit longer than her normal "checking in with me" gaze. On this day I quickly caught her communication, but had I not, her signals to me would have progressed to standing up, looking at me and then at the door, nudging my arm, taking a few steps toward the door and looking back at me, and finally pawing at

the door. Without consciously interpreting them, I instinctively understand her emotions, desires, and intentions.

Here are some common canine body language signals:

Direct gaze: challenge, confidence, or engagement
Averted gaze ("blinking" an object): stress, feeling pressured, deference, or unwillingness to comply
Belly presented: relaxation or deference
Tail and ears up, one forefoot in front of the other: alert, ready to participate
Tail high: confident, high status
Tail low: less confident, lower status, deference, fear
Tail wag: willingness to interact, confident, assertive
Grin: deference, pain, anxiousness, happiness, feeling hot
Hackles raised on neck or base of tail: dominant
Rigid stance, stiff torso musculature: confidence and intent to interact
Ears erect: alert, confident
Ears back: fear
Ears vertically dropped: deference, anxiety
Snarl/growl with only incisors and canines visible: confident, offensively aggressive
Snarl/growl with all teeth and back of throat visible: defensively aggressive, fearful
Body lowered: defensive, fearful, deferential, eye on prey
Licking lips, flicking tongue: appeasement, anxiety (and solicitation of reassurance)
Body bow (paws out, front end down, rump up, tail wagging): invitation to play, and also an announcement that seemingly aggressive actions to follow are intended as play
Mounting or pressing on back of another dog: challenge, marking, claiming, dominance
Licking at corner of another dog's mouth: deference, showing subservience to a more dominant dog

Blowing out lips/cheeks: anticipation (positive or negative), anxiety (if very fast)

Jaw snapping: capitulation, intention to comply as a last resort[7]

Most dogs have a paw preference: they are either right-handed or left-handed. To find your dog's paw preference, watch which paw he uses to hold down a bone to chew or to steady a Kong stuffed with treats. Some dogs show no significant paw preference. These dogs, it turns out, have significantly more noise phobias, becoming very reactive to sounds such as thunderstorms and fireworks.[8] A similar finding has shown that weaker hand preferences in humans are correlated with people suffering extreme levels of anxiety.

In most animals, the left brain specializes in approach and energy enrichment behaviors (love, feelings of safety and calm). The right brain specializes in withdrawal and energy expenditure (fleeing, fear, and depression). The left brain controls the right side of the body and the right brain controls the left side of the body. A dog wags his tail more to the right side of his rump when he is attracted to something, and more to the left when he is fearful of it.[9] (Seeing his owner produces a right wag, while seeing an unfamiliar aggressive dog produces a left wag.)

Here are some ways in which barks may be translated.

High-pitched barks and yaps:

Short bark: A common greeting, or surprise.

Single yap: "Where are you?"

Two short barks: "Look at this!"

Repeated short barks: A call, often used when the dog wants to go outside.

Long and drawn-out barks with pauses between them: Your dog is alone and wants company.

Medium-pitched barks:

One bark: Curious, alert, or happy.

Faltering bark: Asking to play.

Alarm bark: Alert.

Continuous, fast barking: Alert, problem, or someone is entering our territory.

Fast barking with pauses every three or four seconds: Warning of a problem approaching. Your dog is asking you to investigate.

Low-pitched, throaty barks:

Continuous, slow barking: The intruder or danger is close, the dog is prepared to defend himself.

Deep rumbling bark, assertive growl or grunt: Dominant, used for an unexpected guest at the front door.[10]

Stress Indicators

Dogs communicate emotions through subtle changes in their eyes, ears, tail, hackles, stance, lips and tongue, yawning, and sniffing. Most dog owners can read the basic dog body language—curled lips and raised hackles as aggression, and lowered body and tail, or belly display as submission. But they often overlook stress indicators.

When competing in obedience with Chalcy, one exercise requires me to turn my back on her and walk to the opposite side of the ring. This causes her—every single time—to yawn as I leave her. This is a sign of anxiety.

When I ask Chalcy for a behavior she doesn't understand, she predictably sits down and scratches her neck. She is not itchy, but is rather using this as a stalling technique, and it is another stress indicator.

Chalcy is watching me right now as I type, and I turn toward her and ask her for kisses. She doesn't move, except to avert her eyes and head to the side. I laugh and she looks back at me. I ask her again for kisses and she averts again. She's not in the mood to do tricks, and she averts her head to avoid the pressure she feels from my gaze. Avoidance of eye contact, or blinking, is a stress indicator.

Some dogs will turn their heads and pretend to be interested in something else as a way of disengaging from the situation. Avoidance sniffing is a similar stress indicator. Lip licking or tongue flicking is a stress signal (but it may also be an effort by the dog to push air into his Jacobson's organ).

While it's important to be aware of stress indicators in your dog, seeing them doesn't necessarily mean you need to alleviate your dog's stress. As a runner, I know that the stress I put on my muscles and bones causes them to break down and then heal themselves stronger. Allowing your dog to experience a little bit of stress, and having him overcome his fears, can actually teach him to become a stronger, more confident dog.

Teach Your Dog to "Speak" to You

In addition to being a careful observer and recognizing ways in which your dog innately communicates with you, you can also enhance communication by teaching him ways to tell you what he wants. Human babies who are not yet able to communicate verbally can be taught to use sign language. We can similarly teach our dog to express his desires through signals.

TEACH A TRICK! RING A BELL TO GO OUTSIDE

Help your dog communicate with you by hanging a bell on the door and teaching him to ring it when he wants to go outside. Start by wiggling the bell on the floor and encouraging your dog to "get it!" Mark the instant he touches the bell by saying "good bell" and giving him a treat. Next, hang the bell from the doorknob at a low height and encourage your dog to ring it. You may need to hold a treat behind the bell and tease him with it. Reward him as soon as the bell makes a sound.

Get your dog's leash and get him excited to go for a walk. Stop at the door with the bell, encouraging him to ring it. It may take a while, as he will be distracted by the idea of his walk. As soon as he touches the bell, immediately open the door and take him for a walk. In this trick, the reward is a walk instead of a treat, so be sure to introduce this concept early on.

When Chalcy wants to go to our basement training room, she communicates this to me by banging on the dog-sized grand piano next to the basement door. (Hey, don't laugh; my house, my rules!) And when she wants to go for a walk, she lets me know by knocking over software boxes. (Aack! Wait! I thought we got rid of that one!)

Give and Receive Affection

Some people are more touchy-feely than others, and the same goes for dogs. Show your dog your affection by scratching his back and neck and under his arms. Wipe your hand gently over his eyes, and massage the base and the inside of his ears. Get all the places that he can't get himself. Experiment with different grooming brushes and massage techniques until you find the ones that really turn him to mush!

Have conversations with your dog. He might not understand every word, but he will pick up on your energy and appreciate being spoken to. As your dog gets to know you, he will pick up on key words within your sentences, as in "If you can find your **Kong**, I'll fill it with peanut butter for you."

Breath-to-Breath Bonding

A newspaper reporter once asked me what my favorite thing about my dog was. I gave a weird answer, which fortunately she had the good sense not to print. I said, "My dog's breath." Of course, I don't mean that yucky dog breath after the dog has eaten something disgusting in the backyard. But when Chalcy was a puppy, she had this wonderful puppy breath that became ingrained deeply in my brain. Every once in a while I'll smell a trace of that in her breath, and it provokes a deep feeling of love.

In various native cultures across the globe, animal trainers and gentlers have employed a technique of sharing breath with the animal in order to tame it or bond with it. This may have something to do with ingraining your scent into the animal's brain.

In Native American wisdom, a man is thought to link with a horse's spirit by blowing gently into its nostrils, and by their breathing each other's breath.[11] It has been theorized that this same exchange of breath was the secret of the celebrated Irish horse charmers of the nineteenth century who pretended to whisper to the horse and play with its head, and thus probably breathed into its nostrils.[12]

These traditional horse gentling techniques are not without basis in animal behavior. Sharing breath is, in fact, the method of greeting which horses use with each other—exchanging scents by blowing into each other's nostrils.

As a professional animal trainer for twenty-five years, Doug Seus has dedicated his life to raising and training grizzly bears. Seus describes blowing into the nostrils of one of these huge beasts as "throwing your energy into its soul and manifesting yourself in its spirit." It's a way to gain the bear's trust and let the bear know everything is okay. I'll let Seus speak for himself: "I think blowing in an animal's nose, you're giving your soul to them, and there's something about your inner energy that you're throwing into them, and they in reaction, they'll give it back to you. It's something primal and internal and I feel them relax and take in my aura. And it's not a blow like *pwooooh*, it's like *huuuuuuh*, it's out of your soul, it's out of your diaphragm, way down deep."[13]

The late Susan Butcher, legendary American sled dog racer and four-time winner of the grueling Iditarod race across Alaska, is said to have revolutionized the sport by the way she related to her dogs, caring for them with tenderness, training them thoroughly, and inspiring them to excel. From the time a pup was born, she would lift the blind baby and breathe into its nostrils. From that moment she was friend and tutor, comfort and family to the dog.[14]

Share breath with your dog to build a primal bond.

SUMMARY

- **We communicate to our dogs through our energy, informing them of our state of mind and our intentions. We can communicate leadership, pressure, encouragement, or relaxation.**
- **Your dog will do what you expect him to do. Picture what you want your dog to do. Use your body language to convey that mental picture.**

- Nerves travel down the leash. Your stress will increase your dog's stress.
- Dogs follow our body language signals more readily than our verbal cues.
- Dogs read our every twitch, change in breathing, scent secretion, and pupil dilation.
- A deep connection with your dog is achieved through eye-to-eye communication. Encourage your dog to "watch," or look directly into your eyes.
- Convey emotion in the tone of your voice: singsongy for happiness, low or growly for authority.
- Use short, rapidly repeated notes ("tut-tut!") to speed up your dog, and single, continuous notes ("whoooooa") to slow him down.
- Stress indicators in dogs are yawning, scratching, eye or head aversion, lip licking, and avoidance sniffing.
- Teach your dog constructive ways to communicate to you, such as ringing a bell to go outside.
- Share breath with your dog to enhance your bond.

Rule 13: Exercise Together

"Hike!" we yell in unison, and in an instant the carts and scooters jerk forward as the teams of dogs lunge into their harnesses. Nichole's team of Alaskan malamutes, Siberian huskies, and Jindos is ten strong and leading the race, as two by two they fill the width of the narrow dirt trail. Nichole crouches at the back of the team, alternating her feet on the metal skids of the cart. Her commands are directed at her lead dogs, whose leadership makes or breaks the team. "On by!" she calls as the team approaches an offshoot path, and her lead dogs understand to bypass this option. My gentle Weimaraner Chalcy has morphed into a highly driven pack animal, determined to squeeze by Nichole's team and take the lead, pulling me and "Scratch" along with her.

Chalcy and I have been mushing for years now, and have an uncanny feel for each other as we push forward on our scooter through the dirt paths of the Mojave Desert. It wasn't always this easy. When we first were introduced to this sport, we used a variety of borrowed equipment. Enthralled with this exhilarating new activity, I eagerly picked out a shiny new red dog scooter of my own, the Dirt Dawg model, and with Randy's help I assembled it, filled the tires, and tested it in my driveway for the next morning's run. "What should I name it?" I asked Randy. "I was thinking 'Chase' because we'll be going so fast that everyone will have to chase us!"

"Why don't you take it out a few times, and then decide," answered my practical husband, who didn't share the same excitement over my new toy.

The next day was a brilliant, sunny but chilly day—perfect for mushing. Nichole and I took turns riding out ahead and taking pictures of each other as musher and team came roaring past a particularly scenic spot. I crouched down low with my camera, on the edge

of the dirt trail, in order to get the full impact of Nichole's charging team. As her dogs closed in on me, I heard another clamor quickly approaching from behind me. Chalcy, not being able to resist running alongside the pack, was charging toward the team, dragging my new shiny red scooter by its gangline behind her.

After the dust had settled, Nichole and I surveyed the damage to my scooter, bent the front tire back into shape, and readjusted the alignment. I moped that I "didn't even have a chance to name it yet."

"How 'bout 'Scratch'?" offered the ever-helpful Nichole.

Scratch it is.

Bonds are built through shared physical and emotional experiences.

During that day of mushing, Chalcy and I had to communicate with each other, trust each other, act independently but also follow each other's lead. Our adrenaline rushed together as we flew downhill, and we panted in silence together as we hiked uphill. We saw things and heard things that no one else in the world saw and heard that day. We came home tired, fulfilled, happy, and with a connection that we could see in each other's eyes.

"How was it?" asked Randy when we returned home.

"Great!" I answered, but he would never know. He wasn't there, and he didn't go through the experiences with us; he was on the outside of our little world that day.

How would that day have been different if Chalcy and I had spent it watching TV? Unmemorable. We would have learned nothing new about each other, nor about ourselves. She would have been in her world, and I in mine, sitting next to each other on the couch.

THE RULE

Exercise and sports build the bond between you and your dog as you strive side-by-side, as a team, to meet physical and mental challenges.

Side-by-Side

A bond with your dog does not form automatically. Creating a strong bond happens in times when you and your dog focus on each other side-by-side or eye-to-eye. You learn how your dog thinks and reacts, and he learns how you think and react. You get in touch with each other and learn to share information and rely upon each other. All of this builds a sense of camaraderie, teamwork, and oneness that enhances the relationship.

In dog-pack culture dogs do all the important activities together, which helps to build their cohesiveness. They eat together, sleep together, play together, communally raise the young, hunt and defend as a unit, and travel as a unit. This instinctive behavior is part of what bonds the pack together. We can experience the same kind of bond with our dogs by engaging in side-by-side activities, such as walking or running together, training on a dog agility course, hunting together, mushing, and playing Frisbee or ball together.

Try These Sports

"Yes, yes, I've heard all this before: I need to exercise my dog more, go on daily walks, use treadmills, blah, blah, blah, I know . . . but I don't have time. And my dog pulls on his leash. And there isn't any good place to walk him nearby. And he has a big yard. And, and, and . . ."

Well, you know what? Let's make it fun! I'm not a big fan of daily walks with my dog leashed by my side either, so I do a bunch of other physical activities that keep my dog (and me) in shape. This chapter should give you a few ideas. Mush!

Getting Started

Many dog sports have clubs associated with them that can help you get started and provide peer support. (Granted, it's probably a little easier to find a dog-yoga class in Los Angeles than in other parts of the country.) Clubs can be tricky to find, because they aren't usually listed in the Yellow Pages, and don't always have Web sites. It often requires a little legwork to find the club you are looking for. Look in your local paper's classified section for any kind of dog obedience or dog sport club. Call the club and tell the people there what you are looking for, and they may refer you to someone else in the club who is involved in that sport. The dog sport community communicates largely through word of mouth.

When dogs do sports, they *do* get hurt. Just because they have animal instincts doesn't mean they are protected from overexertion and injury. Before you start, do your job and use your human intelligence to consider possible dangers (such as a slippery floor surface or broken glass or fishhooks at a lake). Make it your primary concern to look out for your dog's safety. Maintain regular veterinary checkups and inspect your dog's feet, ears, mouth, and coat often.

Check your equipment for nails, splinters, and places where your dog's foot could get stuck. Work on a soft ground surface and make sure the equipment your dog works on has a high-traction surface. When jumping, your dog should land straight, not twisting, and largely horizontal. Increase difficulty gradually, as a bad experience may set progress back significantly. Your dog will benefit from stretching, and a warm-up/cool-down. There are even some books available on dog massage. Be especially cautious of heat stroke, especially with large or overweight dogs.

Nowadays you can buy a wide variety of sporting equipment for dogs: backpacks, life vests, boots, hydration packs, coats, cool coats, goggles, paw wax, first aid kits, and hands-free leashes. Don't skimp on the equipment—get your dog the proper gear.

Some of the activities listed below may be new to you. You may have seen some of them on TV, but never thought of getting involved yourself. It's time to plunge right in and explore—you and your dog will be glad you did. Below are some sports that may tickle your fancy. Try something new this year!

Running/Walking Sports

Hiking: There are thousands of dog-friendly parks and trails across the United States. Check out a book on dog hiking trails in your area.

Canicross (cross-country running with a dog): In canicross your dog wears a harness and pulls you by a shock cord attached at your belt. There are canicross competitions in Europe, but in the United States it is more common to see leashed dogs at "run with your dog" foot races.

Tracking: In this sport, a dog wears a harness and tracks a scent trail made by a human. Try it out at a grass park. Keep your dog in the car as you track a straight line through the grass, dropping pieces of hot dog every six feet or so. Put a big reward at the end of the track. Use garden flags to help you remember your track. Let your harnessed dog pull you along the track, gobbling up hot dogs along the way!

Canine Search & Rescue (SAR): Search & Rescue dogs detect human scent and track lost persons via air scenting or ground tracking. Volunteer groups offer their services when local disasters or avalanches happen, and set up periodic practice sessions to hone their skills. They can always use another volunteer.

Obedience Variations

Obedience: Dog obedience is a competition sport in which you can earn titles and rankings. The novice-level exercises consist of things like sit-stay, down-stay, on-leash heeling, and recall.

Rally-O: Rally obedience is a quickly growing sport preferred by many because its rules allow the handler to talk to and encourage their dog throughout the competition. In a traditional obedience ring no more than one command per exercise is permitted.

K-9 Drill Team: An offshoot of obedience, this sport is a combination of heeling and formation marching. Teams often perform in parades.

Dog Dancing / Musical Freestyle: This sport puts a little spin on traditional heeling exercises by setting them to music and adding flashy spins, weaves, hops, and figure-8's.

Water Sports

Water Work: Enrich your dog's experience with real-life wet challenges—from swimming with a person or diving for lost gear to rescuing a stranded boater. Testing events gives you achievement goals and a chance to earn water-work titles.

Dock Diving: A dog and handler work as a team to achieve the greatest distance jump for the dog. The handler throws a retrieve object into an above-ground pool or lake and the dog runs down a forty-foot dock that stands twenty-four inches above the water and then leaps out as far as he can. The sanctioning body, DockDogs, holds hundreds of competitions each year.

Kayaking: You row your boat and your pup can alternate between sitting in the kayak and paddling alongside it. Some kayak rental facilities specialize in dogs. A dog life vest provides an easy handhold for getting your dog back into the kayak.

Surfing: There are "canine surf academies" (in California, anyway) where you and your dog go in the ocean together and learn to hang eight!

Snow Sports

Mushing / Dogsledding: "Mushing" is a general term for a dog-powered transport method such as dogs pulling a sled on snow. The term is thought to come from the French word *marche,* meaning to go or run. Commands are "gee" (pronounced JEE; turn right), "haw" (turn left), "on by" (bypass a road or distraction), "whoa" (stop), and "line out" (to tell the lead dogs to straighten out the team and keep the line taut and untangled while stopped. "Lead dogs" are at the front of the team, followed by "swing dogs," which swing the team on curves; "team dogs" are in the middle, with "wheel dogs" closest to the sled or cart. Dogs wear harnesses and travel two by two, attached to a gangline.

Skijoring (cross-country skiing with a dog): Skijoring is an exhilarating and fast-growing winter sport that combines cross-country skiing and mushing. Skijoring is simply connecting the skier and dog or dogs in harness together via a specially designed belt and tugline. **Pulka driving** is a related sport that involves skijoring with a small sled (pulka) between skijorer and dog.

Wheel Sports

Land Mushing: When the snow melts, trade in your sled for a three-wheel land cart and enjoy all the fun of dogsledding! The driver stands on metal skids, and occasionally walks between the skids through difficult patches.

Carting / Draft Dog / Sulky Driving: In this large-breed dog sport, the dog pulls a two-wheel cart or four-wheel wagon filled with supplies like firewood or farm goods, or even people.

Scootering: Scootering is another mushing sport, whereby one to three dogs pull a driver on an unmotorized scooter. Scootering is a good workout for both human and canine participants, because the driver often dismounts and runs, or assists the dog(s) by kicking with one foot.

Bikejoring: In this variation of mushing, you ride a bicycle with your dog pulling you. Bikejoring is primarily a vehicle for exercising and training your dog rather than gaining a workout for yourself.

Roller Skiing / In-line Skating: Skijorers in warmer climates can trade their skis for roller skis, two-wheeled thin skates that mount onto ski boots.

Racing and Jumping Sports

Agility: In this competition sport the handler must quickly and accurately guide his or her dog through a course made up of obstacles such as tunnels, bar jumps, tire jumps, teeter-totters, and weave poles. The handler guides his or her dog using verbal commands and body language while running alongside the dog. In every competition the obstacles are arranged in a different order, and a course map is given to the handler on the day of the race. The dog never has a chance to practice-run the specific course.

Flyball: Flyball is a relay wherein teams of dogs race side-by-side against each other. Leaving his owner at the starting line, the dog runs a straight line, jumping over four hurdles, at the end of which is a spring-loaded box that releases a tennis ball when the dog presses it. The dog grabs the ball and carries it back over the line of hurdles to his owner, at which time the next dog on the team is released to do the same thing.

Flygility: This relatively new sport combines elements of flyball and agility. As in flyball, the dog is sent to fetch a ball from a flyball box and return it to the handler. The course, however, is longer, and it uses agility obstacles such as tunnels, ramps, and jumps.

Scent Hurdling: Scent hurdling is similar to flyball. The dogs jump over a line of hurdles, but instead of retrieving a ball at the end, the dog must find the one dumbbell in the pile that has the scent of his owner, and not of the other owners. This lesser-known sport combines high physical energy with intense mental concentration.

Working Sports

Hunting/Retrieving: According to their breed, dogs point or flush and retrieve upland game birds and waterfowl in dog sport competition. Although this is traditionally a male-dominated sport, more women are participating in competition and having good success with alternate training methods (typically using more praise and "happy voices").

Horseback Riding: Pointing dogs hunt birds as their owners ride horseback in field trials. Your high elevation allows you to keep an eye on your dog when he ranges out.

Herding/Sheepdog: Herding breeds compete to move sheep around a field, gates, fences, or enclosures as directed by their handlers.

Handlers use commands such as "come bye" and "away" to send their dog clockwise or counter-clockwise around the herd. This sport relies heavily upon teamwork.

Schutzhund / Ring Sport: Protection sports test the ability of the dog to protect himself and his handler. The sport trials are similar to the work performed by police dogs, and include skills such as guarding an object.

Lure Coursing: This chase is performed by sighthounds such as greyhounds, salukis, and Afghan hounds, who chase an artificial lure in an open field. Dogs are judged on overall ability, speed, endurance, agility, and how well they follow the lure.

Disc and Acrobatics

Disc Dog: Disc dog is a competitive sport whereby handler and dog work together to successfully throw and catch a disc. There are event categories such as Toss and Fetch (geared toward beginners; a sixty-to-ninety-second opportunity to get as many successful catches as you can), Distance/Accuracy, Furthest Catch, and Freestyle (routines using multiple discs and choreographed to music).

Dogrobatics: In this athletic sport, dog and handler perform choreographed synchronized acrobatics. It features energetic tumbling maneuvers, such as the dog jumping over the handler's back, or through his legs while the handler is in a handstand. Hoops or batons may be used. The dog runs back and forth between diagonally placed targets, executing an acrobatic jump over the handler, who is located in the center of the square. Dogrobatics was first developed by stunt dog team Kyra Sundance and Chalcy.

Dog Tricks

Dog Tricks: You can achieve a full mental and physical challenge for your dog by training a variety of tricks. There are often dog trick contests at dog events, but aside from that, it's just cool to have one really killer trick that you can show off! Chalcy's killer trick

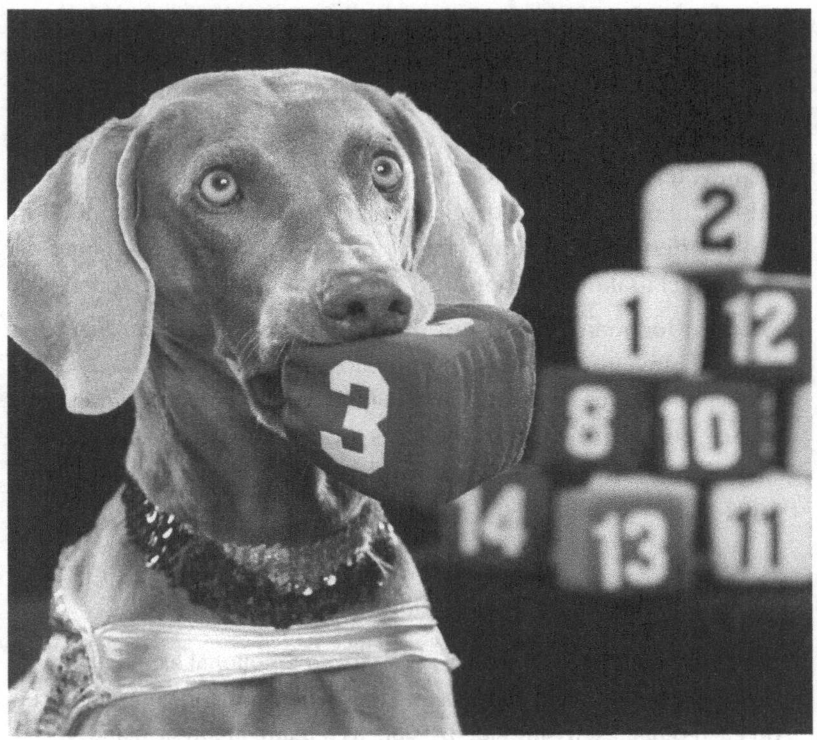

earned her a hefty sum when she won in the "Pet Star $25,000 Championships" TV contest! Chalcy's trick? She demonstrated her ability to read numbers! Check out *101 Dog Tricks* for ideas.

Therapy Dog (in hospitals/schools): Dogs can be trained and certified as Therapy Dogs. These dogs cheer people up by visiting them in institutions or hospitals and performing a few dog tricks.

More

Doga (dog yoga): The concept may seem tongue-in-cheek, but this has actually caught on as a health-and-fitness partner activity that facilitates bonding while giving your dog attention and praise. The idea is not necessarily to stretch your pet to his limits, but rather to let him be involved in as much of your life as possible. The dogs do sun salutations and downward dog, and you'll learn specific massage techniques to calm your dog and aid his circulation and digestion processes.

Dog Camps: An excellent way to explore new dog activities, dog camps feature a bunch of sports, seminars, and clinics scheduled throughout the week. Some camps are intended as an introduction to a variety of dog sports, while others cater to people at competition level looking to improve their skills in a particular sport.

Games: Too many people just don't know how much fun their dog can be. Invent a game with your dog! Dogs actually take to the concept of rules in a game very readily. Watch your dog and try to figure out what he thinks the rules are. Formulating these complicated game rules builds teamwork skills between you and your dog.

SUMMARY

- **Bonds are built through shared physical and emotional experiences.**
- **Creating a strong bond happens in times when you and your dog focus on each other. Exercising side-by-side, as a team, in physical and mental challenges enhances that bond.**
- **Try some new sports!**

Rule 14. Forgive

If we really want to love, we must learn how to forgive.
—Mother Teresa

This is a short chapter. Not because the rule is an unimportant one, but rather the contrary. I'd say this is the MOST important rule. It's a short chapter because it's about a straightforward concept. Forgiveness.

When we argue with our spouses, we can bring up events that happened *years* ago: "You're *always* late! Just like the time you were late for our anniversary!" We can't do this with our dogs. We can't do it because dogs don't understand complex sentences, and because dogs don't remember every little thing, and because it just isn't fair. If your dog has done something wrong, take care of it—discipline him, teach him, do what you need to do—and then move on.

Do you remember the anecdote in the chapter *The Seven Tenets of 'Come'* when Chalcy ran up the hillside and I had to bring her down and discipline her? I put her in time-out for a while, and then I brought her to the front lawn and gave her another chance to obey my "come"

command. When she did it, I praised her sincerely, holding no grudge about her past misdeed.

Give your dog infinite second chances. Always give her a new opportunity to be a "good dog."

14 THE RULE

Be forgiving with yourself and with your dog. All relationships include mistakes—learn from them, don't repeat them. Don't hold a grudge—deal with misbehavior and let it go. Always give your dog another chance to be a "good dog."

Give Them Their Best Shot

Whether you have a puppy, an adult dog, or a senior, you'll want to give your dog his best shot at a healthy and enjoyable life.

Each person in your family will have a distinct relationship with your dog, and if you have more than one dog, you'll have a relationship with each dog as an individual. Give each dog his own play sessions and training sessions, and his own time with you. Otherwise one dog may not want to play if the other dog is around, because the other dog perhaps is too pushy or plays too roughly.

Some of this time with your dog needs to be spent away from the house. If you have multiple dogs, take them on individual outings whenever possible instead of always taking them out as a group. If they always go out together, they are less likely to focus on and bond with you, and they can also learn bad habits and fears from one another.

The Puppy

Puppyhood is a critical time in which the dog can learn to bond with a human. During the first three weeks of his life, a puppy reacts only to the need for warmth, food, sleep, and a mother. During his fourth week, the puppy begins to use his senses and become aware of his environment; this is the week in which emotional and social stresses have

their greatest impact and traumatic events at this time can stay with a puppy for life. From week five through week seven, the puppy begins to venture away from the litter to explore adjacent areas. It is recommended that at the end of week seven the puppy be taken from the litter.[1] The human now takes the place of the puppy's mother and the bond of attachment is established that will have a permanent effect on the dog's ability to bond with a human.

Bonding with your dog does *not* require that you adopt him as a puppy. It's actually not important that you be the person in his life that he initially bonds with. But it is only important that he had that bonding experience with *someone* during his puppyhood. Dogs routinely form new bonds with humans at all stages of life. A service dog or police dog, for example, may be in his fourth home when he forms his closest bond. It's the *ability* to bond that is formed through this early experience. If a puppy does not have the opportunity to bond with a human during this critical socialization period, he will likely never be able to form a bond with any human during his life.

We see a similar detachment disorder in children who are not nurtured during their early years. In its series *This American Life,* Chicago Public Radio presented a story about an American couple who adopted a boy from a Romanian orphanage in which he was given little attention.[2] Soon after his adoption, the boy started to rage and was diagnosed with **detachment disorder.** Because he had not had a bonding experience when he was very young, he was now unable to bond with any person—to be affectionate, to trust, and to empathize.

Treatment for this detachment disorder involved an intense program of approximating what occurs in the healthy attachment cycle of an infant. The adoptive mother and the child remained in constant close physical proximity, and mother and child spent long periods of time focused on each other, looking into each other's eyes.

Puppies also gain attachment through physical proximity and eye contact. Here's how to help your puppy form a bond with you:

- Keep your puppy in the same room with you as you move around the house. Some trainers even suggest tethering your puppy to your waist. This gets him used to following you around, and allows you to give him constant feedback on his actions.
- Groom your puppy daily, combing his coat, massaging his ears, and handling his toes to condition him to human handling and to your touch in particular.
- Take care of your puppy's needs. Prove yourself a dependable and caring leader.
- Actively seek out eye contact with your puppy. Communicate with your eyes more than with your voice.
- Take your puppy on regular walks. This will establish you as a leader, and as a provider of fun activity.
- Take advantage of your puppy's eagerness and begin training immediately. The myth that you should wait a year or two to begin training because "the dog won't have a brain until then" is nonsense. The earlier you begin training the better!
- And most important, don't kill your puppy's spirit! If he is a little rambunctious now, you can always rein him in later.

> But if you break his spirit by riding him too hard when he is young, it is unlikely you'll be able to instill that confidence and initiative in him later.

In dog packs, adult dogs are extremely tolerant of puppies, giving them "puppy license" up until they are about four or five months old. Puppies are allowed to bully adult dogs and be mischievous.[3] Past this point, puppies need to learn to control themselves and behave more politely. They still make many mistakes and errors, but are readily forgiven.

The Adolescent Dog

Dog adolescence begins at about four or five months of age, lasts until about two years of age, and consists of several stages. Adolescent dogs:

- Like action and speed
- Want to play a lot
- Prefer to be with other dogs of their same age and activity level, which is important in developing their social skills
- Get easily bored when nothing is happening
- Have little self-control when something exciting happens, such as a rabbit running by
- Have a hard time concentrating for a long period of time

For an adolescent dog, training in short, fun sessions is best. Give the dog breaks in a training session to allow him to regain focus.

Allow a young dog to explore his surroundings and test things out. Have boundaries, but don't make your dog a prisoner without the freedom to explore and learn on his own. When a young dog is difficult or stubborn, it is not necessarily because he is trying to take the alpha position. He may just be experimenting and figuring out how things work, testing the reactions he will get. Don't overreact, just turn your back and ignore him. Be considerate—your dog needs time to grow up.

The Older Dog

I love seeing older dogs. It means a family has taken good care of them their whole life. It is truly our privilege to care for an animal that has given so much to us. Savor this time.

One of the wonderful aspects of owning a dog is the changing dynamics that come about as the years pass. In the beginning we are older (comparatively) than our dog. Then at some point we are both the same age. Eventually, if all goes well, our dog grows older than we are and we need to care for him a little more.

Every dog has a right to his dignity, and this is especially important when he is older. Help him clean himself if he is unable to; change his bedding if he accidentally soils it; help him get around the house so that he doesn't fall on his face or into his bowl. Anticipate his needs.

The passage from one life stage to another is often blurred, and owners don't always recognize the signs that their dog is getting old. The rule of thumb is that every dog year is equal to seven human years, but old age comes at different times for different breeds. Giant breeds tend to age early, with a life expectancy of generally less than eight or ten years. Large and medium-sized breeds have a life expectancy of eleven to fourteen years, and small breeds can live fifteen years or more. A strong, healthy dog will probably age later than a dog that is stressed by disease or environment early in his life.

An overweight, couch potato dog may be happy being pampered, but he will live longer if he slims down and takes a few more walks. Even old dogs generally like to play with a favorite toy for a few minutes each day, or take a walk to the corner and back. Dogs that enjoyed off-leash walks their entire life may actually appreciate being tethered to you as they get older.

To ensure that your old dog continues to learn new tricks, make sure he gets regular physical activity, mental stimulation, and a diet rich in antioxidants to help keep his aging brain in top shape. A two-year study of older dogs (ages seven to eleven) found they performed better on cognitive tests and were more likely to learn new tasks when they were fed a diet fortified with plenty of fruits, vegetables, and supplemental vitamins; were exercised at least twice weekly; and were given the opportunity to play with other dogs and a variety of stimulating toys.[4]

The antioxidant-fortified diet consisted of standard dog food supplemented with tomatoes, carrot granules, citrus pulp, spinach flakes, vitamin E, vitamin C, and two mitochondrial cofactors: lipoic acid and carnitine.

There's No Shame in Where You Are

"Don't worry about it," I tell a humiliated novice obedience competitor after her dog ran zoomies and bolted from the competition ring. "Chalcy and I failed many competitions before getting our titles."

"I didn't fail," she asserts, "I non-qualified."

Technically, she was correct. The judge's scorecard has three checkboxes: "Qualify," "Non-Qualify," and "Excused." "Excused," by the way, means your dog relieved himself in the ring, or bit someone, or did something offensive enough to be asked to leave immediately. What I find remarkable is the lengths to which we go to avoid the word "fail," when it's not really that bad of a word!

Our reluctance to use the word is symbolic of our extreme distaste for the condition—in our society, we *hate* to lose. We hate it so much that we often avoid situations where we are not certain of our ability to prevail. We hate to try something new, we hate to put ourselves out there, because we are afraid of looking stupid.

But the way I look at it, winning and losing are the same thing. All that really matters is the effort. If you feel a little in over your head, then you're on the track to growth.

Chalcy and I perform halftime shows at professional sporting events. At the age of thirty I enrolled in a tumbling class at the local cheerleading school to work on some new stunts. I felt the stares of my preteen classmates as they giggled and frantically changed places so as to avoid lining up behind the grown-up.

Did I feel like an idiot? Totally! It was uncomfortable enough to have made most people in my situation quit the class. But just be-

ADA CENTRE

9
24
15
00

cause something is uncomfortable, or new, or scary, or hard is not enough reason to quit.

Starting new training classes or dog sports is difficult too—you don't know the rules, and you are the worst ones in the class. But don't ever apologize for the level you're at. Everybody had to start at the beginning, and there is no shame in that.

Change—Just Do It

"But I AM afraid to fail, and I DON'T have self-confidence, and I NEVER try new things."

Here's the biggest myth in our culture today: that we should love ourselves for "who we are." You know what? If you don't like something about yourself, change it! It's not that hard; just decide to change . . . and change! You're shy and you want to be outgoing? Just be outgoing! You want to be assertive? Be assertive! You want to lose weight? Lose weight! How you behave is who you are. And think of all the trees we'll save when we put the self-help industry out of business!

SUMMARY

- Don't hold a grudge when your dog misbehaves—deal with it and let it go. Always give your dog another chance to be a "good dog."
- Puppies: Encourage bonding by being dependable, staying in close proximity, and seeking out eye contact.
- Adolescent dogs: Forgive readily. Give them the freedom to explore, test, and figure things out.
- Older dogs: Encourage exercise and feed a diet rich in antioxidants to help keep their aging bodies and brains in top shape.
- Don't apologize for the level you're at. Everybody had to start at the beginning, and there is no shame in that.
- If you don't like something about yourself, change it!

Do More With Your Dog!®

That's it. That's The Rules. You now have the complete dog-training tool kit with the tools to overcome any hurdle or tackle any challenge. It's not magic, and it's not going to happen overnight. All good things take work. But now, instead of frustration, you'll have the knowledge and confidence to lead your dog in the best direction.

Invest your time and energy in your dog, as a passion, as a challenge, as a goal. You'll be enriching the life of your family member, and deepening the connection between the two of you.

As I'm writing this manuscript downstairs by the fire, I send my print job to the printer in Randy's office upstairs. I give it a few minutes, and then send Chalcy up to "find Randy." A minute later she comes tearing back down the stairs, clutching a stapled (and slightly slobbery) set of papers in her mouth. She's excited, she's proud, she accomplished a mission. It's not much, but it's another way I can interact with her during the course of my day. It's a way to do more with my dog.

Look for ways to incorporate your dog into your daily life. Do you like to cook? How about trying your hand at some tasty dog recipes (with you-know-who as chief product tester)? Knit a sweater for your dog, teach your dog tricks, make a daily routine of getting the newspaper, take your dog to work with you (National Take Your Dog to Work Day is in June!). Enter a pet parade, take your dog to a pet store, take your dog on errands with you—some home improvement chains, for example, allow you to bring your well-behaved dog.

Bring your dog to the movie theater (check the theater's rules first), or to an outdoor shopping mall or restaurant. Take your dog to the lake (try a retrieving-dog lake for off-leash access) or a pet-specific swimming facility. Visit a dog park—a great place to meet like-minded dog owners. For kids, 4-H programs and the Boy Scouts and Girl Scouts have great dog projects. Throw a doggy birthday party. (C'mon! It's fun!)

Make your dog a top priority—because, seriously, what's more important than your dog? If that proposal at work were *really* so important, your boss would have done it himself. And the housework doesn't *really* need to be done until you have a visitor. And your kids . . . Well, it's probably good they learn a little independence anyway!

The rewards are in the journey, and the successes are measured in the smiles, barks, and tail wags that you and your best bud share. This is the beginning of your best-possible life together in the pursuit of a great dog-owner relationship.

Whether he's young or old, athletic or lazy, quick-witted or dumb as a rock—he's YOUR dog and his success need only be measured in YOUR eyes. I hope this book inspires you to "Do More With Your Dog!®"

Do More
With Your Dog!®

Notes

Rule 1: Be Honest

1. Cell Press, "Dogs Copy Other Dogs' Actions Selectively, the Way Humans Do," *ScienceDaily*, April 27, 2007, http://www.sciencedaily.com/releases.
2. Adám Miklósi et al., "A Simple Reason for a Big Difference: Wolves Do Not Look Back at Humans, but Dogs Do," *Current Biology* 13, no. 9 (April 29, 2003): 763–66.
3. Discoveries & Breakthroughs inside Science, American Institute of Physics in partnership with National Science Foundation and Ivanhoe Broadcast Network, 2006.

Rule 6: Attention Is a Reward

1. LRS was developed by trainers at Sea World in 1985.

Rule 10: Benevolent Leadership

1. Nicholas H. Rodman et al., "Comparison of Personality Inventories of Owners of Dogs with and without Behavior Problems," *International Journal of Applied Research in Veterinary Medicine* 2, no. 1 (2004): 55–61.
2. A. L. Podberscek and J. A. Serpell, "Environmental Influences on the Expression of Aggressive Behaviour in English Cocker Spaniels," *Applied Animal Behaviour Science* 52, nos. 3–4 (1997): 215–27.
3. Valerie O'Farrell, "Owner Attitudes and Dog Behaviour Problems," *Applied Animal Behaviour Science* 52, nos. 3–4 (1997): 205–13.

Rule 12: Communicate

1. Amanda C. Jones and Robert A. Josephs, "Interspecies Hormonal Interactions between Man and the Domestic Dog (*Canis familiaris*), *Hormones and Behavior* 50, no. 3 (September 2006): 393–400, http://sciencedirect.com/journals.
2. Kerstin Ackerl, Michaela Atzmueller, and Karl Grammer, "The Scent of Fear," *Neuroendocrinology Letters* 23, no. 2 (April 2002): 79–84.

3. Josep Call et al., "Domestic Dogs (*Canis familiaris*) Are Sensitive to the Attentional State of Humans," *Journal of Comparative Psychology* 117, no. 3 (2003): 257–63.
4. Patricia McConnell, *The Other End of the Leash: Why We Do What We Do Around Dogs* (New York: Ballantine Books, 2002), 56–58.
5. J. Neitz, T. Geist, and G. H. Jacobs, "Color Vision in the Dog," *Visual Neuroscience* 3 (1989): 119–25.
6. Paul McGreevy, Tanya D. Grassi, and Alison M. Harman, "A Strong Correlation Exists between the Distribution of Retinal Ganglion Cells and Nose Length in the Dog," *Brain, Behavior, and Evolution* 63, no. 1 (2004): 13–22.
7. Karen L. Overall, "How Animals Perceive the World: Non-verbal Signaling," (paper presented at the Atlantic Coast Veterinary Conference, Atlantic City, October 9–11, 2001).
8. N. J. Branson and L. J. Rogers, "Relationship between Paw Preference Strength and Noise Phobia in *Canis familiaris*," *Journal of Comparative Psychology* 120, no. 3 (August 2006): 176–83.
9. A. Quaranta, M. Siniscalchi, and G. Vallortigara, "Asymmetric Tail-Wagging Responses by Dogs to Different Emotive Stimuli," *Current Biology* 17, no. 6 (March 20, 2007): R199–R201.
10. Bash Dibra with Mary Ann Crenshaw, *DogSpeak: How to Learn It, Speak It, and Use It to Have a Happy, Healthy, Well-Behaved Dog* (New York: Simon & Schuster, 1999; Fireside, 2001).
11. Wa-Na-Nee-Che with Eliana Harvey, *White Eagle Medicine Wheel: Native American Wisdom as a Way of Life* (New York: St. Martin's Press, 1997), 25.
12. A. J. Ellis, *Horse Training*, 1842.
13. "Growing Up Grizzly," an Animal Planet special feature produced by Arden Entertainment (2001).
14. Source: Lois Rodden's AstroDatabank, 2006, http://www.astrodatabank.com.

Rule 14: Forgive

1. John Paul Scott and John L. Fuller, *Genetics and the Social Behavior of the Dog* (Chicago: University of Chicago Press, 1998; originally published 1965).
2. "Unconditional Love," *This American Life*, episode 317, Chicago Public Radio / Public Radio International (September 15, 2006).
3. Turid Rugaas, "The Puppy and the Young Dog—About Growing Up," 2008, http://www.turidrugaas.com.
4. NIH/The National Institute on Aging, "Diet, Exercise, Stimulating Environment Helps Old Dogs Learn," *ScienceDaily*, January 21, 2005, http://www.sciencedaily.com.

Index

About the Author

Kyra Sundance and her Weimaraner Chalcy have earned worldwide acclaim for their stunning acrobatic stunt dog team routines performed in live shows and television appearances. Their teamwork, obvious love for each other, and joy in working together are an inspiration to animal enthusiasts, and something which Kyra says is not achieved

merely with treats. "It is truly a testamant to my dog's commmitment to our relationship and bond, and something which touches my heart deeply."

The two have performed together on some of he world's premier stages. They were honored to star in a command performance for the king of Morocco at his royal palace in Marrakech, and they have been on *The Tonight Show, Ellen, Entertainment Tonight,* and *FOX News Live;* at NBA, MLB, and AFL halftime shows; and have starred in Disney's *Underdog* stage show in Hollywood.

Kyra embodies her tagline of "Do More With Your Dog!®" having spent years achieving nationwide ranking in competitive dog sports. Kyra also works as a movie-dog trainer, and she teaches dog tricks classes designed to encourage students to rediscover the joy of being with their dogs.

Kyra authored the industry-standard training book *101 Dog Tricks: Step-by-Step Activities to Engage, Challenge, and Bond with Your Dog.*

With her extensive and varied experience in dog sports training, Kyra contends that the training methods are not so important as the underlying commitment to the relationship. "Build a foundation based upon rules of trust, communication, and respect," she says, "and the rest will fall into place."

ÉDOUARD DRUMONT ET CIE

DU MÊME AUTEUR

Histoire politique de la revue « Esprit », 1930-1950
Éd. du Seuil, coll. « L'univers historique », 1975

La République se meurt. Chronique 1956-1958
Éd. du Seuil, 1978

EN COLLABORATION AVEC J.-P. AZÉMA

Les Communards
Éd. du Seuil, 1964, 1970
éd. revue et complétée en 1971

Naissance et Mort de la IIIe République
Calmann-Lévy, 1970
éd. revue et complétée en 1976
rééd. en 1978 sous le titre
La Troisième République
Le Livre de poche, coll. « Pluriel »

ÉDITION CRITIQUE

La Gauche depuis 1900
Jean Touchard, Éd. du Seuil
coll. « Points-Histoire », dernière éd. 1981

Les Congrès de la IIe Internationale
Genève, Minkoff Reprint, 1975 sq.

Mémoires d'un communard
Jean Allemane, Maspero
coll. « Actes et mémoires du peuple », 1981

MICHEL WINOCK

ÉDOUARD DRUMONT ET CIE

ANTISÉMITISME ET FASCISME EN FRANCE

ÉDITIONS DU SEUIL
*27, rue Jacob, Paris VIe*

ISBN 2-02-006088-4

Introduction

A la fin du mois de janvier 1910, Paris patauge. La Seine en crue a submergé ses berges. Dans les quartiers riverains du fleuve, on doit bientôt emprunter des barques ou des radeaux de fortune. Édouard Drumont, publiciste devenu célèbre par vingt-cinq ans de campagne antisémite effrénée, doit fuir son appartement du VIIe arrondissement, après que l'eau eut imbibé ses tapis.

Qui a fait le coup ? Car, dans toute catastrophe, fût-elle « naturelle », il faut chercher la main coupable. Drumont s'y emploie comme toujours. Point d'accident de chemin de fer, point d'émeute sanglante, point de calamité publique dont il n'ait traqué et trouvé le responsable. Pour dire vrai, ce Sherlock Holmes de boulevard ne varie pas dans ses conclusions. Immanquablement, il nous assène les preuves de la récidive : c'est le Juif, encore le Juif, toujours le Juif.

Il y faut parfois une bonne dose d'imagination. Le drôle en a toujours à revendre. Tout de même, l'inondation de Paris, où trouver les fils de David dans ce clapotis ? Élémentaire, mon cher Watson, nous dit Drumont. Si l'eau déborde, c'est qu'elle n'a pas été retenue en amont. Or en amont de Paris on a pratiqué des déboisements récents ; dans les sociétés qui s'en sont chargées, n'y avait-il pas des cousins de Rothschild ? Donc : « Les déboisements furieux opérés par les Juifs furent incontestablement la cause principale de l'inondation. »

Comme Léo Taxil, son contemporain, on pourrait imputer à l'aliénation mentale ce qu'il appelle la « juivomanie » de Drumont. N'était que celui-ci avait des centaines de milliers de lecteurs ; qu'il avait été élu député à Alger en 1898 ; qu'il ne comptait plus ses admirateurs et ses disciples. Paranoïaque ? Peu importe : il est lu, célébré, on le prend au sérieux. Du coup, il n'est pas négligeable.

Ce qui suit, à propos des grandes eaux de Paris, mérite d'être cité car c'est un échantillon de la démarche paralogique qui est habituelle à Drumont et à ses amis :

« Les " coupes à blanc d'étoc " des forêts de France, que l'on a signalées de toutes parts, ne furent pas autre chose qu'un nouveau " signe de la fin " ajouté à tous les autres symptômes de décomposition que nous avons eu l'occasion d'observer depuis vingt ou trente ans. »

Décomposition, dégénérescence, décadence... La première grande vague d'antisémitisme moderne qu'inaugure *la France juive,* publiée par Drumont en 1886, se développe dans les craquements sinistres d'une société qui se lézarde. A tout le moins est-ce l'avis des antisémites car la réalité est peu compatible avec leurs contes noirs et leur esprit de catastrophe. Il se trouve que, au moment même où tant de Français s'imaginent vivre « l'apogée » de la Civilisation ou une étape radieuse dans la « marche irréversible du Progrès », beaucoup d'autres éprouvent de l'anxiété, étourdis par cette fin de siècle électrique et républicaine. Le premier texte qu'on lira se propose d'évoquer, à travers un fait divers — l'incendie du Bazar de la Charité —, les frissons apocalyptiques qu'une partie de la société française se donnait à elle-même. L'antisémitisme a été une des « réponses » à la prétendue décadence dont la littérature conservatrice ou nationaliste a cru voir la France accablée.

« Nous retrouvons ici, d'ailleurs, poursuit Drumont, l'éternel microbe que nous avons invariablement découvert chaque fois que nous avons analysé et étudié une de nos maladies nationales. Ce sont des Juifs, et, qui plus est, des Juifs allemands la plupart du temps, qui ont formé ces sociétés financières dont le but fut de raser impitoyablement, par milliers d'hectares, nos plus belles futaies. »

Notre deuxième texte s'attache à replacer Drumont dans notre histoire politique. Son œuvre constitue, on n'ose pas dire la première synthèse — conglutination serait plus exacte — de l'antisémitisme moderne, rassemblant l'héritage antijudaïque de la tradition chrétienne, l'anticapitalisme judéophobe des couches populaires et socialistes, enfin les thèses racistes de la nouvelle science anthropologique. Car Drumont saisit — et n'importe des contradictions ! — tout ce qui peut stimuler son obsession. Il en appelle à la religion tout en rompant des hallebardes avec les curés ; il fraternise avec les socialistes mais pour mieux lacérer leur drapeau rouge ; il se pique d'arguments et d'un vocabulaire scientifiques (« microbe », « analyse », « maladie ») mais, croyant au Diable et à ses cornes, il sait décréter quand il le faut la « faillite de la Science ». Simpliste, Drumont ? Bien sûr. Mais un des tout premiers il a compris qu'en cette époque de journalisme triomphant, où l'opinion devient un enjeu, la propagande politique visant les « masses » ne procède pas par syllogismes mais par pétitions de principe, gros effets et sentimentalisme.

« Là encore, continue Drumont, remarquez-le bien, le Juif est dans son rôle constitutionnel et atavique. Privé de sa patrie et dépossédé de tout territoire national, le Juif est, par essence, un voyageur et un nomade. Il ne séjourne pas, il ne fait que passer ; il n'habite pas, il campe. Il n'a donc aucune raison sérieuse de ménager sa maison… »

Dans le mouvement nationaliste, qui emplit de ses clameurs la fin du XIXe siècle, le Juif trouve sa fonction. Il est, par effet de répulsion, le révélateur de l'identité nationale. Être français, nous dit-on alors, c'est, par excellence, être non-Juif. Simultanément deux mythes-forces et antagoniques se structurent : celui de Jeanne d'Arc, l'héroïne positive, et celui de l'archétype juif, son négatif. C'est le sujet de notre troisième chapitre.

A la même époque, au cours de l'affaire Dreyfus, au moment où le nationalisme se localise nettement à droite, l'antisémitisme va cesser de figurer dans les rangs de la gauche. L'histoire des relations entre la gauche et les Juifs, qui ne manque pas de rebondissements, c'est ce que nous avons tenté de retracer dans le chapitre 4.

Les quatre derniers textes qui composent la seconde partie de cet ouvrage sont consacrés à la période plus contemporaine qui commence au lendemain de la Première Guerre mondiale. J'ai voulu esquisser d'abord l'itinéraire d'un fascisme français, dans ses rapports avec l'antisémitisme (chap. 5) ; examiner, subsidiairement, les relations des catholiques avec ce fascisme (chap. 6) ; analyser de plus près le roman d'un écrivain fasciste, *Gilles,* de Drieu La Rochelle, qui nous livre quelques-unes des continuités de notre histoire idéologique (chap. 7) ; consacrer enfin à Georges Bernanos une attention particulière : cet adversaire intransigeant du fascisme, du nazisme et des œuvres plus mièvres du maréchal Pétain, ne fut-il pas néanmoins un antisémite (chap. 8) ?

Paradoxalement peut-être, les Juifs ne sont guère présents dans ce livre. Non que je doute de leur existence ; ils ne sont pas le seul produit imaginaire des antisémites. Certes, bien des Juifs en voie d'assimilation ou assimilés ont-ils découvert ou redécouvert tardivement leur *judéité* dans l'œil du raciste. En ce sens, l'antisémitisme est créateur du Juif. Mais l'existence juive a d'autres racines. Elle est fondée sur une culture et une histoire, inséparables d'une foi — gardée ou perdue —, et tout cela lui est propre. Je ne m'interdis nullement de parler des Juifs, quand bien même, issu de père et de mère catholiques, je compte probablement parmi mes ancêtres quelques antisémites très ordinaires. Mon sujet est ailleurs, voilà tout ; il part d'un étonnement qui n'est pas : « Comment peut-on être Juif ? », mais : « Pourquoi a-t-on été antisémite ? »

Nous sommes d'un pays qui, le premier des États chrétiens, a « émancipé » formellement les Juifs — autrement dit, qui a fait d'eux des citoyens comme les autres. Cela s'est passé sous la Révolution, dont ce n'est pas le moindre mérite. Mais aussi, nous sommes de ce pays qui, s'abandonnant dans la défaite au maréchal Pétain et au régime de Vichy, a eu le déshonneur d'inscrire dans la loi un Statut des Juifs qui effaçait cent cinquante ans de liberté ou autant vaut. C'est ce sentiment conjoint de fierté et de honte qui est sans doute à l'origine des pages qui suivent [1].

1. Les huit chapitres qui composent cet ouvrage sont issus, au moins en partie, d'articles publiés dans diverses publications, entre 1971 et 1981. Les références en sont données en fin d'ouvrage, avant la bibliographie.

1

Un avant-goût d'apocalypse : l'incendie du Bazar de la Charité

Le 4 mai 1897, vers quatre heures et demie, le petit Paul Morand, accompagné de sa grand-mère qui était venue le prendre comme chaque jour à la sortie de l'école, regagne son domicile rue Marignan. Passant par la rue Jean-Goujon, le futur écrivain est témoin d'un des faits « catastrophiques » les plus célèbres du siècle : l'incendie du Bazar de la Charité.

Cette institution avait été fondée en 1885 par des membres de la haute société catholique. Le président en était le baron de Mackau, le secrétaire le baron Robert Oppenheim, et le comité d'organisation était pareillement composé de représentants authentiques de l'aristocratie. Chaque année, au printemps, le Bazar rassemblait un certain nombre d'œuvres de charité (Petites sœurs de l'Assomption, écoles libres de la paroisse Saint-Louis-en-l'Isle, cercles catholiques d'ouvriers, œuvres des enfants et des jeunes filles aveugles de Saint-Paul, etc.), lesquelles disposaient chacune d'un comptoir, où s'affairaient des dames patronnesses offrant à la générosité des visiteurs les objets variés que le comité avait réunis. Cette pieuse et philanthropique manifestation était aussi une des dates les plus importantes du calendrier mondain, « un des lieux de rendez-vous les plus élégants et les plus aristocratiques », dit *l'Éclair,* ajoutant : « Sous le couvert de la charité, bien des choses étaient permises qu'en toute autre occasion prohibait le code mondain. Moyennant une poignée de louis, la jeune et jolie baronne de Z... laissait ses adorateurs déposer sur sa joue un baiser. " C'est pour mes pauvres ", disait-elle en rougissant de bonheur [1]. »

Cette année-là, le Bazar s'était installé sur un terrain vague de la rue Jean-Goujon. Sur quatre-vingts mètres de long et vingt mètres de large, on avait reconstitué en bois une vieille rue de Paris, dans un décor moyenâgeux, chaque comptoir ayant son enseigne pittoresque, *L'Écu d'argent, Le Pélican blanc, Le Lion d'or,* etc. Dans un coin du bazar, une nouveauté dont on attendait un grand succès : un appareil de cinématographe. On accédait à la salle de projection par un tourniquet moyennant une pièce de cinquante centimes. Le tout était surmonté d'un vaste vélum, qui rendait en ces journées ensoleillées la chaleur encore plus étouffante.

On comprend que le lieu insolite et distingué, la concentration de tant de jolies femmes et finalement la catastrophe qui s'abat sur ce Moyen Age de carton-pâte aient inspiré à Paul Morand une de ses nouvelles — *Bazar de la Charité* — où l'on peut lire la description la plus saisissante du sinistre, au milieu de l'intrigue imaginaire du conte : « ... Clovis se retourna et vit une flamme se dresser sur l'estrade. Elle s'enrubanna autour du cinématographe qui, dans un grésillement instantané, se mit à fondre avec toutes ses pellicules. Les gestes qu'on pouvait faire pour se protéger ou pour fuir arrivaient trop tard, car l'incendie avait déjà lancé son coup de gueule au ciel, ses griffes à travers la foule.

» Le vélum tendu au-dessus du Bazar se gonfla d'air chaud

1. Ce chapitre a été écrit à partir principalement d'un volumineux dossier de presse, conservé aux Archives de la Préfecture de police (Ba/1313 et BA/1314). Sur la littérature de l'époque, un ouvrage particulièrement suggestif est celui de Mario Praz, *la Chair, la Mort et le Diable dans la littérature du* XIXe *siècle. Le romantisme noir,* Denoël, 1977.

comme une montgolfière, fit craquer ses cordages, tendit une vaste bannière mouchetée de jaune, puis de roux, enfin de noir, qui se perfora, avant de se déchirer. Les têtes levées, aveuglées par le soleil, ne voyaient pas que le plafond de toile brûlait ; ce ne fut que lorsqu'il eut cédé au passage de l'appel d'air, qu'il fléchit sous son poids et se rabattit sur les assistants.

» Avant de comprendre qu'ils allaient être rôtis, avant de chercher une issue, ceux-ci reçurent l'averse de feu sur les épaules. Les ruchés et les festonnés, la paille des grands chapeaux, la mousseline des robes, le taffetas des volants et la soie des ombrelles, les voilettes, les rubans et les plumes, l'organdi et la percale, tous les tissus légers comme des vapeurs qui habillaient les corps des femmes, heureuses de s'abandonner à un précoce été, s'allumèrent comme des feux de joie, flambèrent dans l'air tiède, imprégné de parfums exquis et de lotions ambrées. »

Cet incendie mémorable ne vaut pas seulement pour son intérêt anecdotique et littéraire. Il s'offre à l'historien, ainsi que d'autres faits divers exemplaires, comme un catalyseur : la réaction qu'il provoque dans la société de l'époque révèle sur celle-ci des réalités profondes brutalement mises à nu. Le journal — et spécialement le quotidien —, qui est alors à son apogée, régnant sans partage sur les médias, amplifie la « réaction » jusqu'au moindre village. D'une rumeur les linotypes désormais font un vacarme ; le feu n'est plus circonscrit à un quartier de Paris, c'est tout le pays qui s'embrase. Le journal diffuse les horreurs du charnier, relatant jour après jour les détails les plus intimes et les plus épouvantables. L'effroi puis la commisération laissent bientôt place aux commentaires discordants ; l'union sacrée devant la mort s'abolit, le conflit des interprétations éclate au-dessus des tombes à peine refermées. L'événement devient une nourriture idéologique ; les sauveteurs ont tiré les baronnes du feu au profit des doctrinaires.

Saveurs macabres.

L'incendie de la rue Jean-Goujon déclenche dans la presse une effervescence qui va durer presque tout au long du mois de mai, pendant que sur les lieux du sinistre, devenus lieux de pèlerinage, des camelots vendent aux badauds des complaintes fraîchement imprimées :

> *L'or affluait au milieu des sourires,*
> *De jolis doigts le faisant ruisseler,*
> *Quand tout à coup vibre un cri de délire :*
> *Dans le Bazar le feu vient d'éclater.*

Comme disait *l'Éclair,* en matière de poésie « la hâte est mauvaise conseillère ».

Si l'incendie du Bazar provoque un tel flux de commentaires plus ou moins rimés, c'est certainement en raison de son ampleur et de sa brutalité. Toutefois, comme on le fera remarquer, les autres grands drames — ceux des mines par exemple — ne donnent pas lieu à tant d'émotion. C'est la qualité sociale des victimes, presque toutes issues de l'aristocratie ou de la haute bourgeoisie ; c'est aussi l'écrasante majorité de femmes parmi elles qui sont la cause du retentissement de ce fait divers : « La Mort a, cette fois encore, écrivait Drumont, choisi les têtes les plus charmantes et les plus nobles. Rien n'y manque, pas même une archiduchesse, la sœur de l'impératrice d'Autriche… » Le contraste violent entre les « toilettes pimpantes », les « visages rayonnants », les « êtres contents de vivre », et « l'effroyable catastrophe » devient un cliché sous la plume de tous les journalistes, avant de devenir un thème de réflexion politique et métaphysique.

La rencontre imprévue de la Beauté (une assemblée de femmes du monde, raffinées) et de la Mort (soudaine, hasardeuse) fascine d'autant plus qu'elle est un des grands thèmes du romantisme, tel que tout le XIXe l'a illustré — mais un thème qui, dans les vingt dernières années de ce siècle, comme l'a analysé Mario Praz, se pare de toutes les obsessions du « décadentisme ». La peinture de Gustave Moreau, qui reprend en chacune de ses œuvres le thème de « la fatalité du Mal et de la Mort, incarnés dans la Beauté féminine », les eaux-fortes de Félicien Rops — pour qui le Mal est personnifié dans la femme —, la littérature de Huysmans, de Barbey, de Villiers de L'Isle-Adam, celle de Jean Lorrain, de Marcel Schwob, du jeune Barrès mélangent à l'envi « fleurs et supplices ». Barrès écrivait dans ses *Cahiers :* « Il y a dans ces imaginations de supplices je ne sais quelle sombre et étrange volupté que l'humanité savourera avec délice pendant des siècles. »

Cette fin de siècle est en effet sadique. Sa littérature et son art se complaisent dans les spectacles d'horreur, les scènes frénétiques, la description des perversions rares, le goût du sacrilège :

Le meurtre, le viol, le vol, le parricide
Passent dans mon esprit comme un farouche éclair

disait Maurice Rollinat, ce sous-Baudelaire, et René Vivien :

Je savoure le goût violent de la mort.

Or il est patent qu'entre les récits journalistiques sur l'incendie du Bazar et cette littérature « décadente » il existe des liens profonds. La complaisance avec laquelle les journaux de l'époque décrivent non seulement le drame mais surtout ses suites : le transfert des cadavres plus ou moins calcinés de la rue Jean-Goujon au Palais de l'Industrie où ils sont exposés pour être reconnus par les familles, la description minutieuse des dépouilles, le tri des objets trouvés, les scènes de lamentation, témoignent d'une évidente propension au sadisme. Ajoutons qu'en ce siècle où triomphe l'esprit objectif, scientifique, statistique, la curiosité malsaine du journaliste se masque d'une prétention à la froideur de la médecine légale — qui ne fait qu'ajouter à l'horreur grand-guignolesque de ses articles.

On lit ainsi dans *le Soleil* du 6 mai la liste des ossements retrouvés : « 2 fragments de crâne, 2 fragments de côte,

1 fragment d'os long, 1 apophyse épineuse de vertèbre, 1 fragment de peau et 3 paquets de cheveux » ; le 12, *Liberté* annonce que « le total des objets divers que le tri a fait découvrir se monte à 427 », et, plus loin, précise que « ce matin, vingt-huit tombereaux à un cheval et trente et un à deux chevaux ont transporté quatre-vingt-dix mètres cubes de cendres, poussière et débris à la décharge publique, porte Brancion à Bagnolet ». Bilan quasi anodin en regard des descriptions horribles dont ce public est abreuvé dans les jours suivant le drame. Il y est question de jeunes filles et de femmes nues, au cou desquelles « on aperçoit des médaillons de piété » ; de cadavres « entièrement nus, sauf une bottine et un bracelet » ; d'abominables mutilations dont on peut à peine supporter la vue ; de corps décapités ; de crânes scalpés ; d'entrailles qui se répandent, maintenues par un reste de jupe ; de débris « incomplets : jambes, mains carbonisées, restes informes »... On a beau dire que « la tête tourne, que le cœur manque », on continue néanmoins la description lugubre, allant jusqu'au détail le plus affreux : « Une petite fille — quatre ou cinq ans à peine — montre dans sa nudité sa chair toute rose encore. » Ou bien : « Le peigne en écaille que Mlle Rosine Morado portait dans les cheveux a fondu sous l'action de la chaleur, et fait partie aujourd'hui du cuir chevelu de la malheureuse dont les souffrances sont épouvantables. »

Les scènes d'identification des corps sont narrées avec une précision à nos yeux insolite. On nous raconte comment les dentistes, appelés à la rescousse, examinent les mâchoires de leurs supposées patientes ; comment les chirurgiens cherchent les traces d'opérations les plus intimes ; comment les familles se disputent les dépouilles : « On se précipite sur les cadavres, on retourne d'une main fiévreuse des lambeaux d'étoffes, on examine des bijoux posés sur les morts [...]. Les mâchoires en étau se refusent à tout examen. Il faut recourir au scalpel. On fend les joues d'une large entaille. Les molaires apparaissent et avec elles les plombages révélateurs. » Outre l'inventaire, chaque jour affiné, des chevelures, des tibias et même des « kilogrammes d'intestins » retrouvés, on est surpris de l'étonnante minutie avec laquelle on répertorie les dessous féminins, grâce auxquels on finit par reconnaître les siens : boutons de jarretelle, lambeaux de cache-corset, morceaux de jupons — « en soie, à raies gris-bleu sur fond blanc [qui] indiquent une certaine richesse », jupon de dessous en soie noire, jupon dentelé et mille autres éléments du plus macabre fétichisme.

Le troisième jour qui suit l'incendie, six victimes restent anonymes. Sans scrupule, les journaux donnent alors « les renseignements les plus complets tels [qu'ils les ont] pris sous la dictée de M. le Dr Socquet ». Rien ne nous est épargné, comme en témoigne la fiche signalétique du « cadavre n° 5 » :

« Une femme mesurant 1,60 m environ, bien constituée, sur l'abdomen des vergetures anciennes et nacrées prouvant la maternité. Les jambes sont un peu velues. Cors sur les deuxième et quatrième orteils du pied droit. Portait des jarretières au-dessus du genou. Sur elle : un débris de pantalon festonné à jour avec six petits plis. Un lambeau de chemise avec large ourlet en fine toile. Deux jarretières élastiques sans boucles, dont la couture à l'une d'elles est faite de points grossiers au fil noir. Une bottine claquée à bout pointu, talon moyen, 22 centimètres de longueur de semelle. »

Toute cette presse morbide, nécrophile, fétichiste, qui se réclame de la science et de l'amour du genre humain pour mieux savourer le carnage, favorise, sans le savoir, l'assimilation de la Femme et de l'Enfer — comme tout le romantisme noir contemporain. « L'amour et la volupté, la douleur et l'amour s'appellent les unes les autres dans notre imagination », dit le Barrès de *Du sang, de la volupté et de la mort.*

Guerre des sexes.

L'attraction-répulsion du sexe opposé se traduit par l'ambivalence des attitudes en face des victimes. Après qu'on les a dénudées, qu'on a fouaillé leurs entrailles et qu'on les a réduites à la plus funèbre des nomenclatures, voici qu'on se porte à leur secours. En quelques heures, la rumeur se propage que les hommes présents au moment de l'incendie, ne pensant qu'à leur propre fuite, ont tout mis en œuvre pour se tirer des flammes, n'hésitant pas à bousculer, piétiner, user de leur force pour se frayer le passage, au détriment des femmes livrées au feu.

Au 16 mai 1897, on fait les comptes. 121 personnes ont péri pendant ou des suites de l'incendie. Sur 116 identifiées, 110 étaient du sexe féminin et 6 seulement du sexe masculin. Cette disproportion encourage la rumeur selon laquelle les hommes présents se sont conduits comme des brutes.

« C'est maintenant un fait malheureusement avéré », écrit *la Libre Parole* du 16 mai 1897, « que dans la catastrophe du Bazar de la Charité, les hommes ont eu la plus déplorable attitude. Il n'est pas douteux que quelques-uns se sont, à coups de poing et à coups de canne, frayé un chemin à travers les groupes de femmes affolées. » Les anecdotes, dès lors, vont bon train sur ce que *l'Intransigeant* appelle les « actes de férocité commis au Bazar de la Charité, par les francs-fileurs [2] du grand monde ». *L'Éclair* trouve la formule : il s'agit d'« un Azincourt féminin ». On récolte les témoignages : « Les femmes qui ont pu échapper aux flammes, revenues de leur stupeur, commencent à parler aujourd'hui ; elles attestent la lâcheté des hommes et leur brutalité. » On s'avise que « des chapeaux d'ecclésiastiques » ont été retrouvés sur le lieu du sinistre, que leurs propriétaires n'ont eu garde de venir réclamer ; on narre qu'un jeune homme, qui avait conduit deux dames de ses amies au Bazar, s'est esquivé au bon moment, puis, rendu à son cercle tranquillement, a déclaré à voix haute : « En ce moment, les petites femmes de Paris sont en train de griller » *(Gil Blas) ;* un valet de pied raconte qu'une amie de sa maîtresse a eu l'épaule démise par le coup de canne d'un

2. Le terme de « franc-fileur » est emprunté à l'histoire du siège de Paris (1870-1871) : il s'agissait alors de ceux, généralement riches, qui avaient pu fuir Paris avant le blocus imposé par les Prussiens. *L'Intransigeant* est le journal de Rochefort, ancien communard passé au socialisme national.

monsieur, qu'un autre a mordu l'oreille d'une jeune fille, que des malheureuses soignées à l'hôpital ne cessent de pleurer dans leur délire : « Voici encore des hommes qui vont me piétiner... » Il n'est bientôt bruit que de la pusillanimité des hommes présents, que de leur cynisme et de leur férocité. Selon des rapports de police, inconnus des journaux, « certains assurent que le duc d'Alençon s'est servi de sa canne et même d'un stylet pour écarter ceux qui entravaient sa fuite. Cela se répète et on croit devoir en faire part sans autre affirmation ».

La légende des « Gardénias » s'impose. Plusieurs journaux s'amusent et s'indignent de ces jeunes élégants, la fleur à la boutonnière, qui ont manqué à tous leurs devoirs. On distribue dans la rue des placards pour brocarder le « royal-fuyard », le « baron d'Escampette », « l'art et la manière de se tirer des pieds sans se les faire griller », les « chevaliers de La Frousse »...

Femmes, soyez des femmes.

Cette attitude de lâcheté dénoncée, quelques commentateurs tentent d'en chercher la cause dans « les transformations des mœurs ». Furetières, dans *le Soleil,* regrette ainsi que « le culte de la femme » s'affaiblisse — mais il en rend responsables les femmes elles-mêmes : « Lors du premier congrès féminin, je m'élevai avec force contre les velléités révolutionnaires de quelques-unes des meneuses qui trouvaient insultante la politesse des hommes à l'égard des femmes. » Il y a désormais, dit-il, trop de familiarité entre les jeunes gens et les jeunes filles : « La promenade en commun, à cheval, à bicyclette, la promiscuité d'une existence de camaraderie » laissent prévoir pour demain une concurrence sur le marché de l'emploi, alors qu'il convient d'épargner à la femme « un travail contraire à sa nature ou qui peut contrarier sa mission providentielle : la maternité ».

Dans *le Temps,* cependant, on note que la guerre des sexes risque de s'étendre à toute la société. Voici qu'à l'École des Beaux-Arts, où tout récemment on avait admis les femmes à certains cours, un violent charivari a été organisé contre le « deuxième sexe », nécessitant l'intervention de la police. Une bonne partie de la presse défend les étudiants : une femme architecte, a-t-on idée !

Que la femme reste femme, et les hommes resteront chevaleresques — telle est la morale de la fable. Mais qu'est-ce que rester « femme » ? Probablement, ressembler à ce portrait que l'on doit à M. de Kerohant dans *le Soleil :* « Oui, dans toutes les classes de la société, la femme sait être héroïque parce qu'elle a du cœur. La tête est souvent légère — tête de linotte — mais le cœur est bon », et c'est le cœur qui inspire l'esprit de sacrifice, qui suggère les actes de dévouement et d'abnégation. Victor Hugo a écrit là-dessus un de ses plus beaux vers :

Quand tout se fait petit, femmes, vous restez grandes.

Le débat sur la valeur des femmes et la couardise des hommes tourne court cependant. Car les hommes dont il s'agit ne sont pas n'importe qui, ce sont des hommes de la « haute » comme on dit alors. C'est pourquoi quelques journaux s'emploient à démolir la rumeur. *Le Gaulois* entreprend une grande enquête auprès des rescapés — hommes et femmes — de l'incendie et établit le caractère mensonger, en tout cas exagéré de la rumeur. Peut-être y a-t-il eu quelques mauvais gestes dus à la panique, ils ne furent qu'exceptionnels. La question devient alors sociale et politique, la guerre des sexes va laisser place à la lutte des classes :

« Eh bien ! écrit *le National,* le sang de ces victimes crie et veut être vengé. Si les Parisiens tenaient entre leurs mains les distingués et sélects personnages qui n'ont pas seulement lâché les femmes à côté desquelles ils flirtaient une minute avant mais qui les ont abominablement sacrifiées pour s'échapper de la fournaise, si les Parisiens les tenaient, ils auraient vite fait de leur appliquer la loi de Lynch. » L'article s'intitule : « Les muscadins impunis ».

Comme les dames du Bazar survivantes reviennent sur leurs premières déclarations et affirment la parfaite dignité de la conduite des hommes présents, Henri Rochefort dans *l'Intransigeant* déclare : « Ces dames savent que les individus dont elles font leur société et qu'elles donnent quelquefois pour maris à leurs filles sont ce qu'on peut rêver de plus lâche, de plus abject et de plus méprisable ; mais elles continueront tout de même dans l'intérêt de la religion et de l'aristocratie, à feindre de croire à leur honorabilité. »

Lutte des classes.

La « lâcheté des petits Messieurs », comme dit *la Patrie*, exprime moins les faiblesses du sexe masculin que le déclin, irréversible, des anciennes classes dirigeantes : à cette veulerie, la presse républicaine, en effet, se plaît à opposer la bravoure et la témérité des enfants du peuple dans la personne des généreux sauveteurs, ces fugitifs de la « une », vers qui les ferveurs populaires vont se porter quelques semaines durant.

Dans les jours qui suivirent le sinistre, la presse déjà s'était fait l'écho de quelques voix discordantes, contredisant cette belle unanimité dans la commisération dont les éditorialistes faisaient leur morceau de bravoure. « Deuil de riches ! » entend-on ici et là, devant les décombres calcinés. Dans un article retentissant, intitulé « Esprit de classe », Clemenceau dénonce la récupération que l'État et l'Église font de l'« affreux sinistre dans l'intérêt de l'esprit de classe ». Il déplore qu'on s'émeuve inégalement en face des victimes du coup de grisou et des victimes du Bazar, comme si pour celles-ci « il y [avait] un criminel contre-sens de la destinée alors que pour celles-là, il n'y [a] rien d'extraordinaire qui suscite plus de deux jours de plaintes banales et d'aumônes bruyantes ». Il termine par l'image antagonique des muscadins fuyards et des sauveteurs issus du peuple : « Voyez ces jeunes gens du grand monde qui frappent à coups de canne, à coups de botte les femmes affolées, pour s'esquiver lâchement du péril. Voyez ces domestiques sauveteurs. Voyez ces ouvriers, venus de hasard, qui exposent héroïquement leur vie, le plombier Piquet, qui sauve vingt créatures humaines et, tout brûlé, rentre à l'atelier sans rien dire. Méditez là-dessus, si vous pouvez, derniers représentants des castes dégénérées et gouvernants bourgeois de l'esprit de classe » (19 mai 1897).

Pendant plusieurs jours, les quotidiens républicains donnent à qui mieux mieux dans l'hagiographie populaire. On trace le portrait des sauveteurs : le plombier Piquet, reparti à son atelier après avoir arraché du feu vingt personnes, « sans s'apercevoir qu'il avait le visage balafré d'horribles brûlures » ; le cocher Eugène Georges, « le héros qui, au moins dix fois, probablement plus, pénétra dans le brasier de la rue Jean-Goujon » ; le cuisinier Gaumery de l'hôtel du Palais qui, après avoir descellé les barreaux d'une fenêtre donnant sur le terrain vague qui séparait l'hôtel des bâtiments du Bazar, fit passer des dizaines de femmes par cette issue inespérée ; le cocher Vast ; le palefrenier Trosch ; le vidangeur Dhuy…, c'est « la généreuse vaillance des enfants du peuple » que *le Jour* entend célébrer, en organisant en leur honneur un « banquet des sauveteurs ».

« Et c'était le peuple — le peuple anonyme — qui, dans la personne de ces vaillants de rencontre, révélait par l'héroïsme de quelques-uns des siens, passants obscurs, inconnus et ignorés qu'il est le dépositaire du principe d'action et de vie. »

Le 20 mai, le banquet des sauveteurs a donc lieu, dans la salle du Gymnase de la rue Huyghens. « Il a été, commente le chroniqueur du *Jour,* des plus brillants. » Musique, discours, toasts : le principe ne soulève aucune objection. Toutefois les interventions de quelques orateurs attirent les foudres de la presse de droite, qui s'en prend aux « malotrus de la libre pensée », aux « sales communards » qui ont pris la parole et ont essayé « d'insulter Dieu et les prêtres ».

Le Soir, qui exprime l'avis des classes dirigeantes, fustige la campagne de presse qui, « sous prétexte de glorifier les petits, [couvre] de boue ceux qui n'ont pas eu la chance de naître plombiers : il reste à souhaiter que les polémiques vaines et inconsidérées, déchaînées au sujet d'une catastrophe qui ne comportait pas de déductions politiques et sociales, soient définitivement closes. Les uns et les autres — peuple, bourgeoisie et aristocratie — ont fait leur devoir : l'oligarchie du courage n'est pas plus tolérable que celle de la politique, et, pour augmenter la ration d'éloges qui revient aux vidangeurs, on n'a pas le droit de prendre sur celle des fils de croisés » (22 mai 1897).

Le conflit de classes cependant se donne encore libre cours lors d'une séance à la Chambre, à la fin du mois de mai. L'intervention d'Albert de Mun, député catholique, provoque l'hostilité de l'extrême gauche, qui lui rappelle son passé de « versaillais » contre la Commune : « Vous avez insulté nos cadavres », lui lance l'ancien communard Pascal Grousset.

« Le comte de Mun, " ce pourvoyeur de mitrailleuses ", oublie trop facilement, commente *la Petite République,* que ce sont les fils des communards qu'il a fait massacrer qui sont seuls capables aujourd'hui de sauver du danger les femmes et les filles de toute son aristocratique bande » (30 mai 1897).

L'Ange exterminateur.

Dans le débat qui suit l'incendie, le conflit des classes, pourtant manifeste, prend cependant moins d'acuité que le conflit métaphysique. Ou plutôt, dans une large mesure, la lutte des classes s'exprime à travers la question religieuse. A la veille de l'affaire Dreyfus dont l'un des aboutissements sera la séparation des Églises et de l'État, la France est toujours profondément divisée entre catholiques, qui se réclament généralement des valeurs de l'Ancien Régime, et libres penseurs, qui sont le solide soutien du « parti républicain ». Depuis 1879, c'est-à-dire depuis que Mac-Mahon a quitté la présidence, la République a été laïcisée progressivement, au grand dam du « parti clérical ». C'est ce grand péché de la France, « fille aînée de l'Église », qui se trouve stigmatisé par le RP Ollivier, dominicain, lors de la cérémonie commémorative de Notre-Dame, à laquelle assistent le président de la République, Félix Faure, et des membres du gouvernement Méline.

Le père Ollivier saisit l'occasion — trop belle en vérité — pour réaffirmer la vocation catholique de la France. Si Dieu a permis cet épouvantable incendie, c'est qu'Il a voulu avertir le peuple de ce pays. Il a voulu « donner une leçon terrible à l'orgueil de ce siècle, où l'homme parle sans cesse de son triomphe contre Dieu ». Et notre dominicain, faisant allusion à la cause immédiate du sinistre, dû, pense-t-on, à l'éclatement d'une lampe de cinématographe, d'ironiser sur « les conquêtes de [la] science, si vaines quand elle n'est pas associée » à la science de Dieu. Le siècle scientiste est puni : « De la flamme qu'il prétend avoir arrachée de vos mains comme le Prométhée antique, vous avez fait l'instrument de vos représailles. »

En présence des représentants athées et francs-maçons de la IIIe République, le dominicain impétueux dénonce la cause profonde du désastre : « La France a mérité ce châtiment pour un nouvel abandon de ses traditions. Au lieu de marcher à la tête de la civilisation chrétienne, elle a consenti à suivre en servante ou en esclave des doctrines aussi étrangères à son génie qu'à son baptême. » La France ayant pris le mauvais chemin de l'apostasie, « l'Ange exterminateur a passé ».

Ce thème du sacrifice des innocents pour régénérer la France pécheresse va inspirer d'inépuisables gloses ainsi que des œuvres de patronage, s'efforçant de mettre en alexandrins le sermon du père Ollivier. Citons, par exemple, *l'Incendie du Bazar de la Charité,* mystère en deux tableaux, du chanoine L.M. Dubois, publié par la Librairie salésienne, en 1899.

Dans ce morceau mirlitonesque, destiné aux « pensionnats à clientèle distinguée », le bon chanoine s'efforce de démontrer, à la *lueur* de l'incendie, que la France doit revenir, repentante, à la foi de ses pères. Après quelques dialogues évanescents, « l'Ange de l'expiation » donne la morale de l'histoire :

Ah maintenant de deuil que votre cœur s'emplisse ;
Recueillez tout le sang versé dans un calice.
Le Seigneur a fauché sa divine moisson,
Dans un monde incroyant, il a pris sa rançon.

C'est aussi ce qu'exprimait *la Croix,* le journal des assomptionnistes, au lendemain de la catastrophe — une catastrophe si soudaine, si extraordinaire, qu'on ne pouvait « méconnaître un dessein providentiel ». Faisant allusion au sacrifice de Jeanne d'Arc, qu'on fête en mai, *la Croix* écrivait : « Il n'y a pas de rémission sans effusion de sang, et si la fondation de l'Église a été scellée par le sang de trois millions de martyrs choisis venant faire cortège au Crucifié, pourquoi le rétablissement d'une vie plus chrétienne en notre France ne serait-il pas annoncé par ce bûcher, où les lys de la pureté ont été mêlés aux roses de la charité ? » (7 mai 1897).

Cette interprétation catholique par le châtiment divin et le sacrifice nécessaire à la rechristianisation de la France, il va sans dire que la presse républicaine, radicale, socialiste, la rejette avec véhémence. Le sermon du père Ollivier, prononcé en présence des autorités les plus hautes de l'État, soulève des répliques vengeresses. C'est en octosyllabes que, lors du banquet des sauveteurs, un chansonnier exprime l'indignation laïque :

De quel limon sont donc pétris
Les tonsurés au cœur de pierre
Qui verraient flamber tout Paris
Sans une larme à leur paupière ?

Tribuns d'Église, ivres de fiel
Et de rancune apostolique,
Qui prennent à témoin le ciel
Des crimes de la République ?

L'extrême gauche ne se contente pas d'attaquer dans la presse « cet ignoble père Ollivier » (H. Rochefort), « ce prêtre prêchant dans la chaire du vagabond de Judée » (Clemenceau)… Là où la presse cléricale voit le signe d'une intervention divine, les républicains s'enchantent de cette preuve de l'inexistence de Dieu. La catastrophe ayant éclaté aussitôt après la bénédiction et le départ du nonce du pape dans un endroit catholique et voué à une œuvre de charité, il devient aisé de se livrer à des commentaires « sur la conduite illogique, inqualifiable *de ce Dieu-là,* conduite qui serait criminelle, si cet être mythique existait réellement » (*la Lanterne,* 6 mai 1897). D'où ce commentaire, qui s'impose, du *Radical :* « Le jour où, à toutes nos préoccupations de fantaisie, d'imagination et de foi ridicule, se sera substitué, nettement, pratiquement, l'esprit de science, de calcul, d'assurance et de prophylaxie, ce jour-là nous aurons dominé la nature et nous aurons rempli notre mission d'hommes » (12 mai 1897). Quant au président de la Chambre, Henri Brisson, il récuse, lors de la séance du 18 mai, « la conception d'un Dieu qui, non content d'avoir frappé notre pays il y a vingt-six ans, aurait encore pris une centaine de généreuses femmes en otage de nos crimes [applaudissements prolongés et répétés] et qui poursuivrait la France de sa colère jusqu'à ce qu'il l'ait forcée à rétablir chez elle l'unité d'obéissance [nouveaux et vifs applaudissements] ».

Le conflit devient politique à propos de la présence du président de la République, le franc-maçon Félix Faure, à la cérémonie de Notre-Dame : « Quel beau spectacle, celui de ces athées, de ces francs-maçons en tartufferie de prières pour de nobles dames qui ne prononçaient pas leur nom sans se signer » (Clemenceau). Ce spectacle n'est pas davantage au goût de l'extrême droite. *L'Autorité,* le journal de Paul de Cassagnac, rappelle que la République « spolie les congrégations, …chasse l'Église et Dieu des écoles et des hôpitaux ». Mais c'est surtout l'extrême gauche qui s'indigne de l'eau bénite que Félix Faure a reçue sans broncher. C'est à la Chambre que le gouvernement Méline devra se justifier devant les champions de la Laïque, qui lui rappellent que le père Ollivier, appartenant à l'ordre des dominicains — congrégation dissoute —, avait déjà provoqué le scandale, au temps de Mac-Mahon, en déclarant du haut de la chaire de Notre-Dame-de-Lorette : « Les républicains, c'est comme le fromage : plus il y en a, plus ça pue. »

« Un commencement de justice ».

On doit noter cependant que, dans le camp catholique, quelques caractères indépendants affirment leur dissonance. Ainsi les allusions, dans la presse de province, au refus des classes dirigeantes catholiques de suivre loyalement les recommandations de Léon XIII en matière de politique sociale. Tout autre mais plus tonitruante est la réaction de Léon Bloy. Cet écrivain, pauvre jusqu'à la misère, visionnaire incantatoire, théologiquement intégriste, démolisseur de bourgeois, fulminant comme un prophète, vitupérateur d'un catholicisme tombé dans une sinistre médiocrité, ne pouvait « lire » dans le drame de la rue Jean-Goujon qu'une vérité inconnue de la hiérarchie catholique : il s'agit bien d'un châtiment — mais de celui dont Dieu punit la compromission scandaleuse de l'Église et de l'Argent :

« J'espère, mon cher André, ne pas vous scandaliser en vous disant qu'à la lecture des premières nouvelles de cet événement épouvantable, j'ai eu la sensation nette et délicieuse d'un poids immense dont on aurait délivré mon cœur. Le petit nombre des victimes, il est vrai, limitait ma joie.

» Enfin, me disais-je tout de même, enfin, ENFIN ! voilà donc un commencement de justice.

» Ce mot de " Bazar " accolé à celui de CHARITÉ ! Le Nom terrible et brûlant de Dieu réduit à la condition de génitif de cet immonde vocable ! ! !

» Dans ce bazar donc, des enseignes empruntées à des caboulots, à des bordels, *A la truie qui file,* par exemple ; des prêtres, des religieuses circulant dans ce pincement aristocratique et y traînant de pauvres êtres innocents !

» Et le nonce du pape venant bénir tout ça ! »

Deux pages suivent, fulgurantes, à la gloire du Saint-Esprit vengeur :

« Tant que le nonce du pape n'avait pas donné sa bénédiction aux belles toilettes, les délicates et voluptueuses carcasses que couvraient ces belles toilettes ne pouvaient pas prendre la forme noire et horrible de leurs âmes. Jusqu'à ce moment, il n'y avait aucun danger.

» Mais la bénédiction, la Bénédiction, indiciblement sacrilège de celui qui représentait le vicaire de Jésus-Christ et par conséquent Jésus-Christ lui-même, a été où elle va toujours, c'est-à-dire au FEU, qui est l'habitacle rugissant et vagabond de l'Esprit-Saint.

» Alors, immédiatement, le FEU a été déchaîné, et TOUT EST RENTRÉ DANS L'ORDRE. »

Fin de siècle.

La fin du siècle étant marquée dans nos esprits par l'affaire Dreyfus, nous avons peut-être trop tendance à imaginer la psychologie de cette société 1900 plus rationnelle qu'elle n'était : entre ceux qui s'affirment pour la justice avant tout et ceux qui avant tout combattent pour l'ordre et la nation, on imagine l'opposition de deux thèses rationnellement défendables. De fait, entre la gauche dreyfusarde et cette droite antidreyfusarde dont Maurras devait déduire, positivement, son système monarchiste, les arguments échangés, malgré les passions, en appellent souvent à la raison.

Néanmoins, le triomphe de la raison, en dépit des « progrès de la science », des conquêtes de l'instruction publique et de la laïcisation progressive de l'État, est loin d'être évident. On peut mentionner au moins deux phénomènes qui témoignent alors de la résistance profonde à cette raison conquérante : l'essor des sciences occultes, de la magie noire, du satanisme, et, deuxièmement — mais ceci étant psychologiquement lié à cela — le développement extraordinaire de l'antisémitisme depuis les années 1880.

Les journaux les plus sérieux répandent le bruit que l'incendie du Bazar de la Charité avait été prévu, notamment par Mlle Couédon, célèbre voyante, un an plus tôt, dans les salons de Mme de Maille. Devant un large auditoire, elle aurait déclaré, après avoir invoqué « l'Ange Gabriel » :

Près des Champs-Élysées,
Je vois un endroit pas élevé
Qui n'est pas pour la piété
Mais qui en est approché
Dans un but de charité
Qui n'est pas la vérité...
Je vois le feu s'élever
Et les gens hurler...
Des chairs grillées,
Des corps calcinés.
J'en vois comme par pelletées.

Les personnes qui l'écoutaient devraient être épargnées. De fait, rapporte *le Gaulois* (15 mai 1897), « aucun des invités de cette soirée, tous plus ou moins assidus des ventes de charité, ne périt ou même ne fut blessé dans l'affreuse catastrophe du 4 mai dernier ».

Autre histoire de pressentiment. Toute la presse se fait l'écho d'« un singulier phénomène ». Le matin du désastre, la sœur Marie-Madeleine, de l'orphelinat des Jeunes Aveugles, avait affirmé à ses amies : « Vous ne me reverrez plus ; on me rapportera brûlée vive. » La religieuse devait effectivement mourir dans l'incendie l'après-midi.

Cette fin de siècle se montre curieuse des sciences occultes et de tous les phénomènes métapsychiques. Les romans de quatre sous comme la littérature de l'élite, aussi bien que les journaux, racontent à foison des affaires d'envoûtement, de messes noires, de meurtres rituels. C'est dans ce contexte qu'un Drumont a écrit ses propos antisémitiques les plus délirants.

L'antisémitisme n'avait aucune raison apparente de se manifester dans cet épisode. Les responsabilités de l'incendie n'étaient juives d'aucune façon. Même, l'hôtel Rothschild étant contigu au terrain du Bazar, ce fut dans les écuries du célèbre baron juif que maintes femmes purent être recueillies et sauvées. Pourtant, sachant l'obsession antisémitique de cette fin de siècle, je m'attendais, en dépouillant ce dossier de presse, à une de ses manifestations aussi intempestives qu'habituelles. Elle eut lieu, en effet, là où je ne l'attendais plus. Pour compenser les pertes dues à l'incendie, *le Figaro* avait pris l'initiative d'organiser une souscription. Ce fut un succès dès le premier jour. Mais voici qu'un donateur anonyme adresse d'un coup près d'un million de francs, afin de porter au crédit du Bazar de la Charité le produit exact de la vente de l'année précédente. Après quelques jours d'incertitude, *le Figaro* croit pouvoir révéler que le don exceptionnel proviendrait de la baronne Hirsh — c'est-à-dire d'une Juive. Celle-ci dément aussitôt. Tollé ! Le 19 mai, Paul de Cassagnac signe, dans *l'Autorité,* un article intitulé « Trop, trop de Juifs ». Les Juifs, dit-il, ne sont pas plus généreux que les chrétiens : ils sont tout simplement plus riches. Mais puisqu'on sait que cet argent est d'origine chrétienne, alors l'attitude du *Figaro* est odieuse, d'avoir voulu « exalter les Juifs et ravaler le mérite des catholiques. *La Libre Parole* de Drumont, moniteur français de l'antisémitisme, en bonne règle, ne pouvait gâcher pareille aubaine. Lorsque est rendue publique la provenance du don fameux — Mme Lebaudy, une catholique —, *la Libre Parole* exalte la charité chrétienne, « d'origine et d'allure si françaises », si digne de « notre race » — qui préfère l'anonymat — et conspue « la charité ostentatoire de la haute juiverie, transformant en almanach du Golgotha les colonnes du *Figaro* » et de déchirer à pleines dents « cette cynique ploutocratie de l'or... » (*la Libre Parole,* « Les deux charités », 19 mai 1897).

L'antisémitisme qui, dans les mois qui vont suivre, va déferler et trouver dans la condamnation du capitaine Dreyfus la preuve judiciaire de ses fantasmes, exprime à sa manière pathologique l'angoisse profonde d'une société qui tremble sur ses assises. La doctrine de Drumont, soutenue par les ligues, une presse puissante et le dessus du panier souvent des classes dirigeantes, permet à la petite-bourgeoisie française de se rassurer en face des transformations qui affectent la vieille civilisation rurale. L'antisémitisme apparaît alors comme une réaction à la peur éprouvée devant la modernité. L'industrialisation, l'urbanisation, et, allant de pair, la laïcisation de la société française, la vague d'anarchisme, les progrès du mouvement ouvrier, ont provoqué, en de nombreuses couches de la société, une inquiétude profonde et durable. De ce point de vue, l'œuvre de Drumont — avec toutes ses hallucinations, ses obsessions, ses phobies — est révélatrice, dans la mesure même où elle a eu une audience extraordinaire.

Le XIXe siècle s'achève dans un climat de trouble et d'incertitude — comme en fait foi la vogue du décadentisme en littérature, cette littérature profuse en catastrophes et imprégnée de l'idée du déclin : « Se dissimuler l'état de décadence où nous sommes arrivés serait le comble de l'insenséisme. Religion, mœurs, justice, tout décade... La société se désagrège sous l'action corrosive d'une civilisation déliquescente », écrivait déjà *le Décadent,* en 1886.

L'incendie du Bazar de la Charité a été interprété comme un signe annonciateur. De quoi ? Là-dessus les avis divergent. Mais, contre une petite minorité d'esprits forts qui expliquent le sinistre par le hasard et le hasard par le calcul des probabilités, la plupart des contemporains refusent les raisons des instituteurs. Des lois secrètes régissent ce monde. Les catholiques rappellent leur *credo,* tout en interprétant diversement, on l'a vu, ce *signe* divin. Mais, catholiques ou non, les Français ont l'impression de vivre sous la menace du Destin. Le catholique Bloy clame alors : « Attendez-vous..., préparez-vous à bien d'autres catastrophes auprès desquelles celle du Bazar infâme semblera bénigne. La fin du siècle est proche et je sais que le monde est menacé comme jamais il ne le fut. » Un observateur moins prophétique, Henry Céard, écrit en ce même mois de mai 1897 : « Dans un aveuglement d'autruche nous refusons de nous persuader que, à toutes les heures, [la vie] nous menace, et ce jour où j'écris est plein de périls et de crainte. » Sous la menace de ce *demain* qui fait peur, chacun se rassure à sa manière, au nom de la science, au nom des pratiques occultes, au nom de la foi, au nom de chimères diverses… Et la politique même, bien souvent, n'est qu'un lieu parmi d'autres où l'homme d'Occident contemporain transfère, en la travestissant, son obsession de la Mort.

L'histoire de l'angoisse, immense sujet pour l'historien.

2

Édouard Drumont et Cie

L'antisémitisme moderne a été et reste un des phénomènes sociopolitiques majeurs de notre siècle. Or, frappés que nous sommes par l'énormité du massacre perpétré par les nazis sur la personne de plusieurs millions de Juifs, indignés ensuite par les iniques procès d'une Union soviétique paraissant vouloir honorer l'héritage des *progromchtchiki,* nous savons mal, ou nous ne voulons pas savoir, qu'aux origines de ce délire devenu, sous le IIIe Reich, système de gouvernement, des Français ont pris une part qui n'est pas si négligeable.

On a souvent évoqué à propos du nazisme le nom de Gobineau. Mais celui-ci n'était pas à proprement parler antisémite ; sa phobie était le mélange des races, il y voyait la cause de la dégénérescence humaine. Au demeurant, il ne fit guère d'adeptes en France. Sans doute son nom est-il à retenir dans le développement du « racisme biologique », tel qu'on l'observe dans la seconde moitié du XIXe siècle ; il faudrait y joindre les noms de Vacher de Lapouge, de Jules Soury, de bien d'autres [1]. Mais ces hommes de cabinet ou de laboratoire n'ont pas eu d'influence politique. Tout autre est le cas de Drumont.

Lui, on aurait plutôt tendance à le sous-estimer. Son nom

1. Voir Z. Sternhell, « Les origines intellectuelles du racisme en France », *L'histoire,* n° 17, novembre 1979.

figure bien dans les manuels mais on se rend mal compte de l'extraordinaire faveur dont il a joui dans tous les milieux. Écrivain de troisième rang, certes, mais démagogue de premier ordre ! C'est lui qui a donné son impulsion définitive à l'antisémitisme français. Or celui-ci, au moment de la première grande vague, qui se déroule dans les vingt dernières années du siècle, n'est pas seulement un salmigondis de préjugés bêtes et méchants. C'est un instrument d'une utilisation politique qui peut aller loin — qui ira loin. Notamment, la dualité gauche/droite, sur laquelle fonctionne le système idéologique du pays, pourrait être remise en question, au profit d'une monade politique dont l'idée et le nom restaient à inventer.

Dans la décennie qui suit le krach de la banque catholique l'Union générale (1882), on assiste en effet à la naissance d'une nouvelle droite. Celle-ci se dégage des références conservatrices — même si, profondément, elle signifie le rejet de la société démocratique et industrielle ; elle s'affirme populaire. Elle veut capter les forces croissantes du mouvement ouvrier et les unir aux nostalgies des catholiques vaincus, aussi bien qu'au patriotisme cocardier. Dans cet effort de fusion, l'antisémitisme va s'imposer comme l'indispensable catalyseur : Drumont, le premier, devait en user systématiquement ; son échec final n'en laissa pas moins à ses héritiers spirituels une méthode dont l'Allemagne et le monde entier ont connu la terrible efficacité.

La personnalité et les œuvres de Drumont paraissent bien aujourd'hui tombées en désuétude. Sait-on pourtant que le slogan rageur : « La France aux Français », qui déshonore toujours les murs de nos cités, était le sous-titre de son journal, *la Libre Parole ?* Entre les deux guerres et pendant l'occupation allemande, Drumont avait été redécouvert. Pour ne citer qu'un de ses plus illustres admirateurs, Bernanos, dans sa phase maurrassienne, lui avait consacré une biographie assez distraite qui n'en contenait pas moins l'affirmation : « Dégagé des hyperboles ridicules, l'antisémitisme apparaîtra ce qu'il est réellement : non pas une marotte, une vue de l'esprit, mais une grande pensée politique [2]. » C'est de 1941 que date la dernière édition, par Flammarion, de *la France juive.* Le contexte de cette dernière résurrection semblait condamner à tout jamais Drumont, jusqu'au jour où M. Emmanuel Beau de Loménie s'offrit « de remettre en lumière la carrière et l'œuvre d'Édouard Drumont » et publia un recueil largement commenté de ses meilleurs morceaux [3].

Cette anthologie est d'un admirateur, mais d'un admirateur embarrassé. S'il ne dissimule pas qu'à son avis la « réhabilitation » de Drumont s'impose, s'il y travaille avec conviction, M. Beau de Loménie s'efforce toutefois, tout au long de son discours et dans le choix même des textes qu'il présente, de minimiser le plus possible l'antisémitisme de Drumont ; à tout le moins, d'en faire un élément accessoire et excessif d'une pensée qui a pour noyau l'*anticapitalisme national* — comme si l'antisémitisme n'avait pas été en France (et le temps passé est-il de rigueur ?) le corollaire nécessaire de cet « anticapitalisme » de propriétaires. Vaille que vaille, M. Beau de Loménie veut nous faire accroire que, des œuvres de Drumont, *la France juive* (201 éditions) est finalement la moins importante : « Sa thèse, nous dit-il, était trop unilatérale, trop peu mesurée, trop systématique » ; ce sont les œuvres postérieures à *la France juive* « qui sont les plus riches d'enseignements toujours valables ». De telle sorte qu'il y aurait une manière de « coupure épistémologique » dans l'œuvre de Drumont : à une première partie, œuvre de jeunesse, plus sentimentale, s'opposerait une seconde, autrement scientifique, autrement admirable et malheureusement méconnue. La thèse est peu défendable : si Drumont compte dans l'histoire, ce n'est pas pour avoir posé les hypothétiques fondements ration-

2. G. Bernanos, *La Grande Peur des bien-pensants,* Grasset, 1931.
3. *Édouard Drumont ou l'anticapitalisme national,* présenté par E. Beau de Loménie, Pauvert, 1968.

nels du poujadisme (« l'anticapitalisme national »), mais bien pour avoir le premier fait de l'antisémitisme un système d'explication globale. Je ne vois pas qu'il y ait renoncé dans les œuvres postérieures à *la France juive ;* bien au contraire, je lis clairement le résumé de ce système dans *la Fin d'un monde,* que M. Beau de Loménie prise tant : « La force des Juifs, y écrit Drumont, est de ne plus procéder comme autrefois, par des méfaits isolés ; ils ont fondé un système où tout se tient, qui embrasse le pays tout entier, qui est muni de tous les organes nécessaires pour fonctionner, ils ont fortifié les points sur lesquels on pourrait les prendre, ils ont modifié sans bruit les lois qui les gênaient ou obtenu des arrêts qui paralysent l'action de ces lois, ils ont soumis la presse au capital, de façon qu'elle soit dans l'impossibilité de parler. »

Avant d'en arriver aux sources et au contenu des idées de Drumont, il n'est pas inutile d'ouvrir une parenthèse sur les idées mêmes de M. Beau de Loménie, auteur prolixe qui a déjà écrit une monumentale *Histoire des dynasties bourgeoises,* où le meilleur avoisine le pire. La documentation de l'auteur, souvent sérieuse, est en effet gâchée par un esprit de système que l'on impute généralement à l'historiographie « de gauche ». Cette histoire, d'inspiration légitimiste, s'emploie à expliquer toute la France contemporaine par l'accaparement des biens dont la bourgeoisie révolutionnaire s'est rendue coupable entre 1789 et 1815, et par la volonté subséquente dont cette bourgeoisie, devenue conservatrice, a fait preuve, à travers tout le XIXe siècle et le XXe siècle, pour protéger et faire fructifier les positions acquises par les bâtisseurs de ces multiples « dynasties » illégitimes qui ont ruiné l'ancienne France. C'est le propre des historiens « de droite » de tout expliquer par le complot. Drumont avait déjà dénoncé la « gigantesque spoliation » de la Révolution française, mais le vrai complot, à ses yeux, était le complot juif, lequel a l'avantage décisif de synthétiser tous les complots réunis : depuis celui de la Haute Banque jusqu'à celui de l'Internationale socialiste. Si cette explication globale paraît un peu primaire à M. Beau de Loménie, il lui arrive cependant de considérer l'antisémitisme avec une tolérance... qui ne me paraît guère tolérable. Que si publier aujourd'hui des textes de Drumont, une étude sur Drumont qui se flatte d'objectivité, n'a pas besoin de justification, en revanche accepter cette anthologie et cette étude d'un auteur qui, sauf à gourmander un peu Drumont pour ses « hyperboles », n'hésite pas à en actualiser les paraboles donne matière à l'étonnement. Voici deux échantillons qui illustrent mon propos : « Qu'aurait-il [Drumont] dit s'il avait pu voir, comme nous le voyons aujourd'hui, la publicité journalistique accaparée par la firme Publicis de M. Bleustein-Blanchet ; et s'il avait pu considérer la place tenue dans les rubriques de télévision par un Zitrone et tant d'autres ? » (p. 81) ; faisant allusion à la guerre des Six-Jours et aux intempérances verbales de M. Edmond de Rothschild, M. Beau de Loménie dénonce la solidarité des Juifs avec Tel-Aviv, pour conclure : « Il est difficile d'imaginer plus éclatante preuve de la valeur lucide et prophétique de certaines des thèses de Drumont que ces déclarations émanant de quelques-uns des plus qualifiés de nos Israélites d'aujourd'hui » (p. 83-84). Par un joli saut-de-mouton dialectique au-dessus du génocide nazi — soit la cause directe de la naissance d'Israël et de la solidarité juive avec Tel-Aviv —, M. Beau de Loménie fait de son maître à penser, dont les thèses ont contribué à l'institution des camps de concentration, ce tranquille devin qu'on aurait dû prendre en France un peu plus au sérieux.

Ces exemples confirment en tout cas notre hypothèse, selon laquelle il n'y a guère en France d' « anticapitalisme national » sans antisémitisme. Les autres défauts du livre sont moins graves : les pointes antisorbonnardes contre une Sorbonne imaginaire, la nostalgie « Algérie française » évoquant le « temps des abandons gaullistes », les attaques contre ce « pauvre Albert Camus » qui fait ici fonction de baudet — un baudet qu'on étudierait trop, paraît-il, à l'Université, au préjudice des bons auteurs tombés dans l'oubli, d'un Drumont par exemple... Tout cela prêterait plutôt à sourire s'il n'y avait dans ce livre, malgré ces calembredaines, de bonnes analyses. Comme dans ses ouvrages précédents, mais ici avec plus d'éclat peut-être, notre auteur n'a pu se corriger des simplifications abusives et des naïvetés de l'extrême droite.

Mais revenons à Drumont. Son rôle, disions-nous, a été de désigner le Juif comme le principe universel des désordres et des malheurs de la France depuis la Révolution. « Le jour où vous attaquez le Juif, écrit-il, vous prenez la réalité corps à corps, vous vous mesurez avec votre véritable ennemi. » Drumont marque une étape importante dans l'histoire de la contre-révolution : c'est dans le mythe force de l'antisémitisme qu'il concentre les attaques dirigées contre la France issue de 1789, qu'il trouve le moyen d'un rapprochement entre la pensée contre-révolutionnaire traditionnelle catholique et l'anticapitalisme socialiste populaire.

L'antisémitisme chrétien.

On doit au livre de Pierre Pierrard, *Juifs et catholiques français* [4], d'éclairer les sources de Drumont : « Drumont, écrit-il, contribua largement au scandale de l'assimilation du catholicisme à l'antisémitisme. » Si Pierre Pierrard commence son étude à la Révolution française, on sait depuis longtemps que les « racines chrétiennes de l'antisémitisme » remontent à l'antijudaïsme de certains Pères de l'Église [5]. L'élément nouveau, pendant et après la révolution de 1789, c'est, aux yeux de

4. P. Pierrard, *Juifs et catholiques français,* Fayard, 1970. Le livre de M. Pierrard est un riche tableau de l'antisémitisme catholique. C'est aussi la description optimiste mais sans complaisance de l'itinéraire suivi par les catholiques français, depuis la Révolution jusqu'au concile Vatican II, dans leurs sentiments à l'égard des Juifs. Cette étude est utile par la richesse de sa documentation ; elle est sympathique par la fermeté de son propos (l'auteur est professeur à l'Institut catholique) ; on regrettera seulement son parti pris d'en rester au stade purement descriptif.

5. Voir J. Isaac, *Genèse de l'antisémitisme,* Calmann-Lévy, 1956.

nombreux auteurs catholiques et contre-révolutionnaires, la responsabilité prise par les Juifs dans la chute de l'Ancien Régime. La Révolution qui avait émancipé les Juifs ne pouvait avoir été que l'œuvre des Juifs : tel est le sophisme qui triomphe dans une série d'ouvrages cités par Pierre Pierrard, et qui aboutit à la formule de Drumont : « Le seul auquel la Révolution ait profité est le Juif. Tout vient du Juif. Tout revient au Juif. »

Cette histoire « occultiste » qui vise à l'explication de tous les phénomènes sociaux et politiques par le complot juif a commencé avec l'abbé Augustin de Barruel, pour lequel 89 avait été l'aboutissement « de la conspiration des sociétés secrètes ». Auteur de cette thèse qui est l'argument de son *Mémoire pour servir à l'histoire du jacobinisme,* Barruel reçut en 1806 la lettre d'un certain Simonini, lequel désignait les vrais coupables, derrière les francs-maçons et les illuminés fauteurs de révolution : les Juifs. Que les sociétés antichrétiennes fussent organisées et entretenues par ceux qui, du fait de leur religion, étaient tenus en respect par la société chrétienne, c'était une hypothèse défendable. Mais Simonini allait plus loin : il révélait que les Juifs « se promettaient, dans moins d'un siècle, d'être les maîtres du monde ». Les élucubrations de ce soi-disant capitaine piémontais n'eurent pas d'effet immédiat ; mais sa lettre fut publiée à Paris en 1878, puis reproduite dans de nombreux ouvrages antisémitiques [6].

Toutefois, sans atteindre les hauteurs de cette absurdité, qu'on peut mettre au rang des sources de ces *Protocoles des Sages de Sion,* faux historique dont un Maurras autant qu'un Hitler faisaient leurs délices, de nombreux auteurs hostiles à la Révolution, tel Bonald, mêlèrent l'antijudaïsme « chrétien » à leur antilibéralisme. Il semble que, sous le second Empire, cette littérature fut féconde : Pierre Pierrard énumère une liste de romans pieux aux titres suggestifs et évoque ces *Mémoires d'un*

6. Voir l'excellente étude de Norman Cohn, *Histoire d'un mythe. La « conspiration » juive et les « Protocoles des Sages de Sion »,* Gallimard, 1967.

ange gardien (1862), dont le succès fut vif et durable, où l'on voit un petit garçon « horrifié par la cruauté des Juifs, bourreaux de Jésus » ; il cite aussi des ouvrages plus « sérieux », notamment celui de Gougenot des Mousseaux, paru sous le titre : *le Juif, le Judaïsme et la Judaïsation des peuples chrétiens* — passé d'abord inaperçu, appelé à devenir par la suite, selon le mot de Norman Cohn, « la Bible de l'antisémitisme moderne ». Pour cet auteur imaginatif, la Cabale préconisait l'adoration de Satan, et les Juifs cabalistes ne visaient rien de moins que le règne de l'Antéchrist. Dans la lutte qui opposait alors l'Église et la franc-maçonnerie, l'ouvrage de Gougenot des Mousseaux s'en prenait simultanément aux Juifs et aux maçons — confusion désormais classique : Pie IX félicita l'auteur. A une époque où la chrétienté médiévale paraissait s'écrouler par pans entiers, où le pouvoir temporel du pape allait être bientôt réduit à sa plus simple expression, où les idées nouvelles remettaient en question la dogmatique romaine, de nombreux auteurs catholiques furent tentés de dénoncer à l'origine de ces multiples dangers autant de conspirations, où la franc-maçonnerie machinait ses desseins en compagnie des Juifs. A titre d'exemple, la « question romaine » suscita la fable selon laquelle le complot contre la papauté était mené par un certain « Piccolo Tigre », Juif franc-maçon ; Mgr Gaston de Ségur, fils de la célèbre comtesse, en fit un livre, *les Francs-maçons* (1867), qui compta, nous dit Pierre Pierrard, trente-six éditions en cinq ans.

La guerre de 1870-71, la prise de Rome par les patriotes italiens, la Commune, l'avènement de la IIIe République, alimentèrent en nouveaux prétextes la littérature antijuive. Tandis que la *Civiltà cattolica* des jésuites romains accumulait « sur la tête des *Hébreux* tous les crimes de la terre », en France, les lois scolaires de Ferry accréditèrent le dogme du « complot judéo-maçonnique ». Dans le foisonnement des publications cléricales qui reprenaient et illustraient ce thème, on peut retenir la naissance, en 1884, de *la Franc-maçonnerie démasquée,* revue catholique mensuelle qui dura jusqu'en 1924 ; l'un de ses rédacteurs écrivait, en 1885, soit un an avant le livre de Drumont mais un an après l'encyclique *Humanum Genus,* qui condamnait la franc-maçonnerie : « Le Juif est l'homme de la loge, parce que la loge est essentiellement pour lui le moyen de parvenir. » On saisit la double équation : République = franc-maçonnerie = juiverie. De son côté, le journal *la Croix* entreprenait une ardente campagne contre les loges et, insensiblement, comme l'écrit Pierre Sorlin dans une étude consacrée au journal des assomptionnistes, « elle en vient à associer le Juif et le maçon [7] ».

Le vieil antijudaïsme médiéval se trouvait donc nettement renouvelé près d'un siècle après la Révolution française. Le Juif, émancipé par la loi révolutionnaire, était désormais considéré par les antisémites chrétiens comme l'inspirateur occulte de 1789, l'animateur de la franc-maçonnerie, l'instigateur des lois laïques, le promoteur de l'anticléricalisme, l'ennemi acharné de la religion et de la civilisation chrétiennes. Il est, selon le mot de Gougenot des Mousseaux, « l'ingénieur en chef des révolutions » (cité par Jeannine Verdès-Leroux, voir plus loin).

Cet antisémitisme « religieux » se frottait déjà de nationalisme chez quelques auteurs, prompts à assimiler France et chrétienté. Un Louis Veuillot est caractéristique de ces catholiques-et-français-toujours, qui écrit, par exemple, en novembre 1870, dans *l'Univers :* « Moi, chrétien catholique de France, vieux en France comme les chênes et enraciné comme eux, je suis constitué, déconstitué, reconstitué, gouverné, régi, taillé par des vagabonds d'esprit et de mœurs. Renégats ou étrangers, ils n'ont ni ma foi, ni ma prière, ni mes souvenirs, ni mes attentes. Je suis sujet de l'hérétique, du Juif, de l'athée et d'un composé de

7. P. Sorlin, « *La Croix* » *et les Juifs,* Grasset, 1967. Très bonne monographie sur une des manifestations les plus importantes de l'antisémitisme catholique. C'est après la publication de *la France juive* que *la Croix* se déchaîne contre les Juifs, au point de se proclamer, en 1890 : « Le journal le plus antijuif de France, celui qui porte le Christ, signe d'horreur aux Juifs. »

toutes ces espèces qui n'est pas loin de ressembler à la brute [8]. »

Ces quelques exemples suffisent à montrer que la flore de Drumont ne manquait pas de terreau, qu'un public catholique, comme le fait observer Pierre Pierrard, était, à la veille de *la France juive,* en état de réceptivité. « Partout, dira Drumont, vous retrouvez le Juif essayant de détruire directement ou indirectement notre religion. Le divorce est d'institution juive, le Juif Naquet fait passer le divorce dans nos lois. Nos belles cérémonies funèbres irritent le Juif, c'est un ingénieur du nom de Salomon qui se met à la tête d'une société pour la crémation qu'il voudrait rendre obligatoire. C'est un Juif, Camille Sée, qui organise les lycées de jeunes filles, de façon à en exclure tout enseignement religieux [9]... » Etc.

L'antisémitisme « économique ».

Dans son livre sur le krach de l'Union générale [10], Jeannine Verdès-Leroux, après avoir noté « le rôle moteur des catholiques

8. Cité par Pierre Pierrard, *op. cit.*
9. *La France juive, op. cit.,* t. 2, p. 443.
10. J. Verdès-Leroux, *Scandale financier et antisémitisme catholique. Le krach de l'Union générale,* Éd. du Centurion, 1969. Ce livre contient quelques rappels historiques importants et situe bien la genèse de l'antisémitisme moderne en France ; c'est aussi un utile répertoire de la littérature portant sur la question. Toutefois, il importe de signaler que l'auteur semble mal connaître certaines des œuvres qu'elle cite. Le cas est particulièrement net à propos de Léon Bloy, dont elle fait un « antisémite de droite » plein de « haine [...] à l'égard des Juifs ». Or si Bloy a eu une phase antisémite (voir *le Désespéré*), tout lecteur de son *Journal* sait fort bien qu'il a par la suite répudié ses sentiments de jeunesse : « Il ne me coûte rien d'avouer, écrivait-il le 23 juin 1911, qu'à l'époque, lointaine déjà, du *Désespéré,* sans remonter aux temps mythologiques de mes années de lycéen, j'ai pu dire ou écrire des sottises que mon âge plus mûr a restituées au néant. J'appelle ça un changement heureux et normal. » *Le Salut par les Juifs,* d'autre part, est un livre à interpréter avec prudence : Jeannine Verdès-Leroux ne veut y voir qu'antisémitisme ; c'est oublier : 1) que le livre contient une attaque féroce contre Drumont, 2) que Bloy s'est expliqué lui-même sur l'aspect antijuif de sa deuxième partie (il écrit ainsi en janvier 1896 au grand rabbin : « Il me fallut donc adopter la méthode recommandée par saint Thomas d'Aquin, laquelle consiste à *épuiser d'abord l'objection* avant de conclure. Méthode

dans l'élaboration et la diffusion de l'antisémitisme en France », rappelle la deuxième source de l'antisémitisme moderne : l'antijudaïsme « économique ». Parallèlement à (et parfois indépendamment de) l'antisémitisme « religieux » s'est développé au XIXe siècle un mouvement d'hostilité, qu'on pourrait qualifier « de gauche », aux Juifs confondus avec les milieux financiers dominants. Le nom de Rothschild évoque encore aujourd'hui les séquelles d'un antisémitisme populaire, à fondement anticapitaliste, qui était, entre autres choses, l'expression naïve d'une lutte des classes qu'on ne savait pas mieux exprimer. De nombreux auteurs qui se réclament de la Révolution française ou qui comptent parmi les pionniers du socialisme en France ont souvent confondu dans leur réprobation Juifs et capitalistes, et opposé le peuple producteur à la « finance juive » : un Michelet, un Fourier, un Proudhon ont nourri de leur prose l'antisémitisme moderne. Mais, par un glissement sémantique, le terme « juif » est souvent pris chez eux comme un synonyme d'« usurier », sans

---

excellente et d'une grande loyauté philosophique, mais qui me fit malvenir de ceux mêmes que je prétendais honorer comme nul chrétien ne l'a fait, je crois, depuis dix-neuf siècles »), 3) que Bernard Lazare a loué le livre de ce « philosémite ». Mais l'ignorance de Bloy par l'auteur va jusqu'à lui faire classer son *Je m'accuse* dans les écrits des apologistes de Drumont. Rappelons que le *Je m'accuse* de Bloy est un pamphlet dirigé contre Zola comme exploiteur de l'Innocence ; on y trouve aussi une jolie volée de bois vert administrée aux folliculaires en soutane de *la Croix ;* qu'on en juge : « Le spectacle sans nom d'un groupe de prêtres acharnés sur un pauvre homme dont ils *savaient* l'injuste condamnation (il s'agit évidemment de Dreyfus), et chaque matin — la bouche pleine du Sang du Christ — léchant les bottes, crottées de sang, des tourmenteurs ! » Il se trouve seulement que l'inclassable Bloy n'était pas du camp des dreyfusards, voyant de tous côtés autant d'imbéciles et de bourreaux ; on peut le regretter mais le placer au rang des antisémites notoires est une erreur d'interprétation. Si, comme Jeannine Verdès-Leroux, on cite telle phrase de Bloy qui évoque « le Crime suprême » des Juifs (*i.e.* la crucifixion), il serait honnête de compléter pareille allusion par ces mots de Léon Bloy : « Que penser des chrétiens qui Le crucifient depuis deux mille ans, *L'ayant reconnu,* sachant qu'ils ont été mis au monde pour L'adorer et comment imaginer l'énormité du châtiment et de la honte qui les attendent ? » En vérité, qu'y a-t-il de commun entre un Drumont et un Bloy ?

référence explicite à l'origine raciale ou religieuse de ceux qu'ils condamnent. Néanmoins, il en va parfois différemment. Si Proudhon, par exemple, définit le Juif comme l'*anti-producteur,* de sorte que l'on pourrait en déduire que tout intermédiaire, quelle que fût son origine, est « juif », il se laisse aller à pétitionner, entre autres mesures souhaitables, l'abolition des synagogues [11]. Toutefois, aucun de ces auteurs n'a traité de la question à fond. C'est Toussenel, avec ses *Juifs rois de l'époque,* publiés en 1845, qui fut la « source de gauche » de Drumont, lequel a pu en parler comme d'« un chef-d'œuvre impérissable ».

A vrai dire, l'ouvrage de Toussenel est plein de la même équivoque linguistique observée chez son maître Fourier et chez les autres socialistes antijuifs. D'une part, il fait l'assimilation complète et réciproque du Juif et du financier, au point de condamner sous le vocable de « Juifs » les spéculateurs protestants et catholiques ; d'autre part, il lui arrive de préciser que les Juifs dont il parle sont bien issus du peuple de la Bible. Ainsi, dans l'introduction de son livre fameux, Toussenel affirme : « J'appelle, comme le peuple, de ce nom méprisé de Juif, tout trafiquant d'espèces, tout parasite improductif, vivant de la substance et du travail d'autrui. Juif, usurier, trafiquant sont pour moi synonymes. » Mais il donne un peu plus loin cette précision que le Juif est inséparable de la Bible. Or : « Je ne sais pas les grandes choses, dit-il, qu'a faites le peuple juif, n'ayant jamais lu son histoire que dans un livre où il n'est parlé que d'adultère et d'inceste, de boucheries et de guerres sauvages ; où tout nom qu'on révère est souillé d'infamie ; où toute grande fortune débute invariablement par la fraude et par la trahison ; où les rois, qu'on nomme saints, font assassiner les maris pour leur voler leurs femmes ; où les femmes qu'on nomme saintes entrent dans le lit des généraux ennemis pour leur trancher la tête… » Et

11. Voir L. Poliakov, *Histoire de l'antisémitisme,* Calmann-Lévy, 1968, t. 3.

plus loin : « Je n'appelle pas peuple de Dieu le peuple qui met impitoyablement à mort tous les prophètes inspirés de l'esprit saint, qui crucifie le Rédempteur des hommes, et l'insulte sur la croix… »

Nous voilà donc renseignés : les Juifs, pour Toussenel, ne sont donc pas n'importe quels usuriers, mais bel et bien ceux que l'ancienne liturgie catholique du Vendredi saint nommait les *perfidi,* qu'on appelait depuis des siècles « déicides ». Eh bien non ! Ce serait trop clair ! Toussenel ajoute en effet : « Qui dit juif, dit protestant, sachez-le. » D'où il résulte que l'Anglais, le Hollandais ou le Genevois sont tous pareillement « juifs » et que le livre de Toussenel, violente diatribe contre la ploutocratie triomphante sous la monarchie de Juillet, n'était pas exactement d'un antisémite. Comme le fait remarquer Léon Poliakov, dans son ouvrage déjà cité : « Nombreux sont les chapitres des *Juifs rois de l'époque* dans lesquels il n'est pas question des Juifs du tout. En réalité, le véritable propos de Toussenel était de dénoncer le règne de l'argent… » Il n'empêche que, par ses ambiguïtés, par certaines de ses formules (« Force au pouvoir ! Mort au parasitisme ! Guerre aux Juifs ! Voilà la devise de la révolution nouvelle »), Toussenel devint l'un des pères nourriciers des antisémites, à telle enseigne que sa « seule ambition » était, dira Drumont, de se montrer digne de ce prestigieux « prophète ».

Dans ce courant, nous pouvons négliger les appréciations méprisantes de Marx sur les Juifs : encore largement méconnu en France à l'époque de Drumont, il ne peut l'avoir influencé. Mais ce rappel pour mémoire d'un « antisémitisme juif » (Poliakov) nous donne la mesure des sentiments antijuifs qu'on peut observer d'un bout à l'autre de la famille socialiste. Le développement du capitalisme financier ne pouvait que renforcer cette tendance : à la misère ouvrière il fut aisé d'opposer la richesse honteuse du Juif Rothschild.

Ajoutons enfin, pour enrichir le tableau, qu'un certain antisémitisme de gauche pouvait avoir un tout autre contenu. C'est ainsi que fut publié, en 1884, à Bruxelles, l'ouvrage du blanquiste Gustave Tridon : *Du molochisme juif.* L'auteur, ancien communard, avait, dans ce livre posthume, comme jadis un Diderot ou un Voltaire, accusé les Juifs d'être les initiateurs de la religion catholique, ce qui, évidemment, ne manquait pas de vérité. L'antisémitisme chrétien se trouvait donc ainsi légitimement complété par l'antisémitisme anticlérical et athéiste. Au nom du principe selon lequel « chaque progrès est une victoire remportée sur Dieu », Tridon dénonçait dans les Juifs les fondateurs de ce monothéisme sanguinaire qu'était le christianisme. Livre donc encore plus antichrétien qu'antijuif, sans portée immédiate, mais qui nous révèle les inépuisables fonctions de l'antisémitisme, gigantesque marmite idéologique apte à faire bouillir un semblant d'unanimité contre le Juif-Protée.

Racisme et occultisme.

On doit tenir compte d'un dernier élément qui grossit encore la confluence de l'antijudaïsme chrétien et de l'antisémitisme « économique » : je veux parler de la faveur dont ont joui dans la seconde partie du XIXe siècle les thèses racistes, à fondement prétendument scientifique, et dont Drumont a usé comme d'un ingrédient supplémentaire pour l'enrichissement de sa synthèse.

Prêt à saisir tout ce qui lui tombe sous la main pour discréditer la communauté juive, il ne manque pas de reprendre à son compte les théories qui ont opposé alors, sur le plan biologique autant qu'historique, les « aryens » aux « sémites ». Dans *la France juive,* sans toujours donner ses sources, il évoque au moins trois auteurs : Taine, Gellion-Danglar (*les Sémites et le Sémitisme,* 1882), et Renan surtout, dont l'*Histoire générale et système comparé des langues sémitiques* l'a visiblement influencé. Ces auteurs et d'autres qu'il ne cite pas l'ont amené à considérer la dualité aryen/sémite comme une des clés majeures de l'histoire universelle. Il fait sienne l'idée de Renan selon laquelle « la race sémitique, comparée à la race indo-européenne, représente éternellement une combinaison inférieure de la nature humaine [12] ». D'où s'ensuit ce combat de l'Ange et de la Bête qui résume l'histoire de l'humanité :

« Dès les premiers jours de l'histoire, nous voyons l'aryen en lutte avec le sémite [13]. »

« Ce fut une guerre de races : aryens contre sémites, que cette guerre de Troie ; guerre de races encore : l'invasion de l'Espagne et du midi de la France par les Sarrasins ; la revanche héroïque des croisades dont l'effort superbe dura trois siècles [14]. »

« De quoi se compose une vraie révolution ? Elle a toujours pour base une question de race [15]. »

On devine qu'au moment de l'affaire Dreyfus la culpabilité de celui-ci tombait sous le sens. On la déduisait de « sa race », comme dit Barrès ; Drumont était du même avis : « C'est une question de race et tous les raisonnements métaphysiques n'y feront rien [16]. »

Autour de ces deux pôles ethniques, dont les origines se perdent dans la nuit des temps, se sont fixés sous forme de stéréotypes des caractères millénaires, « observables » encore dans nos sociétés, et dont l'antagonisme se perpétue. Pour tout dire, l'aryen est l'homme de l'idéal, du dépassement, de la transcendance ; le sémite est l'homme de la réalité, du positif, de la matière. Le premier a pour milieu naturel la forêt ; le refuge du second est le désert.

Entre l'homme de la forêt et « l'homme de proie des sables d'Arabie », entre « le fils du ciel, sans cesse préoccupé d'aspirations supérieures » et l'éternel errant seulement soucieux de « la vie présente », il n'est rien de commun : « Le sémite est mercan-

12. E. Renan, *Histoire générale et système comparé des langues sémitiques,* 1855.
13. *La France juive, op. cit.*, t. 1, p. 7.
14. « Guerre de races », *La Libre Parole,* 7 décembre 1898.
15. *La Libre Parole,* 27 septembre 1900.
16. *Ibid.*, 2 novembre 1897.

tile, cupide, intrigant, subtil, rusé ; l'aryen est enthousiaste, héroïque, chevaleresque, désintéressé, franc, confiant jusqu'à la naïveté [17]. »

La physionomie des Juifs n'en est que mieux repérable, tandis que leur physiologie présente des caractères propres :

« Les principaux signes auxquels on peut reconnaître le Juif restent donc : ce fameux nez recourbé, les yeux clignotants, les dents serrées, les oreilles saillantes, les ongles carrés, le pied plat, les genoux ronds, la cheville extraordinairement en dehors, la main moelleuse et fondante de l'hypocrite et du traître ; ils ont assez souvent un bras plus court que l'autre [18] » ; « il sent mauvais [19] » ; « il est sujet à toutes les maladies qui indiquent la corruption du sang [20] » ; mais, « par un phénomène que l'on a constaté cent fois au Moyen Age et qui s'est affirmé de nouveau au moment du choléra, le Juif paraît jouir vis-à-vis des épidémies d'une immunité particulière, il semble qu'il y ait en lui une sorte de peste permanente qui le garantit de la peste ordinaire [21] ».

On pourrait continuer longtemps cette anthologie burlesque ; bornons-nous pour en finir au principal, qui explique tout scientifiquement : « Ces gens n'ont vraiment pas le cerveau conformé comme nous ; leur évolution est différente de la nôtre, et tout ce qui vient d'eux est exceptionnel et bizarre [22]. »

Toutefois, si le racisme de cette seconde moitié du XIXe siècle se prévaut de la science — l'anthropologie, la biologie, la linguistique... —, l'œuvre de Drumont qui en diffuse les « découvertes » trempe aussi (mais est-ce bien contradictoirement ?) dans le climat fin de siècle où d'autres sciences, occultes celles-là, connaissent un regain d'éclat. « Entre 1885 et 1890 », écrit Victor-Émile Michelet, un initié, « deux mouvements d'esprit,

17. *La France juive, op. cit.*, t. 1, p. 9.
18. *Ibid.*, p. 34.
19. *Ibid.*, p. 104.
20. *Ibid.*, p. 103.
21. *Ibid.*, p. 104.
22. É. Drumont, *De l'or, de la boue, du sang,* 1896.

proches par les tendances sinon par leurs points d'appui, s'élancèrent pour bousculer les délétères croyances alors à la mode, soit le matérialisme scientifique, et son succédané, le naturalisme littéraire. Ces deux mouvements parallèles [étaient] le symbolisme et l'occultisme [23]. » C'est en 1884 qu'était publié *le Vice suprême,* premier roman du Sâr Péladan, qui fit sensation : « Il éclatait comme une bombe, nous dit Victor-Émile Michelet, au-dessus de la marécageuse littérature naturaliste d'alors, et répandit au-dehors les vapeurs exaltantes du monde occulte. » Comme le disait Papus, pseudonyme du Dr Encausse, dans son *Occultisme contemporain,* datant de 1887 : « la science ne repose sur aucun fondement véritable... ». Une autre science doit être retrouvée : la science du caché, réservée aux initiés. Au rationalisme qui est au pouvoir, il convient d'opposer une connaissance supérieure des choses ; à la physique, une méta-physique ; à la chimie, l'alchimie ; à la négation de Dieu, l'affirmation des correspondances entre l'homme et l'univers. Ce retour en force de l'occultisme est accompagné d'une ferveur publique pour tout ce qui a trait au spiritisme, au satanisme, à toutes ces pratiques étranges et sulfureuses, dont le roman de Huysmans, *Là-bas,* a superbement illustré la vogue.

Or Drumont, à ce sujet, garde une attitude ambiguë. D'un côté, il réprouve cette « sorcellerie », œuvre des cabalistes, des talmudistes, des Juifs par excellence qui, depuis des siècles, perpétuent « d'abominables mystères » dans leurs ghettos. D'un autre côté, il résiste mal à la fascination. S'il lui arrive de faire tourner les tables, c'est — nous dit-il — seulement « par hasard [24] ». En revanche, il déclare nettement : « J'avoue croire, dans une certaine mesure bien entendu, à cette chiromancie, que Dumas appelait " la grammaire des sociétés à venir " ; j'y crois non comme à la bonne aventure, mais comme à une science [25]. »

23. V.-É. Michelet, *Les Compagnons de la hiérophanie,* 1937, p. 31.
24. É. Drumont, *La Dernière Bataille,* 1890, p. 512.
25. Lettre à Jules Mery, citée par Byrnes, *Antisemitism in Modern France,* New Brunswick, Rutgers University Press, 1950.

Mais surtout il croit aux maléfices diaboliques : « Remarquez qu'il y a cent ans à peine que le Démon est affranchi de toute surveillance et déjà les suicides ont décuplé, les maisons de fous sont pleines, on ne parle que de la " grande névrose ". Tous les Jotums scandinaves, tous les Cabires de l'Afrique, tous les thaumaturges, tous les faiseurs de philtre, tous les trouble-cervelles de la Rome impériale ou d'Alexandrie sont déchaînés sur Paris [26]. » Or Drumont est lui-même un initiateur, un révélateur, celui qui, derrière la science sociale officielle, décrypte le Mal juif. « La vérité est que nous sommes enveloppés de mystère, que nous vivons dans le mystère [27] », dit-il ; du moins, lui, Drumont, peut-il percer celui de notre décadence. Il Sait. Il a trouvé l'explication. Il connaît le Secret.

Ce goût du secret, du caché, du souterrain — dont tout son antisémitisme est nourri —, Drumont le cultive aussi par la lecture des romans populaires. « J'ai toujours eu un faible, je ne le cache pas, pour ces individualités exceptionnellement organisées qui nous transportent dans un monde d'idées différentes de celui dans lequel nous vivons, qui parfois soulèvent le voile de l'avenir sur des horizons inattendus [28]. » Et il dit de manière plus explicite : « Figurez-vous ce que penseront nos fils en constatant que les aventures imaginaires de Rocambole ne sont rien à côté de ce que nous avons vu se passer réellement depuis que les Juifs sont les maîtres chez nous [29]. »

Drumont, à son insu, situait le niveau de sa littérature : dans cette catégorie du rocambolesque où Ponson du Terrail avait gagné son opulente notoriété. Ses livres ressortissent tous par quelque côté au roman-feuilleton, où les Juifs invariablement malfaisants tiennent les rôles de méchants, dont l'âme populaire dans les chaumières exige le châtiment.

26. *La Dernière Bataille, op. cit.,* p. 513.
27. *Ibid.,* p. 517.
28. *La Libre Parole,* 10 mai 1894.
29. *Ibid.,* 4 mai 1893, cité par Stéphane Khémis, *les Juifs selon Édouard Drumont,* Université de Paris-VIII, 1972 (mémoire de maîtrise).

L'antisémitisme comme doctrine.

Toutes ces influences éparses, voire contradictoires, prouvent que le terrain de l'antisémitisme comme doctrine politique était préparé ; les années qui précèdent *la France juive* devaient créer les conditions de sa naissance. D'un côté, le triomphe idéologique et politique des républicains renforce le public catholique dans sa conviction qu'il existe une alliance perverse entre Juifs, francs-maçons et républicains ; simultanément, le krach de la catholique Union générale, dont on rend la banque juive responsable, va échauffer l'antisémitisme « économique », dont la flamme pouvait être entretenue par les débuts d'une longue période de crise et de chômage... N'y avait-il pas là l'occasion de rassembler le peuple catholique et le peuple ouvrier sous une même bannière ? Ce que l'on voit s'ébaucher sous le boulangisme, cette esquisse de réconciliation, contre la République opportuniste, entre classes populaires et conservateurs catholiques, il appartenait à Drumont d'en fixer dans ses ouvrages le principe directeur pour l'avenir : c'était l'antisémitisme.

C'est Drumont qui, par la fonte de tous les éléments antijudaïques, judéophobes et antisémitiques, exprimés avant lui, a su élever le mythe juif à la hauteur d'une idéologie et d'une méthode politique. Son œuvre est « un carrefour dans l'histoire de l'antisémitisme, le point d'aboutissement de deux courants, le catholique et le socialiste » (Pierrard). De fait, sur des positions fondamentalement réactionnaires, débordant de sympathies monarchistes, Drumont tenta, sans doute avec plus de naïve sincérité que de machiavélisme, d'ébranler le régime républicain avec la complicité des troupes révolutionnaires socialistes. Cette alliance contre nature qu'il espérait avait alors apparemment quelque chance de réussite : l'antisémitisme devait justement la sceller. Drumont, de livre en livre, manifesta un sentimentalisme social, un « vague socialisme » de plus en plus accentué, sans abandonner pour autant son antisémitisme. Ainsi, après la fusillade qui avait eu lieu à Fourmies, lors de la manifestation du

1er mai 1891, il publia un ouvrage fracassant qui, pour ne pas infirmer la tradition de cette historiographie contre-révolutionnaire selon laquelle tout événement est le fruit d'une conspiration, porte le titre significatif : *le Secret de Fourmies*. Quel est donc ce « secret » de Fourmies ? C'est, révèle Drumont, que le préfet et les sous-préfets du département du Nord, que les responsables donc de la fusillade du 1er mai sont... vous l'aviez deviné ? des Juifs (voir encadré).

Tout aussi remarquable est la vision de la Commune de Paris qu'a peu à peu élaborée Drumont. Hostile à la révolution parisienne au long des soixante-douze jours de son existence, il se montre au fil de son œuvre de plus en plus « compréhensif » à l'égard des communards. Cette sympathie tardive a pour but d'utiliser le souvenir de la Commune, les couches populaires qui y sont attachées, contre la mauvaise République, celle qui, grâce aux francs-maçons, aux Juifs, aux opportunistes, s'est imposée contre le spectre de la République sociale autant que contre le sceptre de la monarchie restaurée. « A la prochaine Commune, écrit-il, comptez sur nous, m'ont dit des officiers traînés dans la boue par les journaux juifs pour avoir été à la messe. Nous ne toucherons plus à nos ouvriers, et, quand ils auront les mains noires de poudre, nous ne nous en apercevrons pas. Nous savons maintenant sur qui frapper et quels sont les vrais fauteurs des guerres civiles » *(la France juive devant l'opinion)*. On voit la fécondité d'une pareille entente cordiale entre l'armée française et le peuple révolutionnaire. L'ennemi à abattre leur est désormais commun : c'est la République juive, capitaliste et anticatholique. Dans *la Fin d'un monde,* il s'emploie à glorifier l'honnêteté des ouvriers communards ; s'il y a eu « férocité » dans les rangs de la Commune, elle est toute d'origine bourgeoise : « L'école des Frères où la plupart des ouvriers avaient été élevés, produisit moins d'instigateurs de tueries que l'Université. » On saisit le dessein d'une affirmation aussi piquante : le rêve de l'unité des catholiques et des ouvriers contre la République libre penseuse, juive et bourgeoise. Immanquablement, le lecteur a le droit

Un problème résolu : le secret de Fourmies.

Énoncé : Le 1er mai 1891, Fourmies, petite ville textile du Nord, est le théâtre d'un affrontement sanglant entre l'armée et les ouvriers grévistes. Bilan : dix morts et des dizaines de blessés. Parmi les victimes, la ville pleure un enfant de douze ans. Ce drame douloureux a nécessairement une raison cachée puisque, à Fourmies, tout le monde est gentil. « Une population de tisseurs et de fileurs [...] douce comme les moutons dont elle peigne et travaille la laine » ; « des rapports très cordiaux entre ouvriers et patrons » ; « un humble curé » à « l'âme héroïque », un « bon pasteur » veillant sur son troupeau, bref une petite ville de la chrétienté française, où l'on se chamaille bien de temps en temps, mais sans gravité. Comment expliquer que nos braves soldats aient pu tirer dans ce bon peuple ?

Solution : Des socialistes ont parlé de la responsabilité du maire, un négociant en laines, qui, poussé par les industriels — ses clients —, a fait appel à la troupe. Non ! Drumont a saisi tout de suite d'où venait le drame. Le 4 mai, il adresse ce télégramme au député Albert de Mun : « Le sous-préfet juif Isaac, fils d'un naturalisé de Crémieux, a fait essayer le Lebel sur des ouvriers français. Ceux qui vous aiment toujours espèrent que c'est vous qui prononcerez les paroles vengeresses pour flétrir l'assassin. Le préfet Vel-Durand est juif aussi, ils sont tous juifs là-dedans » (AN F7 12527, tél. intercepté).

Son siège étant fait, Drumont n'a plus qu'à partir faire... son enquête. Il en publie les résultats dans son livre, *le Secret de Fourmies,* en 1892. C'est bien une histoire juive. « Peut-être Isaac a-t-il voulu simplement célébrer à sa façon le centenaire de l'émancipation des Juifs en 1791 que certains journaux toute honte bue ont eu l'aplomb de rappeler comme une date glorieuse ? »

Conclusion morale et politique : « Le Juif, qui est devenu notre maître en faisant battre les Français entre eux, verra un jour tous les Français se réconcilier sur sa peau. » **CQFD.**

de connaître le « secret » de la Commune. Pourquoi tant de Français se sont-ils battus contre tant de Français ? Encore une fois, vous l'aviez deviné, c'est en raison du double jeu des banquiers juifs : « A Versailles, ils affichaient des sentiments d'indignation ; à Paris, ils subventionnaient l'insurrection afin de satisfaire leur haine contre les prêtres et, en même temps, de compliquer la situation politique pour se faire payer plus cher leur concours financier. »

On pourrait prendre d'autres exemples : comment Drumont parle de Jules Guesde, quelle sympathie il témoigne aux blanquistes, comment il va jusqu'à encenser le *Molochisme juif* de Tridon, dont la thèse anticatholique est aux antipodes de la sienne, justifier les attentats anarchistes... Telle est l'astucieuse nouveauté : ameuter contre l'œuvre de la Révolution française (personnalisée par le Juif) les forces populaires qui s'en réclament encore.

Dans cette entreprise, Drumont n'a pas toujours été compris des siens. Les conservateurs pressentis se sont bien vite effarouchés du caractère social que prenait son antisémitisme : son anticapitalisme juif risquait d'atteindre au rebond les bastions du capitalisme catholique. Ils surent finalement trouver leur compte à l'épouvantail sémitique, lors de l'affaire Dreyfus, tout en se riant des rêveries socialisantes de Drumont. « Ces milieux-là, en effet », dit M. Beau de Loménie des milieux d'affaires, « n'avaient eu que fort peu de goût pour l'antisémitisme de réformes économiques et sociales du Drumont des débuts, qui risquait de menacer dangereusement leurs privilèges. Mais ils étaient prêts maintenant à accueillir le nouvel antisémitisme orienté vers la lutte contre le sémitisme antimilitariste, anticlérical et marxisant. »

Que de nombreux conservateurs fussent séduits par « une thèse qui tendait à accuser de tous nos maux les Juifs seuls » n'est pour étonner qu'un naïf comme Drumont, ou comme son biographe. Telle est bien au contraire la véritable fonction politique de l'antisémitisme : dès lors qu'on désigne aux yeux des foules indigentes, aux petits commerçants et aux artisans victimes de l'évolution économique, aux ouvriers exploités et aux paysans contraints à l'exode rural, les Juifs responsables de tous leurs maux, on offre une arme inestimable à la conservation sociale qui, forte de son contrôle sur la presse, va orchestrer le développement du mythe à son propre usage. Les conflits de classes s'envolent : il ne reste plus qu'une minorité de profiteurs juifs écrasant l'immense majorité de leurs victimes aryennes et catholiques.

Mais si l'antisémitisme est, comme le disait Bebel, « le socialisme des imbéciles », il pouvait se révéler à l'occasion une excellente formule politique capable, de manière affective et irrationnelle, de concilier les contraires, de rapprocher les extrêmes opposés et de fanatiser les masses en vue de la conquête du pouvoir. Pour inconséquent qu'il fût, on peut tenir l'antisémitisme de Drumont comme la sincère tentative d'un bourgeois révolté par les effets sociaux de l'essor capitaliste pour rassembler le petit peuple et l'ancienne France contre le monde moderne [30]. Idéologiquement, on sait que cette entreprise ne fut pas sans lendemain : de Maurice Barrès à Drieu La Rochelle, les thèmes de la décadence unis à ceux du misonéisme eurent l'antisémitisme comme dénominateur commun. Mais, surtout, au-delà des sensibilités littéraires, Drumont avait mis au jour une méthode d'action. En établissant l'antisémitisme comme système d'explication universelle, il faisait du Juif le pôle négatif des mouvements nationalistes : c'est par rapport au Juif, c'est contre le Juif,

30. Sur la « sincérité » de Drumont, sur sa personnalité, on se reportera à l'article de Jean Bastaire, « Drumont et l'antisémitisme » (*Esprit,* mars 1964). Bastaire y a voulu « faire le point » sur le cas Drumont, se tenir « à égale distance de la louange et de l'invective ». Mon propos ici ne vise pas à la « compréhension » de l'homme Drumont, mais la place qu'il occupe dans l'histoire politique, non à ses intentions profondes (la « dénonciation implacable du règne de l'argent » selon Bastaire) mais aux effets de son œuvre. L'article de Jean Bastaire fournira donc au lecteur un utile contrepoint à cette chronique. Comme l'auteur le dit fort bien, chez Drumont l'on trouve conjointement « une indignation sincère » et « une analyse exécrable ».

que le nationaliste va définir son identité française ou allemande, fier qu'il sera d'appartenir à une communauté et de connaître clairement l'adversaire qui en menace l'unité et la vie. Comme le dit Maurras : « Tout paraît impossible, ou affreusement difficile, sans cette providence de l'antisémitisme. Par elle, tout s'arrange, s'aplanit et se simplifie. Si l'on n'était antisémite par volonté patriotique, *on le deviendrait par simple sentiment de l'opportunité* [31]. » C'est par le truchement de ce mythe protéiforme, l'antisémitisme, que l'on peut rêver, en effet, d'unir les forces populaires anticapitalistes aux capitalistes eux-mêmes ; les catholiques aux athées ; les petits commerçants aux actionnaires de monopoles ; les ouvriers aux patrons... S'il est abusif de faire de Drumont un prénazi, il n'est pas exagéré de dire, en revanche, que son expérience et ses idées ont été une des sources françaises du national-socialisme.

De la théorie à la pratique.

Le philosophe et historien allemand Ernst Nolte, dans sa grande étude sur le fascisme, a placé Drumont, aux côtés de La Tour du Pin et de Barrès [32], sous la bannière du « conservatisme radical », qui apparaît comme une des préfigurations de la démarche fasciste : « Dans les conditions politiques de la République, le conservatisme radical tend [...] à capter la force qui pousse le mouvement ouvrier en combattant lui-même avec énergie le monde bourgeois et en substituant, à l'image détestable du capitaliste, l'image détestable du Juif. Étant donné sa tendance, le conservatisme radical doit chercher à soulever les masses populaires, et il est antisémite. C'est précisément son

31. *L'Action française,* 28 mars 1911. Cité par C. Capitan, *Charles Maurras et l'idéologie d'Action française,* Éd. du Seuil, 1972.

32. Sur Maurice Barrès, voir Z. Sternhell, *Maurice Barrès et le nationalisme français, 1884-1902*, Colin, Fondation nationale des sciences politiques, 1972. On y lit ceci, entre autres : « Dans l'antisémitisme moderne Barrès découvre le moyen d'intégration par excellence du prolétariat dans la communauté nationale. »

radicalisme qui le rend plus moderne que les autres formes de conservatisme [33]. » Or, si Drumont, promoteur du mythe, n'a pas été homme d'action, il n'a pas manqué de disciples prêts à mettre en pratique les plus dynamiques de ses idées, notamment le singulier marquis de Morès, que son biographe américain, Robert F. Byrnes, a désigné comme le « premier national-socialiste [34] ».

Ce fringant cavalier, saint-cyrien démissionnaire, gendre d'un richissime Yankee, prompt à dilapider une bonne partie de la fortune de ses beaux-parents en multiples projets successifs (ranch dans le Dakota du Nord, coopérative à New York, chemin de fer au Tonkin), bagarreur éternel, infatigable batteur de fer, chasseur de tigre au Népal, découvre en 1888 dans *la France juive* l'explication de tous ses déboires : la main du Juif y a trempé. Au moment du boulangisme déclinant, il bat la campagne politique avec la même audace et la même imprévoyance qu'il avait manifestées dans l'élevage et le commerce des bovins. Du moins a-t-il une idée, celle de la fusion nécessaire entre le nationalisme et le socialisme, entre l'« ouvrier révolutionnaire » et le « conservateur chrétien ». Impatient, impétueux, Morès clame son avidité d'action : « La vie n'a de valeur que par l'action », et — ce que Drumont n'avait jamais conçu — ce marquis dévoyé qui s'était jadis acoquiné dans le Middle West avec les vagabonds et les voleurs de bétail décide de fonder, à l'indignation de sa respectable famille, une étonnante association, « Morès et ses amis », qu'on peut considérer comme une sorte de modèle, sur le mode mineur, des futures sections d'assaut : on trouve sous les ordres du preux chevalier, revêtus d'une chemise rouge de cow-boy et couverts d'un large sombrero, une bande hétéroclite d'antisémites, d'anarchistes, d'anciens boulangistes, de chô-

33. E. Nolte, *Le Fascisme dans son époque,* t. 1, *L'Action française,* Julliard, 1970.

34. R. F. Byrnes, « Morès, The First National Socialist », article paru dans *The Review of Politics,* 1950. Cet article est en fait un des chapitres du livre de R. F. Byrnes, *Antisemitism in Modern France, op. cit.*

meurs, d'hommes sans foi ni loi, auxquels s'adjoint le renfort de bouchers de La Villette séduits par le Mousquetaire depuis qu'il a fustigé une firme juive coupable d'avoir vendu de la viande avariée à l'armée... Avec sa troupe, il organise des coups de main qui visent à effrayer les financiers de la Bourse ; bat la grosse caisse dans les campagnes électorales ; claironne qu' « au temps de la Commune on a tué 35 000 hommes [et qu'] il suffira, cette fois, que l'on tue 200 ou 300 usuriers », serre publiquement Louise Michel sur son cœur ; en appelle à l'armée pour lui demander de se ranger du côté des ouvriers en chômage ; écope de trois mois de prison ferme pour ses provocations ; dès sa remise en liberté apporte son suffrage aux grévistes ; lâche ses troupes contre les manifestations juives ; rédige des programmes de félicité universelle en pillant Louis Blanc et Proudhon, tout en jurant fidèle respect à « la religion, la patrie, la famille et la propriété » ; dénonce bientôt au nom du « socialisme » les socialistes français, tous vendus à l'Allemagne, à l'Angleterre ou à la juiverie ; déclare bien haut que la nouvelle société aura pour base la paysannerie, la classe ouvrière et l'armée ; rêve d'une alliance avec les Arabes pour contrecarrer l'expansion anglaise ; bref, en tous lieux et à toute occasion, se déchaîne, jusqu'à ce qu'il commette l'erreur de s'en prendre à Clemenceau, accusé par lui d'être un « espion anglais » — ce qui déclenche, *primo,* une contre-attaque foudroyante du leader radical incriminant ce champion de l'antisémitisme d'être le débiteur de Juifs notoires ; *secundo,* une brouille avec Drumont ; *tertio,* son départ pour l'Algérie, à la fin de l'année 1893. Là, il tente d'intéresser des bailleurs de fonds à ses rêves de conquête, n'y parvient pas, monte alors étourdiment une expédition suicidaire vers le Sud, où il trouve la mort au cours d'un combat avec les Touaregs.

Lors de ses obsèques, le 19 juillet 1896, Drumont réconcilié prononce l'oraison funèbre, dans laquelle il dit notamment : « Il voulait que tous les enfants de cette Patrie redevenue grande fussent heureux, qu'ils aient le droit à la vie, qu'ils ne fussent pas condamnés à nourrir de leur travail une poignée d'exploiteurs, de parasites et de mercantis. Voilà pourquoi il a combattu la juiverie. [...] Il a rêvé comme Boulanger de rendre à lui-même le pays, qui se noie dans la boue parlementaire, de substituer l'activité saine de la vie à ce régime qui exhale une odeur de corruption et de décomposition et sous lequel la France étouffe [35]. »

On voit, d'après le résumé de cette vie de Morès, que ce qu'on a pris l'habitude d'appeler le « proto-fascisme » l'Allemagne n'en a pas été le théâtre exclusif. Nolte, à ce propos, s'il a tort de négliger quelque peu les racines proprement allemandes du national-socialisme, a raison en revanche de faire grief à Shirer *(le IIIe Reich)* de « considérer l'Allemagne isolément » et « le national-socialisme comme l'inévitable résultat de toute l'histoire de l'Allemagne [36] ». Norman Cohn, de son côté, nous montre que, à l'époque où un Morès achevait ses prouesses en France, dans la Russie de Nicolas II on voyait à l'œuvre les membres de ces Centuries noires, qui ne manquaient pas d'avenir non plus : tout aussi attachés que les disciples de Drumont au trône et à l'autel, ces « aventuriers politiques lancés dans l'agitation antisémite et le terrorisme [...] faisaient un large appel à la démagogie extrémiste [...], se servaient de criminels de droit commun pour perpétrer [dépassant en cela Morès] des assassinats et pour provoquer des pogromes [37]... ».

Une nouvelle droite est bien née à la fin du XIXe siècle, parallèlement à l'essor de l'industrie et du mouvement ouvrier, une extrême droite restée attachée aux thèmes réactionnaires fondamentaux, mais qui a tenté d'emprunter quelques-uns des mots d'ordre ou des caractères du socialisme montant, en les assimilant à l'antisémitisme, ce lieu géométrique introuvable des aspirations contradictoires et des classes antagonistes. La personnalité d'un Morès indique aussi l'importance du rôle que peuvent jouer certains individus déclassés, d'une vitalité aussi effrénée

35. É. Drumont, *Les Héros et les Pitres,* 1900.
36. E. Nolte, *op. cit.*
37. N. Cohn, *op. cit.*

que leur démagogie, habiles à se servir du mythe [38]. Marx disait, à propos de Napoléon III, « le neveu », que les événements et les personnages historiques surviennent pour ainsi dire deux fois, « la première fois comme tragédie, la seconde fois comme farce ». De Morès à Hitler, l'évolution fut inverse : la farce a précédé la tragédie [39].

38. Qu'on songe encore à cet autre aristocrate en dérogeance qu'était Henri Rochefort, matamore de l'opposition à la fin du second Empire, qui fut successivement communard, boulangiste, antisémite et antidreyfusard, et qui, lors de sa mort, en 1913, eut le talent posthume de réunir autour de sa dépouille des représentants de l'extrême gauche et de l'extrême droite. Un livre a été consacré à cet autre marquis : *le Prince des polémistes : Henri Rochefort,* par Roger L. Williams, Trévise, 1971. Hélas ! malgré les références à des sources sérieuses, c'est une étude bien plate qui ne nous apprend rien de vraiment neuf sur ce personnage qui fut plus souvent « pitre » que « héros ». Son antisémitisme, seulement évoqué, ne prête à aucun essai d'interprétation. De plus, l'auteur paraît bien peu familiarisé avec l'histoire du socialisme en France, voyant des « marxistes » partout, aussi bien en la personne de Lissagaray, ce qui est erroné, qu'en celle de Benoît Malon, ce qui est grotesque ; sur la Commune, il use d'un ton qu'on croyait banni de l'historiographie universitaire (ex. : les élus de la Commune sont « une bande [*sic*] de *vieux* [*sic*] révolutionnaires et de journalistes de gauche »), commet des erreurs flagrantes (faisant vivre par exemple le Comité central de la garde nationale plusieurs mois avant sa naissance, ne sachant pas orthographier le nom de Chaudey qu'il écrit à plusieurs reprises Chaundey...) ; sur la période suivante, il continue de plus belle : il confond la *Société* des droits de l'homme avec la *Ligue* du même nom, cite, à propos du boulangisme, maintes œuvres mineures, mais ignore la thèse de Jacques Néré qui est capitale ; fait de Barrès un adhérent de l'Action française, etc. Quant à la traduction, elle n'est ni plus ni moins scandaleuse. Le traducteur, ignorant catégoriquement les textes originaux en français, transpose de l'anglais des formules très célèbres, d'où résulte parfois la franche gaieté du lecteur. Tout le monde connaît, par exemple, le mot de Gaston Crémieux lancé à l'Assemblée de Bordeaux : « ruraux ! » ; tout le monde connaît l'Assemblée des « ruraux », sauf notre traducteur, lequel, d'une application zélée, nous donne du « péquenots », et répète le mot — avec guillemets s'il vous plaît, comme s'il n'inventait rien ! Le plus fort est qu'il cite la source française avec exactitude (Maurice Reclus) et qu'il ne s'est même pas donné la peine d'y aller voir.

39. Farce encore, mais point négligeable, que l'histoire de cet autre antisémite de foire qui s'appelle Jules Guérin. Ancien bras droit de Morès, authentique escroc, noceur prodigue, bravache aimant faire tâter ses biceps par ses hommes de main — « Morès et Matamorès », comme on disait

L'antisémitisme moderne est un phénomène complexe, dont les nombreuses causes, religieuses, économiques, sociales, psychologiques, sont difficiles à hiérarchiser. Notre propos était seulement, ici, de montrer une des fonctions politiques du mythe juif, qui apparaît comme le principe fédérateur de forces diverses, voire contradictoires, mises au service de la contre-révolution. Drumont, Morès et leurs successeurs n'ont cependant pas réussi dans leur dessein. La fin du XIXe siècle semblait pourtant devoir favoriser l'entreprise : les milieux socialistes et les classes populaires étaient loin d'être débarrassés de leur antisémitisme « économique », comme l'attestent, par exemple, les écrits d'un Lafargue [40] ou les exemplaires de *la Revue socialiste* des années 1885-1890 ; le parti monarchiste divisé et vaincu ne savait plus à quel saint se vouer ; de plus, à partir de 1882, la crise économique qui atteint la France provoque une longue période de difficultés sociales… Arme universelle, l'antisémitisme visait la République (juive par origine et par nature), la défense du catholicisme (attaqué par la franc-maçonnerie juive), la défense du peuple

plaisamment —, il rencontra une éphémère popularité grâce à l'épisode tragi-comique du « Fort Chabrol », hôtel particulier où il resta barricadé avec ses troupes six semaines durant, en 1899. Délégué général de la Ligue antisémitique (devenue Grand Occident de France), il publie *l'Antijuif* et s'attire une clientèle populaire, à laquelle il prêche le coup d'État : « Si le coup d'État, dont on parle, s'accomplissait et si un homme honnête, énergique et bon Français, osait balayer l'ordure juive qui souille la France, pour réaliser le programme républicain, que des républicains ont oublié depuis plus de vingt ans, il est bien possible que la France tout entière soit du côté de cet homme-là » (*l'Antijuif,* 20 janvier 1899). Il avait su se faire subventionner par le duc d'Orléans, promettant au prétendant de rallier à sa cause des associations ouvrières et des syndicats. Son affaire se termine piteusement par une condamnation à la prison puis au bannissement, ternie par une guerre intestine féroce entre guérinistes et drumontistes. L'antisémitisme d'action s'achevait en France dans le ridicule ; au demeurant, les « brigades de marche » de Guérin, qui avait réemployé des bouchers de la Villette à l'âme nationaliste, en annonçaient d'autres. Pour plus de détails, on verra Z. Sternhell, *la Droite révolutionnaire,* Éd. du Seuil, 1978.

40. Voir C. Willard, *les Guesdistes* (Éditions sociales, 1966), qui montre les ambiguïtés des rapports qu'ont entretenus les guesdistes avec l'antisémitisme. Signalons aussi au passage la récente présentation de *Paul Lafargue. Textes choisis,* par Jacques Girault, Éditions sociales, 1970.

contre le capitalisme (usuriers juifs, Banque juive). Mais l'affaire Dreyfus paraît, en France, décisive : tandis que l'antisémitisme achève de se fixer à droite, le mouvement socialiste semble nettoyé de ses dernières séquelles antijuives. L'Action française ne fut jamais, malgré qu'elle en eût, un mouvement populaire ; dans les années 1936-1944, c'est Drieu La Rochelle et Doriot qui paraissent avoir repris la leçon de Drumont, mais sans plus de succès que leur maître. Le régime républicain, qui s'était imposé et consolidé par un combat continu avec les forces contre-révolutionnaires, semble avoir sécrété des contrepoisons efficaces. Mais il convient d'observer que, si le mouvement ouvrier et socialiste international a su dénoncer les pièges de l'antisémitisme dans les rangs de la classe ouvrière, les autres fractions des couches populaires ne furent pas aussi bien immunisées. Sans véritables organisations de classe, sans idéologie propre, les « classes moyennes », menacées par l'évolution économique et la concentration capitaliste — petits patrons, petits commerçants, rentiers ruinés par l'effondrement des monnaies, etc. —, purent trouver dans l'antisémitisme cette nostalgie d'un âge d'or détruit par l'« invasion juive ».

Il serait dangereux de croire qu'aujourd'hui en France l'antisémitisme est mort. Certes, les effets de la décolonisation, et particulièrement la guerre d'Algérie, le conflit israélo-arabe ont brouillé les cartes : l'extrême droite française, dans son ensemble, découvrant que les Juifs, à l'occasion, peuvent être aussi de bons défenseurs de « l'Occident », a mis en veilleuse sa passion antisémitique. Mais si l'extrême droite prend désormais ses précautions avec les Juifs, le lecteur attentif de ses feuilles hebdomadaires sait bien que ce « philosémitisme » est tout d'opportunité et que le vieux mythe est toujours prêt à renaître de ses cendres chaudes. Par ailleurs, on a vu le conflit du Proche-Orient redonner vie à un certain antisémitisme de gauche dont n'est pas toujours exempt l' « antisionisme [41] ». De l'exis-

41. Voir plus loin, « La gauche et les Juifs ».

D'une pierre deux coups : Drumont propose de régler conjointement la question juive et la question sociale.

« Sur qui pèse le plus durement le régime actuel ? Sur l'ouvrier révolutionnaire et sur le conservateur chrétien. L'un est atteint dans ses intérêts vitaux ; l'autre est blessé dans ses croyances les plus chères.

Pour l'ouvrier, la Révolution sociale est une nécessité absolue... Je suis convaincu, pour ma part, qu'ils ne réussiront pas ; ils mettront très facilement la main sur Paris, mais ils ne pourront se saisir de la France...

Ce but, que poursuivent les ouvriers, et qu'ils n'ont pas tort de poursuivre à leur point de vue, ne pourrait-il pas être atteint pacifiquement ? Pourquoi un prince chrétien, un chef aux conceptions fermes et larges qui, au lieu de voir les questions des lieux communs, les regarderait en face, ne confisquerait-il pas les biens des Juifs ? » (*la France juive, op. cit.,* t. 1, p. 517 *sq.*)

Drumont fixe à cinq milliards le montant de ce capital juif à confisquer. Se présentant aux élections municipales de Paris en 1890, dans le quartier du Gros-Caillou, dans le VIIe arrondissement, il déclare dans sa profession de foi :

« Avec cinq milliards, demain, nous nous chargeons de résoudre la question sociale, sans secousse, sans violence. »

La majorité des votants resta sceptique. Pour se venger de son échec, Drumont rédigea incontinent son *Testament d'un antisémite,* où il dit : « Les conservateurs n'ont pas eu le courage de s'unir à nous pour essayer de reconstituer la société française sur les bases de la justice ; ils ont préféré associer leur cause à celle de la Juiverie moribonde ; ils s'effondreront avec elle. »

L'idée, pourtant, comme on sait, avait de l'avenir.

tence et de l'évolution d'un État israélien, l'antisémitisme de droite lui aussi peut tirer de nouveaux prétextes — comme le prouvent les commentaires cités plus haut de M. Beau de Loménie. Il n'est donc pas superflu d'évoquer la vigilance nécessaire : l'antisémitisme n'est pas seulement une monstruosité morale et une ineptie intellectuelle ; instrument des politiques réactionnaires, il est, par-dessus les notions de droite et de gauche, en résumant tous les racismes, la négation de la société pluraliste, l'exaltation imbécile du moi national et finalement un des levains de la barbarie totalitaire.

3

Jeanne d'Arc et les Juifs

Jeanne d'Arc n'a pas quitté l'histoire sur le bûcher de Rouen. Comme quelques-unes des grandes figures de notre passé national, elle survit au long des siècles non seulement grâce aux poètes et aux historiens mais encore, et peut-être surtout, parce que le sujet historique qu'elle était est devenu un objet symbolique, un enjeu dans la guerre partisane que se livrent les idéologues français, tout particulièrement depuis la fin du XIXe siècle.

Le titre de ce chapitre peut surprendre : qu'y a-t-il de commun à l'histoire de Jeanne et à l'histoire des Juifs français ? Tout simplement la place de choix, le tout premier rôle, que nos antisémites ont réservé par prédilection à la « Bonne Lorraine ». Celle-ci, vouée au culte patriotique par les républicains modérés, désireux d'utiliser l'image de Jeanne comme un instrument de consensus dans un pays profondément divisé, a été captée finalement — au moins en partie — par cette lignée de journalistes et d'écrivains qui se sont employés à diffuser le mythe du Juif en France ou plus tard à y naturaliser les délires nazis. Jeanne et les Juifs ? Disons plutôt : Jeanne contre les Juifs.

L'exaltation de Jeanne d'Arc comme héroïne nationale est d'abord plutôt de gauche comme en témoigne l'œuvre de Michelet. La défaite de 1871 consommée et l'échec confirmé des tentatives de restauration monarchique, c'est un député républicain, Joseph Fabre, qui, en 1884, défend l'idée d'une fête nationale consacrée à Jeanne. Fabre, devenu sénateur, récidive dix ans plus tard devant l'assemblée du Luxembourg, qui approuve son projet. La conjoncture est particulière : les républicains modérés viennent de gagner les législatives de 1893 mais l'extrême gauche devient inquiétante. Plus encore que les émotions provoquées par les attentats anarchistes, l'arrivée massive d'une cinquantaine d'élus socialistes au Palais-Bourbon donne à penser. Or voici que, menacés sur leur gauche, les modérés peuvent espérer un renfort décisif sur leur droite grâce à l'attitude politique du pape Léon XIII, qui a préconisé aux catholiques français leur « ralliement » au régime républicain. Dès lors, la fête nationale en l'honneur de Jeanne d'Arc, dont Fabre s'est fait l'inusable propagandiste, apparaît comme un de ces ferments de l'unité nationale, dont les extrémistes de gauche et de droite doivent faire les frais. Le président du Conseil, Charles Dupuy, soutient le projet de Fabre à la Chambre, le 8 juin 1894 : « Il n'y aura, dit-il, qu'une chose nous dominant tous : le patriotisme sous le nom de Jeanne d'Arc. » La fête nationale du 14 juillet répugnant encore aux catholiques, en raison de son estampille révolutionnaire, une fête nationale, complémentaire, offerte à Jeanne d'Arc, pouvait sceller, dans l'univers affectif des symboles, la réconciliation des centres (gauche et droit) dans la République des honnêtes gens. Jeanne la chrétienne ayant eu le bon goût d'être condamnée par un homme d'Église, elle pouvait plaire également aux cléricaux et aux anticléricaux, chacun y reconnaîtrait la sienne. Les Juifs ne manqueraient pas à cette unanimité : ne comparaient-ils pas Jeanne à Déborah, à la reine Esther ou à Judith ? Voilà ce qu'on avait entendu, en 1890, à la synagogue de Nancy, lors d'une cérémonie en l'honneur de Jeanne d'Arc, dont une statue avait été offerte à la municipalité par un certain Osiris. Alphonse de Rothschild fit un présent semblable, deux ans plus tard, au musée de Cluny [1].

1. Voir M.R. Marrus, *les Juifs de France à l'époque de l'affaire Dreyfus*, Calmann-Lévy, coll. « Diaspora », 1972, p. 142-143.

Las ! le zèle clérical, aiguillonné par l'extrême droite, le disputa en tapage au zèle anticlérical, excité par l'extrême gauche, de sorte que l'estimable projet centriste de fraternisation derrière l'étendard de la Pucelle échoua sous les feux croisés de la loge et de la chapelle. « Est-ce que l'on va continuer de se battre autour de la statue de Jeanne d'Arc, à coups de couronnes et d'emblèmes ? », demandait l'éditorialiste du *Jour* (1er juin 1894). De fait, celle que l'Église venait de déclarer Vénérable (décision de la Sacrée-Congrégation des Rites de janvier 1894) n'était plus pour la gauche qu'un agent idéologique au service des prêtres et des réactionnaires [2].

L'anniversaire de la mort de Jeanne d'Arc n'ayant pas été voté par les deux assemblées comme fête nationale, la droite cléricale et nationaliste s'en empare. Chaque mois de mai devient une occasion d'affrontement entre nationalistes et républicains libres penseurs. Très vite, les manifestants d'extrême droite qui se pressent devant la statue de l'héroïne, place des Pyramides, associent dans leur enthousiasme la ferveur pour Jeanne d'Arc et la haine des Juifs. Les antisémites parisiens ont ainsi trouvé un lieu saisonnier de pèlerinage. La presse et les rapports de police relatent les échauffourées annuelles. Le slogan « Mort aux Juifs ! » se confond avec les « Vive Jeanne d'Arc ! » ; les manifestants de droite ne se contentent pas de le scander : munis de timbres de caoutchouc, ils l'impriment sur les murs, y compris « sur les parois des chalets de nécessité » (*l'Événement,* 19 mai 1896).

L'affaire Dreyfus achève de structurer le nationalisme français autour du mythe « Juif ». Les cérémonies de mai 1898 en faveur de Jeanne portent au plus haut point la complémentarité des deux cris : « Vive Jeanne d'Arc ! », « A bas les Juifs ! » A Alger, Édouard Drumont est élu député le 8 mai. Le lendemain *la Croix* d'Alger écrit : « Le 8 mai, fête de Jeanne d'Arc, la libératrice de

2. Sur tout cet épisode, voir Rosemonde Sanson, « La fête de Jeanne d'Arc en 1894. Controverse et célébration », *Revue d'histoire moderne et contemporaine,* XX, juill.-septembre 1973.

la France, le soleil s'est levé radieux dans un ciel d'azur, nos âmes ont tressailli d'un noble enthousiasme, comme au matin d'une bataille où l'on va défendre, contre la souillure étrangère et cosmopolite, les trois couleurs de notre drapeau. Etc. » (signé « Le Croisé »). Par un processus d'identification, les antidreyfusards font de la haute figure de Jeanne un archétype du nationalisme français, l'antipode de Dreyfus. La libératrice du territoire et le traître juif s'apparient désormais comme deux pièces antagoniques d'un même système.

L'affaire Thalamas, en 1904, offre un nouvel exemple de fusion entre les deux mythes — celui, positif, de Jeanne et celui, négatif, du Juif. Les suites de l'affaire Dreyfus ont conduit au pouvoir Émile Combes. La droite nationaliste se déchaîne contre le général André, le ministre des « fiches ». Au mois de mai, les fêtes de Jeanne d'Arc ont donné lieu à de nouveaux incidents. Laurent Tailhade, dans *l'Action,* a traité Jeanne d'Arc d'« idiote ». Le détournement de l'héroïne par les nationalistes a provoqué en effet les injures des anticléricaux contre la « Pucelle clérico-militaire », contre la « Mascotte militaire », contre « l'Idole clérico-laïque dangereuse à toute pensée libre » (*l'Action,* 23 avril 1904). La localisation du symbole à droite et à l'extrême droite explique l'affaire Thalamas qui éclate en novembre. Mince affaire, à l'origine, d'un professeur de seconde du lycée Condorcet, pris à partie par ses élèves pour avoir douté du caractère sacré de la vierge lorraine. Mais l'incident est savamment exploité par les nationalistes jusqu'à faire l'objet d'une discussion à la Chambre des députés, le 1er décembre 1904. Occasion de quelques échanges colorés entre la gauche et la droite, au cours desquels Jaurès notamment est accusé de proférer « des paroles d'Anglais ».

Nationalistes et antisémites ont trouvé une noble cause à défendre contre un régime qui a livré « le pays aux Juifs et aux francs-maçons » (*la Libre Parole,* 25 novembre 1904). Le 29 novembre, Drumont, y allant de ses objurgations courantes, déclare : « Ils sont toute une bande dans les établissements d'enseignement, dans les sociétés savantes, dans les revues, dans les académies, tous Juifs, protestants, francs-maçons, qui se sont fait, mutuellement, la courte échelle et qui ont réussi à faire croire qu'ils avaient régénéré, transformé, rénové la Littérature, l'Histoire et la Science. »

Les jours suivants, *la Libre Parole* brode sur la liaison complice du régime en place avec les francs-maçons et les Juifs. La relation : Thalamas = franc-maçon = Anglais = Juif, inspire, par exemple, un article de Gaston Méry, « De Cauchon à Thalamas » (2 décembre 1904). Le 5 décembre, lors d'un meeting, François Coppée est applaudi avec frénésie et salué par le cri : « A bas les Juifs ! » Le journal de Drumont fait ce commentaire : « C'est comme un signal, toute la salle répète ce cri, véritable signe de ralliement. » Sur ces entrefaites, on apprend la mort de Gabriel Syveton, celui qui avait osé gifler le général André, le ministre de Combes. Lors de ses funérailles, les nationalistes entonnent : « Vive Jeanne d'Arc ! » et « A bas Thalamas ! » Enfin, le 15 décembre, a lieu la grande réunion que tiennent, salle des Horticulteurs, les différents chefs du nationalisme français « contre les insulteurs de Jeanne d'Arc ». Plus que Thalamas, c'est Dreyfus qui est traîné au banc d'infamie. Un message de Drumont lu à la tribune soulève, à propos de Jeanne d'Arc, les cris rituels : « Vive Drumont ! A bas les Juifs ! »

Cette association entre la religion de Jeanne et l'antisémitisme ne prend pas fin avec la Grande Guerre et l'Union sacrée. La victoire du Front populaire et la fin des années trente vont mêler de nouveau ces cris d'amour et de haine dans les publications et dans les rangs d'un nationalisme français, attiré de plus en plus par l'exemple fasciste. De Dreyfus, on était passé à Blum. Que le chef du Front populaire fût juif, il n'en fallait pas plus pour que l'extrême droite y vît la source des malheurs nationaux. Tout est prétexte, par exemple, à *Je suis partout* pour faire un mauvais parti au leader socialiste. Le 15 mai 1937, Jean-Jacques Brousson doit y reconnaître que « M. Léon Blum n'a pas osé supprimer la fête nationale de Jeanne d'Arc » — ce qui ne l'empêche pas d'affirmer : « Visiblement la sainte de la patrie n'est pas en odeur chez les fanatiques de la Pasionaria. Une vierge qui croit à Dieu et à la patrie ! Ah ! s'il y avait eu une manifestation en faveur de cette Judith qui se glissa dans la tente d'Holopherne, et lui trancha gentiment le col ! Mais une héroïne qui offre la paix avant la bataille... »

Comme le constatait avec jubilation Rebatet, dans le même journal, le 1er avril 1938 : « L'antisémitisme renaît en France avec une singulière vigueur. » Il appartint au régime de Vichy de le rendre légal. Le culte Jeanne d'Arc fut simultanément des rites ordinaires du régime pétainiste. Jamais peut-être notre sainte nationale ne fut si bien traitée qu'au temps où les Juifs étaient persécutés au nom de la loi. Car par un paradoxe singulier, le régime de « la Grande Culbute », comme l'appelait Bernanos, s'ingénia à faire de l'épopée de Jeanne l'allégorie de sa légitimité. L'imposture s'achevait en point d'orgue : le symbole de la Résistance était l'objet du plus inique des détournements par le régime de la Capitulation : « Si les moyens diffèrent, avec Pétain comme avec Jeanne, le combat reste identique [3]. »

Ceux qui, abusant du nom de Jeanne d'Arc, avaient décrété le statut des Juifs mettaient un point final à cette singulière entreprise de récupération. La France libre et la Résistance intérieure trouvèrent des raisons plus fondées d'exproprier les antisémites de la Bergère héroïque.

L'Anti-Juive.

En un demi-siècle, cette Jeanne d'Arc des nationalistes antisémites s'est donc imposée dans leurs écrits comme un mythe d'identification, opposable au mythe juif de répulsion. Les qualités, les attributs et les emblèmes de Jeanne sont, en effet, exactement inverses de ceux que l'antisémite réserve aux Juifs. Jeanne incarne la francité, la quintessence de la civilisation

3. Brochure anonyme, *Jeanne d'Arc, sa mission, son exemple,* Paris, 1942.

française, son point de sublimation, là où le Juif, quels que soient ses avatars historiques — Dreyfus ou Blum —, cristallise les éléments de rejet sous la figure inquiétante de l'Autre, de l'Étranger introduit dans le cercle de famille dont il va s'acharner à la destruction. Il suffit d'indiquer sous la forme d'un bref échantillonnage quelques correspondances entre les deux mythes pour prendre la mesure de leur complémentarité.

LE MYTHE JEANNE D'ARC	LE MYTHE JUIF
1. La Terre, les racines	**1. L'Errance, la ville**
• *La paysanne*	• *Le nomade*
« C'est une *terrienne,* fille de laboureurs... Elle est élevée en paysanne, en bonne paysanne de France, vigoureuse, de sens solide et d'humeur gaie [5]. »	« Ils [les Juifs] sont spéculateurs, usuriers, brocanteurs, syndics de faillite, ergoteurs, politiques [4]... » « C'est une race de nomades et de bédouins [6]. »
• *Le travail, l'effort*	• *La spéculation, le capitalisme*
« Non. Jeanne n'appartient pas aux capitalistes internationaux. » Jeanne appartient au nationalisme français dans ce qu'il a de plus réaliste, de plus profond et de plus attaché à la	« Les immenses fortunes juives ne sont le fruit d'aucun labeur effectif, d'aucune production [7]. » « C'est lui [le Juif] qui a donné à la féodalité internationale du capitalisme sa forme la plus

4. J.-J. Brousson, « Rétablissez l'Édit de Nantes en faveur des chrétiens », *Je suis partout,* 20 novembre 1937.
5. H. de Sarrau, *La Leçon de Jeanne d'Arc,* 1941.
6. É. Drumont, *La France juive, op. cit.,* t. 2, p. 16.
7. *Ibid.,* t. 1, p. 2.

terre. Au petit peuple des villages, à ses fêtes, à ses fées, à ses travaux [...].

» Jeanne n'appartient pas à l'argent, aux idéologues, aux faux défenseurs d'une civilisation pourrie, puisqu'elle appartient à la jeunesse éternelle et à la vivacité créatrice [9]. »

« Jeanne était une fille du vrai peuple travailleur [10]. »

inhumaine et la plus tentaculaire [8]. »

• *La vie saine et naturelle*

« Elle fut amenée à partager les simples et fortes émotions de cette vie des champs. [...]

» Un milieu populaire sain à l'âme et au corps [12]. »

« Elle a aimé les choses naturelles d'une passion qu'on ne retrouvera pas, jusqu'à Jean-Jacques [14]. »

• *Un monde morbide*

« Ils [les Juifs] se plaisent dans les détritus et les lamentations, comme Job sur son fumier [11]. »

« Il [le Juif] est sujet à toutes les maladies qui indiquent la corruption du sang [13]. »

• *Le peuple*

« C'était une enfant du peuple [15]. »

« Si comme elle le déclarait...,

• *Les intellectuels*

« La plus frivole des Juives

8. L. Rebatet, « Le fait juif », *Je suis partout,* 14 janvier 1944.
9. R. Brasillach, « Devant l'avenir », *Je suis partout,* 12 mai 1941.
10. G. Valois, *Le Fascisme,* 1927, p. 82.
11. J.-J. Brousson, *loc. cit.*
12. Abbé J. Ygouf, *Panégyrique de Jeanne d'Arc,* 21 mai 1905.
13. É. Drumont, *La France juive, op. cit.*, t. 1, p. 104.
14. J.-J. Brousson, « La fête nationale de Jeanne d'Arc, de Voltaire à Léon Blum », *Je suis partout,* 15 mai 1937.
15. Abbé J. Ygouf, *loc. cit.*

elle ne savait " ni A ni B ", elle était par contre animée de cette foi ardente, de cette foi agissante qui soulève les montagnes [17]. »

vous jette à la figure la Bourse et la Sorbonne [16]. »

---

2. La Patrie

● *L'unité nationale*

« Suivant la forte expression du maréchal, Jeanne d'Arc est [...] l'héroïne de l'unité nationale [18]. »

2. L'Anti-France

● *L'agent de la décomposition*

« Le Juif, qui est l'être antisocial par excellence, ne peut être qu'un dissolvant ; il a recommencé son éternel rôle de destructeur ; il a mis le feu à la nouvelle Patrie qu'on lui avait faite, comme il avait mis le feu à Jérusalem [19]. »

« Tout Juif est de nécessité un traître pour le pays où il a dressé sa tente de nomade [20]. »

« Israël trahit forcément comme le bœuf rumine et comme l'éléphant a une trompe [21]. »

16. P. Drieu La Rochelle, *Gilles,* Le Livre de poche, 1962.
17. H. de Sarrau, *loc. cit.*
18. *Ibid.*
19. É. Drumont, *La Libre parole,* 7 mars 1893, et préface à Octave Tauxier, *De l'inaptitude des Français à concevoir la question juive,* Paris, 1900.
20. J. Soury, *Campagne nationaliste 1899-1901,* cité par *l'Action française,* 1er janvier 1904.
21. L. Daudet, *L'Action française,* 6 mars 1908.

• *La servante de la royauté*

(Par définition.)

• *Le profiteur de la Révolution*

« Le Juif a confisqué la Révolution à son profit, il en a été le seul bénéficiaire [22]. »

• *Contre les Anglais*

« On comprend que les partisans d'un Juif qui rêvait de livrer la France à l'étranger [Dreyfus] aient gardé rancune à la jeune et touchante créature qui nous a délivrés du joug de l'Angleterre [23]. »

• *Juifs-Anglais*

« Vous savez de quel nom nous appelons l'Ennemi qui a remplacé chez nous l'Anglais envahisseur du XVe siècle et qui essaie de nous asservir par la puissance corruptrice de l'or, comme l'Angleterre voulait nous asservir par la force brutale du fer. Cet Ennemi s'appelle pour nous le Juif et le franc-maçon [24]. »

« Les Anglais plus encore peut-être qu'au XVe siècle veulent la destruction de la France en tant que nation unie, grande et libre [25]. »

---

3. La Spiritualité

• *La sainte catholique*

« La figure de Jeanne d'Arc apparaît comme un point noir

3. Le Matérialisme

• *Le déicide*

« Le Juif fit mourir le Rédempteur et depuis le jour où ce

22. É. Drumont, préface citée.
23. H. Rochefort, « La non-pucelle d'Orléans », *L'Intransigeant,* 27 novembre 1904.
24. É. Drumont, lettre citée par *l'Action française,* 15 décembre 1904.
25. Dorsay, « Toute la France derrière Pétain contre l'Anglais », *Je suis partout,* 13 mai 1944.

dans l'azur immaculé du matérialisme triomphant [26]. »

forfait fut consommé, le peuple déicide, sur qui pèse la malédiction du ciel, est dispersé sur la terre, odieux à tous, maudit de tous [27]... »

• *Le surnaturel*

« Le cauchemar du rationalisme et de la libre pensée [28]. »

• *L'utilitarisme*

« Le sémite est mercantile [...] ne voyant guère rien au-delà de la vie présente [29]. »

• *La virginité*

« Messieurs, avez-vous observé ceci : que de toutes les héroïnes qui ont paru sous l'Ancien Testament, aucune n'était vierge. Déborah était la femme de Lapidoth... Judith était veuve. Esther avait remplacé Vasthi auprès d'Assuérus...

» Quelle supériorité dans Jeanne d'Arc !

» Elle est vierge, et cette fois l'amour de la patrie n'est plus contraint de se faire aider des artifices d'un amour inférieur [31]. »

• *La prostitution*

« Ce sont les Juives qui fournissent le plus fort contingent à la prostitution des grandes capitales [30]. »

26. É. Schuré, *L'Ame celtique et le Génie de la France,* 1921.
27. P. Bellet, « L'invasion juive », *Revue du monde catholique,* t. IX, 1er janvier 1887.
28. J.-B. Ayroles, *M. Thalamas contre Jeanne d'Arc,* 1905 (à propos du procès de réhabilitation).
29. É. Drumont, *La France juive, op. cit.,* t. 1, p. 9.
30. *Ibid.,* p. 90.
31. Abbé J. Lémann, *Jeanne d'Arc et les héroïnes juives,* 1873.

4. La race supérieure

« Le premier jet du sang gaulois [32]. »

« On supplie les Français de ne pas faire du plus haut symbole de leur race une bien-pensante héroïne de patronage [34]. »

« C'est une Celte que Jeanne d'Arc, qui sauva la Patrie [35]. »

« Elle a su communiquer son ardeur guerrière aux meilleurs soldats de son époque [38]. »

« Encore Jeanne seule a-t-elle ce clair génie inimitable, qui est celui de sa race, la beauté naïve [39]... »

4. La race inférieure

« Je suis le premier à reconnaître que la race sémitique, comparée à la race indo-européenne, représente une combinaison inférieure de la nature humaine [33]. »

« Ce n'est que depuis quelques années que l'on s'aperçoit que le Juif est un être très particulier, organisé d'une façon distincte de la nôtre, fonctionnant tout à fait en dehors de notre fonctionnement à nous, ayant des aptitudes, des conceptions, un cerveau qui le différencient absolument de nous [36]. »

« ... Sans aucun courage militaire [37]. »

« Après des siècles, les Juifs portent sur leur figure les stigmates de l'infamie de leur sang [40]... »

32. Agathon, « Béatification de Jeanne d'Arc », *La Revue,* 15 avril 1894.

33. E. Renan, *Histoire générale et système comparé des langues sémitiques,* 4e éd., p. 4, repris par J. Soury et M. Barrès, voir Z. Sternhell, *Maurice Barrès et le nationalisme français, op. cit.*

34. R. Brasillach, « Pour une méditation sur la raison de Jeanne d'Arc », *Je suis partout,* 13 mai 1938.

35. É. Drumont, *La France juive, op. cit.,* t. 1, p. 427.

36. É. Drumont, *La Libre Parole,* 2 août 1893.

37. L. Rebatet, *loc. cit.*

38. H. Rochefort, *loc. cit.*

39. R. Brasillach, *loc. cit.*

40. R. Bergot, *L'Algérie telle qu'elle est,* 1890, cité par J. Verdès-Leroux, *op. cit.*

Cet antagonisme *essentiel* entre Jeanne d'Arc et les Juifs devait inspirer une hypothèse audacieuse mais qui ne manque pas de lien logique avec ce qui précède. Un harangueur de droite, M. de Kérohant, la formula en 1894, au moment où les républicains modérés, nous l'avons vu, tentaient de faire de Jeanne un symbole réconciliateur. Il s'agit de l'évêque Cauchon. De l'encombrante mémoire de l'évêque Cauchon. Vous ne voyez pas ? Bon sang ! mais c'est, bien sûr ! Il aurait été... Juif [41] !

41. Agathon, *loc. cit.*

4

La gauche et les Juifs

La Dépêche de Toulouse est un journal républicain, un quotidien de gauche. En 1895, Jaurès y donne des articles toutes les semaines. Au mois de décembre précédent, l'ex-capitaine Dreyfus a été condamné à la déportation, pour fait d'espionnage. Ce n'est pas encore une affaire ; ce n'est pas encore « l'Affaire » ! A la date du 13 mars, le regard est attiré par la déclaration d'un député radical-socialiste de la Dordogne, Raymond Gendre, qui s'exprime sur « les Juifs ». Tiens donc ! les députés de la gauche sont ainsi tenus de donner leur « avis » sur les Juifs, en ce temps-là ? Mais l'étonnement redouble quand on lit sous la signature de l'honorable parlementaire : « J'estime que la juiverie politique et financière qui nous ronge est la plus grande plaie sociale du jour. » Qui est ce Gendre-là ? Le *Dictionnaire des parlementaires* signale que Gendre a bien été élu à Sarlat contre un candidat conservateur ; il se réclame de « l'idéal républicain ». Précisément, dans sa lutte « pour une République honnête, économe et populaire », il dénonce la collusion au pouvoir de l'opportunisme (le centre gauche) et de « la juiverie ». Quel est le commentaire de *la Dépêche ?* Aucun. Pas un mot d'objection.

Le rejet de l'antisémitisme par les hommes de gauche n'a donc pas toujours été une évidence, un impératif catégorique. Les préjugés « de race » n'ont pas seulement été le monopole de la droite ou de l'extrême droite. Mais on ne peut s'en tenir à cette constatation générale qui ramènerait l'antisémitisme au parterre des lieux communs. Il s'agit de savoir plus précisément quels ont été, depuis 1789 — c'est-à-dire depuis que la gauche existe —, les rapports de celle-ci avec la communauté juive en France. C'est en prenant la mesure de cette longue durée qu'on y verra peut-être plus clair.

Si l'on prend d'abord une grosse lunette pour balayer prestement quelque deux siècles d'histoire française, trois reliefs successifs émergent comme autant de moments de solidarité entre la gauche et les Juifs : la Révolution, l'affaire Dreyfus et la lutte antihitlérienne. Au cours de ces trois « crises » de nature différente, la gauche, en affirmant et en développant ses idéaux, a été amenée à trancher dans ce qu'il a été assez tôt convenu d'appeler la « question juive ». Toutefois, si l'on troque les jumelles contre une loupe d'historien, on doit vite convenir que cette bonne intelligence entre la gauche et les Juifs, proclamée trois fois avec éclat, est loin d'épuiser le problème. La réalité n'a pas toujours été aussi lumineuse que les grands principes. Les grands principes eux-mêmes n'ont pas été sans effets pervers.

L'ère nouvelle de la Liberté.

Au début de cette histoire donc, un monument glorieux : l'émancipation des Juifs par l'Assemblée constituante, le 28 septembre 1791. Dès les premières semaines de l'Assemblée, en 1789, l'abbé Grégoire, un des membres les plus en vue de la gauche, attire l'attention de ses collègues sur la question. Dans sa *Motion en faveur des Juifs,* il affirme : « Les Juifs sont membres de cette famille universelle, qui doit établir la fraternité entre les peuples ; et sur eux comme sur vous la Révolution étend son voile majestueux. Enfants du même père, dérobez tout prétexte à la haine de vos frères, qui seront un jour réunis dans le même bercail ; ouvrez-leur des asiles où ils puissent tranquillement reposer leurs têtes et sécher leurs larmes ; et qu'enfin le Juif, accordant au Chrétien un retour de tendresse, embrasse en moi son Concitoyen et son Ami. »

Ces paroles généreuses n'étaient pas du goût de tous les députés. A côté d'un Mirabeau, d'un Clermont-Tonnerre, d'un Robespierre, qui mêlèrent leurs voix à celle de l'abbé Grégoire, le droite réussit à retarder l'événement. L'abbé Maury, tout en se proclamant hostile à toute « oppression », dénia aux Juifs la qualité de Français, et partant de citoyens. C'était aussi l'idée du député alsacien Reubell, qui fut l'adversaire le plus acharné de l'émancipation. Depuis le début de la Révolution, l'Alsace, où résidaient la majeure partie des Juifs français, était le théâtre de véritables pogromes à l'occasion du mouvement agraire. Reubell introduisait dans la discussion une contestation qui n'était pas celle d'un homme de droite — mais d'un futur Montagnard. Il n'y eut donc point d'unanimité de gauche en faveur des Juifs. Toutefois, le décret de 1791 scellait l'alliance de la Révolution et du judaïsme [1]. Il « libérait, écrivit plus tard Bernard Lazare, tous ces parias d'une séculaire servitude ; il rompait tous les liens dont les lois les avaient chargés ; il les arrachait aux ghettos de toute sorte où ils étaient emprisonnés ; de bétail qu'ils étaient, il en faisait des hommes [2] ».

Aux 50 000 Juifs français émancipés par la Révolution allaient être ajoutés les centaines de milliers d'autres Juifs européens, émancipés par les armées de la République et de l'Empire. En Hollande, en Italie, en Allemagne… Henri Heine a raconté comment les armées de Napoléon sont entrées dans les villes d'Europe sous les acclamations des Juifs. « La France », avait dit Samuel Lévy, dans une lettre à l'Assemblée constituante, « la France […] est notre Palestine, ses montagnes sont notre Sion, ses fleuves notre Jourdain… La liberté n'a qu'une langue,

1. Il s'agit de l'émancipation des Juifs d'Alsace et de Lorraine, représentant à eux seuls les neuf dixièmes des Juifs de France ; les autres — Juifs de Bordeaux, de Bayonne, du Comtat — avaient été faits citoyens français dès 1789.

2. B. Lazare, *L'Antisémitisme, son histoire et ses causes,* 1894, p. 195.

et tous les hommes savent son alphabet. La nation la plus asservie priera pour elle qui a délié les chaînes des esclaves. La France est le refuge des opprimés. »

Ces noces sublimes de la Révolution et de la Liberté, la gauche en a gardé la gravure émouvante dans son album de famille. D'autant plus qu'après cette vague émancipatrice les Juifs devaient subir de rudes retours de bâton. D'abord, en France même, quand Napoléon prit en 1806 des mesures restrictives concernant les Juifs. Puis, dans la plupart des pays d'Europe repris en main après 1815 par la contre-Révolution, une législation antijuive fut rétablie. Ce fut la gloire d'une autre révolution française, celle de 1848, que de donner le signal d'une nouvelle libération, dont profitèrent notamment les Juifs d'Allemagne et d'Autriche. A la fin du XIXe siècle, seules la Roumanie et la Russie maintenaient dans leurs frontières un antijudaïsme légal.

Le mouvement contre-révolutionnaire avait dénoncé très tôt cette « collusion » des Juifs et de la Révolution. En 1806, Bonald écrivait : « Les Juifs ne peuvent pas être et ne deviendront jamais, quelques efforts qu'ils fassent, des citoyens d'un pays chrétien, tant qu'ils ne seront pas devenus chrétiens eux-mêmes. » L'antisémitisme d'extrême droite en viendra à dénoncer dans les Juifs, émancipés par la Révolution, la raison secrète de la Révolution même [3]. A sa manière, il consolidait les liens entre la gauche et les Juifs.

Rothschild brouille les cartes.

La Révolution avait donc été émancipatrice, point de doute là-dessus. Cependant, par ses proclamations universalistes et le culte de la Raison qui l'illustra quelque temps, elle pouvait faire renaître une « question juive » — celle d'un particularisme rebelle à l'assimilation et, de surcroît, d'un particularisme religieux contraire à la nouvelle religion nationale. Au moment de la

3. Voir P. Pierrard, *Juifs et catholiques français, op. cit.*

fête de la Fédération, les députés des provinces rivalisèrent de professions de foi unitaires. Il n'y avait plus ni « Bretons » ni « Auvergnats » ni « Provençaux », mais des Français d'une même nation. L'année suivante, Clermont-Tonnerre, lors des débats de l'Assemblée sur la citoyenneté active, avait clairement affirmé : « Aux Juifs, en tant que *nation,* il faut tout refuser ; mais aux Juifs, en tant qu'*hommes,* il faut tout accorder [...] ; il ne peut y avoir de nation dans la nation. » On voit qu'en poussant un peu loin ce précepte, en soi légitime, on pouvait s'acheminer vers l'alternative suivante : ou les Juifs perdent leurs particularités — ils s'assimilent complètement (renoncent au sabbat, à l'alimentation *cawchère,* etc.) —, et dès lors ils sont pleinement français car ils ont cessé d'être juifs ; ou bien ils gardent leurs coutumes et leurs lois, et dès lors ils doivent être « expulsés ». Tandis que la droite (l'abbé Maury notamment) disait : respectons les convictions religieuses des Juifs mais n'en faisons pas des citoyens, la gauche, elle, pouvait, en offrant la citoyenneté aux Juifs, leur interdire à terme ce qu'on n'appelait pas encore le droit à la différence.

Cette tendance hyper-assimilatrice prit un tour terroriste en 1793. L'athéisme militant des sans-culottes ne livra pas seulement combat à l'Église catholique. La Convention dut résister aux mandements des sections populaires qui réclamaient qu'on interdît la circoncision, la célébration du sabbat, et l'on vit dans certaines villes des marchands juifs tenus par la pression populaire d'ouvrir leurs magasins le samedi.

Un antijudaïsme de « gauche », à fondement antireligieux, venait ainsi compléter le séculaire antijudaïsme catholique. Déjà Voltaire, dans son zèle à « écraser l'Infâme », s'en était pris maintes fois à la Bible et aux Juifs. Dans son *Dictionnaire philosophique,* il avait écrit à l'article « Juifs » : « ... vous ne trouverez en eux qu'un peuple ignorant et barbare, qui joint depuis longtemps la plus sordide avarice à la plus détestable superstition... » C'est le caractère irréductible de la religion juive qui perpétuait le Juif dans les nations, en empêchant son assimilation. Diderot l'avait dit clairement : « La religion des Juifs et celle des peuples chez lesquels ils habitent ne leur permettent pas de s'incorporer avec eux ; ils doivent faire une nation à part [4]. »

Les tendances les plus irréligieuses de gauche continuèrent au XIXe siècle à stigmatiser la religion juive, coupable notamment d'avoir enfanté le christianisme. A la fin du second Empire, les étudiants révolutionnaires militant dans les rangs blanquistes et se désignant comme « hébertistes » furent des plus acharnés contre Dieu en général, et contre les Juifs en particulier. C'est à ce milieu révolutionnaire qu'appartenait Gustave Tridon, dont le livre posthume publié en 1884, *Du molochisme juif,* lui valut, malgré son antithéisme, l'éloge d'Édouard Drumont. Il s'agissait d'une déclaration de guerre au monothéisme judéo-chrétien, auquel Tridon opposait l'antique Hellénie païenne et la science moderne.

Toutefois, cet antisémitisme antireligieux (visant « le sémitisme et son produit immédiat, le christianisme [5] ») a occupé moins d'esprits « progressistes » qu'une autre forme d'hostilité aux Juifs, d'origine plus ancienne mais renforcée par les progrès mêmes des Juifs dans les sociétés modernes, une fois acquise leur émancipation. Le régime de la monarchie de Juillet fut le moment d'une ascension sociale de bon nombre de familles juives, entre lesquelles celle des Rothschild prit une dimension quasi mythologique.

Louis-Philippe fut un des monarques les plus favorables à la communauté juive. Le 1er février 1831, la Chambre des pairs confirmait à une large majorité un projet de loi de la Chambre des députés, plaçant la religion juive au rang des autres confessions émargeant au budget des Cultes. Comme dit Bernard

4. Pour Voltaire, Diderot, les Encyclopédistes, voir L. Poliakov, *Histoire de l'antisémitisme, op. cit.,* t. 3.

5. A. Regnard, *Aryens et sémites,* 1890. Cet ouvrage avait d'abord été publié dans sept livraisons de *la Revue socialiste,* de juin 1887 à octobre 1889.

Lazare : « C'était l'écroulement définitif de l'État chrétien [6] ... » De manière plus sensible à l'opinion, des noms juifs apparaissaient désormais aux premiers rangs. On en vit à la Chambre (Crémieux, notamment, élu en 1842), à la scène (Rachel), à l'affiche des concerts (Meyerbeer), et surtout dans les affaires financières, dans la banque, à la Bourse. James de Rothschild, le plus jeune de la célèbre famille francfortoise, y avait acquis une position de puissance indiscutable. La fortune colossale que les Rothschild accumule ne se fait pas discrète. Les journaux sont bientôt pleins de leurs splendeurs. En 1836, Henri Heine dépeint d'une phrase l'hôtel des Rothschild de la rue Saint-Florentin : « C'est le Versailles de la souveraineté absolue de l'argent [7]. » Ce luxe ostentatoire favorise un antisémitisme populaire qui, de Rothschild, passe aisément à l'ensemble des Juifs, tous plus ou moins « Rothschild ». De sorte que la haute finance, dont l'ascension est remarquable sous la monarchie de Juillet, devient bientôt un synonyme de « finance juive », malgré les noms bien chrétiens de Casimir Perier, Laffitte ou Schneider.

Aussi dans les années 1840, un antisémitisme « socialiste » va enrichir l'antisémitisme de gauche. Ce ne fut pas le fait des saint-simoniens, prophètes de l'industrialisme ; de nombreux Juifs furent même de ce « nouveau christianisme ». Mais les autres écoles y donnèrent de la voix ou de la plume, peu ou prou. En 1844, Marx, dans *la Question juive,* avait écrit, entre autres : « L'argent est le dieu jaloux d'Israël, devant qui nul autre dieu ne doit subsister. » Mais nul n'était besoin de Marx. Les disciples de Fourier trouvèrent dans l'œuvre de leur maître défunt quelques formules encourageantes, que l'un d'eux, Alphonse Toussenel, développa dans un livre publié en 1845, *les Juifs rois de l'époque.* Ouvrage fort confus au demeurant, faisant du terme « Juif » la notion la plus élastique, mais bourrée de formules à ravir Drumont, qui voyait en ce livre un « chef-d'œuvre impérissable ». « Les Juifs, y lisait-on, sont une nation dans la nation,

6. B. Lazare, *op. cit.*
7. Voir J. Bouvier, *les Rothschild,* Fayard, 1967.

quoi qu'ils fassent et qu'ils disent, et ils y seront la nation conquérante et dominatrice avant peu. » Sans doute Toussenel entendait-il par « Juif » « tout trafiquant d'espèces » et visait-il avant tout la « féodalité financière », mais ses attaques contre la Bible et le fait d'assumer la confusion langagière généralisée du « Juif » et de l'« usurier » le classent bien parmi les antisémites ; les citations qu'il fait de Fourier indiquent la filiation et la continuité du phénomène. Des contemporains de Toussenel, eux aussi adversaires du capitalisme, l'illustrèrent. A l'antisémitisme du jeune Marx, en Allemagne, faisait écho celui qui allait devenir son rival et adversaire en France, Joseph Proudhon. Dans ses *Carnets* posthumes, publiés voilà une vingtaine d'années, on tombe sur des sentences qui ressemblent à des appels au pogrome.

Ainsi, devant l'élévation sociale des Juifs émancipés, dont certains occupent des positions de tout premier rang, et quand bien même il ne s'agit que de quelques-uns, une hostilité nouvelle s'exprime. A côté d'un antijudaïsme contre-révolutionnaire, dont on suit la trace continue sous la monarchie de Juillet et le second Empire, des voix se font entendre dans ce que l'on peut appeler, au sens large, la famille révolutionnaire et socialiste. Un discours antijudaïque s'y donne libre cours, sur deux registres, bien souvent confondus : hostilité à la religion juive, hostilité à la haute finance — entendons la Banque juive, la partie étant ici prise pour le tout. D'autre part, relayant la Révolution qui les avait émancipés, des régimes politiques fort peu de gauche, ceux de Louis-Philippe et de Napoléon III, se montrent favorables aux Israélites. La solidarité entre la gauche et les Juifs y perd sa nécessité première ; il faut attendre l'affaire Dreyfus pour la revoir s'affirmer dans l'éclat d'un drame national.

L'effet Drumont.

Jusqu'aux années 1880, il n'y a pas véritablement de « question juive » en France. Les dix premières années de la IIIe République sont tout occupées par le conflit central entre monarchistes et républicains. Bon nombre de Juifs français, quatre-vingt-dix ans après leur émancipation, ont quitté la religion de leurs aïeux. Ils sont en voie de s'assimiler complètement à la nation française. Alfred Naquet — qui avait épousé une catholique — pouvait ainsi dire dans un discours à la Chambre, en mai 1895 : « Pendant plus de trente ans, je n'ai fréquenté à peu près que des non-Juifs. » Cette intégration totale de la communauté juive avait été théorisée par les Juifs eux-mêmes sous le nom de « franco-judaïsme ». Certains auteurs, comme Théodore Reinach, allait jusqu'à imaginer l'extinction du judaïsme par l'assimilation complète : « Que l'émancipation, l'égalité pénètrent partout, non seulement dans les lois, mais dans les mœurs et dans les idées, le sentiment juif perdra de plus en plus de son âpreté, et finira sans doute par s'éteindre complètement [8]. » Cette tendance à l'assimilation a cependant été arrêtée par deux faits concomitants : les mouvements d'immigration des Juifs venus de l'Est et le développement en France d'un antisémitisme de combat.

Plusieurs facteurs, au début des années 1880, ont contribué à nourrir un courant antisémite. Ainsi après l'attentat perpétré contre Alexandre II, la Russie connaît une période de violente répression, au cours de laquelle les pogromes se trouvent légalisés par des mesures antijuives officielles. Des milliers de Juifs russes gagnent alors l'Occident, et notamment la France. L'année suivante, un millier de Galiciens, fuyant l'Autriche-Hongrie à la suite de persécutions, trouvent refuge à Paris. De 1881 à 1939, la composition de la communauté juive française va, en plusieurs vagues successives, se trouver bouleversée. Ces immigrés d'Europe orientale exercèrent, selon l'expression de Pierre Vidal-Naquet, une « constante pression antiassimilationniste [9] ».

Ce phénomène ne fait que s'amorcer au début des années 1880. D'autres facteurs, plus décisifs, ont joué. Premièrement, le

8. Cité par M.R. Marrus, *op. cit.*, p. 137.
9. P. Vidal-Naquet, préface à Marrus, *op. cit.*

triomphe définitif des républicains sur leurs adversaires monarchistes et cléricaux. En 1883, on voit paraître un hebdomadaire au nom sans vergogne : *l'Anti-Sémitique,* portant en épigraphe une formule aussi claire que son titre : « Le Juif, voilà l'ennemi ! ! ! » Journal sans audience considérable, qui cesse de paraître dès 1884, mais qui exprime déjà une bonne partie des thèmes que développera Drumont, avec un succès retentissant, dans sa *France juive* en 1886. Transformé en principe d'explication universelle, le Juif est accusé par Drumont d'avoir détruit l'ancienne chrétienté, mis en place la République franc-maçonne, affamé le prolétariat et dirigé de manière occulte les destinées de la France. Le signal de départ du mouvement antisémite est véritablement donné. Vont suivre la création de la Ligue antisémitique de Jules Guérin, le lancement de *la Libre Parole,* quotidien auquel fait écho *la Croix* des assomptionnistes.

Devant cet antisémitisme d'extrême droite, que fait la gauche ? Quand on lit la presse de gauche de cette époque, et notamment les journaux socialistes des années 1890, on est frappé par le peu d'intérêt qu'il suscite. Pis : un certain nombre de personnalités, socialistes ou radicales, peuvent avancer des opinions antijuives sans susciter apparemment aucune indignation. Car il s'agit bien d'« opinion » : on peut être ou ne pas être antisémite ; cela ne semble pas tirer à conséquence.

Nous avons vu plus haut comment un député radical pouvait faire des déclarations antijuives dans *la Dépêche* de Toulouse sans s'attirer les foudres. Mais les socialistes ? Leurs positions théoriques sont en principe contraires à l'antisémitisme. Ainsi, l'hebdomadaire guesdiste *le Socialiste* explique à ses lecteurs, le 26 juillet 1892 : « Il s'agit de sauver l'exploitation capitaliste en amusant les travailleurs avec les " youtres ", comme on dit, devenus des boucs émissaires... Quel répit pour la société actuelle si, au lieu de se poursuivre entre possédés et possédants pour l'expropriation de ces derniers, la lutte pouvait être déplacée, limitée entre " sans prépuce " et " avec prépuce " ! »

Le vocabulaire de cette mise au point laisse déjà subodorer une certaine complaisance pour un antisémitisme vulgaire. De fait, les journalistes socialistes reprennent sans problème de conscience les injures populaires et les brocards éculés sur les Juifs. Le mot de « Juif » lui-même, comme l'attestent les dictionnaires du temps, est entendu généralement comme une insulte. C'est pourquoi certains dreyfusards, un peu plus tard, préconiseront de rayer « le vocable " Juif " » du langage, et de ne garder le terme d'« Israélite » que pour évoquer le culte et la religion [10]. En termes clairs, on ne prend pas de gants pour parler des Juifs, même si tous les socialistes n'usent pas du terme de « youpins » que l'on note régulièrement dans le journal anarchiste d'Émile Pouget, *le Père Peinard.*

Avec habileté, Drumont et ses disciples font de leur mieux pour flatter socialistes et syndicalistes sur le dos des Juifs. Face au capitalisme (forcément juif pour Drumont !), même combat ! Cette espèce de complicité est notable lors de certaines réunions publiques, y compris celles des marxistes du parti ouvrier [11]. Elle est même redoutée par certains observateurs, tel Anatole Leroy-Beaulieu.

Le 27 février 1897, Leroy-Beaulieu, catholique, républicain libéral, donne une conférence à l'Institut catholique de Paris sur le thème de l'antisémitisme. Devant un auditoire largement noyauté par des militants antisémites qui l'interrompent tout au long, il démontre l'inconsistance intellectuelle de l'antisémitisme. Mais l'un de ses arguments est notable du point de vue qui nous occupe. Ce défenseur de la société libérale dénonce dans l'antisémitisme son anticapitalisme, son « socialisme ingénu ». Et plus loin : « Une sorte de socialisme *sui generis,* socialisme de droite, si vous voulez, socialisme déguisé sous de vagues formules chrétiennes » *mais* « travaillant, qu'il le veuille ou non, au profit

10. Voir J. Psichari, à l'assemblée générale de la Ligue française pour la défense des droits de l'homme et du citoyen, 4 juin 1898.

11. Voir C. Willard, *les Guesdistes, op. cit.,* notamment ch. XXI, p. 410 *sq.*

de l'autre socialisme, du socialisme athée, du socialisme révolutionnaire [12] ».

Certains socialistes ont perçu cette convergence comme profitable à leur projet politique. Ces foules populaires que Drumont entraînait derrière lui, au nom du « socialisme ingénu », on pourrait peut-être les suivre jusqu'à un certain point, profiter de leur dynamique, les amener ensuite au « vrai » socialisme. De là résultent d'étonnantes rencontres. Naquet, dans le débat à la Chambre de 1895 évoqué plus haut, avait ainsi attiré l'attention de ses collègues sur ce qu'il appelait « la politique de la *trouée* » de certains socialistes pensant : « Quand les antisémites auront ouvert la brèche, nous y passerons. » Or la sténographie du débat note des « marques d'assentiment sur divers bancs à l'extrême gauche », et le député socialiste Rouanet de dire clairement, lui qui n'est pourtant pas antisémite : « C'est pour cela que j'approuve la campagne de M. Drumont. »

Édouard Drumont, au moins jusqu'à l'affaire Dreyfus, ne jouit donc pas d'une trop mauvaise réputation parmi les socialistes. L'année même de la publication de *la France juive,* Benoît Malon lui avait consacré dans sa *Revue socialiste* un important compte rendu. Malon, faisant la part des « injustices » contenues dans *la France juive,* n'en déclarait pas moins que « ce livre mérite [...] d'être discuté ». Et, tout en faisant observer que le capitalisme « tout entier » et pas seulement le capitalisme juif était coupable, Malon se laissait aller à des commentaires sur la « haute juiverie » et sur la « noble race aryenne » qui étaient des signes du temps.

En 1890, Albert Regnard, collaborateur de la même *Revue socialiste,* publiait un ouvrage intitulé *Aryens et sémites.* S'inscrivant dans la même perspective que le blanquiste Tridon, dont il se réclamait explicitement, il renouvelait l'antimonothéisme de gauche, le mêlant à des considérations « scientifiques » désormais répandues sur les idées raciales. Or cet homme d'extrême gauche reconnaissait à Drumont un « immense mérite » et lui savait gré

12. A. Leroy-Beaulieu, *L'Antisémitisme,* 1897, p. 61.

— nonobstant ses erreurs — d'avoir réaffirmé une « éclatante vérité ». Laquelle ? L'infamie du capitalisme ? Certes, mais mieux encore : « La réalité et l'excellence de la race aryenne, de cette famille unique à laquelle l'humanité doit les merveilles du siècle de Périclès, la Renaissance et la Révolution — les trois grandes époques de l'histoire du monde — et qui seule est en mesure de préparer et d'accomplir l'achèvement suprême de la rénovation sociale. »

Voilà ce qu'un socialiste pouvait imprimer quelques années avant l'affaire Dreyfus, sans convaincre peut-être la majorité de ses camarades mais sans soulever davantage la protestation.

Sur les « races », on devisait, on ergotait, on se livrait à des classements. Les Juifs eux-mêmes admettaient comme les autres cette distinction entre une « race sémite » et une « race aryenne ». Répétons-le : avant Hitler, rares sont ceux qui voient dans l'antisémitisme une doctrine de mort. Pour bien des gens de gauche, les antisémites étaient des imbéciles ; ils n'étaient pas des bourreaux en puissance.

Et Jaurès ?

Dans cette confusion il est important d'observer le comportement de Jaurès. Lui est un intellectuel, qui ne se laisse pas dominer par les passions et sait faire les distinctions doctrinales qui s'imposent. Or lui, le « pur », le « clairvoyant », plus attaché que d'autres aux principes immortels de la Révolution et de la République, converti au socialisme depuis 1892, année au cours de laquelle il devient un des ténors de l'extrême gauche à la Chambre, il faut bien convenir que sa vigilance antiraciste n'est pas évidente. Il est même « quelque peu effleuré, nous dit Madeleine Rebérioux, par le courant antisémite populaire où il lui était arrivé de déceler " un véritable esprit révolutionnaire " [13]. »

13. Art. « Jaurès », in *Dictionnaire biographique du mouvement ouvrier français 1871-1914,* t. XIII.

Certes à plusieurs reprises, Jaurès se défend d'être antisémite. « Je n'ai pas de préjugé contre les Juifs », écrit-il en 1889. Mais, au moment de l'affaire du Panama, dont se saisit Drumont pour en faire une affaire « juive », on le voit plus attentif aux thèses de l'antisémitisme. Ses rapports avec Drumont, jusqu'à l'affaire Dreyfus, sont de bonne compagnie, Drumont ne tarissant pas d'éloges sur ce socialiste de terroir. Mêmes relations cordiales avec le marquis de Rochefort, ancien communard, ancien boulangiste, qui trempe de plus en plus dans le nationalisme, l'antisémitisme, avant de devenir un des champions de l'antidreyfusisme.

En avril 1895, Jaurès va passer quelques courtes vacances en Algérie. Il y découvre l'existence d'un antisémitisme virulent. Loin de le réprouver, il va en rendre raison dans *la Dépêche* de Toulouse. Dans deux articles, publiés les 1er et 8 mai 1895, il explique que « sous la forme un peu étroite de l'antisémitisme se propage en Algérie un véritable esprit révolutionnaire ». Et Jaurès de reprendre à son compte les arguments du lobby antisémite contre « la puissance juive ». Que la majorité des Juifs d'Algérie, émancipés par le décret Crémieux de 1870, appartiennent aux couches pauvres de la société n'est pas connu de Jaurès : il n'a vu que « l'usure juive » qui réconcilie contre elle « l'Européen » et « l'Arabe ».

Résumons-nous. Jusqu'en 1898, l'antisémitisme n'est perçu par l'ensemble de la gauche — et particulièrement par les socialistes — ni comme un opprobre ni comme une menace sérieuse. Lors du congrès international socialiste de Bruxelles, en 1891, un délégué juif américain avait demandé la condamnation ferme de l'antisémitisme. Le congrès, ne jugeant pas « nécessaire » la discussion, se contenta d'une motion, où l'on flétrit *également* « les excitations antisémitiques *et philosémitiques* » — ce dernier adjectif ayant été rajouté au texte initial à la demande de deux délégués français, Regnard et Argyriadès.

Dans les années qui suivent, rien ne vient frapper d'interdit l'antisémitisme dans les rangs de la gauche. Les plaisanteries sur les Juifs sont monnaie courante dans tous les secteurs politiques. Le mouvement antisémitique, dont les socialistes se démarquent sur le plan théorique, apparaît à beaucoup d'entre eux néanmoins comme riche de virtualités révolutionnaires. Socialistes et antisémites se rencontrent en certaines réunions et en certaines batailles électorales face à un adversaire commun : la République opportuniste, la République affairiste, la République du Panama, dans laquelle on stigmatise la présence « juive ». Allant plus loin, certains socialistes n'hésitent pas à reprendre à leur compte les théories racistes sur la supériorité des « aryens » sur les « sémites ». A des degrés divers, comme on le voit, l'antisémitisme a eu droit de cité au sein de la gauche.

La « révolution dreyfusienne ».

Point de rupture dans cette histoire des relations entre la gauche et les Juifs, l'affaire Dreyfus va avoir pour effet de couper net aux relations semi-complices entre la gauche et les antisémites. Au demeurant, cette coupure nous paraît plus évidente par le recul dont nous disposons ; à l'heure des choix, on a longtemps tergiversé. Du reste, ce ne fut pas un homme politique qui le premier se dressa avec éclat contre la guerre nouvelle que l'on faisait aux Juifs. L'initiative en revint à Émile Zola, avant même qu'il fût convaincu de l'innocence de Dreyfus par Bernard Lazare. Le 16 mai 1896, *le Figaro* publie son article, « Pour les Juifs », où Zola exprime sa « surprise » et son « dégoût croissant » devant la campagne qui se développe contre les Juifs ; il dénonce le « fanatisme » et en appelle à l'« universelle fraternité ».

C'est le même Zola, soutenu par Clemenceau, qui, en lançant son « J'accuse » dans *l'Aurore,* le 13 janvier 1898, deux jours après l'acquittement d'Esterhazy par le Conseil de guerre, déclenche ce qu'on appellera la « révolution dreyfusienne ». La gauche est loin d'être unanime. A côté d'un Clemenceau, entré dans la bataille depuis le mois d'octobre 1897, et qui jusqu'en décembre 1899 va accumuler article sur article en faveur de la révision ; qui trouve le titre simple mais génial donné à la lettre de Zola : « J'accuse » ; qui fait de la cause dreyfusienne une ultime bataille de la Révolution française ; à côté de lui, la tendance est plutôt de ne pas remettre en cause la chose jugée et de préserver l'Armée de tout soupçon. Le 19 janvier, après que les poursuites ont été lancées contre Zola, un manifeste est publié par 32 députés socialistes qui se déclarent au-dessus de la mêlée.

Les élections législatives doivent avoir lieu au mois de mai 1898. Or les socialistes parlementaires sont sensibles à la pénétration des mots d'ordre nationalistes et antisémites dans les couches populaires. La popularité d'un Rochefort est significative à cet égard. Lui, l'ancien communard, l'ancien évadé de la Nouvelle-Calédonie, le « marquis rouge », est resté une des « idoles » du peuple parisien, quoiqu'il soit devenu nationaliste (le mot vient d'être inventé) et antisémite.

C'est moins du côté du Parlement qu'on trouve le premier foyer de résistance au nationalisme et les premiers bataillons dreyfusards, que dans les tendances antiparlementaires du mouvement ouvrier : dans le groupe allemaniste et dans les colonnes de son journal *le Parti ouvrier,* et chez les anarchistes qui entourent Sébastien Faure et *le Libertaire.* Dès la fin de l'année 1897, ils ont fait leur choix et bravent Rochefort sans complexe. Le 17 janvier, Jules Guérin ayant organisé une réunion antisémite au Tivoli-Vauxhall, les anarchistes de Faure et les allemanistes prennent d'assaut l'estrade et dispersent la réunion.

Ces groupes antiparlementaires avaient perçu avant les députés socialistes le péril antisémite. Tout ce mois de janvier résonne, après l'article de Zola, des manifestations antijuives. Dans toutes les grandes villes, on brise des devantures de magasins juifs, on assiège des synagogues, on porte la main sur des particuliers. De Rennes à Grenoble, de Lille à Marseille, les mêmes slogans retentissent : « Mort aux Juifs ! Mort à Zola !

Mort à Dreyfus ! » Le comble est atteint en Algérie où, à partir du 18 janvier, la chasse aux Juifs est lancée à Alger. Quatre jours durant, une foule excitée par Max Régis, suggérant « d'arroser de sang juif l'arbre de la liberté », se déchaîne contre les boutiques juives, fracturées, dévastées, pillées, tandis que bientôt Constantine et Oran suivent l'exemple.

Jaurès, dès lors, ne voit plus dans l'antisémitisme cet « esprit révolutionnaire » un peu fruste qu'il avait cru discerner trois ans plus tôt en Algérie. Au cours de ce mois de janvier, il entre dans la bataille dreyfusienne. Le procès d'Esterhazy auquel il a assisté, le cri accusateur de Zola, l'influence de quelques amis comme Lucien Herr et de jeunes normaliens comme Charles Péguy, et, brochant sur le tout, cette violence antisémite de la rue concourent à le lancer dans le combat, après des mois d'hésitations [14].

L'article de Zola a agi comme un détonateur. Son courage a donné du courage. Une pétition circule en faveur de la révision du procès Dreyfus. Véritable acte de naissance d'une gauche intellectuelle, elle rassemble plusieurs milliers de signatures. Quelque chose a changé dans la vie de la plupart des signataires. « L'affaire Dreyfus, écrira Julien Benda, m'a fait passer de l'intellectualisme à l'action intellectuelle, de la pensée fière et lointaine à celle qui descend dans la rue [15]. »

C'est au moment du procès Zola, entre le 7 et le 25 février 1898, qu'est fondée la Ligue des droits de l'homme, sur l'initiative du sénateur Trarieux. Le 4 juin, au cours de sa première assemblée générale à l'hôtel des Sociétés savantes, Trarieux en trace le programme : « Défendre contre des menaces sourdes de contre-révolution les principes fondamentaux de la *Déclaration*

14. Sur les hésitations de Jaurès, voir notamment M. Rebérioux, « Zola, Jaurès et France : trois intellectuels devant l'Affaire », *Cahiers naturalistes,* n° 54, 1980. Et aussi E. Cahm, « Le mouvement socialiste face au nationalisme au temps de l'affaire Dreyfus », *Bulletin de la Société d'études jaurésiennes,* n° 79, oct.-décembre 1980.

15. J. Benda, *La Jeunesse d'un clerc,* Paris, Gallimard, 1968, p. 120.

des droits de l'homme, sur lesquels repose depuis cent ans l'égalité de la patrie. » Entre la Révolution et l'affaire Dreyfus, la continuité était de nouveau proclamée.

Cependant, il est notable que bien des hommes de gauche renâclent au dreyfusisme, même après les élections de mai 1898, qui ont permis à 26 nationalistes et antisémites, Drumont en tête, élu par Alger, d'entrer à la Chambre. Dans le camp socialiste, les guesdistes vont garder tout au long de l'Affaire un quant-à-soi qu'ils justifient par la lutte de classe. Le 9 juillet 1899, Paul Lafargue se gausse encore dans *le Socialiste* des « dreyfusards bourgeois qui nous ont tant embêtés avec leur Justice imprescriptible ». Toutefois, en leur congrès de septembre 1898, les guesdistes ont affirmé le caractère *réactionnaire* de l'antisémitisme — « misérable contrefaçon » et « piège à travailleurs » que « Bebel a pu justement appeler *le socialisme des imbéciles* ».

Qu'elle est longue à aboutir, cette « Vérité » qui s'est mise « en marche » ! L'antisémitisme, progressivement, se fixe à l'extrême droite. Entre l'anticlérical Rochefort et les assomptionnistes de *la Croix,* entre Drumont et Déroulède, quel plus efficace dénominateur commun pourrait-on imaginer en dehors de l'antisémitisme ? C'est l'appel à la guerre contre les Juifs, si apte à entretenir les passions populaires, qui soude leur nationalisme autant que la défense sacrée de l'Armée. Il ne fait plus de doute que l'antisémitisme est bien une arme de la « réaction ». Oui, mais... Tout en combattant la démagogie nationaliste, maints socialistes éprouvent encore bien de la peine à se débarrasser de leurs présomptions contre les Juifs. Encore une fois, Jaurès est un bon révélateur. Lui, qui est entré avec tout le poids de son influence, avec tous les dons de son esprit et les feux de son éloquence dans cette mêlée, où il s'agit de défendre un homme et un principe, on le surprend encore, en juin 1898, déclarer dans un discours au Tivoli : « Nous savons bien que la race juive, concentrée, passionnée, subtile, toujours dévorée par une sorte de fièvre, par la fièvre du gain quand ce n'est pas par la fièvre du prophétisme, nous savons bien qu'elle manie avec une particulière habileté le mécanisme capitaliste, mécanisme de rapine, de mensonge, de corruption et d'extorsion. Mais nous disons, nous : Ce n'est pas la race qu'il faut briser ; c'est le mécanisme dont elle se sert, et dont se servent comme elle les exploiteurs chrétiens [16]. »

Tout de même, en 1899, il semble bien que les jeux soient faits. Le peuple républicain, appelé à plusieurs reprises à descendre dans la rue pour défendre le régime, s'oppose désormais aux ligueurs de Guérin et aux imprécations de Rochefort. Péguy a raconté la grande manifestation du 11 novembre 1899, pour le « Triomphe de la République ». Il dit bien comment « l'acclamation au nom de Dreyfus, l'acclamation publique, violente, provocante » fut « la plus grande nouveauté de la journée, la plus grande rupture, la plus grande effraction de sceaux de ce siècle [17] ». Ce « *Vive Dreyfus !* » poussé par le peuple parisien, soumis depuis une dizaine d'années à la propagande de haine des antisémites, marquait effectivement une étape : la gauche se nettoyait des préjugés racistes.

Et pourtant, car jamais rien en histoire n'est totalement consommé, les attaques contre les Juifs n'y auront pas complètement disparu entre la fin de l'Affaire et 1914. Les suites politiques de la grande bataille autour de Dreyfus amenèrent la victoire du Bloc des gauches et du combisme. Le socialisme, derrière Jaurès, parut aux yeux de l'extrême gauche s'abîmer dans les délices parlementaires. C'était une nouvelle trahison de la lutte des classes ! En 1906, l'arrêt de la Cour de cassation réhabilitant Dreyfus provoque un article de Robert Louzon dans *le Mouvement socialiste :* « La faillite du dreyfusisme ou le triomphe du parti juif », où l'on apprend « qu'il existe un parti dont le judaïsme, grâce à sa puissance d'argent, à son activité commerciale et intellectuelle, est le chef »...

On connaît le dérapage de Georges Sorel, ancien dreyfusard,

16. *La Petite République,* 9 juin 1898.
17. Ch. Péguy, « Le “ Triomphe de la République ” », in *Œuvres en prose, 1898-1908,* Bibliothèque de la Pléiade, p. 103-122.

collaborateur à la même revue, où il avait publié en 1906 ses *Réflexions sur la violence* à la gloire de la CGT. Son antiparlementarisme et le déclin du syndicalisme révolutionnaire le poussèrent vers 1910 dans les bras tendus des théoriciens de l'Action française. S'il n'y reste que l'espace de quelques années, du moins son évolution indique-t-elle la fragilité d'une certaine extrême gauche face aux tentations renouvelées de l'antisémitisme. S'il en fallait un autre exemple, moins célèbre, on pourrait évoquer celui d'Émile Pataud. Un rude gaillard, secrétaire du Syndicat des électriciens, qui avait subitement plongé dans la nuit noire la ville de Paris en mars 1907, par une grève surprise. Attiré lui aussi par les militants de l'Action française, on le voit en 1911 devenir l'orateur principal d'un meeting antisémite ; son Syndicat des électriciens refuse de l'exclure en dépit des protestations. Ce n'est qu'en 1913 que la CGT peut le rejeter, à la suite d'une agression qu'il a lancée avec des amis sur des rédacteurs de *la Bataille syndicaliste.* Un chiendent d'antisémitisme restait donc accroché aux organisations syndicales.

En gros, cependant, l'affaire Dreyfus avait purgé la gauche de cet antisémitisme plus ou moins vivace qu'on avait pu y observer au début des années 1890. Sans doute l'affaire Dreyfus n'a-t-elle pas opposé face à face antisémites et philosémites. L'enjeu de la bataille était plus complexe, à la fois moral et politique. Sur le plan moral, les dreyfusards avaient défendu les causes universelles de la Justice et de la Vérité contre la cause particulière de la Raison d'État. Sur ce terrain, tous les dreyfusards n'étaient pas de gauche, même s'ils étaient plus nombreux du côté des libres penseurs que du côté des catholiques. Sur le plan politique, il s'était agi de préserver les institutions républicaines, les libertés démocratiques, contre un mouvement nationaliste décidé à jouer son va-tout. Mais sur ces deux plans la question juive interférait. La condamnation inique de Dreyfus et l'acquittement d'Esterhazy n'étaient pas indépendants du fait que le premier fut juif. Quant au nationalisme, dont les fièvres et les audaces ont fait trembler le régime, il avait privilégié l'antisémitisme comme l'un de ses thèmes fédérateurs et mobilisateurs. A cette droite extrême qui hurlait contre les Juifs, la gauche répondit bientôt en faisant la guerre aux « curés ». Émile Combes en fut le général en chef ; la séparation des Églises et de l'État, l'aboutissement. Jamais, depuis la crise du 16 mai 1877, on n'avait vu un tel corps à corps entre la gauche et la droite. Du même coup, les centristes et autres catholiques dreyfusards ou démocrates-chrétiens se trouvaient coincés : l'anti-antisémitisme s'imposant d'autant mieux à gauche.

Dans le légendaire de la gauche, la victoire dreyfusiste occupe une place de choix. Les funérailles d'Émile Zola, en octobre 1902, y figurent comme une des nobles scènes du théâtre républicain. Anatole France, libre penseur et dreyfusard, prononça au cimetière Montmartre l'oraison funèbre du grand écrivain. Après avoir rappelé ce que Jules Guesde avait désigné comme « le plus grand acte révolutionnaire de ce siècle » — il parlait du « J'accuse » —, Anatole France finit par ce cri de fierté : « Il n'y a qu'un pays au monde dans lequel ces grandes choses pouvaient s'accomplir. Qu'il est admirable, le génie de notre patrie ! »

L'accusé Blum.

Une troisième séquence de notre histoire contemporaine a noué entre 1933 et 1945 des liens plus étroits entre la gauche et la communauté juive : la lutte commune qui les engagea contre le nazisme.

C'est au cours de cette période que la France a connu un second déchaînement d'antisémitisme. La Grande Guerre, la « solidarité des tranchées », la prospérité retrouvée n'avaient pu abolir tous les préjugés antisémites dans les années vingt. A tout le moins ne faisaient-ils pas le fond des éditoriaux ordinaires ; ils ne présidaient même pas à la formation du premier fascisme français — ce Faisceau, dont le fondateur Georges Valois avait pourtant donné sa voix avant 1914 aux thèses antijuives. Rabi y voyait un « antisémitisme de bonne compagnie » par rapport à celui qui sévit dans les années trente [18].

Cette recrudescence de racisme s'inscrit dans un contexte général de xénophobie, suscitée par la crise économique [19]. En décembre 1931, un député peut déclarer à la Chambre : « Nous ne souffrons pas d'une crise de chômage national mais d'une crise d'invasion étrangère. » Cette explication simpliste exprime une idée largement reçue. *L'Humanité* ne reconnaît-elle pas les ravages qu'elle fait jusque dans les rangs communistes [20] ? L'extrême droite entonne tous les couplets de la chanson que Drumont a mise au goût du jour : « La France aux Français ! » Toutefois, cette hostilité clamée contre l'étranger a l'occasion de monter de plusieurs tons, après l'avènement de Hitler au pouvoir en 1933. Par dizaines de milliers, des proscrits gagnent la France. Les Juifs, victimes désignées du nouveau régime, en représentent le plus fort contingent. Une entraide française est organisée ; des personnalités de tous milieux et de toutes convictions offrent leur soutien. On doit à Camille Chautemps, ministre de l'Intérieur, l'affirmation solennelle et rassurante d'avril 1933, selon laquelle la France resterait « fidèle à [s]es traditions généreuses d'hospitalité ». Ce qui n'empêche point le gouvernement français de mettre en garde les départements sur l'« extrême circonspection » avec laquelle on doit laisser introduire en France « des Israélites chassés d'Allemagne [21] ».

Cette prudence officielle dans l'accueil à réserver aux premières victimes du nazisme est déjà peu flatteuse pour le centre gauche au pouvoir. Mais que dire du flot de haine raciale dont la presse d'extrême droite, fort prospère en ces années-là, fait déborder ses colonnes ? On voit même reparaître le titre du

18. W. Rabi, *Anatomie du judaïsme français,* Éd. de Minuit, 1962.
19. Voir R. Schor, *l'Opinion française et les Étrangers en France, 1919-1939,* Nice, 1980, thèse multigraphiée pour le doctorat ès lettres, 5 vol.
20. *Ibid.*
21. *Ibid.*, p. 102.

journal de Jules Guérin : *l'Antijuif ;* cette fois, son directeur s'appelle Louis Darquier de Pellepoix. Quant à *la Libre Parole* de feu Drumont, elle reprend vie sous la responsabilité d'Henri Coston. D'une manière générale, au moins jusqu'au décret-loi du 20 mars 1939 qui interdit en France toute propagande raciste, ce fut un concours d'antisémitisme dans les grands journaux dits nationaux, tels que *l'Ami du Peuple, l'Action française, Je suis partout* et *Gringoire,* dont l'écho était démultiplié par une séquelle de publications plus obscures et plus acharnées.

La victoire électorale du Front populaire et bientôt la guerre civile en Espagne sont l'occasion de nouvelles véhémences. Pour la première fois, un fils d'Israël, Léon Blum, devient président du Conseil — ce qui est dénoncé à la Chambre même, par Xavier Vallat, comme une honte infligée à ce vieux pays « gallo-romain ». L'extrême droite transfère toute sa haine sur Blum. Jean-Pierre Maxence la résume d'une phrase : « M. Léon Blum par toutes ses fibres représente l'étranger. » Discours, articles, caricatures, livres mêmes s'accumulent contre « le Juif Blum ». En 1938, paraît encore aux Éditions Baudinière l'ouvrage d'un certain Laurent Viguier, *les Juifs à travers Léon Blum,* dont le sous-titre précise : *Leur incapacité historique de diriger un État.* En substance, ce pamphlet expose le « diagnostic » énoncé dès la première page : « Le mal vient du Juif. » Ce n'est là qu'un exemple de cette rhétorique de la violence, de ce pogrome qui n'était encore que papier.

En tout cas, le Front populaire se trouvait accusé par les plus virulents de ses adversaires non seulement de faire cause commune avec les « Juifs » mais d'être l'expression politique de ceux-ci, la nouvelle étape dans leur conquête du pouvoir universel. Quelle que fût sa timidité (notamment dans sa politique d'immigration [22]), le Front populaire représentait en France le pôle politique de la résistance au nazisme et s'affirmait comme la

22. Ralph Schor note ainsi que, contrairement à l'accusation lancée par la droite, le Front populaire dans les années 1936-1937 n'a pas augmenté sensiblement le nombre des naturalisations.

sauvegarde des communautés juives menacées. Cependant, au crépuscule du Front populaire, en mai 1938, les radicaux au pouvoir n'hésitèrent pas à promulguer des décrets-lois visant l'immigration, ce qui amena socialistes et communistes à additionner leurs protestations contre « ces textes draconiens ».

La « solution finale » et ses lendemains.

Après une première période d'incertitude [23], la Seconde Guerre mondiale prit l'aspect d'un affrontement planétaire entre les « démocraties » et les « fascismes ». L'alliance précieuse de l'Armée rouge valait bien aux yeux des alliés occidentaux cette approximation. Le procès de Nuremberg en 1945 confirma solennellement la victoire du Bien sur le Mal. La lutte contre le nazisme et la cause juive s'étaient confondues ; elles étaient inséparables ; elles étaient également sacrées. Le Juif était l'antipode du nazi. Qui avait lutté contre celui-ci avait lutté pour celui-là. Les « collabos », ceux qui avaient pris le parti du bourreau, monopolisaient alors officiellement l'antisémitisme. Le régime de Vichy, qui se défendait d'être pronazi, n'en était pas moins le régime du Statut des Juifs et de la Milice. La France résistante — dans sa réalité et dans son mythe — portait l'étendard de l'antiracisme. Certes, toute la droite n'avait pas été collaboratrice — de Gaulle en était la preuve vivante —, ni toute la gauche résistante. Mais ce sont les communistes et les

23. La résistance communiste avant l'entrée en guerre de l'URSS est un sujet de controverse mille fois abordé. Il faut rappeler ici simplement les attaques communistes de cette période contre Léon Blum, en particulier l'article signé Maurice Thorez, publié dans le journal suédois de langue allemande *Die Welt* en 1940, dont le caractère antisémitique a été plusieurs fois relevé. Voir A. Kriegel, *le Pain et les Roses,* 10/18, p. 391 *sq.* Sur l'attitude générale du PCF pendant la guerre face à la question juive, voir du même auteur, « Résistants communistes et Juifs persécutés », in *H/Histoire,* n° 3, novembre 1979, et encore d'A. Kriegel, « Vérité historique et mensonges politiques », *Commentaire,* n° 12, hiver 1980-1981.

socialistes qui cueillent les fruits politiques de l'après-guerre et de l'après-Vichy.

Le parti communiste, devenu le plus fort des partis de gauche, ne ménage pas ses déclarations d'amitié à l'égard des survivants d'Auschwitz et des autres camps de la mort. Tout comme la diplomatie soviétique, les communistes français apportent leur soutien à l'État d'Israël qui naît dans la douleur. Les Juifs français sont nombreux dans « le parti des fusillés ». En mai 1948, Florimond Bonte s'écriait devant une foule rassemblée au Vélodrome d'Hiver : « Au nouvel État juif, surgi au milieu des plus pénibles souffrances de l'enfantement et au cœur des combats héroïques des meilleurs fils d'Israël, j'apporte ici le chaleureux salut de bienvenue du parti communiste français, toujours solidaire des combattants de la liberté, de la démocratie et de l'indépendance. » Ce fut sans doute l'apogée de la solidarité entre la gauche et les Juifs.

Plus encore qu'après l'affaire Dreyfus l'antisémitisme était condamné par la gauche. L'horreur des charniers nazis paraissait devoir refouler à tout jamais la haine du Juif dans tous les secteurs de l'opinion. Mais la gauche, revendiquant l'héritage de la Résistance, se trouvait des raisons supplémentaires pour aimer et protéger les rescapés de ce qu'on appellera l'Holocauste.

Les ambiguïtés de l'antisionisme.

Il faut en convenir : cette idylle de l'après-guerre a passé. Si aujourd'hui l'ensemble des organisations de gauche restent intransigeantes sur les principes, on doit constater qu'entre un certain nombre d'entre elles et les Juifs un contentieux s'est créé.

La crise a été entamée dès 1949. Staline lance alors en URSS la première d'une série de campagnes dont les Juifs vont faire principalement les frais. On assiste d'abord à une ubuesque dénonciation du « cosmopolitisme » — grossier camouflage des nouvelles purges auxquelles sont exposés les Soviétiques « d'origine juive ».

Cet « anticosmopolitisme » est relayé assez vite par l'« antisionisme », autre manière d'éclaircir les rangs des communistes d'URSS et des démocraties populaires et de tenir en sujétion les communautés juives, en les privant notamment de leurs moyens d'expression propres. Le procès Slansky, à Prague, en 1952, est l'acte le plus connu de ce nouvel assaut. Entre autres indignités, l'épouse d'un accusé — Lise London — réclame au tribunal le châtiment « le plus rigoureux [24] » pour son conjoint ; un fils, la mort pour son père, devenu son « pire ennemi [25] ».

Quelles sont alors les réactions de la presse de gauche ? *L'Humanité,* dépourvue de toute curiosité journalistique quant aux ressorts de ce procès truqué, souscrit sans rechigner aux explications officielles : « C'est contre leur pays et son régime de démocratie populaire que de prétendus nationalistes juifs — des sionistes — qui sont purement et simplement des espions, se sont mis au service des États-Unis où sévit l'antisémitisme » (25 novembre 1952). Le ton est donné. Le thème du complot, repris de la presse soviétique, fleurit de nouveau. Mais si des observateurs ont le mauvais goût de suspecter de l'antisémitisme dans ce procès d'un prétendu « sionisme » où une majorité de communistes juifs sont mis en cause, le parti communiste retourne incontinent l'accusation : les antisémites, ce sont les autres !

Est-ce l'avis du reste de la gauche ? De fait, écrit François Honti, dans un article du *Monde :* « L'antisionisme n'est pas l'antisémitisme. » Tout de même, nous dit-il, « le président [du tribunal] n'a [...] pas manqué une occasion pour faire ressortir comme une tare, ou du moins comme une circonstance aggravante, cette origine israélite en même temps qu'il qualifiait le sionisme de “ pire ennemi de la démocratie populaire ” »

24. *L'Humanité,* 29 novembre 1952, et A. London, *l'Aveu,* Gallimard, 1969.
25. Voir la lettre de Thomas Frejka au tribunal, *le Monde,* 27 novembre 1952.

(29 novembre 1952). La distinction entre antisionisme et antisémitisme n'est pas dans les faits aussi évidente que l'affirment les communistes. Peu de jours après, *le Monde* revient sur la question. Dans un article beaucoup plus fouillé que le précédent, Georges Penchenier démontre que les régimes communistes, « sous couvert d'antisionisme », font « bel et bien de l'antisémitisme » (3 décembre 1952). Les mêmes avis contradictoires se retrouvent dans les colonnes de *l'Observateur,* hebdomadaire de la gauche intellectuelle et neutraliste. Tandis que Claude Bourdet dénonce « l'excitation systématique de la passion antisémite » à l'occasion du procès de Prague, Gilles Martinet rédige un contrepoint rassurant : « L'antisionisme ne doit pas être confondu avec l'antisémitisme. »

L'année suivante éclate à Moscou l'affaire du « complot des blouses blanches ». Des médecins, juifs en majorité, comptant parmi les autorités médicales de l'URSS, auraient été stipendiés par les services israéliens et américains pour attenter à la vie des dirigeants soviétiques. La mort de Jdanov leur serait due. Le scénario est rocambolesque mais la nature antisémitique des attaques staliniennes n'échappe à personne, communistes mis à part. *L'Humanité* publie glorieusement, le 27 janvier 1953, une déclaration de dix sommités médicales françaises (au rang desquelles quelques communistes juifs) selon laquelle « la mise hors d'état de nuire, en URSS, du groupe de criminels a rendu un très grand service à la cause de la paix ». Une nouvelle fois, le PCF entérine les aberrations staliniennes, sans l'ombre apparente d'un doute. L'antisémitisme est impossible en URSS, parce que *impensable :* « Les criailleries sur le châtiment mérité de quelques criminels sionistes attachés aux services d'espionnage américains ne peuvent faire oublier que, dans notre propre pays, les principaux pourvoyeurs des charniers hitlériens sont en liberté et se préparent à reprendre du service lorsque ce n'est déjà fait. » Ainsi conclut François Billoux, dans *l'Humanité* du 18 février 1953.

Alexander Werth, journaliste progressiste britannique, qui a vécu plusieurs années en URSS, écrit de son côté dans *l'Observateur :* « Que les autorités soviétiques soupçonnent gravement les Juifs, notamment ceux qui se proclament Juifs avant tout, c'est l'évidence même. La suppression du seul journal yiddish de Moscou, le *Einheit,* la liquidation de la maison d'édition juive, du " Comité juif antifasciste " et du théâtre juif en sont la preuve » (29 janvier 1953).

Seul donc le parti communiste, jusque-là, semble donner prise au soupçon, par les silences et les justifications dont il gratifie l'antisémitisme stalinien. La suite des événements devait faire sortir le PCF de son isolement.

La fin des années cinquante et les années soixante sont marquées par les phases successives et accélérées de la décolonisation. En France, la guerre d'Algérie met la gauche au pied du mur. Le gouvernement socialiste de Guy Mollet assume la responsabilité de la répression des « rebelles algériens ». Pour atteindre leur principal soutien extérieur, le colonel Nasser, il lance à l'automne 1956, en accord avec les conservateurs britanniques, l'expédition de Suez. Cet épisode militaire et diplomatique est condamné par l'ensemble de l'opinion internationale, Américains et Soviétiques en tête. Du moins, le gouvernement israélien, impliqué dans cette affaire douteuse, se trouve-t-il complice du gouvernement Mollet. Socialistes français et Israéliens resteront toujours en bons termes, pour le meilleur et pour le pire.

Cette guerre de 1956 est lourde de conséquences sur les relations entre Israël et le reste de la gauche. L'idée qu'on avait de l'État hébreu s'est brusquement modifiée. Le couple que formaient la gauche et le Juif en est troublé.

A côté des communistes, qui condamnent l'expédition et le comportement du gouvernement Ben Gourion, une nouvelle gauche, surtout intellectuelle, définie par ses positions anticolonialistes, découvre l'État juif avec d'autres yeux. Il n'est plus la terre d'asile promise aux victimes des persécutions et aux rescapés des camps mais un allié du colonialisme. Comme l'a écrit François Furet : « L'Israélien vainqueur [prend] dans la configuration nouvelle la place qu'occupait le ploutocrate juif dans l'imaginaire de droite ou de gauche au XIXe siècle [26]. » C'est un dilemme difficile à éviter pour les Juifs de la Diaspora : ou ils restent solidaires d'Israël, mais en assumant *volens nolens* cette figure du « colonialiste juif » ; ou ils refusent de se laisser confondre avec l'Israélien conquérant, mais c'est au prix des liens de communauté qui les rattachent aux autres Juifs.

Moins de neuf ans plus tard, la guerre des Six-Jours achève la métamorphose. Le thème de l'impérialisme, succédant à l'anticolonialisme, unifie les militants et les intellectuels d'une gauche dont la guerre du Vietnam a du reste aggravé l'antiaméricanisme. Israël est désigné comme le complice — « objectif » dans le meilleur des cas — de l'impérialisme américain. La cause palestinienne a relayé la cause algérienne. L'antisionisme prend en France une ampleur sans précédent.

De l'antisionisme à l'antisémitisme, il n'y a pas de pente fatale — l'expression d'*antisionisme* se référant à des attitudes politiques fort diverses [27]. Mais à partir de la fin des années soixante, l'hostilité déclarée à Israël est soupçonnée à plusieurs reprises d'être un « néo-antisémitisme [28] ».

Pour les maos de *la Cause du Peuple,* il faut dénoncer « le complot impérialiste et sioniste » (février 1969). Pour ceux de *l'Humanité nouvelle,* « le sionisme [est] le fer de lance de l'impérialisme au Moyen-Orient » (25 mai 1967). Pour ceux de *l'Humanité rouge,* « le sionisme, c'est le fascisme » (4 janvier 1973). Pour les trotskistes de *Rouge,* « la nature fondamentale du

26. F. Furet, « Entre Israël et la gauche française : trente ans de malentendus », *le Nouvel Observateur,* n° 705, 15 mai 1978.

27. On ne saurait confondre l'antisionisme des membres de la Diaspora qui refusent de reconnaître en Israël la centralité du monde juif, l'antisionisme religieux des ultra-orthodoxes, l'antisionisme des communistes qui ne remet pas en cause officiellement le droit d'Israël à l'existence, l'antisionisme de l'OLP qui se fixe pour objectif la disparition de l'État juif, etc.

28. Voir notamment J. Givet, *la Gauche contre Israël,* Pauvert, 1968, ou L. Poliakov, *De l'antisémitisme à l'antisionisme, op. cit.,* 1969.

projet sioniste [est] expansionniste, raciste, colonialiste » (24 août 1973). Cette presse gauchiste, tout en refusant « la confusion entre antisionisme et antisémitisme », dénie à l'État d'Israël le droit d'exister : « C'est l'existence même de l'État d'Israël qui est la source du conflit qui ravage le Proche-Orient. Et derrière Israël, c'est avant tout l'aigle américain qui est responsable. C'est l'impérialisme américain qui arme ce gendarme de ses intérêts économiques dans la région, qui soutient cette enclave créée de toutes pièces, qui est prêt à nourrir Israël jusqu'à la dernière goutte de pétrole arabe » (*Rouge,* 12 octobre 1973).

De *l'Humanité* à *l'Humanité nouvelle,* de *Rouge* à *l'Humanité rouge,* une évidence en forme d'équation s'impose : Israël = impérialisme américain. Le dilemme auquel les Juifs de la Diaspora se trouvent confrontés se resserre. S'ils ne s'affichent pas clairement en faveur de la cause palestinienne, ne risquent-ils pas d'être mis au banc des accusés par la gauche anti-impérialiste ? Ceux qui, sans accepter les yeux fermés les choix politiques d'Israël, veulent néanmoins défendre son droit à l'existence contestée ne risquent-ils pas d'être suspects *ipso facto* ?

Le glissement de l'antisionisme déclaré à l'antisémitisme de fait — notamment au moment de la guerre du Kippour en 1973 — est moins repérable en France que dans d'autres pays [29].

29. Voir en particulier la théorie et la pratique du terrorisme allemand, in A. Geismar, *l'Engrenage terroriste,* Fayard, 1981, et H.-J. Klein, *la Mort mercenaire,* Éd. du Seuil, 1980.

En ce qui concerne la France, l'observateur soucieux d'exactitude devrait s'interdire tout amalgame entre les différents courants gauchistes des années soixante-dix. Un de mes lecteurs de *L'histoire,* lorsque ce chapitre parut d'abord sous forme d'article, me reprocha de ne pas avoir suffisamment nuancé mon propos — et particulièrement de n'avoir pas distingué nettement *l'Humanité rouge,* des « maoïstes orthodoxes », qui « revendiquaient hautement l'héritage du " génial Staline " sans omettre les plus petites purges », de l'organe de la Ligue communiste, *Rouge,* où l'« on trouve au contraire l'exaltation du passé révolutionnaire juif, du ghetto de Varsovie, etc. ». J'en donne bien volontiers acte à mon correspondant. Il n'était pas question pour moi, dans un article embrassant près de deux siècles d'histoire, d'entrer dans la sociologie des groupes et sous-groupes politiques. C'est aussi la raison pour laquelle je n'ai pas voulu évoquer

Toutefois, on peut être troublé par l'analogie des *structures* entre le complot sioniste/impérialiste, dénoncé aussi bien par le parti communiste français que par de nombreux groupes gauchistes, et le vieux complot juif universel. Simple coïncidence ? Pour Alain Finkielkraut, « l'antisémitisme change parfois de nom, mais jamais d'intrigue [30] ».

Quoi qu'il en soit, il est désormais fini, le temps où la gauche unanime et les Juifs chantaient à l'unisson. Les luttes anti-impérialistes prévalant, à cause d'Israël le torchon brûle chez les militants. L'antisionisme, dans ses diverses variantes, a heurté de front les anciennes solidarités.

La barbe de Marx et des Prophètes.

Pouvons-nous tirer quelques conclusions ?

1° Si l'on veut bien accepter l'idée — discutable — selon laquelle la vie politique en France est principalement organisée autour de ces deux pôles qu'on appelle la droite et la gauche, on doit tenir pour établie la tradition philosémite de celle-ci : la Révolution émancipatrice, l'affaire Dreyfus et la Résistance ont rythmé l'histoire d'une alliance aux couleurs républicaines. La communauté juive française en a bien conscience s'il faut en juger par un sondage de l'IFOP publié par *le Point* du 30 janvier 1978. Celui-ci faisait apparaître que 56 % des Juifs « pratiquants » votaient à gauche. Remarquons cependant la très nette préférence de cet électorat pour le parti socialiste. Cela ne saurait étonner, vu l'attitude du parti communiste et de l'URSS face aux problèmes du Proche-Orient. Il n'existe pas pour autant de « vote

---

l'affaire Faurisson — ce négateur des chambres à gaz soutenu par des sympathisants de la Vieille Taupe, communistes libertaires ou « anarcho-marxistes », qui mérite à elle seule une étude approfondie (voir notamment à ce sujet P. Vidal-Naquet, « Un Eichmann de papier », *Esprit,* septembre 1980). J'ai simplement voulu mentionner comment l'antisionisme pouvait être facteur de néo-antisémitisme, précisant que de l'un à l'autre il n'y avait pas de nécessité.

30. A. Finkielkraut, *Le Juif imaginaire,* Éd. du Seuil, 1980.

juif ». Une forte minorité donne ses voix à la droite. Outre que les Juifs ne se déterminent pas seulement en tant que Juifs, qu'ils appartiennent à des classes sociales différentes et ont des idées et des intérêts variés comme les autres Français, il convient d'observer que, depuis la monarchie de Juillet, un courant de la droite modérée a entretenu un philosémitisme durable. Représentatif surtout d'une certaine bourgeoisie libérale, d'abord orléaniste puis républicaine, il s'est trouvé souvent pris entre les feux croisés de la gauche et de l'extrême droite. Une minorité de catholiques, républicains libéraux notamment, ont été de cette famille traditionnellement à l'abri des préjugés antisémites [31]. Il n'y a donc jamais eu de coïncidence exacte entre la gauche et l'anti-antisémitisme.

2° La vigilance face à l'antisémitisme n'a pas été indéfectible à gauche. Les préjugés antijuifs, avoués jusqu'à l'affaire Dreyfus, plus discrets par la suite et interdits après Hitler, n'en ont pas moins été toujours décelables [32]. D'autre part, il est patent que, jusques et y compris lors de la Seconde Guerre mondiale, l'antisémitisme a rarement été pris pour ce qu'il était, c'est-à-dire un danger *en soi.* Voici des exemples, entre autres, de cette carence répétée de l'analyse.

En 1942, au moment des grandes rafles, la résistance communiste répand un tract : « A bas l'antisémitisme ! » On y proclame la solidarité du peuple français avec les Juifs, « nos frères » : « Ripostez aux mesures barbares et sadiques des boches et vichyssois en manifestant en toute circonstance votre sympathie et votre solidarité aux Juifs persécutés et en entourant leurs enfants d'une chaude affection. » Compassion et action. C'est impeccable. Mais de quelle manière le tract communiste apprécie-t-il les raisons de cet antisémitisme ? En fait, les thèses

31. Voir ainsi J.-M. Mayeur, « Les catholiques dreyfusards », *Revue historique,* CCLX1/2.

32. Voir ainsi le sondage de l'IFOP publié par *le Nouvel Adam,* n° 5, 1966. On y observe des préjugés antisémites encore tenaces dans l'opinion de gauche.

racistes de Hitler sont réduites au rang de simples procédés : « De même qu'en Allemagne les campagnes antisémites ont eu pour objet de masquer au peuple allemand ses véritables ennemis : les ploutocrates et leurs chiens de garde nazis, de même les hitlériens voudraient déchaîner la haine du Juif pour faire disparaître la haine du boche [33]. » Déjà, le 11 novembre 1938, au lendemain de la « Nuit de cristal », *l'Humanité* avait expliqué à ses lecteurs les raisons cousues de fil brun du déchaînement raciste : « M. Hitler avait besoin d'un prétexte [l'assassinat du nazi von Rath par un Juif à Paris] pour faire retomber sur les Juifs les fautes et les erreurs de son régime. » *Mein Kampf* n'a jamais été considéré, du point de vue communiste, que comme l'idéologie fumeuse des « chiens de garde » du grand capital allemand.

Si l'on prend en compte cette longue histoire, on peut considérer que le marxisme, dont une bonne partie de la gauche se réclame, a sous-estimé le problème du racisme en vulgarisant la primauté de l'économique sur le culturel et en ramenant l'histoire à une seule de ses intrigues, celle de la lutte des classes. De même que les guesdistes reléguaient l'antisémitisme au rang des accessoires idéologiques de la réaction capitaliste, de même le Comité de vigilance antifasciste a interprété le nazisme comme une variante germanique du fascisme, lequel n'était qu'un produit du grand capital « aux abois ». Dans cette vision « matérialiste » de l'histoire, où banquiers et P-DG complotent nos destins, les cultures, les religions et les mentalités font figure de comparses, transitoires superstructures et décors idéologiques promis à l'évaporation, sous la chaleur rayonnante du socialisme vainqueur.

Cette représentation simplifiée de la tragédie humaine, *l'Humanité* en exprimait clairement les conséquences sur la question juive, au moment de la guerre des Six-Jours : « La discrimination raciale, l'antisémitisme sont le fait de la réaction, des classes

33. Ce tract est publié *in extenso* dans le recueil sur *la Presse antiraciste sous l'occupation hitlérienne 1940-1944,* Centre de documentation de l'UJRE, 1950.

sociales exploiteuses — et non pas le fait de tel ou tel *peuple* en tant que tel [...]. Les massacres d'Auschwitz, de Buchenwald, etc., furent le fait du *fascisme,* c'est-à-dire de la forme la plus bestiale du capitalisme. La solidarité des victimes du racisme est donc et doit être la solidarité contre le fascisme, contre les couches sociales qu'il représente. Et elle passe par la solidarité de tous les adversaires du fascisme, et plus généralement du capitalisme qui en est " le ventre toujours fécond ", que ces adversaires soient Juifs ou non » (le 20 juin 1967).

En d'autres termes, à l'issue de ce raisonnement en forme de sorite : antisémitisme = fascisme = réaction = capitalisme, on voit que l'antisémitisme est finalement assimilable au capitalisme; que lutter contre celui-ci, c'est lutter contre celui-là. En suivant ce raisonnement, il appert que : a) l'URSS, puissance socialiste, ne peut être en aucun cas taxée d'antisémitisme, ou ce serait une contradiction dans les termes ; b) que l'anticapitalisme peut dispenser de l'anti-antisémitisme puisque celui-ci est contenu dans celui-là ; c) que la plupart des Juifs étant, au nom d'une double fidélité à leur pays et à Israël, dans le camp de l'impérialisme, donc du capitalisme, ce sont eux les véritables antisémites. CQFD.

La vérité est que les Juifs ont été persécutés depuis deux millénaires non pas en tant que capitalistes ou prolétaires mais en tant que Juifs. Il s'ensuit que le raisonnement marxiste-léniniste est à bout de souffle face aux mesures antijuives quand elles sont prises par des États « socialistes » et « impérialistes ». Nous sommes alors devant une situation dont l'*impensabilité* dispense de toute conjecture. Il n'y a plus qu'à donner au chat sa langue de bois.

Étiemble écrivait ceci, en 1957, qui devrait donner à réfléchir : « Si je cherche aujourd'hui la cause première des vices les plus graves de notre société, je trouve que l'esprit de classe lui-même commet moins de meurtres sans doute, en tout cas moins d'abjections que le préjugé de race. » Tant que la gauche, marxiste-marxisante, pratiquera la réduction de l'histoire à son plus simple antagonisme : bourgeoisie/prolétariat, impérialisme/anti-impérialisme, sionisme/antisionisme, il est à craindre qu'entre elle et les Juifs le malaise ne persiste. Le fait juif, dans sa tragique complexité, est absolument irréductible à l'un ou l'autre terme de cette triple alternative. Comme d'autres faits, celui-ci est têtu, pour parler comme Lénine.

5

Le fascisme en France

Combien de monde contient la salle Wagram à Paris ? 3 000, 4 000, 5 000 places ? Les avis divergent dans les reportages. En tout cas, en ce 11 novembre 1925, c'est plein à craquer, d'un public attentif, de gens très comme il faut : ingénieurs, voyageurs de commerce, employés des assurances. La date de la réunion n'a pas été choisie au hasard : la salle est décorée de drapeaux tricolores et les anciens combattants sont en majorité. L'un deux, Georges Gressent, qui depuis longtemps signe des articles et des livres « Georges Valois », domine la tribune, flanqué d'un ancien officier, Jacques Arthuys, et du fils d'un écrivain célèbre mort depuis peu, Philippe Barrès.

Dans la foule, les indicateurs du préfet de Police enregistrent consciencieusement les thèmes des discours. Le gouvernement en place, celui du Cartel des gauches, et présentement le troisième cabinet Paul Painlevé — un mathématicien, ce Painlevé, mais aussi impuissant que ses prédécesseurs à enrayer la chute du franc ! —, subit les foudres des orateurs. Le régime parlementaire au rancart ! Les vieux partis à la décharge ! Ils ont trahi la paix ! Ils entraînent le pays dans le naufrage monétaire et économique ! Il est temps de réagir !

Ce jour-là était fondé dans l'enthousiasme et accueilli par une vibrante *Marseillaise* le premier parti fasciste français : le Faisceau des combattants et des producteurs. Il s'assignait un but tout simple : créer, au-dessus des partis et des classes, un véritable État national.

Origines françaises du fascisme.

Un commentaire s'imposait le lendemain : le fascisme italien, au pouvoir depuis l'automne 1922, avait trouvé un client en France pour ses exportations idéologiques. Le mouvement de Valois ne s'appelait-il pas le Faisceau ? Quant aux chemises noires, les « légionnaires » les troquaient contre des chemises bleues (comme la ligne bleue des Vosges). Du reste, Valois ne cachait pas son admiration pour Mussolini : « A l'Italie, écrivait-il le 3 décembre 1925, reviendra l'honneur d'avoir donné un nom au mouvement par lequel l'Europe contemporaine tend à la création de l'État moderne [1]. »

Toutefois, comme Valois devait l'écrire quelques années plus tard : « A l'origine du Faisceau, en France, il y a une foule de malentendus [2]. » Retenons-en deux pour notre part :

1° le fascisme que Valois et ses amis voulaient donner à la France n'était pas un mouvement d'extrême droite de plus, à la manière des Jeunesses patriotes de Pierre Taittinger, destiné à protéger les intérêts de la bourgeoisie face au péril rouge. Non seulement Valois affirmait son fascisme « antiploutocratique », ce qui pouvait ne faire de mal à personne, mais il se montrait partisan résolu d'un syndicalisme ouvrier « absolument libre » et en appelait aux producteurs, sans lesquels — disait-il — il n'y avait rien à espérer ;

2° loin d'imiter Mussolini, Valois eut à cœur de rappeler à plusieurs reprises que c'était au contraire les précédents français qui avaient inspiré le fascisme italien. Mussolini avait inventé le mot ; l'idée était née en France, avant 1914. Georges Valois

1. Cité par Pierre Milza, *l'Italie fasciste devant l'opinion française 1920-1940,* Colin, coll. « Kiosque », 1967.

2. G. Valois, *L'Homme contre l'argent,* Librairie Valois, 1928, p. 179.

lui-même avait contribué à son accouchement. « Nos emprunts au fascisme italien se réduisent au choix de la chemise comme pièce caractéristique de l'uniforme, et à une conception de l'opération révolutionnaire inspirée de la marche sur Rome [...] c'est tout. Pour le reste, conception de la structure de l'État moderne, c'est nous les inventeurs, et c'est nous que l'on copiait en Italie [3]... »

Dans un livre qu'il publie en 1927, Valois définit le fascisme par la fusion de deux courants jusqu'alors contradictoires : le nationalisme et le socialisme. Le nationalisme et le socialisme ne doivent plus se faire la guerre mais se réconcilier ; ils ont le même ennemi, l'individualisme triomphant du XIXe siècle et ses corollaires : le libéralisme et le régime parlementaire. Cette fusion eût été possible dans le socialisme français, blanquiste ou proudhonien, mais, dit Valois, « le marxisme l'a rendue impossible ». La synthèse désirée doit donc être opérée dans un nouveau mouvement : telle est la vocation du fascisme [4].

En d'autres termes, le fascisme est défini comme étant « à la fois à gauche et à droite ». A gauche, parce qu'il a pour objectif de satisfaire aux « besoins du peuple » et de « défendre celui-ci des grands et des puissants » ; à droite, parce qu'il en appelle à l'autorité d'un État restauré.

Dans la genèse de l'idée fasciste, Valois insiste sur la dette qu'il a contractée envers Maurice Barrès. Le Barrès boulangiste, le député « révisionniste » élu en 1889, le journaliste franc-tireur : « Sa *Cocarde,* faite avec des républicains, des royalistes, des socialistes, c'était la préface de notre œuvre [5]. »

Le mot, donc, n'existait pas, en cette fin du XIXe siècle — mais l'idée, oui. Mais qu'est-ce qu'une idée, si elle ne sort pas des livres, des journaux ou des salons où quelques esprits distingués l'échangent contre une tasse de thé ou un petit four ? Or le préfascisme — appelons ainsi ces mouvements divers qui avant la

3. G. Valois, *L'Homme...*, *op. cit.*, p. 264-265.
4. G. Valois, *Le Fascisme,* 1927.
5. G. Valois, *L'Homme...*, *op. cit.*, p. 184.

Grande Guerre concouraient à rassembler des forces apparemment hétérogènes venues et de gauche et de droite contre le régime en place —, ce préfascisme ne resta pas dans le monde des idées pures ; il prit forme, se métamorphosa, échoua finalement, mais non sans laisser des traces durables et des germes que l'ébranlement de la guerre et de l'après-guerre fit croître. Zeev Sternhell a étudié dans un livre récent [6] ces racines françaises du fascisme, où s'enchevêtrent, à moins qu'ils ne se succèdent, le boulangisme, les ligues, les syndicats jaunes, voire les convergences inattendues entre des nationalistes de l'Action française et des théoriciens du syndicalisme révolutionnaire.

L'événement provoque généralement ces alliances contre-nature : les crises épisodiques, en relançant les attaques contre la République parlementaire et contre la République bourgeoise (c'est tout un !), les favorisent. Mais il leur faut un catalyseur, faute duquel la formule « fasciste » (socialisme + nationalisme) reste inopérante. Ce fut la trouvaille de cette fin de siècle, le sésame de cette nouvelle droite qui se constitue dans les années 1880 : à ces bourgeois et à ces prolétaires qu'on voulait unir, il fallait un ennemi commun ; en 1886, Édouard Drumont le leur offrit dans un gros bouquin frénétique, qu'on dévora à pleines dents : *la France juive.* Le 20 octobre 1889, Henri Rochefort dénonçait « le triomphe de la juiverie ». C'était dans *le Courrier de l'Est,* le journal de Barrès. Une longue et sinistre histoire commençait. Jusqu'en 1914, toutes les aventures préfascistes repérables en France eurent recours à l'antisémitisme. Georges Valois ne fait pas exception à la règle.

Il a pourtant appris le *b a ba* politique dans les feuilles anarchistes. A vingt ans, il est dreyfusard. Mais, précisément, il va faire partie de cette petite cohorte d'intellectuels dreyfusards qui sont bientôt déçus par l'œuvre de la gauche parlementaire accédant au pouvoir, sous les auspices de Combes et avec l'appui de Jaurès. Selon le mot de Péguy, qui est un de

6. Z. Sternhell, *La Droite révolutionnaire, op. cit.*

ces dreyfusards dépités, la « mystique » dreyfusarde est tombée en « politique ». L'intrigue, la brigue et le sectarisme ont fait leur lit dans celui de la justice. Toutefois, à partir de 1906, un fait nouveau pourrait bouleverser les données de la politique : la montée en force de la CGT révolutionnaire, dont Georges Sorel, autre combattant désabusé du dreyfusisme, se fait le théoricien contre le « socialisme parlementaire ».

Ce sont ces deux hommes, Georges Valois et Georges Sorel, qui vont certainement compter le plus dans la genèse doctrinale du fascisme. Sorel, tout nourri de Marx et de Proudhon, futur admirateur de Lénine et de Mussolini, se rapproche des nationalistes à partir de 1910. Valois, lui, tout monarchiste qu'il est devenu depuis 1906, ne s'estime pas moins solidaire de la classe ouvrière. Il formule même l'idée d'une « monarchie ouvrière » dans laquelle le syndicalisme, organisation de classe authentique, défendrait « la vie ouvrière » sous l'autorité du roi, conservateur de « l'énergie nationale ». Le second dira du premier : « Le père intellectuel du fascisme, c'est Georges Sorel [7]. »

Les deux hommes et leurs amis finissent par se rencontrer. En définitive, cela ne donne lieu qu'à quelques projets avortés et à quelques revues (*l'Indépendance*, les *Cahiers du Cercle Proudhon)*, mais cette convergence insolite d'hommes et d'idées si différents est virtuellement destructrice du régime établi : l'antidémocratie de gauche et l'antidémocratie de droite, l'une inspirée de la révolte ouvrière et l'autre de l'activisme monarchiste, tel est, sans oublier le catalyseur antisémitique, le nouveau mélange explosif. Édouard Berth, disciple de Sorel, résume ainsi cette rencontre : « Deux mouvements synchroniques et convergents, l'un à l'extrême droite, l'autre à l'extrême gauche, ont commencé l'investissement et l'assaut de la démocratie ; pour le salut du monde moderne et la grandeur de notre humanité latine [8]... »

7. G. Valois, *Le Fascisme, op. cit.*, p. 5.
8. É. Berth, *Les Méfaits des intellectuels,* Rivière, 1914.

L'illusion de Valois.

Quand Valois fonde son Faisceau, ce passé est encore vivant mais la guerre a provoqué une nouvelle donne. Trop d'hommes jeunes sont morts pour la patrie ; les survivants n'ont pas le droit de trahir leur sacrifice. La victoire oblige. Or le régime en place, surtout depuis le Cartel des gauches, révèle jour après jour son impuissance. Valois est resté à l'Action française mais l'économiste et l'organisateur qu'il est prend des initiatives. En 1922, il lance la formule des États généraux, qui doivent représenter l'ensemble des intérêts de la nation. Il ne parle plus de monarchie. Un chef responsable, oui, mais qui pourrait rallier les différentes familles politiques. Un État dans lequel la bourgeoisie garderait sa fonction de gestionnaire économique (contrairement à ce qu'a fait Lénine) mais serait chassée de la direction politique ; une classe ouvrière organisée ; un État arbitre, responsable, au-dessus des classes. Et comment réaliser cet État national ? Grâce à une élite qui a fait ses preuves : celle des combattants qui ont placé la patrie au-dessus de leurs intérêts propres.

En février 1925, il lance un hebdomadaire, *le Nouveau Siècle.* C'est là qu'est publié son « Appel aux combattants ». Avec ceux qui viennent à lui, il crée des « légions » destinées à militer contre le parlementarisme. Caillaux et le banquier Horace Finaly sont ses cibles favorites au cours de ses campagnes pour le franc. Mais l'antisémitisme n'est plus de ses discours, comme si les souffrances et les souvenirs des combattants de la Grande Guerre étaient devenus le nouvel élément unificateur.

La fondation du Faisceau provoque les attaques du parti communiste. Valois, cependant, ne cesse d'appeler à lui les militants ouvriers. Des communistes, il dit : « Il n'y a pas de différence très profonde entre eux et nous. Ils sont comme nous en rébellion contre le règne de l'argent » (*le Nouveau Siècle,* 19 mars 1925). En mars 1926, Valois est payé de ses efforts d'une manière éclatante : le maire communiste de Périgueux, Delagrange, qu'il a affronté naguère en réunion publique, donne son adhésion au Faisceau.

Victoire plus symbolique que substantielle. Peu d'ouvriers s'engagent au Faisceau dont la composante bourgeoise prédomine [9]. Malgré ses désirs de dépasser l'opposition gauche/droite, le fascisme de Valois reste embourbé à droite. C'est aussi de la droite qu'il reçoit les coups les plus durs. Principalement ceux de l'Action française, qui, après quelques semaines de neutralité, passe à l'offensive verbale, puis à l'action de commando.

Pendant les premiers mois suivant la fondation, Valois obtient cependant quelques beaux succès. S'inspirant de la marche sur Rome, il met au point une marche sur Paris — en plusieurs mois et en plusieurs étapes : Verdun, d'abord, et puis Reims, Meaux... Les premières réunions attirent un grand public. Trains spéciaux et autocars drainent les fascistes dans les hauts lieux. Ils sont sans doute alors 25 000, mais le mouvement s'affaiblit en se divisant. L'arrivée de Delagrange et les discours ouvriéristes de Valois déplaisent à la plupart des adhérents. Georges Valois, malgré ses qualités intellectuelles et son sens pratique, n'est pas et ne veut pas être le chef « charismatique » qui semble indispensable au succès des fascismes. Enfin Poincaré vient, rétablit la droite au pouvoir en 1926 et le franc sur ses bases en 1928. A la même date, Valois est exclu de son propre mouvement. Son évolution personnelle vers la gauche est alors entamée.

Le deuxième souffle des années trente.

Le monde, un moment stabilisé comme le franc Poincaré, est de nouveau menacé du chaos par la grande crise économique partie des États-Unis en 1929. En France, la victoire électorale de la gauche en 1932 agit comme un déclic : les ligues de droite

9. Voir Z. Sternhell, « Anatomie d'un mouvement fasciste en France. Le Faisceau de Georges Valois », *Revue française de science politique,* février 1976.

renforcent leurs effectifs et l'on voit naître de nouvelles organisations de type fasciste. La victoire de Hitler, qui prend le pouvoir en janvier 1933, suscite à droite des comparaisons vengeresses contre le régime parlementaire et l'alliance radicalo-socialiste, incapables de remettre de l'ordre dans les finances et l'économie du pays. Ces premières années de la décennie voient éclore une série de petites revues, *Réaction, Esprit, Ordre nouveau,* etc., autant d'expressions d'une nouvelle génération intellectuelle qui, en dépit de ses différences, communie dans la même aversion de la République parlementaire et bourgeoise.

Le 6 février 1934, après un mois de campagne de presse et de manifestations provoquées par l'Action française et les ligues de droite, qui se servent de l'affaire Stavisky comme d'un bélier contre le gouvernement et le régime en place, la Chambre des députés se trouve investie au cours d'une journée d'émeute assez confuse, dont le résultat le plus clair est la démission d'Édouard Daladier de la présidence du Conseil et la formation d'un nouveau cabinet d'Union nationale sous la direction de Gaston Doumergue.

Les commentateurs ont souvent vu dans cette journée fameuse comme la tentative *avortée* d'un putsch fasciste. Ce fut en fait une manifestation d'intimidation *réussie* par les ligues contre un gouvernement de gauche qui doit finalement laisser la place. Si quelques-uns des meneurs du 6 février espéraient le putsch, le manque total de coordination des différents groupes manifestants aussi bien que le refus délibéré de certains d'entre eux, comme les Croix-de-feu du colonel de La Rocque, de forcer les barrages fragiles de la police, montrent assez bien le caractère classique de cette « journée ». Comme en 1926, la gauche doit, malgré sa victoire électorale deux ans plus tôt, passer les rênes du pouvoir à la droite, les radicaux assurant cette nouvelle majorité, en échangeant leurs alliés socialistes d'hier contre de nouveaux alliés « modérés », sous couvert d'« union nationale [10] ».

10. S. Berstein, *Le 6 février 1934,* Gallimard, coll. « Archives », 1975.

Mais, loin de perpétuer la droite au pouvoir, la journée du 6 février provoque un sursaut des organisations de gauche qui, malgré leurs querelles, lancent une contre-attaque et des manifestations qui préfigurent le Rassemblement populaire et sa victoire aux élections du printemps 1936. Cette victoire des forces de la gauche un moment réconciliées grâce à une révision tactique de l'Internationale communiste a été remportée au nom de l'antifascisme. Les menaces fascistes étaient surtout visibles à l'extérieur : conquête de l'Éthiopie en 1935 par Mussolini, renforcement de la dictature hitlérienne et remilitarisation de la Rhénanie en mars 1936 par l'Allemagne, pronunciamiento lancé en juillet de la même année contre la République espagnole et début de guerre civile de l'autre côté des Pyrénées, sans compter en mai les succès électoraux du rexisme de Léon Degrelle en Belgique, au mois d'août le coup d'État de Metaxás en Grèce, et, en ce même été, comme une apothéose, les jeux Olympiques de Berlin. Pour bien des gens de droite, une conclusion s'impose : tandis qu'en France les grèves et les occupations d'usines laissent craindre la bolchevisation du pays, les États étrangers savent prendre les mesures d'autorité nécessaires face au « spectre du communisme » qui hante de nouveau l'Europe.

« Gringoire » et « Je suis partout ».

Ce sont ces réflexes de classe assez communs qui ont certainement alimenté la diffusion en France d'un état d'esprit fasciste. Mais cette peur sociale, somme toute banale, ne suffit pas à expliquer l'espèce d'« imprégnation fasciste », selon l'expression de Raoul Girardet[11], qui pénètre la France au cours de ces années-là. Car, plus que par un ensemble d'organisations, dont nous parlerons plus loin, une partie de la droite française a été

11. R. Girardet, « Notes sur l'esprit d'un fascisme français, 1934-1940 », *Revue française de science politique,* juillet-septembre 1955.

conquise ou contaminée par une idéologie de guerre civile, que la puissante presse de droite de l'époque porta jusqu'au fond des départements.

Une école de violence existait à droite depuis longtemps : l'Action française et le quotidien du même nom, que dirigeait Charles Maurras, auréolé en 1936 par sa condamnation à huit mois de prison pour ses appels au meurtre. L'Action française n'est pas spécifiquement fasciste mais elle constitue depuis longtemps une école de pensée extrémiste qui, par le mépris des institutions libérales et des traditions républicaines, l'exaltation du « coup de force » et des pouvoirs autoritaires, et peut-être plus encore par l'apprentissage d'un certain style, fait d'invective, d'outrance, de calomnie, d'attaques *ad hominem,* a largement contribué à former des « têtes » fascistes. Ce sont les maurrassiens de la nouvelle génération qui, derrière leur aîné Pierre Gaxotte, animent *Je suis partout :* Robert Brasillach, Maurice Bardèche, Pierre-Antoine Cousteau, Lucien Rebatet, Georges Blond, Alain Laubreaux… A côté, les grands hebdomadaires *Gringoire* et *Candide,* dont le tirage dépasse plusieurs centaines de milliers d'exemplaires, distillent une violence, sinon fasciste à proprement parler, du moins, selon leur expression, « anti-antifasciste » (« Le fascisme est pour beaucoup une réaction vitale, une sorte d'anti-antifascisme [12] », écrit Brasillach en 1938). *Gringoire,* en particulier, journal fondé par Horace de Carbuccia, où collaborent Henri Béraud, Philippe Henriot, Jean-Pierre Maxence, etc., s'illustre en 1936 par la campagne qu'il déchaîne contre le ministre de l'Intérieur socialiste Roger Salengro, acculé au suicide.

La véhémence, mêlée au vieil antisémitisme resurgi, est tout spécialement dirigée contre le chef du Front populaire, Léon Blum, que Maurras avait appelé « détritus humain » et que Gaxotte résume par ces mots : « Il incarne tout ce qui nous

12. Cité par P.-M. Dioudonnat, *Je suis partout 1930-1944 ; les maurrassiens devant la tentation fasciste,* La Table ronde, 1973, p. 418.

révulse le sang et nous donne la chair de poule. Il est le mal, il est la mort [13]. »

Ce « bréviaire de la haine » que composent jour après jour la presse et la littérature d'extrême droite est balancé par l'éloge des grandes réalisations des dictatures. Au fil des discours fascistes ou fascisants de l'époque, la France du Front populaire est peinte sous les couleurs sombres de la décadence : chute démographique, alcoolisme, « invasion juive », intellectualisme... *Bagatelles pour un massacre,* de Céline, comme plus tard *les Décombres* de Rebatet, exprime ce dégoût physiologique pour un peuple avili ; à la même époque, les livres de Drieu La Rochelle et de Brasillach, qui diagnostiquent le même délabrement physique et moral du pays, en appellent à l'idéal héroïque du guerrier, chantent l'exaltation du corps, du plein air, du sport, de l'action. Ce qui donne ainsi, sous la plume de Brasillach, des morceaux « antibourgeois » du genre : « De graves personnes, pleines de leur droit, de ce-qui-est-à-moi-est-à-moi, protestèrent contre l'auto-stop, que pratiquaient depuis vingt ans les Allemands, les Américains. Ils n'avaient évidemment pas l'esprit fasciste [14]. » Pour ces intellectuels, le fascisme défiait sur son propre terrain le communisme qui prétendait devenir « la jeunesse du monde ».

Uniformes et grandes manœuvres.

Cet état d'esprit fasciste où le romantisme juvénile, l'esthétique aristocratique le disputent à l'antimarxisme, à l'antisémitisme le plus haineux et à l'exaltation des pouvoirs hiérarchiques s'est donc répandu à doses plus ou moins fortes dans la droite du pays. On ne peut pas dire que les gens de gauche en furent complètement préservés, comme en témoigne la scission des « néo-socialistes » qui sortent de la SFIO derrière Marcel Déat en 1933. L'un de ceux-ci, Montagnon, avait déclaré au 30e congrès

13. P. Gaxotte, « L'homme maudit », *Candide,* 7 avril 1938.
14. R. Brasillach, *Notre avant-guerre,* Grasset, 1941, p. 193.

du parti socialiste, en juillet 1933, à la Mutualité : « La naissance du fascisme, la force du fascisme, vient de la nécessité qui semble évidente partout d'un État fort, d'un État puissant, d'un État d'ordre. » Le pacifisme intégral et l'anticommunisme viscéral amenèrent aussi un certain nombre de syndicalistes ou de personnalités de gauche sur des positions assez proches des formules fascistes ; l'échec du Front populaire qui se désagrège en 1938 ne fait que les encourager. De ce point de vue, est significative l'évolution d'un Gaston Bergery et de son hebdomadaire *la Flèche,* dont l'anticapitalisme pouvait ainsi s'exprimer en 1939 : « Il est certain que Léon Blum faisant la pause en 1937 accomplissait un geste de soumission que n'aurait accompli ni M. Hitler ni M. Mussolini. » Ce fut enfin un ancien communiste, Jacques Doriot, qui créa la formation fasciste la plus influente : le parti populaire français.

Entre 1933 et 1936, on assiste à la création d'au moins cinq organisations fascistes ou de type fasciste :

— La *Solidarité française,* fondée en 1933 par François Coty, parfumeur, qu'on trouve jusqu'à sa mort, en 1934, à l'origine de multiples financements de journaux et d'organisations de droite. Bernanos disait joliment de lui : c'est un Birotteau qui se prend pour un César. Grâce à *l'Ami du Peuple,* quotidien populaire et xénophobe qu'il avait lancé en 1928, il avait acquis de l'audience. A sa mort, c'est le commandant Jean Renaud qui prend la tête de la Solidarité française, dont les membres sont des plus actifs lors du 6 Février. Les milices de la SF portaient la chemise bleue de rigueur, des bottes, un ceinturon et saluaient « à l'antique ». Une panoplie de grades, d'écussons, de brassards ajoutait encore à l'allure martiale qu'on voulait imprimer à ces corps d'élite. La Solidarité française n'a guère survécu à la mesure de dissolution qui la frappe en même temps que les autres ligues en juin 1936.

— Le *Francisme* est créé en septembre 1933 par Marcel Bucard, ancien combattant et blessé de guerre, qui avait été du Faisceau de Valois, et collaborateur de Gustave Hervé à *la*

Victoire. Admirateur de Mussolini, Bucard est reçu par le Duce à Rome en septembre 1935. Il réunit quelques milliers de fidèles, dont les plus actifs défilent avec la chemise bleue, la cravate marine, le ceinturon baudrier et le béret basque. Le parti est dissous en juin 1936 mais le 11 novembre 1938 Bucard, qui entre-temps a fait un séjour en prison, fonde le parti unitaire français d'action socialiste et nationale, dont le manifeste annonce le double objectif de combat : « A la fois contre la réaction ploutocratique et contre le judéo-marxisme. » En 1941, Bucard lui redonnera vie sous le nom de parti franciste.

— Le *parti populaire français :* la dérive de Jacques Doriot du communisme au fascisme s'est faite en plusieurs étapes [15]. Précurseur du Front populaire au moment où il est exclu du parti communiste, Doriot, grâce à la popularité acquise à Saint-Denis, dont il est le maire, tente d'abord de s'imposer entre communistes et socialistes par le biais du « Rayon majoritaire de Saint-Denis ». Mais le rapprochement et l'accord final entre communistes, socialistes, puis radicaux, vont l'exclure du Rassemblement qu'il souhaitait à l'origine. En avril 1936, il est élu contre le candidat du Front populaire. Fort de son succès, il fonde le 28 juin le parti populaire français qui, pendant deux ans, va conquérir une certaine audience. La base ouvrière de Saint-Denis donne à son parti une assise prolétarienne tandis que son éloquence de tribun le désigne, lui, comme le nouveau Mussolini. Des intellectuels, séduits, le rejoignent, les uns après être passés par le communisme comme Henri Barbé, ou Paul Marion passé aussi par le parti socialiste ; d'autres sont issus de l'Action française comme Claude Jeantet ; les adhérents les plus connus restant Alfred Fabre-Luce, Bertrand de Jouvenel et Drieu La Rochelle. Grâce notamment à Pierre Pucheu, directeur du service d'exportation au Comptoir sidérurgique de France, Doriot bénéficie de l'aide financière d'industriels et d'associa-

15. Voir J.-P. Brunet, « Doriot, du communisme au fascisme », *L'histoire,* n° 21, mars 1980, et D. Wolf, *Doriot, du communisme à la collaboration,* Fayard, 1970.

tions patronales, que complètent les subsides de l'Italie fasciste.

Contrairement aux deux formations précédentes, le PPF réussit à devenir un parti de masse. On estime généralement à 100 000 ses effectifs, quand bien même ses vrais militants sont sensiblement moins nombreux. Ceux-ci n'ont pas à porter d'uniforme ; il leur suffit d'un insigne ; du reste, leur parti ne se déclare pas fasciste. Ils saluent toutefois « à la romaine » — geste qui s'oppose au poing levé du Front populaire. Ils ont un hymne, *France, libère-toi ;* ils prêtent serment. Sans oublier, dans toutes les réunions, le portrait géant de Doriot.

En 1938, les accords de Munich et la découverte des liens financiers avec l'Italie provoquent des dissensions au sein du PPF ; c'est le début d'une crise durable, à laquelle le parti de Doriot ne pourra survivre qu'à la faveur de la guerre et de la collaboration.

— Le *CSAR (*la *Cagoule)*. Le Comité secret d'action révolutionnaire, fondé en 1936, appartient à l'histoire des sociétés secrètes plus qu'à celle du fascisme. Mais bien de ses membres adhèrent aux idées fascistes. Il fut créé au lendemain de la victoire du Front populaire par des transfuges de l'Action française décidés à l'action, notamment Eugène Deloncle et Jean Filliol. Administrateur de sociétés, polytechnicien, ancien combattant plusieurs fois cité, Deloncle est particulièrement à l'aise dans l'univers des complots, des serments, des mystères... Pour lui, il importe de lutter par l'action clandestine contre les trois ennemis désignés : le bolchevisme, le Juif et la franc-maçonnerie [16].

Disposant de fonds, d'armes et de munitions, la Cagoule met à son compte un certain nombre d'activités : sabotages sur les avions en transit en France destinés aux républicains espagnols, exécution des frères Rosselli, militants antifascistes réfugiés en France. Mais le but ultime est le coup d'État. A cette fin, la

16. Voir Ph. Bourdrel, *la Cagoule,* Albin Michel, 1970.

Cagoule doit nécessairement entraîner une partie de l'armée. En mars 1937, le maréchal Franchet d'Esperey s'entremet afin d'unir les projets de Deloncle avec les activités du commandant Loustanau-Lacau. Celui-ci avait créé un « réseau Corvignolles », qu'on appela aussi la « Cagoule militaire », destiné à surveiller et faire expulser de l'armée les communistes. Mais Loustanau refuse de participer à tout mouvement putschiste. Sans se décourager, la Cagoule — après quelques attentats provocateurs (par exemple contre le siège de la Confédération générale du patronat français le 11 septembre 1937) — décide le coup de force pour la nuit du 15 au 16 novembre. Mais, faute du soutien de l'armée escompté jusqu'au bout, l'opération est finalement annulée. Les dirigeants de la Cagoule sont arrêtés peu de temps après. La guerre va les faire libérer. L'un de ces « cagoulards » se fera particulièrement connaître sous Vichy : Joseph Darnand, chef de la Milice.

— Un fascisme paysan : les *Chemises vertes* de Dorgères. Henri d'Halluin, fils de petits commerçants, journaliste dans la presse agricole sous le pseudonyme d'Henry Dorgères, se fait vraiment connaître en mars 1935, au cours d'une campagne électorale, à l'issue de laquelle il est battu de peu pour le siège que Camille Chautemps venait de laisser après son élection au Sénat. En quelques mois il devient le chef éloquent d'une *Défense paysanne,* où il sait regrouper des comités de défense paysanne régionaux, dont l'origine remonte à 1929, et qui étaient alors dirigés contre les assurances sociales. Propagandiste de la mythologie terrienne contre la « tyrannie des villes », violemment antiétatiste (« le fonctionnaire, voilà l'ennemi »), antimarxiste, xénophobe, le mouvement de Dorgères se donne des allures fascistes avec la création des Jeunesses paysannes. Vêtus de la chemise verte, décorés d'un insigne (une fourche et une faux entrecroisées sur un faisceau de blé), ils sabotent les réunions des adversaires et se préparent à établir une « Dictature paysanne », par laquelle la France retrouverait ses antiques vertus.

L'apogée du mouvement se situe entre 1936 et 1938. L'Ouest, le Nord, la région parisienne, la région de Nice, l'Algérie furent les plus touchés par le dorgérisme qui put compter sur plusieurs dizaines de milliers d'adhérents, dont 10 000 environ réellement actifs. Il est à noter que son influence dépassa le monde des notables et des petits exploitants, le dorgérisme réussissant à intégrer bon nombre de salariés agricoles [17].

Caporalisme et corporatisme.

Ces mouvements fascistes, avoués ou non, reprennent tous à leur compte la synthèse de Valois (fascisme = nationalisme + socialisme), en lui donnant un contenu variable mais avec cependant des constantes assez nettes. Ces organisations sont nées dans la crise générale des années trente ; elles prétendent faire sortir la France de la décadence. En face des menaces externes (restauration de l'Italie, de l'Allemagne, danger soviétique), elles dénoncent les faiblesses du pays : le régime parlementaire, la lutte des classes, la menace communiste... Changer de régime, mettre en place un État fort, à même de se faire respecter à l'extérieur, de rétablir et de maintenir l'ordre à l'intérieur, tel est le but commun de leur nationalisme. Un nationalisme qui, tôt ou tard, reprend à son compte la panacée antijuive.

Si pour Jean Renaud, de la Solidarité française, la « race aryenne » ne repose que sur des « hypothèses invérifiées », il dénonce en revanche les « puissances occultes de l'Internationale juive », « l'emprise de l'esprit, de la pensée, du travail de la nation par le Juif », car, « de la littérature pornographique au scandale financier ou au meeting révolutionnaire, on trouve au moins un Juif [18] ». Si l'antisémitisme n'apparaît qu'en 1936 dans la propagande franciste, Marcel Bucard comble vite son

17. Voir P. Ory, « Le dorgérisme », *Revue d'histoire moderne et contemporaine,* avr.-juin 1975.
18. J. Renaud, *La Solidarité française attaque,* 1935.

« retard » : « chasser les Juifs » devient chez lui un impératif obsessionnel. *Le Franciste* du 4 juin 1936 déclare que « le Front populaire est une invention juive » ; en 1938, Bucard publie sa déclaration de guerre : *l'Emprise juive*. Jacques Doriot, au début du PPF, ne professe aucun antisémitisme. La guerre d'Espagne venue, son journal, *l'Émancipation nationale,* se met à parler de « judéo-bolcheviks ». Insensiblement, l'organe du PPF se mêle au chœur antisémite, d'abord *mezzo voce,* puis *fortissimo*. Le 23 juillet 1938, Drieu La Rochelle y publie un article, « A propos de l'antisémitisme », où il est dit : « Nous ne pouvons admettre que, dans l'insuffisance actuelle des mœurs et des lois, tant de Juifs tiennent les leviers de commande de l'administration et de la politique. » Dans les mois qui suivent, les expressions « judéo-marxisme » ou « clan juif » deviennent monnaie courante. Entre *le Droit de vivre* de Bernard Lecache, président de la LICA, et *l'Émancipation nationale* de Doriot, la guerre est décidément entamée [19]. Quant aux écrivains de *Je suis partout,* qui se déclarent ouvertement fascistes, ils illustrent leur virulence antisémitique de vieille date par l'accueil qu'ils réservent aux *Bagatelles pour un massacre* de Céline : « La démocratie, partout et toujours, écrit Céline dans son [livre] éblouissant, n'est jamais que le paravent de la dictature juive [20]. » Ces journalistes, dans la droite ligne de Drumont, déposent une couronne au mur des Fédérés, pour l'anniversaire de la Semaine sanglante, tout en rivalisant d'agressions verbales contre les Juifs. Tout se passe comme si, en France, un courant fasciste devait nécessairement se jeter à un moment ou à un autre dans les marécages de l'antisémitisme.

Chaque organisation fasciste se proclame anticapitaliste mais leur « socialisme » ne va pas jusqu'à condamner la propriété privée. L'idéologie sociale des fascismes est très nettement

19. Voir P. Hollemart, *l'Idéologie de « l'Émancipation nationale », 1936-1939,* Institut d'études politiques de Paris, 1980 (mémoire de DEA).
20. P.-A. Cousteau, cité par P.-M. Dioudonnat, *op. cit.,* p. 224.

orientée en direction des classes moyennes : pour la Solidarité française, il faut « faciliter [au travailleur] dans la plus large mesure possible l'accession à la propriété » ; le PPF, lui, propose « le maintien et la défense de toutes les activités moyennes, paysannes, artisanales, commerciales et industrielles, qui constituent l'essence même de la nation »... Ces thèmes préindustriels sont complétés souvent par la nostalgie de la France villageoise. Le francisme préconise le « retour à la terre », le « repeuplement des campagnes », la « réorganisation de la vie rurale », tandis que Dorgères fait de ce retour le grand mythe de son mouvement.

Alors, le socialisme ? La solution au problème social, c'est pour tous le corporatisme. Il faut en finir avec la lutte des classes, l'affrontement entre syndicats et patronat, les idéaux collectivistes. Le corporatisme, c'est sur le plan économique l'unité nationale réalisée par la collaboration harmonieuse des classes dans la profession organisée. L'État doit avoir la faculté d'arbitrage. Il doit aussi veiller aux réalisations sociales d'intérêt général : hygiène sociale, sports, urbanisme, logements — « de façon, dit le PPF, à engendrer une race plus forte, plus saine... ».

Si diverses organisations fascistes récupèrent encore le terme de socialisme, celui-ci n'a plus grand-chose à voir avec les conceptions de Sorel et de Valois. Eux défendaient les principes d'un syndicalisme ouvrier resté libre. Les fascistes des années trente rêvent, pour leur part, de tenir en respect la classe ouvrière dans des institutions corporatistes d'où ses organisations propres seraient chassées. L'Italie et l'Allemagne sont devenues des modèles : « Là-bas, il n'y a plus de grèves ! » L'équation fasciste : nationalisme + socialisme n'est plus que de l'algèbre publicitaire.

Et les Croix-de-feu ?

Nous n'avons pas parlé jusqu'ici d'un mouvement qui symbolisait, plus encore que les précédents, le danger fasciste en France aux yeux des militants de gauche des années trente : les Croix-de-feu. Celles-ci, devenues, après leur dissolution de juin 1936, le parti social français, furent de très loin, au sein des nouvelles formations politiques de l'époque, les plus nombreuses, le PSF comptant jusqu'à 700 000 membres. Mais, quelles que soient les velléités de tel ou tel de ses adhérents — qui passèrent souvent du reste à des groupes plus « musclés » —, le parti de La Rocque ne saurait être considéré comme fasciste puisqu'il avait le souci de se tenir dans une stricte légalité et défendait un programme plus conservateur que « révolutionnaire ».

Au départ, ce n'était qu'une association d'anciens combattants comme tant d'autres. C'est lorsque le comte François de La Rocque, fils du général Raymond de La Rocque, et lui-même militaire à la retraite, devient président des Croix-de-feu en 1931, que l'association se transforme peu à peu en mouvement de masse, ouvert à tout le monde à partir de 1933 par la création de la Ligue des volontaires nationaux. Après la journée du 6 Février, au cours de laquelle les Croix-de-feu refusent de franchir les barrages policiers — La Rocque s'opposant, dira-t-il, « aux contagions de la folie » —, le mouvement attire les volontaires dont le nombre ne va pas cesser de s'élever.

« Fascistes ! » dira-t-on des Croix-de-feu, parce qu'ils constituent bientôt l'organisation anticommuniste la plus puissante ; parce qu'on y pratique la mystique du Chef ; parce qu'on y trouve aussi ces groupes de choc — les Dispos — organisés militairement, à la fois service d'ordre et bataillons de défense contre la subversion bolchevique.

Le PSF constitué le 10 juillet 1936 sous la présidence de La Rocque et la vice-présidence de Jean Mermoz, qui devait se tuer peu de temps après dans un accident d'avion, garde les mêmes caractéristiques que le mouvement Croix-de-feu, à ceci près qu'il se déclare désormais décidé à la conquête du pouvoir par les urnes, alors que la Ligue n'avait pas présenté de candidats officiels aux élections de 1936.

Virtuellement, tout se prêtait à faire du PSF un parti fasciste français : sa clientèle de classes moyennes, l'appui financier que

La Rocque aurait pu obtenir de grands industriels, son anticommunisme et son antisocialisme militants. Mais le colonel de La Rocque, éduqué dans un milieu chrétien social, imprima à l'idéologie et à la pratique de son parti une marque beaucoup plus traditionaliste que fasciste. Son refus de la violence (même si, au cours de certaines manifestations, des bagarres, comme à Clichy en mars 1937, provoquent des blessés et des morts), son refus de l'antisémitisme (même si, dans les rangs, maints Croix-de-feu de la base partagent le même racisme que les fascistes), son catholicisme fervent et les thèmes de la droite conservatrice, seulement retrempés par l'esprit militaire et la mystique ancien combattant qu'il prône, font de son organisation ce qu'on pourrait appeler un parti conservateur de masse. Car telle était la nouveauté du temps par rapport à la droite de naguère : ne pas laisser aux états-majors et aux politiciens l'avenir du pays ; le peuple devait y être activement associé. Mieux : il devait être mobilisé et se tenir toujours prêt. La Rocque comme Mermoz désiraient naïvement appliquer à la vie politique des recettes militaires, ce qui a amené René Rémond à qualifier leur mouvement de « scoutisme politique ».

Cependant, La Rocque joua un rôle appréciable dans l'échec du fascisme en France, dans la mesure où, polarisant la plus grosse partie des opposants de droite (voire d'extrême droite) au Front populaire, il garda une complète autonomie et fit de son mieux pour protéger ses ouailles de la contamination par les mouvements fascistes. On le vit nettement en juin 1937, lorsqu'il refusa d'adhérer au Front de la Liberté que Doriot avait créé pour contrecarrer le parti communiste et le Front populaire. Au cours d'un meeting tenu à l'époque, La Rocque déclara clairement : « Notre entrée dans le Front de la Liberté signifiait la fermeture de nos portes au recrutement populaire. Et nous étions classés fascistes — ce dont nous ne voulons à aucun prix[21]. »

21. Cité par Ph. Machefer, « L'union des droites, le PSF et le Front de la Liberté, 1936-1937 », *Revue d'histoire moderne et contemporaine,* janv.-mars 1970.

Doriot avait escompté attirer les Croix-de-feu pour les noyauter : la victoire du fascisme passait sans doute par là. Mais La Rocque tint ferme et le PPF se désagrégea.

Épilogue.

Ainsi, à la fin de 1938, passé la vague de peur sociale déclenchée par le Front populaire, les mouvements fascistes battent de l'aile. La France de Daladier, à la veille de la guerre, a retrouvé une certaine stabilité politique. La rupture du Front populaire suffirait-elle pour autant à expliquer l'échec du fascisme en France ? Elle y a certes contribué mais l'exemple de l'Italie, qui a vu la montée et la victoire du fascisme *après* et non pas *contre* la vague révolutionnaire de 1920-1921, inclinerait à quelque circonspection.

En fait, si le fascisme en France n'a pas su s'imposer, c'est que la droite française pouvait rester forte à l'*intérieur* de la légalité républicaine. La clientèle habituelle des fascismes — les classes moyennes, artisans, commerçants, employés, exploitants agricoles — était numériquement considérable en France. Mais ces classes moyennes adhéraient, dans une large mesure, à ces traditions républicaines, que le parti radical et aussi la Fédération républicaine de Marin incarnaient encore puissamment à l'époque. Économiquement, ces couches sociales étaient atteintes par la crise ; socialement, elles étaient aussi hostiles au pouvoir des « trusts » qu'aux solutions « collectivistes », mais ce double refus s'est exprimé à travers une grande diversité de choix politiques. Selon les régions et les milieux culturels, les membres de ces classes moyennes étaient soit attirés par les solutions autoritaires (mais La Rocque plutôt que Doriot), soit fidèles à une certaine idée de la République, celle de leurs pères ou de leurs instituteurs.

Un témoignage, saisi au cours d'une enquête, illustrera ce propos. Voici un épicier de la banlieue parisienne ; il lisait *la Victoire* de Gustave Hervé (celui qui publie en 1936 la brochure prémonitoire *C'est Pétain qu'il nous faut*) ; il voue Blum aux gémonies, etc. On lui demande s'il a été Croix-de-feu, comme son voisin le boucher. « Ah ! non ! monsieur, dit-il, moi, j'ai toujours été *républicain !* » Ledit boucher, s'il avait été présent, aurait juré ses grands dieux que, pour lui aussi, la République, c'était sacré.

Or, ni en Italie ni en Allemagne ceux qui ont été sollicités par le fascisme ou le national-socialisme ne pouvaient avoir de ces réflexes. S'il y avait des influences marxistes — au demeurant circonscrites aux milieux ouvriers et intellectuels —, il n'existait pas ce que nous appelons des traditions démocratiques. La République de Weimar avait été d'emblée rejetée par une grande partie de l'opinion, accusée d'être un produit du *Diktat* étranger. Quant à l'Italie, le suffrage universel venait tout juste d'être instauré en 1919.

Depuis les années 1870, la droite française, vaille que vaille, s'était accommodée de la République parlementaire ; elle l'avait en partie colonisée. C'est dans ce cadre politique que les hommes d'affaires avaient pu prospérer ; la petite-bourgeoisie, protéger ses intérêts contre les « gros » ; les ouvriers, défendre leurs organisations de classe ; les employés, espérer par les vertus de l'école laïque la promotion sociale de leurs enfants...

Il est vrai que l'industrialisation du pays, l'essor des grands magasins, l'exode rural, la destructuration progressive de la société villageoise commencèrent, à la fin du XIXe siècle, à remettre en question l'harmonie républicaine. La Grande Guerre, la révolution bolchevique et la crise des années trente achevèrent de la bouleverser. Mais pas au point de remettre en question un cadre politique qui, malgré ses faiblesses et ses corruptions, laissait aux différentes couches sociales au moins l'illusion de vivre dans un pays libre et pacifique.

Or, le fascisme porte en lui l'impérialisme. Il porte en lui la guerre, comme moyen de gouvernement, comme éthique collective, comme mythe national. La nation fasciste, c'est la nation militarisée. Les escouades françaises n'étaient guère destinées à la guerre — comme les squadristes, les sections d'assaut ou les phalangistes. La France n'avait plus de conquêtes à faire depuis 1918 ; le fascisme français avait beau se déclarer nationaliste : il était pacifiste — du moins face à l'Allemagne d'où venait le danger. Ce n'est pas là la moindre de ses contradictions.

Seule la guerre, imposée d'ailleurs et perdue, remet les fascismes en selle. Deloncle crée le MSR (Mouvement social-révolutionnaire), qui s'affirme « national », « socialiste », « raciste » et déclame contre les Juifs, « banquiers internationaux dont la guerre est la principale source de profits ». Déat lance le RNP (Rassemblement national populaire), au moyen d'une brève entente avec Deloncle, en janvier 1941 ; il s'applique à donner à son mouvement une certaine cohérence doctrinale, ce qui l'amène à publier en 1942 *le Parti unique*. L'ancien normalien, l'agrégé de philosophie, l'ancien socialiste, est désormais entré carrément dans la carrière de l'antisémitisme fasciste : « Le problème, l'unique problème, est donc de faire comprendre au peuple français la nécessité d'une défense systématique et résolue contre les infiltrations juives [22]. » Les Français, dit-il encore, « feront aussi cette réflexion fort opportune que notre peuple, plus que d'autres, a besoin de se refaire biologiquement, qu'il lui manque à la fois le nombre et la qualité, que les précautions prises par les éleveurs de bétail seraient utilement appliquées à l'élevage des petits d'hommes, et d'hommes français, et que la pureté de la race est la condition première de tout redressement démographique [23] ». Doriot, lui, relance le PPF et rivalise avec Déat dans la fuite en avant collaborationniste, faisant siens non seulement les idées hitlériennes mais jusqu'à l'uniforme allemand. Le Francisme de Bucard se nazifie sans retenue. Dans le numéro du 27 décembre 1941 de son hebdomadaire, *le Franciste,* on peut lire : « En 1939, 300 000 Juifs vivaient sur le territoire français ; 5 000 ont déjà été déportés. Quand se décidera-t-on à

22. M. Déat, *Le Parti unique,* 1943, p. 129 (recueil d'articles publiés dans *l'Œuvre,* du 18 juillet au 4 septembre 1942).
23. *Ibid.*, p. 131.

coffrer et à éliminer les 295 000 restants ? » Ce fanatisme est loin d'être isolé ; c'est aussi celui de l'équipe de *Je suis partout,* dont fait partie Rebatet. On lit dans *les Décombres,* que celui-ci publie en 1942, au moment des rafles et des déportations : « La juiverie offre l'exemple unique dans l'histoire de l'humanité, d'une race pour laquelle le châtiment collectif soit le seul juste [24]. »

Ce ne sont plus là que des fascismes d'imitation, sécrétant leur fiel et ourdissant leurs menues intrigues sous l'aile tutélaire de l'aigle allemand.

Tous ces nationalistes se mettent par la logique implacable de la situation au service d'un nationalisme étranger, celui — ô ironie ! — de l'« ennemi héréditaire ». Or Hitler, à ces avatars de fascismes vaincus, préfère la collaboration du maréchal-patriarche, qui a reçu les pleins pouvoirs en juillet 1940. Pétain reprend la formule lancée naguère par La Rocque : « Travail, Famille, Patrie. » Mais le régime du maréchal n'a pas les mêmes prudences que le parti du colonel. Il fait entrer l'antisémitisme dans la loi, ce qui apparaît, entre autres mesures contre-révolutionnaires, comme une rupture avec 1789. En 1943, alors que La Rocque est déporté en Allemagne après avoir fourni des renseignements à l'Intelligence Service, Pétain laisse créer la Milice française, dont le futur chef Darnand déclare bientôt sa « volonté de voir instaurer en France un régime autoritaire national et socialiste, permettant à la France de s'intégrer dans l'Europe de demain ».

Nous avons dit plus haut ce qu'était devenu le « socialisme » des fascistes français ; c'est dans l'épreuve de 1940-1944 qu'on a pu mesurer leur « nationalisme ». Lucien Rebatet, formé à l'école du nationalisme intégral, en exprimait la toute relativité dans un article de *Je suis partout* du 28 juillet 1944 : « J'admire Hitler. Nous admirons Hitler, et nous avons pour cela de très sérieuses raisons... C'est lui qui portera devant l'Histoire l'honneur d'avoir liquidé la démocratie. »

24. L. Rebatet, *Les Décombres,* Denoël, 1942, p. 566.

La formule de Valois n'était décidément plus de saison. Mais Valois lui-même, à la veille de sa mort dans le camp de déportation de Bergen-Belsen, avait cessé d'être « fasciste » depuis longtemps.

Le fascisme est intimement lié à la Grande Guerre et aux bouleversements dont elle fut l'origine, jusqu'à la crise des années trente. Il est remarquable cependant que la formule politique, sinon linguistique, en a été élaborée avant 1914 ; qu'en France un certain nombre de tentatives ont été faites pour allier une classe ouvrière révolutionnaire aux couches sociales et aux familles d'esprit contre-révolutionnaires ; que l'antisémitisme a été utilisé comme le détonateur de ce mélange. Les feux ainsi allumés ne furent, en France, que de paille, et les violences restèrent le plus souvent verbales. Le système politique français demeura solidement organisé autour des familles idéologiques qui s'étaient mises en place tout au long du XIXe siècle.

Si la menace fasciste devint plus sérieuse entre les deux guerres, et surtout dans les années trente, en raison notamment des difficultés réelles et des appréhensions vagues éprouvées par les classes moyennes — c'est un fait que la France y résista victorieusement ; que le fascisme y fut surtout un état d'esprit dans une partie de l'opinion ; que les organisations qui en avaient suivi peu ou prou le modèle demeurèrent plutôt faibles.

On a pu dire que les formes atténuées que la crise économique prit en France ont épargné à celle-ci la tentation fasciste. C'est possible mais seulement dans une certaine mesure car les exemples de l'Angleterre et des États-Unis, où la crise fut violente sans menacer les institutions démocratiques, nous montrent bien que d'autres facteurs ont agi, qui ressortissent en particulier aux héritages et aux habitudes culturels des différentes nations. Le succès des fascismes s'est appuyé socialement sur deux masses de manœuvre : la petite-bourgeoisie appauvrie et apeurée, et les ouvriers chômeurs ou en passe de l'être, dans des États tardivement unifiés et sans habitudes démocratiques enracinées. Il n'est pas douteux qu'en France cent cinquante ans d'« esprit républicain » et de résistance périodique aux tentatives contre-révolutionnaires ont mithridatisé dans une large mesure le corps social. D'autre part, l'enthousiasme belliqueux, l'esprit conquérant, l'agressivité impérialiste qui sont au fond des fascismes n'avaient plus cours en France — où le pacifisme de gauche et de droite finit par dominer l'opinion. Cependant, par un effet pervers, contre lequel le pacifisme n'est jamais prémuni, celui-ci devait en définitive faciliter la guerre, la défaite et ainsi la chute de la démocratie. C'est une autre histoire.

Toutefois, quand bien même le fascisme *intérieur* n'a jamais sérieusement menacé les institutions françaises (la dictature pétainiste n'eut droit à l'existence que par la défaite militaire, elle s'évanouit du moment que la France fut libérée), on doit remarquer que dans notre pays presque toutes les tentatives qu'on peut qualifier de « fascistes » ont repris à leur compte l'idéologie antisémite qui, elle, ne manquait pas de continuité. Le Faisceau mis à part, qui fit long feu, toutes les autres figures du fascisme français ont réactivé d'une manière ou d'une autre les formules de Drumont. Pendant une soixantaine d'années, moyennant une accalmie due à la Première Guerre mondiale, l'antisémitisme en France n'a pas désarmé. Il aura fallu précisément la défaite des fascismes pour lui arracher ses dernières prétentions de légitimité.

6

Les catholiques français face aux fascismes

En quoi les milieux influencés par le catholicisme ont-ils été sensibles à l'attrait exercé par les régimes autoritaires ?

Les motivations proprement religieuses du comportement politique sont toujours difficiles à isoler. Ce que l'on peut dire pour les années trente, c'est que la pratique religieuse et l'électorat de droite superposent leurs grandes masses. Il suffit de comparer la célèbre carte de la pratique religieuse dans la France rurale établie par le chanoine Boulard, après la Seconde Guerre mondiale, avec les cartes électorales pour s'en convaincre : le Nord, l'Ouest, l'Est, le sud-est du Massif central, la Haute-Savoie, le Pays basque..., ce sont là des coïncidences d'une grande permanence.

Il est notable, d'autre part, que les élections de 1936 — qui ont divisé la France en deux camps nettement tranchés — ne se sont pas faites, comme c'était le cas en d'autres temps, sur la question religieuse. Si les catholiques, dans leur immense majorité, votent à droite, ce n'est donc pas à cause de la conjoncture particulière des années trente ; c'est en raison de traditions lointaines, d'une histoire qui remonte au moins à la Révolution de 1789, des conditions dans lesquelles le régime républicain s'est imposé et s'est fortifié : par sa lutte contre l'Église.

En théorie, le catholicisme n'est ni de gauche ni de droite.

C'est ce que rappelle, à la veille des élections de 1936, un article de *la Vie intellectuelle :* « Le catholicisme que l'on place à droite serait tout aussi bien — ou tout aussi mal — à gauche. Il est pour l'ordre, pour l'autorité, pour la propriété, pour la patrie, d'accord ! Mais dites-moi, est-ce qu'il serait par hasard contre la justice, contre la liberté, contre le progrès, contre l'État, contre la paix ? » (10 mai 1936).

En fait, il n'est pas douteux que les milieux catholiques sont mieux disposés que d'autres à appeler de leurs vœux un régime fort. Non pas un régime fasciste, à tout le moins le modèle qui s'en est imposé aujourd'hui à nos esprits : les fascismes et l'Église ne font pas forcément bon ménage, car ils se trouvent en concurrence dans le domaine idéologique ; plutôt un régime patriarcal, respectueux de la religion, des traditions, des hiérarchies.

Quelles sont les raisons d'une telle sympathie ?

L'univers mental des catholiques est encore, pour la majeure partie d'entre eux, centré sur une conception du monde préindustriel. Le courant traditionaliste, antilibéral, n'est pas seulement représenté par les journalistes de *l'Action française ;* le catholicisme social en est pénétré ; la crise de 1929 en justifie le bien-fondé. Pour ne prendre que deux noms, fort éloignés l'un de l'autre, Le Cour Grandmaison et Mounier, il est frappant de retrouver dans leur discours des condamnations du libéralisme à peu près identiques. « Le grand reproche, dit le premier, que nous adressons au libéralisme, c'est précisément d'avoir, sous le masque trompeur de la liberté, asservi l'homme à l'homme, le travail à l'argent [1]. » Et le second d'écrire : « Il y a toute une psychanalyse à faire de cet individualisme dont le langage sublimé en termes de liberté, d'autonomie, de tolérance, a couvert le règne brutal des concurrences et des coups de force [2]... » Ce qui ne signifie pas que Mounier, fondateur

1. *Journal officiel,* Débats parlementaires, 15 février 1938, p. 342.
2. E. Mounier, « Refaire la Renaissance », *Esprit,* octobre 1932.

d'*Esprit,* est favorable aux régimes autoritaires ; pourtant, la condamnation du libéralisme par ce catholique d'avant-garde, de même que ses réticences pour le mot de démocratie (il lui préfère celui de « république »), montre bien la force d'une tradition dont les sources remontent haut.

Ce refus du libéralisme masque lui-même une défiance, chez certains une phobie, du monde industriel, une horreur de la lutte des classes, la nostalgie plus ou moins explicite d'un ordre antérieur fondé principalement sur les valeurs religieuses. Mais ce courant est renforcé depuis la fin du XIXe siècle par les couches importantes d'une petite-bourgeoisie (urbaine et rurale) qui n'est pas obligatoirement catholique mais qui, en face de la concentration commerciale et industrielle et des mutations sociales qu'elle provoque, éprouve une angoisse qu'exprime très bien, quoique d'une façon pathologique, toute l'œuvre d'un Drumont. L'hostilité au changement, l'antisémitisme, le thème du retour à la terre (c'est, trente-cinq ans avant la formule pétainiste, le titre d'un ouvrage de Jules Méline), voilà autant d'expressions de cette peur de l'avenir, approfondie par la suite à cause de la guerre et de ses lendemains chaotiques, à cause de la crise économique et des tensions sociales conséquentes... La terre se meurt, les magasins à prix unique menacent les boutiques, les églises se lézardent...

A ces causes anciennes — qui mêlent d'ailleurs catholiques et non-catholiques — il convient évidemment d'ajouter le refus et la peur du communisme. Un régime politique, ouvertement en guerre contre la religion, s'est instauré en Russie ; un immense territoire chrétien a été rayé de la carte de la chrétienté et voici qu'en Occident, en France même, la menace prend forme et bientôt explose dans le succès communiste de 1936 !

On comprend dès lors l'attrait sur bien des catholiques de ces régimes autoritaires qui s'affirment antilibéraux, anticapitalistes, aussi bien qu'anticommunistes ; qui proclament le bienfait des valeurs d'ordre, de famille, de patrie, de travail, bref, qui prétendent fonder, contre le désordre des libéralismes et la tyrannie du communisme, la renaissance d'un monde ordonné, voire patriarcal.

Les mouvements fascistes français et les ligues s'inspirent-ils dans leur doctrine des principes chrétiens ? Avaient-ils une clientèle catholique ?

Dans les slogans des fascismes français (la Solidarité française, le Francisme, le PPF), les allusions aux valeurs chrétiennes sont également rares. Mais les ennemis désignés (l'instituteur laïc, le franc-maçon, le marxiste), de même que les valeurs et les solutions mises en avant (la France rurale, la natalité, la famille, l'union des Français, le corporatisme), sont autant d'éléments doctrinaux et émotionnels sympathiques aux catholiques. Toutefois ces mouvements ont été trop faibles ou trop éphémères... Autrement important est le cas des Croix-de-feu, devenues le PSF de La Rocque, catholique pratiquant notoire. Ses idées sans originalité s'inspiraient d'un « corporatisme d'inspiration sociale-chrétienne » (Machefer). Dans *Disciplines d'action,* en 1940, La Rocque écrira : « L'inspiration reste inchangée ; nous la puisons dans une fidélité immuable à la civilisation chrétienne. » Avant Pétain, le PSF affirmait en 1936 : « L'ordre français a toujours reposé sur trois éléments : Travail, Famille, Patrie. » L'influence de La Rocque sur les milieux catholiques a été indiscutable [3], mais non spécifique, là encore : l'électorat des classes moyennes, que le PSF disputa aux radicaux lors des élections partielles où il se présenta avant la guerre, est mieux accordé à l'image du PSF que sa composante catholique. Quoi qu'il en soit, le succès même du PSF, qui se coupe de l'extrême droite et réaffirme en permanence son légalisme, dans les milieux catholiques tendrait à prouver finalement la résistance de ceux-ci aux solutions vraiment fascistes.

Il reste que, pour parodier une formule de Raoul Girardet, il y a eu une imprégnation autoritaire du catholicisme français

3. A titre indicatif, notons par exemple qu'aux élections de 1936 Georges Bidault, candidat du PDP, est nettement battu en Normandie par un candidat Croix-de-feu.

dans les années trente. Celle-ci s'est affirmée beaucoup moins à propos de l'Allemagne qu'à propos de l'Espagne. La guerre d'Espagne a cristallisé dramatiquement les attitudes politiques des catholiques.

Qu'a représenté le franquisme pour les catholiques français ? Il ne faut pas sous-estimer, il ne faut pas surestimer la division des catholiques français à ce sujet. La sous-estimer serait faire bon marché du pluralisme catholique et, plus encore, méconnaître ce qui prépare, au sein du catholicisme français, ce qu'on pourrait appeler la sortie de leur ghetto, tant il est vrai que le milieu catholique reste clos sur lui-même. Mais surestimer la division, ce serait inversement laisser s'accréditer l'idée qu'une sorte d'équilibre, disons entre les profranquistes et les antifranquistes, se serait réalisée ; or ce ne fut pas le cas. Disons donc tout net que la masse des catholiques pratiquants, lecteurs de *la Croix,* de *l'Écho de Paris* ou de *la France catholique,* s'accordent à tenir pour légitime la « croisade » franquiste contre la révolution anarchiste et communiste.

Qu'on suive, par exemple, *le Nouvelliste,* quotidien conservateur lyonnais, de clientèle catholique, journal rival du *Progrès* radical, et qui a fait l'objet d'une étude récente de la part d'une étudiante américaine [4]. Ce journal provincial est un bon reflet du conservatisme catholique des années trente. L'horreur du Front populaire s'y étale en termes violents ; le spectre de la « soviétisation de la France » le hante. La comparaison avec l'Espagne, où un gouvernement de Front populaire a triomphé, va de soi. Le « poison communiste », le « virus rouge », est à l'œuvre au-delà et en deçà des Pyrénées. Soutenir la rébellion antigouvernementale, quand elle éclate, est donc de toute nécessité :

« Ce que vous appelez fascisme en un terme générique n'est qu'une angoisse, très noble, poussant les individus à se libérer du joug et de l'oppression qu'au nom du Front populaire le

4. Marjorie Anne Sa'adah, *Means and End : The Catholic Conservative Right in France, 1934-1940,* Radcliffe College, mars 1936 (mémoire dactylographié).

gouvernement et les groupes de la majorité imposent à des catégories très nombreuses de l'opinion du pays. C'est là un mouvement de révolte saine et même sacrée qui s'empare du cœur des Espagnols, et contre lequel nous-mêmes nous nous sentons débordés. Vous avez fait, vous ferez une politique de persécution, de violence et d'extermination contre tout ce qui est de droite. Mais vous vous trompez profondément : plus votre violence sera grande, plus la réaction sera forte. »

La guerre d'Espagne, comme le dit un journaliste du *Nouvelliste,* en mars 1939, est « pour nous Français [...] le fait capital de l'après-guerre ». Il y va de la défense de la civilisation occidentale, c'est la lutte ouverte « entre le bolchevisme et la civilisation chrétienne ».

Cette adhésion au franquisme (à la fois contre les rouges et pour la défense des valeurs chrétiennes) se fait sans hésitation, sans trouble de conscience ; c'est une solidarité catholique et conservatrice qui ne se discute pas. Or, on ne voit rien de tel, dans ce même journal, en faveur de l'Allemagne nazie. Au contraire, on y fait — avec modération, certes ! — le procès et de la politique antisémite de Hitler et du régime totalitaire, du régime policier : « Dieu nous préserve de jamais avoir chez nous une Gestapo. »

Il n'en est pas de même pour l'Italie de Mussolini. L'abolition du régime parlementaire, la mise au pas des partis et des syndicats (au pas ou au rancart), les accords du Latran qui ont permis la réintégration des catholiques dans la communauté italienne, le corporatisme vanté par le régime (le corporatisme ! mot magique des années trente ! solution miracle ! et ce ne sont pas seulement les catholiques traditionalistes qui le revendiquent : voir François Perroux, Marcel Prélot, etc.), tout cela a travaillé en faveur de l'Italie mussolinienne — sans compter les options diplomatiques de la droite. Cette sympathie pour l'Italie a été sujette à variations mais, jusqu'à la guerre d'Éthiopie, on peut en déceler la marque jusque dans les pages des publications catholiques « avancées ». C'est ainsi qu'en septembre 1935,

G. Viance, de retour d'Italie, publie dans *la Vie intellectuelle* un article sur « Fascisme et liberté », largement justificateur de l'État fasciste, quand bien même c'est au nom du syndicalisme et de Georges Sorel... Évidemment, après l'Éthiopie, nombre de ces catholiques vont dénoncer Mussolini : le fascisme pour eux découvre alors son vrai visage. Il n'en reste pas moins important de voir combien, jusqu'aux rangs de certains catholiques d'avant-garde, la critique du libéralisme ou celle, comme dit G. Viance, du « démocratisme égalitaire » ont pu favoriser de secrètes sympathies pour les régimes autoritaires.

En quoi cela a-t-il préparé Vichy ?

Pour aller à l'essentiel, je crois bon de revenir à l'observation que je faisais plus haut, quant aux appréhensions du milieu catholique, en particulier de la petite-bourgeoisie. N'oublions pas, d'autre part, la répugnance des catholiques pour la politique — monde de l'impureté, de la compromission, de l'ambiguïté. Les catholiques français d'alors (mais est-ce bien changé aujourd'hui ?) ne pensent pas la politique en termes politiques. Vastes adhésions, refus massifs : le cœur parle plus que la raison. Machiavel autant que Marx leur sont horribles. Rien dans l'éducation chrétienne ne préparait alors à l'« affrontement », comme dira Mounier.

On comprend dès lors la faveur de Vichy pour tant de catholiques. C'est une revanche de la société patriarcale unifiée contre la société industrielle divisée. Revanche des valeurs rustiques sur la ville babylonienne. Revanche de la « morale » sur la « politique » — celle-ci jugée comme chose purement technique confiée à des spécialistes, tandis que le peuple vaque à régénérer la France au moyen des vertus privées et communautaires. La grande peur de mai-juin 1936 est encore dans le subconscient de beaucoup. L'ordre est revenu, la propreté, le respect de l'autorité... Avec Vichy, pour maints catholiques, la parenthèse qui s'était ouverte en 1789 vient de se fermer. La défaite brutale de juin 40 a été le châtiment divin d'une nation qui avait perdu Dieu depuis un siècle et demi. Le vieux maréchal devenait l'instrument de la rédemption française. « Travail, Famille, Patrie : ces trois mots sont les nôtres », dira en 1940 le cardinal Gerlier. La société conflictuelle — que les catholiques ont tant de mal à admettre — a laissé place de nouveau à la patrie familiale sous la trinité du Père, du Chef et du Soldat. « L'air se purifie autour de nous, écrit Mgr Lecœur, évêque de Saint-Flour ; l'atmosphère s'embaume de ces idées de justice, d'honnêteté, de fraternité, d'idéal chrétien dont la sève qui monte dans le grand arbre de France va le faire reverdir. »

Quels sont ceux qui, dans les années trente, ont résisté à ces tendances ?

Dans une très large mesure, la résistance aux courants autoritaires s'est confondue longtemps avec la résistance à l'hégémonie de l'Action française sur le monde catholique. Il est difficile d'imaginer aujourd'hui le formidable empire que Maurras et les siens ont exercé sur les esprits dans l'entre-deux-guerres. De ce point de vue, on peut dire que le pape Pie XI a joué un rôle décisif en condamnant l'Action française en 1926. Mais il fallut bien des années encore pour que les intellectuels et les prêtres formés par Maurras ou modifient leur attitude ou perdent de leur influence. Dans cette lutte contre l'Action française, il faut mettre en première ligne l'ACJF, qui, à partir de 1927, va former des générations de démocrates-chrétiens : ce sont les jeunes gens sortis de l'ACJF qui vont former les cadres du parti démocrate populaire, qui vont faire vivre le journal *l'Aube,* la revue *Politique...,* ce sont eux qui formeront aussi les cadres de la résistance chrétienne et, plus tard, ceux du MRP. On connaît, d'autre part, les publications des dominicains et celles des jésuites, qui ont compté pour beaucoup dans l'émancipation du catholique français, de même que l'influence des grands écrivains : Maritain, Mauriac, Bernanos ; l'action menée par les Semaines sociales... Bref, tout autant de filets d'eau qui ont fini par faire un grand fleuve en 1944. Mais, bien avant l'évolution que l'on constatera après la guerre, une bonne partie de l'Église, des intellectuels, du clergé apparaissent comme des éléments de résistance aux fascismes. Il en résulte souvent une hostilité déclarée à l'Église de la part des milieux d'extrême droite : l'anticléricalisme est une des composantes du fascisme. Un exemple, dans *les Décombres* de Rebatet ; on y lit, entre autres : « A la veille de la guerre, tous les grands organes du clergé étaient passés à l'ennemi : la puissante " Bonne Presse " de *la Croix* avec le démagogue Mercklen et sa bande, le judéo-bolcheviste *Sept* des dominicains, les *Études* des jésuites, les *Dossiers de l'Action populaire,* celle-ci grande idée de Ratti [*i.e.* Pie XI], exprimant les vœux de la catholicité pour le succès économique des Soviets, les grandes maisons de livres, avec leurs collections mystiques et sociales dirigées par des Juifs convertis [5]. » On a vraiment l'impression, à écouter ces gens d'extrême droite, que l'Église a viré au rouge.

Et le rôle d'*Esprit* dans tout cela ?

Mounier, l'animateur de « la fameuse bande d'*Esprit* », en qui le même Rebatet voyait « l'avant-garde du judéo-christianisme », n'appartient pas, paradoxalement, au courant dont on parlait plus haut. Il a toujours affiché une certaine répugnance pour la démocratie-chrétienne, non sans ingratitude. Mais, en 1932, quand il fonde *Esprit,* la vieille lutte sillonniste et démocrate-chrétienne contre l'Action française lui paraît périmée. La condamnation pontificale a levé cette hypothèque intellectuelle. On se moque un peu, à *Esprit,* de ces démocrates-chrétiens dont toute l'ambition est de réconcilier l'Église avec le radical-socialisme. Libéralisme, démocratie parlementaire, ce sont là presque des synonymes associés, dans l'imagerie d'*Esprit,* à l'inconsistant, au flasque, au mou. L'« éloge de la force », tel qu'on le pratique à *Esprit,* aurait pu entraîner la revue à quelque sympathie pour le fascisme. Mais non ! En janvier 1934, dans un numéro spécial sur les « pseudo-valeurs spirituelles fascistes », Mounier déclare sans ambages : « Nous appellerons [...] fascisme, sur le plan politique, social et économique, une réaction de

5. L. Rebatet, *Les Décombres, op. cit.,* p. 547.

défense du capitalisme… » En septembre de la même année, la revue dénonce les « duplicités du corporatisme ». En juin 1935, en face du Rassemblement populaire en formation, la revue prêche la nécessité pour les révolutionnaires « de figurer dans quelque front provisoire de défense non du régime mais du minimum d'humanité et de liberté que porte ce régime, minimum d'humanité et de liberté à son tour menacé » (A. Ulmann, « L'émeute contre la révolution »). La guerre d'Éthiopie, la guerre d'Espagne, l'abdication de Munich…, lors de tous ces grands drames de l'avant-guerre, *Esprit* s'affirme nettement comme adversaire des régimes autoritaires et fascistes — et de tout ce qui peut les favoriser. C'est ainsi que pour répondre à la campagne d'antisémitisme relancée par un numéro spécial de *Je suis partout,* Mounier et ses amis consacrent un numéro du *Voltigeur* (bimensuel, annexe d'*Esprit*), le 1er mars 1939, à la réplique : « L'antisémitisme contre la France ».

Toutefois, on doit à la vérité de dire que si Mounier et *Esprit* sont allés effectivement beaucoup plus loin que les démocrates-chrétiens dans leur volonté de rupture avec « le désordre établi », il n'empêche que, par défiance profonde de la démocratie parlementaire, ils n'ont pas eu le réflexe élémentaire d'un Edmond Michelet en juin 1940. Ces premières hésitations de 1940 aussi bien que les sympathies pour le parti communiste exprimées par la revue après la guerre (et la condescendance pour le parti socialiste) laissent supposer que la laïcisation du politique que Mounier avait su si bien définir et qui, de fait, éloigna toujours la revue des partis plus ou moins confessionnels, n'est pas allée jusqu'à son terme. Dans certaines adhésions comme dans certains refus d'*Esprit,* je me demande si l'on ne retrouve pas parfois la marque profonde et ancienne de l'antilibéralisme catholique.

7

Une parabole fasciste : Gilles *de Drieu La Rochelle*

Malgré leur échec politique en France, les idées fascistes ont pu y trouver un terrain fertile : une famille d'esprits formés par les œuvres de Drumont, de Barrès, de Maurras y inclinait naturellement. N'est-ce pas en France qu'on peut observer les signes — au moins doctrinaux — les plus nets d'un proto-fascisme avant 1914 ? La démarche d'un Drumont et d'un Morès, le « socialisme » d'un Barrès, la convergence d'un Valois et d'un Sorel : autant d'étapes dans la genèse du fascisme, c'est-à-dire l'alliance théorique du nationalisme et du socialisme contre la démocratie libérale et parlementaire. Quoi qu'il en advînt par la suite, le fascisme a été durablement pensé, en effet, par ses adeptes intellectuels français comme le résultat de cette synthèse voulue avant 1914 par la gauche de l'Action française (Valois) et les transfuges du syndicalisme révolutionnaire (Berth, Sorel) : « Ce sont deux mouvements qui semblent, et qui sont, en effet, aux antipodes l'un de l'autre ; et, néanmoins, c'est de leur libre opposition que jaillira le nouvel équilibre social [1]. » Parallèlement à ce qui se passe en Italie à la même époque — la rencontre d'une extrême gauche et d'une extrême droite nationaliste autour

1. É. Berth, cité par P. Andreu, *Notre maître, M. Sorel*, Grasset, 1953, p. 88.

de la *Lupa,* revue dirigée par Paolo Orano [2] —, on observe en France un semblable creuset, ainsi décrit par Drieu La Rochelle :

« Sans doute quand on se réfère à cette époque, on s'aperçoit que quelques éléments de l'atmosphère fasciste étaient réunis en France vers 1913, avant qu'ils le fussent ailleurs. Il y avait des jeunes gens sortis des diverses classes de la société, qui étaient animés par l'amour de l'héroïsme et de la violence et qui rêvaient de combattre ce qu'ils appelaient le mal sur deux fronts : capitalisme et socialisme parlementaire, et de prendre leur bien des deux côtés. Il y avait, je crois, à Lyon, des gens qui s'intitulaient socialistes-royalistes ou quelque chose d'approchant. Déjà, le mariage du nationalisme et du socialisme était projeté. Oui, en France, aux alentours de l'Action française et de Péguy, il y avait la nébuleuse d'une sorte de fascisme [3]. »

Passons sur l'à-peu-près d'une telle évocation ; l'important est ici la définition du fascisme, *tel qu'on y crut* (et non point tel qu'il fut réalisé), cette alliance explosive de deux « absolus » — comme disait encore Berth — que pouvait tenter de structurer Georges Valois en fondant le Faisceau en 1925, sur le modèle mussolinien :

« L'opposition du nationalisme et du socialisme, écrit-il, a paru irréductible dans le régime parlementaire [...]. L'opération salvatrice du fascisme est d'annuler le caractère irréductible de cette opposition [4]. »

Le Faisceau a fait long feu, comme on sait, mais non l'idée qui le sous-tendait — cette fameuse synthèse opératoire. Ce qu'on a parfois appelé « l'esprit des années 1930 [5] » avait bien pour dénominateur commun : le refus de la démocratie bourgeoise et

2. Voir E. Santarelli, « Le socialisme national en Italie », *le Mouvement social,* janv.-mars 1965. L'auteur mentionne l'influence sorélienne dans ce rapprochement.
3. *Les Nouvelles littéraires,* 2 février 1934.
4. *Le Nouveau Siècle,* 25 janvier 1926.
5. Voir J. Touchard, « L'esprit des années 1930 », in *Tendances politiques dans la vie française depuis 1789,* Hachette, 1960.

parlementaire, et la volonté pour édifier un « ordre nouveau », de réunir les énergies de droite et de gauche contre la molle République de concentration. Après février 1934, les « non-conformistes des années 30 [6] » durent choisir leur camp, qui la droite, qui la gauche : décidément, il était difficile de changer la règle du jeu politique en France. C'est à ce moment-là pourtant que Pierre Drieu La Rochelle est saisi d'un nouvel espoir : n'a-t-on pas vu, dans la manifestation du 6 février, des ouvriers communistes marcher du même pas que des bourgeois nationalistes ? Peu de temps plus tard, il se déclare *fasciste* et publie une série d'articles recueillis bientôt sous le titre de *Socialisme fasciste* [7]. En 1936, Drieu pense avoir découvert l'expression politique de ses idées dans le PPF de Doriot — ce maître d'œuvre enfin trouvé de la synthèse fasciste. Pendant deux ans, il va s'affirmer comme un des porte-plume les plus remarqués de *l'Émancipation nationale,* l'organe du PPF, jusqu'à sa rupture avec Doriot en octobre 1938.

A la même époque, un autre écrivain fasciste, Robert Brasillach, suivait un itinéraire parallèle sinon identique. Pour lui aussi, la « grande recherche » était de réaliser « l'idée fasciste ou nationale-socialiste », savoir « l'union d'une doctrine sociale forte et de l'intelligence nationale [8] ».

Si telle est bien, en ses débuts, l'originalité du fascisme, on peut légitimement conclure à son échec : dans les régimes mussolinien et hitlérien montrés en exemple par les écrivains fascistes français [9], on sait à quel point le nationalisme a complètement étouffé le « socialisme ». Mais à rester dans l'œuvre des fascistes français, on peut mesurer la pauvreté de leur propre socialisme : si Valois restait encore proche des concep-

6. J. Loubet Del Bayle, *Les Non-Conformistes des années 30,* Éd. du Seuil-Gallimard, 1969.

7. *Socialisme fasciste,* 1934.

8. R. Brasillach, *Notre avant-guerre, op. cit.,* p. 30.

9. Voir P. Sérant, *le Romantisme fasciste... ou l'œuvre politique de quelques écrivains français,* Fasquelle, 1960.

tions soréliennes, Drieu et moins encore Brasillach ne prenaient au sérieux les fondements les plus communs du socialisme. Le mot était pratique, on en jouait abusivement. Dans le cas de Drieu, on peut même se demander jusqu'où allait son nationalisme : n'était-ce pas le drame des fascistes français, que d'avoir cru voir, au lendemain du 6 Février, « l'aube du fascisme se leve [r] sur la France [10] », et d'avoir eu à subir la victoire du Front populaire deux ans plus tard ? Douter de la France (« est-ce que vraiment on nous fera croire que désormais les grands sentiments sont incompréhensibles à la France ? [11] ») conduisait à espérer dans l'Europe — une Europe qui, en de notables parties, échappait déjà à la décadence libérale. Le nationalisme de Drieu, impraticable dans le cadre français, débouchait logiquement sur un « nationalisme européen » qui annonçait déjà l'impasse « collaborationniste » des années d'Occupation.

Si le socialisme de Drieu est plus que suspect, si son nationalisme est sujet à caution, que reste-t-il de la synthèse fasciste et de la nouveauté fasciste ? Peu de chose, en vérité, comme en témoigne *Gilles,* ce roman-bilan, ce roman autobiographique, que Drieu écrit à la veille de la guerre.

Ce roman s'impose en effet à l'historien des idées politiques. Mieux que la plupart des écrits théoriques, il présente dans le désordre apparent de l'intrigue mais selon une logique propre à l'idéologie de l'auteur, qui avait été pendant deux ans le penseur du PPF, un riche catalogue des idées fascistes, telles qu'elles ont pu s'exprimer dans le cadre français.

Gilles a été publié en octobre 1939 : la censure de guerre avait alors supprimé maints passages du roman ; c'est en 1942 que devait paraître la version intégrale, enrichie d'une préface rédigée par l'auteur au cours du mois de juillet de la même année.

De ce récit qui retrace à sa façon une vingtaine d'années

10. H. Béraud dans *Gringoire,* cité par R. Brasillach, *op. cit.,* p. 151.
11. R. Brasillach, *op. cit.,* p. 273.

d'histoire — de la Grande Guerre à la guerre d'Espagne —, rappelons les grandes lignes :

La première partie du roman, « La permission », narre le retour du front à Paris d'un jeune combattant, Gilles Gambier, qui vient d'être blessé. Sans famille, à l'exception d'un tuteur impécunieux retiré en Normandie, sans argent, mais désireux de jouir au maximum des délices de l'arrière, il parvient à vivre dans l'aisance grâce aux femmes, sur lesquelles il exerce un universel attrait. L'une d'elles réussit à le retenir, Myriam Falkenberg, sœur de deux compagnons d'armes « morts au champ d'honneur ». Elle est jolie, intelligente ; elle est riche surtout. Ce « bon parti » le décide au mariage, malgré ses préventions, cependant qu'à la faveur des relations de sa future épouse il obtient un poste au Quai d'Orsay. A la suite de ce mariage bénéfique mais immoral, un sursaut de dignité renvoie Gilles au front, où de nouvelles amours consomment sa rupture avec une épouse qu'il n'a jamais aimée.

La deuxième partie, « L'Élysée », a pour cadre chronologique les années vingt. Gilles mène à Paris une vie légère, distraite et — malgré ses fonctions au ministère — dépourvue d'ambition. Après avoir divorcé d'avec Myriam, il semble enfin connaître la réussite sentimentale auprès de Dora, jeune femme américaine, mère de deux enfants, jusqu'au jour où, mis l'un et l'autre devant un choix décisif, il éprouve la douleur de perdre sa maîtresse avec la conviction d'avoir été puni pour médiocrité. Une médiocrité qui le dépasse, une médiocrité proprement française, qui tient aussi à son entourage : fréquentant un groupe de littérateurs révolutionnaires dirigé par Caël, il place en ces nouveaux amis l'espoir de détruire ou d'aider à la destruction d'une société bourgeoise qui lui fait horreur. Mais il a tôt fait de s'apercevoir du caractère pusillanime de ces révolutionnaires de café : le complot qu'ils méditent contre l'honneur du président de la République se termine de la façon la plus piteuse et la plus inavouable pour eux.

La troisième partie, « L'Apocalypse », nous transporte dans

les années trente et particulièrement en 1934. Quittant le Quai d'Orsay, optant délibérément pour la pauvreté — une pauvreté qu'il avait toujours redoutée —, Gilles va faire retraite dans le désert algérien d'où il ramène Pauline (qu'il épousera plus tard) et de mâles résolutions. De retour à Paris, il fonde *l'Apocalypse,* journal d'opinion, qui lui permet de gagner modestement sa vie et celle de Pauline : c'est un pamphlet contre la France radicale-socialiste ; c'est aussi, dit-il, une « prière ». Entré désormais dans le jeu politique, Gilles attend le salut, pendant quelque temps, d'une fructueuse alliance des forces vives qui restent à la France : l'extrême droite et l'extrême gauche. Un moment, il croit l'occasion venue lorsqu'il pressent chez Clérences, jeune-Turc radical, des intentions voisines des siennes. Mais le 6 février le porte en quelques heures de la plus grande exaltation au plus profond abattement. Suivi en effet du fol espoir que tout devient possible, Gilles somme Clérences d'agir, mais le caractère décidément velléitaire de son ami le renforce dans le sentiment, menacé l'espace d'une émeute, de l'irrémédiable décadence de la France. C'est à l'occasion de ces journées dramatiques, dernière chance de sursaut finalement gâchée, qu'il se déclare ouvertement « fasciste ».

La guerre d'Espagne est le théâtre de l'« Épilogue ». Gilles y participe du côté de Franco. L'âpre discipline de la guerre le sauve personnellement à ses propres yeux de la chute où son pays est entraîné. L'ascétisme militaire, le goût de l'action, la morale du risque le préparent à tout le moins à une mort héroïque qu'il attend le fusil à la main.

Remarquons, sans nous y attarder longuement, la nature indiscutablement autobiographique de ce roman. Gilles a plus d'un trait caractérologique de Drieu, mais si l'on s'en tient aux seules ressemblances factuelles entre la vie du romancier et celle de son personnage nous pouvons noter des coïncidences évidentes. Le romancier qui publie *Gilles* en 1939 a quarante-six ans ; il est de la classe d'âge de son héros, ancien combattant comme lui, blessé comme lui au combat. L'un et l'autre épousent une jeune fille juive en premières noces ; l'un comme l'autre divorcent. Drieu fréquente les dadaïstes puis les surréalistes comme Gilles s'intègre au groupe Caël — caricature reconnaissable d'André Breton. Et combien d'autres traits communs encore : on sait que le désespoir de Gilles après que Dora l'eut quitté est un épisode authentiquement vécu par son père littéraire en 1925 ; que Drieu a été le collaborateur de Bergery comme Gilles l'ami de Clérences ; qu'il s'est reconnu fasciste enfin en 1934, tout comme son héros... Ces exemples suffisent : sous le masque de la création artistique, un écrivain doublé d'un homme politique se confesse et, du même coup, nous fait prendre la mesure d'une « vocation » fasciste.

Gilles est sans doute d'abord l'analyse, ou l'auto-analyse, d'un cas singulier, celui de Pierre Drieu La Rochelle. Dans une étude récemment parue, le Dr Robert Soucy nous montrait qu'on pouvait expliquer les options politiques et idéologiques de Drieu à partir de ce que l'on peut bien appeler son « complexe d'infériorité [12] ». Ce n'est point là notre propos ; nous voudrions déceler, au contraire, ce que *Gilles,* au-delà de Drieu, contient de plus général ; en quoi les idées, les images, les mythes véhiculés par ce roman ressortissent à une idéologie qui, tout en étant celle de Drieu, est commune, en de multiples aspects, à toute une intelligentsia de droite de son époque. Que la psychanalyse, ou toute autre psychologie, nous permette de mieux comprendre la démarche de Drieu paraît incontestable, mais elle ne peut expliquer à notre sens l'option finalement fasciste de Drieu : les prédispositions à la névrose acquises dans la petite enfance, l'application à vaincre sa peur, la volonté de surmonter son angoisse peuvent décider de tout autres choix. Autrement dit, l'analyse des « idées politiques » ne nous paraît pas superfétatoire : si ces « idées » n'existent pas en elles-mêmes, elles ne sont pas nées pour autant des seuls fantasmes d'un individu isolé ; elles participent d'un milieu et d'un temps ; par là même, elles

12. Dr R. Soucy, « Le fascisme de Drieu La Rochelle », *Revue d'histoire de la Deuxième Guerre mondiale,* avril 1967, p. 61-84.

dépassent celui qui s'en est fait le propagateur. C'est le caractère spécifique de ce roman de Drieu que nous avons voulu retenir, ce qu'il charrie parfois de moins personnel : en quoi il témoigne du fascisme français dans son ensemble. Tel qu'il apparaît dans ce livre, le fascisme fut un violent refus de la France contemporaine, une nostalgie avouée d'un âge d'or révolu, et le rêve moins précis d'un ordre nouveau. C'est dans cette économie secrète que la leçon de *Gilles* se dévoile ; c'est celle-là que nous allons suivre.

Une ultime remarque de méthode s'impose au préalable. Le discours de Drieu se laisse entendre sur trois registres ; c'est d'abord le discours direct, l'auteur exposant sa pensée de manière explicite ; c'est ensuite le discours indirect, symbolique ou parabolique, par lequel l'auteur, en toute connaissance, veut compléter sa leçon par l'exemple et l'image, laissant au lecteur le soin de conclure ; c'est enfin, malgré l'auteur, ce que son récit contient d'aveux inconscients. Dans notre présentation, nous mêlerons ces trois registres par souci de synthèse, ce qui nous conduira à faire simultanément la traduction idéologique du roman telle que Drieu l'eût vraisemblablement acceptée et l'interprétation personnelle à laquelle nous nous risquerons — interprétation d'où la critique ne sera évidemment pas exclue.

La décadence.

Dans la préface de *Gilles,* Drieu enracine son roman — et toute son œuvre même — dans le fumier de la décadence française : « Je me suis trouvé comme tous les autres écrivains contemporains devant un fait écrasant : la décadence [13]. » Le mot (ou l'idée) est le *leitmotiv* de *Gilles* : il n'est pas de fait ni de personnage qui n'en rende compte à sa manière. Qui plus est, cette décadence paraît « irrémédiable [14] », à tout le moins aux yeux de Carentan, le vieux tuteur de Gilles, que Drieu nous

13. *Gilles,* p. 111. Nos références se rapportent à l'édition intégrale de 1949.

14. *Ibid.*, p. 94.

présente comme une manière de Mage, retiré sur ses terres normandes, qu'on vient consulter de temps à autre comme la Pythie à Delphes : « Voici, dit l'oracle, les derniers jours de cette fameuse " civilisation ". L'Europe qui n'a pas croulé en 1918 s'en va lentement en ruine [15]. »

« La France se meurt », de maladies multiples et incurables. Il n'est besoin que de visiter un village normand pour mesurer les ravages de la dépopulation et de l'alcoolisme ; il y a eu les morts de la Grande Guerre, les blessés, les mutilés, survivants sans progéniture, ou ceux qui ont eu des enfants, « tous morts en bas âge ; alcoolisme et syphilis [16]... », et puis tous ceux qui sont partis pour la ville. Le tableau soulève le cœur. La France ne s'est pas remise de la grande saignée, et ceux qui y ont survécu sont abîmés dans l'éthylisme et l'infécondité. Quand la décadence a corrompu jusqu'au village, on imagine dans quelles turpitudes la ville se putréfie. « Les cinémas et les cafés, les maisons de passe, les journaux, les bourses, les partis et les casernes [17] », autant d'attributs infamants du monde moderne. Au nadir, Paris est devenu une concentration d'intellectuels débraillés (qui ont perdu « la dignité des anciennes mœurs [18] »), de noceurs, d'homosexuels (« Il y en a partout. Avec la drogue, c'était la maladie qui lui avait le plus déchiré le cœur à Paris [19] ») ; la peinture de Picasso, les music-halls, les romanciers catholiques, les Juifs, « les cauteleux radicaux francs-maçons [20] »... On jauge la profondeur du mal.

Les prétendues élites donnent d'elles-mêmes un spectacle dégradant ; qu'il se tourne vers les hommes au pouvoir, qu'incarnent les radicaux, ou vers ceux qui représentent la révolte, comme les jeunes gens qui se groupent autour de Caël (*i.e.* les surréalistes), Gilles éprouve la même nausée. Sous la plume

15. *Gilles,* p. 179.
16. *Ibid.,* p. 342.
17. *Ibid.,* p. 340.
18. *Ibid.,* p. 384.
19. *Ibid.,* p. 455.
20. *Ibid.,* p. 455.

mordante de Drieu, le radicalisme est mis en pièces. Herriot, parangon du parlementarisme, pilier de la République bourgeoise, facilement reconnaissable sous les traits caricaturaux de Chanteau, exprime toute l'obésité morale et physique du radicalisme déclinant : ce n'est qu'un paquet de *graisse* [21] (substantif répété avec délectation comme mot clé), incapable d'un sursaut viril, mais roué et satisfait, engoncé dans ce régime républicain dont le personnel « était vraiment un monde d'héritiers, de descendants, de dégénérés et un monde de remplaçants [22] ». Le style de la satire fasciste utilise avec prédilection l'image et le vocabulaire de la sexualité, Drieu n'échappe pas à la règle. Ainsi, entre l'orateur radical et son public, « au lieu d'une saine et féconde rencontre sexuelle, on voyait deux onanismes s'approcher, s'effleurer puis se dérober l'un à l'autre [23] ». Et si ces hommes-là peuvent être au pouvoir, c'est qu'« il y a une puissance de syphilis dans la France [24] ». A l'opposé des radicaux, les petits-bourgeois de la revue *Révolte* ont beau contester la France bourgeoise, ils en sont les parasites. Le portrait que Drieu trace d'eux est souvent d'une honnêteté intellectuelle douteuse : par l'amalgame de faits vrais et notoires (telle phrase publique de Breton, par exemple), pour que nul ne s'y trompe, et d'inventions romanesques où ceux qu'il attaque figurent ignoblement, l'auteur se fait le plaisir de vitupérer ses ennemis au vu de tous mais à l'abri de la fiction. Les surréalistes (qui ne sont jamais appelés par leur nom) sont des révoltés qui tremblent devant les gendarmes ; quand ils se battent, c'est à méchants petits coups de pied, et non à coups de « grande patte fauve [25] », comme font les braves avant de bourrer tranquillement leur pipe. Caël, *alias* Breton, n'est qu'un « grand Inquisiteur de café [26] » ; autour de lui, ce n'est qu'un monde de bourgeois veules, de femmes, et

21. *Gilles,* p. 391.
22. *Ibid.,* p. 386.
23. *Ibid.,* p. 390.
24. *Ibid.,* p. 343.
25. *Ibid.,* p. 211.
26. *Ibid.,* p. 330.

d'*impuissants* qui, malgré leurs propos bravaches contre les nantis, finissent par s'entendre avec ces radicaux précédemment éreintés, par opportunisme politique : le cercle est bouclé, les jeunes bourgeois sont revenus épauler leurs flatulents géniteurs. Politiciens professionnels et révoltés de Montparnasse sont de la même famille.

Deux figures du roman personnifient la décadence française : c'est Gilles lui-même, le premier Gilles, celui qui fait un mariage d'argent, celui qui approuve Carentan, son vieux maître, professant la suppression des maisons closes, mais qui ne peut se résoudre à ne les plus courir ; le Gilles désœuvré, nihiliste, fréquentant la bande de Caël, participant à ses mascarades, pour le plaisir de la destruction, seule force qui lui reste. Un Gilles sans enfant, souffrant du péché d'« avarice ». La seconde figure symbolique est Pauline, ancienne « poule » devenue la compagne de Gilles : elle ne manque pas de vertus, comme la France, mais, comme elle, elle est frappée à mort : « Il s'en approchait maintenant comme d'un temple foudroyé, délabré, où régnait un air troublant de désastre, de ruine, de stérilité [27]. » Comme Gilles a perdu foi en la France, « il ne croyait plus en Pauline, stérile, marquée par la mort, mais surtout devenue bourgeoise [28] ». Et plus loin, pour que l'allégorie soit claire : « La France mourait pendant que Pauline mourait [29]. »

De cette décomposition, quel est le secret ? A y regarder de près, il faut en chercher l'explication la plus profonde dans une sorte de « déterminisme physiologique [30] » : la France meurt de la race. Outre la présence multipliée d'étrangers en France, *bicots, Tchèques, Polonais,* la preuve insigne de la décadence française est l'omniprésence et la puissance occulte des Juifs. Selon Robert Soucy, qui se réfère à un article sur « la question juive » de Drieu,

27. *Gilles,* p. 400.
28. *Ibid.,* p. 408.
29. *Ibid.,* p. 425.
30. Nous empruntons cette expression à Z. Sternhell, *Maurice Barrès..., op. cit.*

celui-ci, en 1938, « n'était toujours pas converti au racisme » : « Ce n'est qu'après la défaite de la France et après que Drieu se fut rallié à la collaboration » que cette conversion se serait faite [31]. La lecture de *Gilles* ne confirme pas cette conclusion : le racisme de Drieu s'y affirme tout au long. Non seulement les Juifs y sont dénoncés comme produits *culturels,* mais — déjà en tant que race biologiquement distincte des autres — comme facteurs de dégénérescence *naturels*.

Le Juif, selon Drieu, c'est le monde moderne qui s'est fait chair : « Moi, dit Carentan, je ne peux pas supporter les Juifs, parce qu'ils sont par excellence le monde moderne [32]. » Ou bien : « Le Juif, c'est horrible comme un polytechnicien ou un normalien [33]. » Ou encore : « La plus frivole des Juives vous jette à la figure la Bourse et la Sorbonne [34]. » Cette modernité du Juif, Drieu ne manque pas d'en rappeler l'explication que l'on trouve dans la tradition antisémitique de droite : « Les Juifs restent stérilement fidèles à 89 qui les a sortis du ghetto [35]. » Nomade, déraciné, le Juif est l'insecte parasite dans le ventre de la nation ; lorsqu'un pays a perdu la sagesse de s'inspirer de ses propres traditions, de s'abreuver à la source de ses vertus séculaires, le Juif, produit de la Révolution, du Capitalisme et du Scientisme, surgit du périmètre réservé où nos ancêtres avaient eu la sagesse de le contenir et, par la ruse et l'argent, s'insinue dans le corps social affaibli : « Il doit y avoir, dans le rôle des Juifs, une nécessité biologique pour qu'on retrouve ainsi toujours leurs mots dans la salive des décadences [36]. » Cette allusion à la biologie n'est encore qu'un trope ; de l'image à l'explication « scientifique », le pas est cependant bientôt franchi.

Le Juif est l'antiphysique, l'esprit désincarné, la valeur fiduciaire prétendant se substituer à la monnaie métallique ; bref,

31. Dr R. Soucy, *loc. cit.,* p. 68.
32. *Gilles,* p. 99.
33. *Ibid.,* p. 100.
34. *Ibid.,* p. 100.
35. *Ibid.,* p. 401.
36. *Ibid.,* p. 387.

une personnalisation de l'abstrait. De Myriam, Drieu donne cette clé : « Dans son milieu, on ignorait toute expérience physique : que ce fût le sport, l'amour ou la guerre [37]. » Ce qui n'est pas une tare familiale, mais bien raciale puisqu'on la retrouve chez les autres Juifs, par exemple chez Cohen, que Gilles rencontre en Espagne lors d'un quiproquo dramatique : alors qu'ils sont réunis dans le même avion en détresse, « Cohen était abominablement exaspéré de ne pouvoir en ce moment rien faire pour ajouter à la chance. Il se heurtait à la nécessité et à la simplicité de l'action physique [...]. Il aurait voulu lui communiquer [au pilote] son astuce, son art de se retrouver dans la vie. Mais comment changer cette monnaie de papier dans l'or d'un travail d'homme ? [38] ». La Bourse et la Sorbonne restent inopérantes dès que l'action physique s'impose ; revanche de la vieille race, de la civilisation paysanne : quand la ruse devient impuissante, la « voix du sang » parle.

C'est qu'en effet les défauts des Juifs ne sont pas exclusivement des phénomènes de culture ; ils sont congénitaux, héréditaires et inévitables. Si *Gilles* met en scène une galerie de Juifs, l'existence de chacun d'eux est subordonnée à une essence supérieure : ils sont consubstantiellement de la *Juiverie,* autant d'hypostases d'une idée pure ; quoi qu'ils disent, quoi qu'ils fassent, ils sont de la race maudite. Car Gilles-Drieu ajoute foi explicitement à la théorie des races : « Oh ! races, races. Il y a des races, j'ai une race [39]. » Une race qui doit se préserver du métissage si elle veut sauvegarder ses qualités intrinsèques ; l'instinct sur ce point ne trompe pas. Gilles épouse la Juive Myriam, parce qu'il a besoin de son argent, mais, en dépit de sa bonne volonté, ce n'est qu'à grand renfort de courage qu'il parvient à remplir ce qui s'appelle strictement ici son devoir conjugal, à telle enseigne que le jour de ses noces il va se redonner du cœur chez une prostituée de ses connaissances ; jamais il ne guérit de son dégoût épidermique,

37. *Gilles,* p. 29.
38. *Ibid.,* p. 447.
39. *Ibid.,* p. 91.

tant qu'à la longue il divorce. Drieu illustre ainsi la prétendue « loi de répulsion » imaginée par Gobineau, qui postule l'opposition instinctive aux croisements [40]. Pour se purifier du commerce sexuel entretenu avec la représentante de la race interdite, Gilles, son divorce prononcé, « s'était précipité en Scandinavie [41] ». L'allusion est claire, Drieu La Rochelle accrédite déjà le mythe aryen. De même que *physiquement* Myriam répugne à Gilles malgré qu'il en ait, de même Dora (c'est-à-dire la *Dorique,* l'Indo-européenne, l'Aryenne) l'attire et le retient victorieusement. « Cette Américaine, avec son mélange de sang écossais, irlandais, saxon, croisait et multipliait plusieurs caractères des peuples nordiques. Or, c'était de ce côté-là que se rassemblaient toutes les émotions de Gilles [42]. » Avoir épousé une Juive est bien, pour Gilles-Drieu, « la tare ineffaçable [43] » ; le « terrible silence de la chair [44] » qui s'est établi entre Gilles et Myriam est dans la nature des choses, on ne peut impunément attenter à la « parenté de sang ». Sans faire appel à la *Blutsverwandschaft* de Büchner qui est devenue un dogme du régime hitlérien, Drieu exprime là des idées puisées dans sa culture française — notamment et principalement chez Barrès dont il est le fervent admirateur [45].

Dans cette description de « l'hiver d'un peuple [46] », il n'est pas difficile, en effet, de déceler l'influence récurrente de Barrès. Roman de la décomposition, *Gilles* multiplie les images de la mort, du néant et de la pourriture. La France y est décrite comme

40. Voir Gobineau, *Essai sur l'inégalité des races humaines,* 1867, p. 208.
41. *Gilles,* p. 182.
42. *Ibid.,* p. 182.
43. *Ibid.,* p. 38.
44. *Ibid.,* p. 64.
45. Drieu : « Barrès est évidemment le prince de la littérature contemporaine et, chaque année, je relis un cycle de ses livres. » Cité par J.-P. Maxence, *Histoire de dix ans, 1927-1937*, Gallimard, 1939, p. 41. Sur le racisme de Barrès et sur l'influence jouée dans celui-ci par Jules Soury, voir la thèse de Z. Sternhell sur Barrès, citée plus haut.
46. *Gilles,* p. 340.

une prostituée moribonde, autour du lit de laquelle des « vieillards débiles et pervers [47] », des « petits intellectuels, dernières gouttes de sperme arrachées à ces vieillards [48] » et des charlatans juifs dessinent une danse macabre grotesque. Le romantisme funéraire de Barrès, sa « hantise du périssable [49] », son obsession de la mort se renouvellent dans ces pages d'un Drieu encore plus persuadé que son maître de l'incurable maladie dont la France est atteinte. Si nous retrouvons décrites sous la plume de celui-là les mêmes images funèbres de la décadence française dont celui-ci était prodigue, nous pouvons y lire aussi la même déception de ne pouvoir compter sur une race française, sur une race « pure » en qui placer l'assurance du redressement national : « Hélas ! *écrivait Barrès,* il n'y a point de race française, mais un peuple français, une nation française, c'est-à-dire une collectivité de formation politique [50]. » Et Gilles-Drieu, considérant avec la même inquiétude la différence lourde de conséquences entre la « pureté » aryenne de Dora et les caractères aléatoires de sa « race latine », s'interroge : « Que savait-il de sa race ? [51] », ce bâtard on ne sait de quelle origine, ce produit on ne sait de quels croisements, tout comme la nation française. Nous pensons voir là certainement une des raisons de l'européanisme de Drieu : de la France métisse, « enjuivée », déclinant « au niveau de la mort [52] », il en appelle à une Europe où l'élément nordique aurait la prééminence — garantie de force et de résistance à la « pétrification ».

47. *Gilles,* p. 403.
48. *Ibid.,* p. 338.
49. J.-M. Domenach, *Barrès par lui-même,* Éd. du Seuil, 1954, p. 74.
50. Barrès, *Scènes et doctrines du nationalisme,* Plon, 1925, p. 74.
51. *Gilles,* p. 89, ou encore : « Je suis bien latin, mêlant la sentimentalité à la cochonnerie. Et moi qui avais joué au Nordique avec elle... », p. 276.
52. *Ibid.,* p. 426.

Le mythe de l'âge d'or.

Le monde contemporain est un univers défruité auquel le héros fasciste ne trouve que la saveur morbide du néant, car c'est un nostalgique des temps révolus d'avant-la-décadence. Les prémices douces-amères du Déclin peuvent avoir été cueillies en des printemps plus ou moins anciens : tel regrette « le siècle de Louis XIV », tel autre « l'âge d'or de la noblesse » qu'il situe entre la guerre de Cent ans et les débuts du XVIIe siècle ; en général, on s'accorde à penser que la décadence est définitive avec le triomphe de la démocratie. Pour Drieu, l'époque lumineuse, c'est le Moyen Age. Le mythe de l'âge d'or est de tous les lieux et de tous les temps ; déjà les poèmes homériques décrivent le passé de manière enchanteresse : c'est l'âge où les mortels vivaient tous comme des dieux, « le cœur exempt de soucis, écrit Hésiode, à l'abri de la fatigue et de l'infortune ». « Et, comparant la misère présente au bonheur dont son imagination colore le passé, le poète oppose avec désespoir les jours sombres de l'âge de fer aux jours ensoleillés de l'âge d'or [53]. » On sait que la conception du Moyen Age a varié selon les siècles : méprisé par les contemporains de Boileau et, plus tard, par ceux d'Émile Combes, le Moyen Age est progressivement devenu, dans l'idéologie de la droite française (et chez de grands écrivains catholiques, que l'on songe à Bloy et à Bernanos), une référence constante. Drieu reprend le mythe à son compte : dans *Gilles,* le monde moderne, contre lequel il n'a pas assez de flèches, a pour antipode rayonnant le temps des Capétiens, époque d'authenticité *foncière,* opposé à la fausseté *mobilière* du monde contemporain. Car la France *vraie* n'est pas le produit de ces valeurs douteuses : Bourse, Sorbonne, Normale, Polytechnique, Franc-Maçonnerie, Juiverie, etc., mais bel et bien celui « [d]es montagnes et [d]es rivières, [d]es arbres et [d]es monuments [...].

53. G. Glotz, *Histoire grecque,* PUF, 1938, t. 1, p. 152.

La pierre construite, cela l'émouvait et le retenait comme encore si proche de la pierre dans la gangue de la terre [54] ». Et la suite, qui nous rappelle encore davantage Barrès : « Il avait entendu son pas résonner solitaire dans toutes les églises de France, les grandes et les petites [...]. Les Français avaient fait des églises et ils ne pouvaient plus les refaire ni rien de semblable : toute l'aventure de la vie était dans ce fait, la terrible nécessité de la mort [55]. » Gilles, périodiquement, se replonge dans la forêt, dans le village, dans la province, pour y retrouver « la valeur d'or », « la valeur primitive, avant toute altération [56] ». La religion fasciste a des aspects nettement chthoniens : on rend un culte à la *Terra Mater,* par lequel on retrouve la source perdue de la Sagesse et de la Race.

Le symbole qui n'est pas nouveau de cette religion qui n'est pas nouvelle est par excellence l'*arbre.* Symbole d'une prodigieuse fécondité dans la littérature traditionaliste française, l'arbre a pris force de signification avec le platane de M. Taine : malheur aux hommes, démontre son disciple Barrès, qui, arrachés à leur milieu naturel, deviennent des *déracinés.* On sait, en effet, que « fils de la terre, l'arbre est ordre, fidélité, tradition. Non liberté, mais nécessité biologique. Non progrès, mais pérennité [57] ». Quand Gilles entraîne Dora en promenade, c'est « toujours vers les forêts [58] ». Pourtant : « Il n'avait jamais osé auparavant emmener une femme parmi les grands arbres [59]. » Cette dernière observation est lourde de sens : le héros de Drieu perçoit bien la communication qui s'établit spontanément entre la forêt sacrée et la représentante des grandes vertus « nordiques » ; car elle aussi « sen[t] [s]es racines [60] ». Quand Gilles vient prendre conseil

54. *Gilles,* p. 393.
55. *Ibid.,* p. 393.
56. *Ibid.,* p. 204.
57. L. Bodin et J.-M. Royer, « Vocabulaire de la France », *Esprit,* décembre 1957.
58. *Gilles,* p. 200.
59. *Ibid.*
60. *Ibid.,* p. 203.

auprès de son vieux tuteur normand, celui-ci lui désigne tout naturellement un hêtre comme détenteur d'éternité : « Ce que dit ce hêtre sera toujours redit, sous une forme ou sous une autre, toujours [61]. » Et lorsque Gilles, dans la forêt avec Dora, pose ses mains sur les troncs d'un hêtre (encore !) [62], il trouve « drôle de voir de telles mains [de longues mains blanches, déliées] sur cette écorce [63] » : la ville l'a efféminé et perverti ; Dora qui comprend le sens de sa réflexion s'empresse de le rassurer : « Vous auriez dû avoir une autre vie [64] », dit-elle. Une vie d'enraciné.

Dans *Gilles,* complainte d'un homme nostalgique sur la « ruine des derniers piliers médiévaux [65] », Drieu chante mélancoliquement le temps des épopées, des cathédrales, des enluminures et des croisades. Quand son héros s'adonne au journalisme, c'est, d'une voix égale, pour déclamer contre le monde moderne et faire, selon sa propre expression, « l'éloge extatique des vérités oubliées dans leur tombe [66] ». Jadis, la vertu avait de préférence les sabots crottés ; la naïveté, la spontanéité l'emportaient sur l'argutie des cuistres. Ce monde viril était en effet guidé par la sensibilité, en quoi il faut voir un des secrets du Moyen Age. « Les Français avaient été des soldats, des moines, des architectes, des peintres, des poètes, des maris et des pères. Ils avaient fait des enfants, ils avaient construit, ils avaient tué, ils s'étaient fait tuer [67]. » Tels sont les héros vrais de la « raison française » qui était tout le contraire du rationalisme : « Oui, il y avait eu une

61. *Gilles,* p. 341.
62. Le hêtre n'est pas pour rien homonyme du verbe être : le jeu de mots n'est sans doute pas involontaire, il est significatif que dans une même phrase de Carentan, à trois lignes d'intervalle, on évoque tour à tour ce *hêtre* et l'*être* (p. 341). La valeur du symbole ontologique du hêtre se trouve ainsi doublée par la phonétique.
63. *Gilles,* p. 201.
64. *Ibid.*
65. *Ibid.,* p. 402.
66. *Ibid.,* p. 364.
67. *Ibid.,* p. 393.

raison française ; mais si vive, si drue, si naïve et si large, embrassant tous les éléments de l'être. Pas seulement le raisonnement mais l'élan de la foi [68]. » Évidemment, la Sorbonne détestée par l'auteur ne fait pas partie de ce Moyen Age rêvé : Thomas d'Aquin est de peu de poids au regard d'un seul croisé. Car le catholicisme était « mâle [69] » (s'opposant probablement à un christianisme femelle, d'origine sémitique) : c'était plutôt celui de Simon de Montfort que celui du Poverello ; le catholicisme chez Drieu tend le sabre de préférence à la joue gauche.

Son idée du Moyen Age, Gilles-Drieu ne l'a pas demandée aux historiens, mais aux « fervents de l'Anti-Moderne, depuis de Maistre jusqu'à Péguy [70] ». C'est dans leurs livres qu'il cherche la règle divine d'une sagesse et d'un ordre perdus. Et si, d'aventure, les hasards de la vie lui offrent, en province (toujours sous le toit de l'auguste Carentan), une réincarnation touchante de l'ancien monde où chacun était à sa place, le voilà qui s'attendrit : « La servante était partie en fermant la porte, en leur jetant un long regard d'orgueil : *elle était fière de servir* [71]. » Tel est le fondement du Moyen Age : c'était une *aristocratie,* un monde hiérarchisé, établi sur la force et l'hérédité des vertus viriles. A lire Drieu, le Moyen Age n'a que des charmes. Violences, famines, épidémies, superstitions, guerres, tout cela n'est que broutilles. Une terre, un roi, une foi, un peuple : voilà le paradis perdu et pleuré.

C'est Carentan, évidemment, qui incarne dans *Gilles* les valeurs médiévales. Il est une manière de revenant, le spectre d'un homme du XIIIe siècle, taillé dans la matière brute, égaré dans la France de M. Doumergue. Il emploie son temps à étudier l'histoire des religions : de l'une à l'autre, il procède comme un alchimiste qui, de distillation en distillation, quête la sagesse éternelle. En France, il est le seul Français — ou à peu près.

68. *Gilles,* p. 392.
69. *Ibid.,* p. 463.
70. *Ibid.,* p. 364.
71. *Ibid.,* p. 102.

Parfois, Drieu accorde encore des vertus ancestrales aux paysans qu'il rencontre, mais ils lui semblent « l'arrière-garde hargneuse d'une armée en déroute [72] » ; un instant, il croit subodorer dans les rangs communistes des « hommes sains et vigoureux [73] », fourvoyés certes ! mais descendant du vieux peuple révolté... Tout compte fait, les vrais Français ont passé l'Atlantique : au Canada, on peut voir « des Français, sur qui n'est pas passé 1789, ni le XVIIIe siècle, ni même somme toute le XVIIe, ni même la Renaissance et la Réforme, c'est du Français tout cru, tout vif [74] ». Rome n'est plus dans Rome, la France est à la semelle des souliers du Québec.

La représentation artificielle du passé français est de toutes les idéologies ; dans la vision de Drieu, le Moyen Age atteste la perfection des origines de la France, ce temps premier d'harmonie avant le déluge. Il est de bonne logique que Gilles-Drieu, son poète, aspire à restaurer un « Nouveau Moyen Age [75] ».

Un ordre nouveau.

Gilles est un roman de la grâce, le récit du cheminement moral d'un homme qui, né au temps de la décadence et nourri de ses fruits amers, tente de transcender son époque qu'il méprise. Dans cette tentative, c'est aux femmes d'abord qu'il est demandé de jouer le rôle médiateur, de permettre d'échapper à la médiocrité contemporaine et de retrouver la trace du paradis perdu. Mais les femmes, à bien considérer, se révèlent paradis artificiels : Gilles, qui use d'un grand nombre d'entre elles, ne parvient pas, malgré le temps, l'affection et l'amour parfois qu'il leur prodigue, à émerger par leur entremise de la décadence ; même, à l'image de Pauline, elles sont trop souvent les vivants symboles de la Chute. Le salut de Gilles, homme de la quête,

72. *Gilles,* p. 339.
73. *Ibid.,* p. 402.
74. *Ibid.,* p. 101.
75. *Ibid.,* p. 340.

chevalier errant et nostalgique, c'est, en définitive, la politique. En elle, Gilles-Drieu découvre enfin le moyen de se dépasser, l'espoir tangible de s'arracher au Déclin, et par-dessus tout sa religion : « Ce serait sa façon de prier [76]. »

La maturation politique de Gilles est lente. De naissance, d'éducation, il dit qu'il est de droite. Mais la droite française, immodérément modérée et bien-pensante, n'a pas plus d'attrait pour un homme d'absolu que le radicalisme. Gilles a d'autres exigences que de défendre la prospérité des notables. Il donne sa sympathie à tout ce qui dans un pays *sénile* comme la France a l'ardeur de la jeunesse, à ceux qui, quel que soit leur drapeau, crachent à la face du vieux monde de la décadence. C'est la raison qui le pousse aux côtés des surréalistes dont l'agressivité verbale et le nihilisme le séduisent par leur énergie suicidaire. Il se sépare d'eux lorsqu'il discerne derrière leur masque le même visage honni des bourgeois *débiles* (autre mot clé). De la même façon, Gilles, qui n'a aucun goût pour le marxisme, n'en témoigne pas moins du respect pour les militants communistes, nous l'avons vu, trompés par les théoriciens, mais capables de la violence qu'il appelle de ses vœux contre le monde moderne. A tout prendre, se demande Gilles à une étape de son évolution, « pourquoi ne pas se jeter dans le communisme ? [77] ». Que la France soit balayée par la destruction. C'est vivre que de hâter la destruction de la mort. « Il voyait dans le communisme non pas une force, mais une faiblesse qui pouvait coïncider avec celle de la France [78]. » Mais ce n'est pas seulement la politique du pire qui attache Gilles-Drieu aux communistes ; à vrai dire, il n'a cessé de rêver à l'union de tous les vaillants, de tous les révoltés, de tous les entrepreneurs de démolition. Ce rêve de renverser « la dictature franc-maçonne [...] par une coalition des jeunes bourgeois et des jeunes ouvriers [79] » n'est pas neuf : Drumont,

76. *Gilles,* p. 358.
77. *Ibid.,* p. 398.
78. *Ibid.,* p. 398.
79. *Ibid.,* p. 422.

Morès, Barrès avaient déjà en leur temps conçu un tel projet ; c'est dans la dernière décennie du siècle passé qu'on avait assisté à la naissance de ce conservatisme radical appelant les ouvriers et les catholiques contre la « République juive ». Mais ce rassemblement des forces vives — jusque-là séparées arbitrairement par les idéologies — a été aussi, d'une autre manière, une des illusions de cet « esprit des années 30 » qu'il serait erroné d'assimiler au fascisme : on rencontre largement exprimées dans *Gilles* ces diverses aspirations à dépasser les traditionnelles oppositions entre la droite et la gauche, pour faire surgir, qui le néo-marxisme, qui le néo-nationalisme. D'un côté, chez les hommes de la tradition, on veut rompre avec les compromissions capitalistes, de l'autre, on veut « fonder un nouveau marxisme en France qui ne [soit] ni dans l'obédience russe ni dans la routine parlementaire des socialistes [80] ». Gilles se joint à ces hommes, venus de tous les azimuts, qui veulent faire table rase ; ils jettent leur dévolu sur un politicien qui pourrait devenir leur chef ; il est encore au parti radical, mais il veut lui aussi sortir du cloaque : c'est Clérences (un composé caricatural de Bertrand de Jouvenel, de Bergery et d'autres radicaux aux idées neuves). Gilles stimule l'énergie de Clérences, participe aux activités de son groupe, avant de se décourager enfin : « Tous ces gens étaient des gens de robe, des clercs comme dit l'autre, tout à fait stériles. Décidément, la vie n'était pas en France [81]. »

Mais sur son chemin de Damas, Gilles est soudain jeté de son cheval par le coup de tonnerre du 6 février 1934. Jusque-là, les orages tant désirés s'étaient tous levés au-delà du Rhin et des Alpes ; le ciel français demeurait terne. Joie ! Le 6 février, la Révolte enfin submergeait Paris : « La France recevait enfin la pensée de toute l'Europe, du monde entier en mouvement [82]. » Le vieux Palais-Bourbon tremble de tous ses piliers ; Gilles crie à Clérences : « Si un homme se lève et jette tout son destin dans la

80. *Gilles,* p. 378.
81. *Ibid.,* p. 408.
82. *Ibid.,* p. 418.

balance, il fera ce qu'il voudra. Il ramassera dans le même filet l'Action française et les communistes, les Jeunesses patriotiques et les Croix-de-feu, et bien d'autres [83]. » Gilles-Drieu nous offre alors une parfaite description de la genèse d'un mouvement fasciste, les premiers éléments de la technique du coup d'État : « Attaque Daladier ou défends-le, mais par des actes qui soient tout à fait concrets. Envahis coup sur coup un journal de droite et un journal de gauche. Fais bâtonner à domicile celui-ci ou celui-là. Sors à tout prix de la routine des vieux partis, des manifestes, des meetings et des articles et des discours. Et tu auras aussitôt une puissance d'agrégation formidable. Les barrières seront à jamais rompues entre la droite et la gauche, et des flots de vie se précipiteront en tout sens. Tu ne sens pas cet instant de grande crue ? Le flot est là devant nous : on peut le lancer dans la direction qu'on veut, mais il faut le lancer tout de suite, à tout prix [84]. »

Encore faut-il un Mussolini, c'est-à-dire, selon Malaparte qui trace ce portrait du Mussolini d'octobre 1922 : « Un homme moderne, froid, audacieux, violent et calculateur [85]. » Las ! La France ne trouve pas son guide et le 6 Février n'a été qu'une journée des dupes. La vieille gueuse reprend vite le dessus et Gilles « regrettait d'être sorti le 6 février, pendant un instant, de son incroyance prophétique. Après ce dernier spasme sans issue, la France ne pouvait plus que descendre au niveau de la mort [86] ». Dès lors, le fascisme de Gilles-Drieu prend ses caractères les plus nets : il s'agit de retrouver, vaille que vaille, malgré ce « peuple de France aux artères asséchées [87] », ce que sa génération a appris de la guerre : l'*idée émouvante de la vie forte* [88].

Le culte de la force *physique,* l'obsession de la *virilité, le mépris*

83. *Gilles,* p. 420.
84. *Ibid.,* p. 421.
85. C. Malaparte, *Technique du coup d'État,* 10/18, 1964, p. 158.
86. *Gilles,* p. 426.
87. *Ibid.,* p. 340.
88. *Ibid.,* p. 423.

des intellectuels sont les expressions multiples d'une apologie de l'instinct. Là encore, Drieu n'invente rien, ne faisant qu'illustrer la leçon de ses maîtres, Barrès avant tout. Ainsi, dans le fascisme de Drieu, s'épanouit la nostalgie de la guerre, du front, du danger : la guerre est l'épreuve de l'homme ; tout y est simple, l'exercice n'est jamais truqué ; face au danger, l'homme est dépouillé, vêtu de sa seule peur et de ses seules forces : nerfs, cœur et muscles : « La Guerre, c'est ma patrie [89] », dit Gilles. Jules Soury, qui a tant appris à Barrès, ne disait-il pas : « La guerre, heureuse ou malheureuse, la guerre éternelle, source de toute vie supérieure, cause de tout progrès sur la terre [90]... » Cette force que la guerre révèle est avant tout celle du corps, car le corps est le tabernacle des principes les plus essentiels, ceux de l'instinct et de la race. A preuve que lorsqu'un Juif, fût-il intelligent et habile, se trouve aux prises avec le danger physique, tel Cohen que nous avons vu précédemment au-dessus de l'Espagne, il doit s'avouer impuissant.

A l'idée de force corporelle est liée celle de *santé*. « Il savait que lui seul dans leur milieu représentait la santé [91]. » Même quand il ne fait pas d'alpinisme, le fasciste est un homme sain, au regard clair, à l'inverse de ces hommes de bibliothèques, cacochymes et myopes : « Tout ce petit monde de bourgeois intellectuels, tremblotant et flageolant, fit grimacer de mépris les agents [92]. » Nous retrouvons ici la même opposition que chez Barrès entre le peuple et les intellectuels. « Le peuple », disait-il, « m'a révélé la substance humaine et, mieux que cela, l'énergie créatrice, la sève du monde, l'inconscient [93] » ; les intellectuels, au contraire, perdus par le kantisme et toutes les autres formes d'abstraction, sont proprement désincarnés, ils n'ont plus corps.

89. *Gilles,* p. 76.
90. J. Soury, *Campagne nationaliste,* p. 185, cité par Z. Sternhell, *Maurice Barrès..., op. cit.,* t. 2, p. 49.
91. *Gilles,* p. 241.
92. *Ibid.,* p. 322.
93. Barrès, *Le Jardin de Bérénice,* Plon, 1891, p. 183.

Le procès de Burdeau-Bouteiller est continué par Drieu : au culte de la raison, il faut substituer celui de l'énergie et de l'action. Dans les années trente, Drieu éprouve le même sentiment que Barrès dans les années quatre-vingt-dix ; celui-ci, méprisant les doctrines, s'écriait : « C'est l'élan que je goûte [94] », et celui-là, rêvant de dissoudre les idées dans la pureté de l'action, s'exclame de dépit devant la France inerte : « Il ne manque qu'une chose : l'élan vital [95]. »

L'anti-intellectualisme de Drieu a pour corollaire la glorification incessante de la virilité. Les intellectuels sont des « impuissants » ; à plusieurs reprises, Drieu les vêt d'une robe (« misérables petits clercs, des petits moines en robe [96] »). Comme dans l'ancienne noblesse, à ces gens de robe s'opposent les gens d'épée. « Penser, c'était finalement donner ou recevoir un coup d'épée [97] », et ceci, plus loin, qui ne laissera plus de doute sur le symbole phallique : « Oui, songeait Gilles, en entrant dans une maison de passe, ce sont des hommes sans épée [98]. » De sorte qu'on peut comprendre qu'entre l'intellectuel de gauche et le fasciste, ce qui les sépare d'abord, c'est la virilité : « Tous ces garçons m'en veulent, dit Gilles, parce que je plais aux femmes [99]. »

Deuxième idée maîtresse : *refaire une aristocratie.* La décadence prend sa source dans la démocratie. Il faut recréer un monde hiérarchisé où les *chefs* pourront à nouveau commander, les chevaliers et non plus les chevaliers d'industrie. « Gilles n'avait jamais cru une seconde qu'il fût possible de croire à l'égalité, au progrès [100]. » Ces idées pernicieuses ont été répandues au XVIIIe siècle : « Il fallait en finir avec toutes ces prétentions absurdes du rationalisme, de la philosophie des lu-

94. Barrès, *Du sang, de la volupté et de la mort,* Plon, 1959, p. 49.
95. *Gilles,* p. 422.
96. *Ibid.,* p. 338.
97. *Ibid.,* p. 339.
98. *Ibid.,* p. 339.
99. *Ibid.,* p. 337.
100. *Ibid.,* p. 367.

mières [101]. » Gilles croit davantage aux forces obscures, aux dons mystérieux qui consacrent un chef. « Je veux, dit-il, détruire la société capitaliste pour restaurer la notion d'aristocratie [102]. » Le meilleur, le chef, ce ne sera plus le riche ni le plus intelligent (l'intellectuel, pour sa part, est tout juste bon à faire un *président*), ce sera l'Homme d'Action, l'Anti-Juif par excellence — le Juif étant, lui, l'Homme de la Transaction et de la Tractation. Comment ne pas évoquer ici encore le Maître Barrès : « Un peuple, une région qui manquent d'aristocratie n'ont plus de modèle, de direction vers laquelle se perfectionner [103]. »

Troisième idée-force : « *Le nationalisme est périmé* [104]. » Lorsque, après le 6 Février, le café du Commerce et les loges ont liquéfié la révolte, Gilles a compris qu'il n'y avait plus rien à espérer de la « France seule ». Gilles a admiré Maurras, mais il le juge désormais « petit et impuissant dans l'immédiat [105] ». Le nouvel ordre doit être européen ou il ne sera pas. Drieu dépasse ici la perspective barrésienne : c'est du fascisme international que va sourdre l'ordre nouveau. Dans ce nouvel ordre, l'Église a son rôle à jouer ; elle doit redevenir l'Église médiévale, et le catholicisme viril devra être le ciment de la nouvelle Europe. « Pour moi, je me suis retiré d'entre les nations. J'appartiens à un nouvel ordre militaire et religieux qui s'est fondé quelque part dans le monde et poursuit, envers et contre tout, la conciliation de l'Église et du fascisme et leur double triomphe d'une nation sur les autres nations [106]. » Quelle que fût son attitude politique après l'invasion allemande, Drieu envisage clairement, en 1939, une guerre fasciste contre l'Allemagne et l'Italie fascistes — n'a-t-il pas rompu avec Doriot après la capitulation de Munich ? Mais, voyant au-delà, c'est « l'invasion de l'Europe par l'armée

101. *Gilles,* p. 368.
102. *Ibid.,* p. 365.
103. Barrès, *Mes cahiers,* Plon, 1917, t. 10, p. 74.
104. *Gilles,* p. 475.
105. *Ibid.,* p. 398.
106. *Ibid.,* p. 475.

russe » qui est prévue ; c'est contre elle que l'Allemagne doit fédérer les patries (non les dissoudre) et faire naître « un esprit de patriotisme européen [107] ». La vocation de l'Allemagne est donc clairement établie : « Par sa force et par la tradition du Saint-Empire romain-germanique, il lui appartient de diriger la ligne européenne de demain [108]. »

Au total, le fascisme de Drieu apparaît comme une volonté de refaire une Europe unie et aristocratique, où les mâles et les chefs commanderont à nouveau aux clercs, aux femmes, aux Juifs et aux manants. Restituer la foi contre le rationalisme, réestimer l'instinct contre l'intellect, la force contre l'argent, noyer le machinisme et le scientisme sous les vertus agraires, tel est le programme.

Le second Gilles — Gilles converti — est le personnage symbolique de cet ordre nouveau, qui plante là Paris pour le service de Franco et du fascisme européen, qui se retrouve dans la simplicité de la guerre, loin des femmes, loin des illusions, à nouveau combattant, et cette fois moine-soldat. La dernière image du livre est particulièrement suggestive : Gilles est seul dans une arène ; il tire au fusil sur les républicains qui approchent. Le lieu de la fin n'est pas choisi au hasard : « Il fallait, écrit Drieu, défendre le lieu des taureaux [109]. »

Dans cet étonnant catalogue des idées fascistes que constitue *Gilles,* il est en vérité bien peu de nouveautés. Nous avons cru déceler une influence centrale sur Drieu, celle de Barrès : tous les thèmes principaux de celui-ci, ou peu s'en faut, sont ici transcrits sous des couleurs à peine différentes. Le sentiment aigu de la décadence française, l'explication raciste qui en est donnée, la nostalgie des valeurs ancestrales, les aspirations aristocratiques, le culte de l'instinct, l'anti-intellectualisme… la filiation est

107. *Gilles,* p. 475.
108. *Ibid.,* p. 476.
109. *Ibid.,* p. 484.

claire. D'autres influences apparaissent, qui déjà avaient convergé en Barrès, nous pensons particulièrement à Nietzsche, évoqué à plusieurs reprises dans *Gilles :* l'hostilité de Drieu contre la « morale d'esclaves » qui est « essentiellement une morale de l'utilité [110] » ; le goût d'une aristocratie de la force et de la volonté de puissance ; l'aspiration, au-delà du nationalisme, à voir naître « l'Européen de l'avenir [111] »... Mais plus que ces influences, ce qui nous paraît distinctif du discours fasciste, c'est, à travers *Gilles,* son caractère mythologique. En compagnie de Drieu, nous voilà assez loin des prétentions positivistes d'un Maurras, loin de la mesure gréco-romaine : c'est des peuples du Nord qu'il s'inspire et c'est la démesure qu'il vante. S'agissant d'un intellectuel, c'est de propos délibéré que le *mythos* est préféré au *logos* car la critique de la France moderne va de pair avec celle du rationalisme dont elle est issue. Sans doute, Drieu n'a-t-il pas tort de dénoncer le mépris de la force répandu chez ses contemporains, la primauté des valeurs intellectuelles dans le système d'éducation français ; sans doute ne manque-t-il pas d'arguments dans son procès de la France de l'entre-deux-guerres. Emmanuel Mounier, en rendant compte de *Gilles,* notait lui-même « que la France d'avant-guerre avait besoin de muscle et d'un peu de sauvagerie [112] ». Mais Drieu juge du déclin français autant sur des billevesées que sur des réalités : à la preuve de la décadence, il apporte sur un même plateau la dénatalité et l'exode rural, soit un trait de déclin et un trait de modernisme ; du même élan : l'alcoolisme et la peinture de Picasso ; la drogue et les écrivains catholiques, etc. Refusant d'analyser sérieusement les maux réels et profonds dont souffre la France, Drieu par magie résume tous ses malheurs dans la personnalité parabolique du Juif, qui représente tout d'un coup l'antiguerrier, le citadin, le banquier, le ratiocinateur, le sorbonnard, le marxiste, bref une épure de tout ce qu'il abhorre. Plus

110. Nietzsche, *Par-delà le bien et le mal,* 10/18, 1962, p. 213.
111. *Ibid.,* p. 203.
112. *Esprit,* avril 1940.

qu'un symbole de la décadence, le Juif est la décadence même, son incarnation : il est l'Homme Moderne comme Dreyfus chez Maurras était *la* République. Cette mutilation volontaire de l'intelligence, cette inclination à l'irrationnel, ce refus, en un mot, du monde réel — dont la complexité exige assurément moins d'explications hâtives que de rigueur et d'humilité intellectuelles — entraînent Drieu dans le rêve : sa conception du Moyen Age n'est rien d'autre qu'un songe doré, le refus, une fois encore, de la réalité (historique, cette fois). A défaut de science, le fasciste préfère s'abandonner au délire d'un prétendu âge d'or (incertain, au demeurant, selon les auteurs) à restaurer, plutôt que de prendre le monde tel qu'il est pour tenter, pas à pas, de le transformer. Nous sommes ici en présence d'une vision eschatologique du monde : il faut faire table rase du présent pour retrouver, *recréer,* par un retour aux sources, la perfection des origines. « N'importe quoi, pourvu que cette vieille baraque là-bas au bord de l'eau craque [113] », dit Gilles du Palais-Bourbon ; l'important, le nécessaire est en effet, par tous les moyens, de « détruire la société actuelle [114] ». Sur cette *tabula rasa,* on prépare une nouvelle naissance du monde. Comme dans la pensée archaïque décrite par Mircea Eliade, « il s'agit toujours, en définitive, d'abolir le temps écoulé, de « revenir en arrière » et de « recommencer l'existence avec la somme intacte de ses virtualités [115] ». Si l'on veut compléter cette analogie entre le comportement de Gilles et la pensée archaïque, on est alors tenté de définir le fascisme comme un rituel plus que comme une politique. Le culte de l'arbre, auquel se livre notre héros, n'est-ce pas ce « retour à l'origine » — « seul moyen que la pensée archaïque croyait efficace pour annuler l'œuvre du temps [116] » ?

113. *Gilles,* p. 417.
114. *Ibid.,* p. 365.
115. M. Eliade, *Aspects du mythe,* Gallimard, coll. « Idées », 1971, p. 106. M. Bardèche, écrivain « fasciste », écrit, quant à lui : « Tout fascisme est réaction par rapport au présent et toute réaction fasciste est résurrection » (*Qu'est-ce que le fascisme ?,* Les sept couleurs, 1960, p. 175).
116. *Aspects du mythe.*

L'action glorifiée est moins une action *en vue de* qu'une action pour l'action : défendre Daladier ou non, n'importe ! mais agir avec fureur, penser avec un pistolet-mitrailleur, « donner, comme dirait Nietzsche, libre cours à sa force », c'est là retrouver le principe même de la vie.

L'incohérence doctrinale et la nature mythologique des idées fascistes étaient autant d'atouts pour servir la réussite de leurs défenseurs dans des sociétés en crise. Là où le fascisme n'a pas su s'imposer, il est resté dans une large mesure — comme c'est le cas en France — une esthétique, une façon de vivre, une façon de ne pas pouvoir vivre *hic et nunc* et, finalement, comme on sait, une façon de mourir. Vivre dans « l'incroyance prophétique », lutter pour une « cause perdue », choisir sa mort, telle apparaît à travers *Gilles* la destinée altière du héros fasciste. Ce qu'il croit faire pour une cause extérieure, il ne le fait en réalité que pour lui-même [117]. Le « Moi » reste l'objet sacré du « culte ».

117. Nous décalquons ici une phrase de Montherlant qui illustre dans le *Solstice de juin* (NRF, Gallimard, 1943, p. 424) une « morale de l'Ordre » voisine de la morale de *Gilles*.

8

Le cas Bernanos

Un homme debout.

> Je suis un homme moyen resté libre, je suis un homme moyen auquel la propagande n'a pas encore appris à sauter dans tous les cerceaux qu'on lui présente... Je suis un homme debout !
>
> *La liberté pour quoi faire ?*

Plus de vingt ans après la mort de Georges Bernanos, on n'entre pas dans son œuvre politique comme dans un jardin à la française ; ce ne sont pas les droites lignes d'un positivisme politique qui l'ont dessinée et, de toute façon, l'esprit de liberté eût tôt fait d'y bouleverser ce que l'esprit de géométrie se fût jamais ingénié d'ordonner. Devant Bernanos, les étiquettes simplificatrices se justifient moins que jamais.

Vu de loin, on pourrait le baptiser réactionnaire. N'est-il pas resté constant, jusqu'à sa mort, dans son option monarchiste ; n'a-t-il pas été l'admirateur attardé de Drumont, auquel il a consacré un de ces livres les plus célèbres [1] — et n'a-t-il pas gardé l'empreinte ineffaçable de l'antisémitisme appris dans *la Libre Parole ?* N'a-t-il pas été, après la Seconde Guerre mondiale, un des plus éloquents champions de l'anticommunisme ? Ces quelques traits pourraient bien lui valoir la sympathie des hommes de droite, mais comment ceux d'entre eux qui n'ont pas la mémoire

1. *La Grande Peur des bien-pensants,* Grasset, 1931.

trop courte pourraient-ils lui pardonner d'avoir dénoncé la campagne d'Éthiopie au moment où l'« élite » intellectuelle française faisait l'apologie du Duce ; d'avoir, écrivain catholique, publié un des pamphlets les plus virulents contre Franco et ses mitres [2] ; de s'être dressé, malgré les patriotes de métier, contre la capitulation de Munich ; d'avoir écrit les pages les plus dures contre le néo-pacifisme de droite, stigmatisé la singulière génuflexion que faisaient devant Hitler ceux qui, peu d'années auparavant, en face d'une Allemagne désarmée, s'indignaient des « générosités » du traité de Versailles et du « pacifisme humanitaire » des socialistes ; d'avoir sans hésitation récusé l'armistice de 1940, acte « strictement conforme à l'esprit de Munich » ; appelé à la résistance face au totalitarisme nazi et à la révolution face aux « saltimbanques de Vichy »... Ce qui ne l'empêche pas, la guerre finie, de retourner ses batteries sur les partis de gauche fondateurs de la IVe République.

On a pu considérer qu'il fluctuait un peu trop et souhaiter qu'il choisisse son camp, une fois pour toutes. Mais si Bernanos est inclassable, ce n'est pas dire qu'il est frivole. Le vrai est qu'il est un homme seul, un homme pauvre, qu'aucune convention sociale, qu'aucune obligation de secte et qu'aucune complaisance de profession n'oblige. C'est sa force. « On aura beau essayer de me tirer à droite ou à gauche, le chemin que je me suis tracé m'est trop familier pour que je ne sois pas capable de m'y conduire, je connais ma route. »

De fait, Bernanos est resté fidèle, sa vie durant, à des valeurs inspirées d'un christianisme fervent — au rang desquelles il convient de placer la double exigence de l'honneur et de la liberté. Son œuvre politique témoigne d'un combat inlassable contre tout ce qui à ses yeux menace les personnes et les peuples du déshonneur de la soumission et de la servitude.

Si la monarchie, à notre étonnement, est pour lui le meilleur des régimes, la conception idéalisée et fort peu théorisée qu'il en

2. *Les Grands Cimetières sous la lune,* Plon, 1938.

a se situe aux antipodes de la monarchie selon Maurras. Là où le disciple d'Auguste Comte voit un corps d'institutions et un ordre hiérarchique, Bernanos défend une forme de gouvernement qui a « une parole d'honneur », soit tout le contraire, à ses yeux, de l'État moderne, qui est toujours le gouvernement des fonctionnaires et des policiers. Son adhésion à l'Action française apparaît comme le fruit d'un malentendu ; devenir camelot du roi avait été pour le jeune Bernanos la seule façon qu'il vît, avant 1914, de s'insurger contre les bien-pensants. Dès lors que l'école maurrassienne lui est apparue comme un des piliers du parti de l'Ordre, il ne s'y attarda pas — même s'il prit la défense de l'AF lorsque celle-ci, en 1926, tomba sous la condamnation de Rome. La montée des dictatures mit clairement au point les relations de Bernanos et de Maurras ; ils n'avaient plus de langue commune. Bernanos avait toujours été du parti du roi ; Maurras n'avait jamais été que du parti de la Ligue.

Bernanos avait tout de même partagé avec Maurras sa condamnation de la démocratie, mais, sur ce mot, il avertit à plusieurs reprises son lecteur : la démocratie qu'il condamne, ce n'est pas la liberté des peuples, c'est la démocratie institutionnalisée qui, soit dans le cadre du parlementarisme bourgeois, soit dans le cadre du communisme soviétique, au lieu de garantir cette liberté tend au contraire à l'abolir. C'est contre le mythe de l'égalité, sur lequel repose la démocratie, que Bernanos nous prévient. La liberté et l'égalité, nous dit-il, ne sont pas compatibles. L'égalité est un principe au nom duquel tous les moyens coercitifs de toutes les tyrannies sont possibles. C'est au nom de l'égalité qu'on institue la terreur ; c'est au nom de l'égalité qu'on instaure la religion de l'État, c'est-à-dire en fin de compte l'apothéose des bureaucrates et des gardes-chiourme. Entre la démocratie occidentale et le communisme, il n'y a qu'une différence de degré : la servitude commence par la conscription obligatoire et elle s'achève par les camps sibériens.

La liberté, selon Bernanos, en effet, n'a rien à voir avec le libéralisme ; il a toujours été convaincu que « dans une société dominée par l'argent la liberté n'est qu'un leurre ». C'est aux hommes d'Ordre, aux bien-pensants, aux profiteurs du régime capitaliste abrités sous les clochers de l'Église et les drapeaux de l'anticommunisme qu'il a réservé ses coups les plus rudes. Dénonçant la peur sociale de tant de catholiques sous le Front populaire, il accuse l'Église officielle de donner sa caution à la bourgeoisie et à ses maîtres : « Il est quand même désagréable d'entendre de bons gras chanoines parler du Sermon sur la Montagne comme d'un manifeste conservateur. » La mission de l'Église est de former des hommes libres, non des hommes d'Ordre.

L'espèce la plus redoutable d'hommes d'Ordre, nous dit Bernanos, ce ne sont pas ceux en définitive qui ont le fusil à l'épaule, c'est la masse moutonnière, ces « majorités silencieuses » ou, comme il dit, les Respectueux, les Circonspects, les Modérés, ceux qui vivant dans la hantise de la sécurité sont prêts à toutes les abdications, à commencer par celle de leur propre liberté. « La pire imprudence est de dédaigner les médiocres ; la médiocrité est un gaz sans couleur et sans odeur ; on le laisse tranquillement s'accumuler, et il explose tout à coup avec une force incroyable. » Bernanos n'a cessé d'être un immodéré : le modérantisme et la médiocrité ont amené Munich et parrainé le vieux maréchal qui en est l'enfant naturel.

Après Hiroshima, Bernanos a consacré une grande partie de ses dernières forces à battre la générale contre le despotisme d'une Technique incontrôlée. De son point de vue, les deux grands régimes en concurrence, capitalisme et communisme, ne sont que les deux faces d'une même anticivilisation dont le trait le moins supportable sera, est déjà la réduction de l'homme à l'état de robot. Non pas que Bernanos préconisât le retour à la terre et au rouet ; ce n'est pas la machine qu'il dénonce, entreprise absurde, c'est l'esprit machiniste, spéculatif et productiviste, qui conduit nécessairement à l'asservissement de l'homme à l'économique et, partant, au monstre étatique moderne.

Bernanos a répudié les idéologies, de droite comme de

gauche : « Au nom de la “ justice sociale ”, comme hier au nom de l’“ ordre social ”, on tue, on déporte, on torture des millions d’hommes, on asservit des peuples entiers, on les déplace d’un lieu à un autre comme des troupeaux. » Mais devant les forces conjuguées des tyrannies, mécanique, étatique, politique, dont les progrès l’ont souvent désespéré, loin de prêcher quelque vague résignation « libérale », il a cru jusqu’au bout que de la France, qui avait tant déçu mais qui gardait en elle tant de réserves de redressement séculaires, partirait « le signal de l’insurrection de l’Esprit ».

« Mon vieux maître ».

L’attitude de Bernanos face aux États totalitaires, particulièrement depuis la conquête de l’Abyssinie, l’a donc situé le plus souvent aux antipodes de son ancienne politique. Du même coup, il s’est acquis un nouveau public, une nouvelle réputation. Les chrétiens de gauche, devenus nombreux dans les années de l’après-guerre, lui ont su gré d’avoir fait entendre une grande voix catholique contre tous les déshonneurs récents de la patrie : Munich, l’armistice, la Collaboration, Vichy béni des évêques... C’était trop rare un écrivain de cette force qui fût un homme de cette trempe. Qui donc, dans le monde des lettres et dans le monde catholique, pouvait bien se vanter d’avoir tenu cette ligne droite face aux avancées de la dictature et de l’impérialisme nazis ? Et ce n’était pas chez lui par un reste de germanophobie maurrassienne car il s’était élevé aussi, et avec quelle véhémence, contre le fascisme italien et la prétendue Croisade du général Franco. Certes, on savait bien que Bernanos se disait toujours monarchiste, mais n’était-ce pas une vieille manie anodine, une singularité qui ne tirait pas à conséquence ? Mais son antisémitisme ? Ne se pourrait-il pas que, dans le même contexte, on l’ait minimisé aussi, ramené à un péché de jeunesse, depuis longtemps pardonné ? Tout admirateur de Bernanos devrait se considérer comme tenu de lever ce doute.

Le premier fait, à ce propos, qui s'impose à nous et ne cesse d'être troublant, est l'admiration continue que Bernanos a vouée à Édouard Drumont, qu'il appelle du reste son « vieux maître ». Quand l'auteur de *la Grande Peur des bien-pensants* qualifie *la France juive* de livre « magique » — ce qu'il est, au demeurant, mais non pas dans le sens flatteur où l'entend notre auteur —, s'agit-il bien, comme le dit Jean Bastaire, d'« un Bernanos aberrant [3] », c'est-à-dire d'un Bernanos momentanément égaré ? Hypothèse difficile à soutenir puisque jusqu'à la fin de ses jours Bernanos s'est appliqué à défendre la mémoire de Drumont et s'est réclamé de lui. Sans doute peut-on soutenir que dans l'œuvre du plus célèbre des antisémites français Bernanos ne voyait pas ce qui crève nos yeux : des appels au pogrome. Il n'est pas douteux qu'il n'a pris chez Drumont que ce qu'il a voulu y prendre : « le procès d'une société sans entrailles [4] ». Et si le Juif avait quelque chose à y voir, ce n'était pas comme agent privilégié ou exclusif de la décadence, mais plutôt comme symptôme de celle-ci. On dira que c'est toujours de l'antisémitisme. N'en doutons pas. La nuance, tout de même, est notable.

L'antisémitisme de Bernanos (il accepte encore le mot en 1936 : « Je m'expliquerai sur *mon antisémitisme* où l'on voudra [5] ») est repérable dès ses premiers articles à *l'Avant-garde de Normandie* [6] jusqu'à la *Grande Peur,* qui en est le point d'orgue. Mais on en trouve encore maintes expressions, quoique atténuées, dans ses écrits ultérieurs. On y reconnaît la combinaison de l'antijudaïsme chrétien et du social-antisémitisme opérée jadis par Drumont, renouvelée par les assomptionnistes de *la Croix,*

3. J. Bastaire, « Drumont et l'antisémitisme », *Esprit,* mars 1964.
4. G. Bernanos, « Édouard Drumont », conférence donnée à l'Institut d'Action française, le 28 mai 1929, in *Écrits de combat I,* Bibliothèque de la Pléiade, p. 1169.
5. *Sept,* 31 juillet 1936, in Bulletin de la Société des Amis de Georges Bernanos, n° 28-29, noël 1956.
6. Voir notamment sa campagne contre « M. Alexandre », commerçant juif de Rouen, in *Écrits de combat I, op. cit.,* p. 930, 952.

répandue largement dans les milieux catholiques d'avant 1914. Premier chef d'accusation : l'antagonisme entre la civilisation chrétienne et la mentalité juive. « Je tiens le Juif pour l'ennemi de la chrétienté », dit-il, ajoutant toutefois : « Je ne le méprise pas [7]. » Deuxième chef d'accusation : l'or juif, l'usure juive, la banque juive. Bornons-nous au résumé de leur œuvre, tel qu'il est formulé dans la conclusion de la *Grande Peur :* « Devenus maîtres de l'or ils [les Juifs] s'assurent bientôt qu'en pleine démocratie égalitaire, ils peuvent être du même coup maîtres de l'opinion, c'est-à-dire des mœurs [...]. Dès la moitié du XIXe siècle, aux premières places de l'Administration, de la Banque, de la Magistrature, des Chemins de fer ou des Mines, partout enfin l'héritier du grand bourgeois, le polytechnicien à binocle, s'habitue à trouver ces bonshommes étranges qui parlent avec leurs mains comme des singes [...], si différents du papa bonnetier ou notaire et comme tombés d'une autre planète, avec leur poil noir, les traits ciselés par l'angoisse millénaire, le prurit sauvage d'une moelle usée depuis le règne de Salomon, prodiguée dans tous les lits de l'impudique Asie [8]... »

Je veux bien croire Bernanos quand il dit qu'il n'est pas raciste, parce que le racisme, c'est la croyance dans une hiérarchie des races et que lui ne distingue pas des races supérieures de races inférieures [9], mais il faut alors convenir que le morceau qu'on vient de lire a dû échapper à sa plume.

Qu'il s'agisse des « seigneurs juifs » ou des « petits youtres roublards de Moscou [10] », Bernanos croit à un « instinct sécu-

7. Lettre à Henry Coston, directeur de *la Libre Parole,* 29 avril 1935, in *Courrier Georges Bernanos,* n° 8, juin 1972.

8. *La Grande Peur des bien-pensants,* in *Œuvres de combat I, op. cit.,* p. 328-329.

9. « Encore la question juive », mai 1944, repris dans *le Chemin de la croix des âmes,* Gallimard, p. 421-424.

10. « Primauté de la peur », *L'Action française,* 5 décembre 1929, in *Œuvres de combat I, op. cit.,* p. 1183.

laire [11] » du Juif qui l'entraîne, soit par le capitalisme, soit par le communisme, à prospérer dans la société moderne, incapable de s'en défendre par paresse et médiocrité.

Au fond, au début des années trente, Bernanos exprime encore les préjugés, sinon tous les stéréotypes, antisémites, propres à sa famille d'origine, catholique et antidreyfusarde. A ceci près, qui n'est pas négligeable, qu'il vomit les conservateurs et les bien-pensants, lesquels précisément font le gros du milieu catholique antidreyfusard. Antisémite, certes, mais au nom d'une monarchie populaire qui n'a rien à voir avec les compromissions de la droite conservatrice et qui n'aura bientôt plus rien à voir avec le monarchisme calculateur et positiviste des maurrassiens.

Dans les années qui suivent sa rupture avec Maurras et l'Action française, Bernanos, tout en se démarquant des antisémites de droite, admirateurs des nouveaux régimes d'ordre installés aux frontières françaises, a continué à évoquer le « problème juif ». En 1939, dans une variante de *Scandale de la vérité,* il déclare *ne rien renier* de l'*antisémitisme* de Drumont. Il concède que le « mot » est « malheureux » mais s'en prend à Jacques Maritain qui vient de parler de « l'impossible antisémitisme ». On ne doit, dit-il, « ni haïr ni mépriser les Juifs » mais constater que leur présence au sein de la communauté nationale pose un problème qui doit être réglé pacifiquement et juridiquement. « Je ne suis pas antijuif, je crois seulement que chaque État chrétien devrait traiter avec ses Juifs selon les règles de l'équité... Pourquoi les États ne traiteraient-ils pas avec eux comme ils traitent avec l'Église ? [12] » Et Bernanos d'entrer dans quelques détails de ce *traité* (il n'est point question d'un quelconque « statut » imposé ou octroyé) : il souhaite qu'on réserve aux Juifs un « grand nombre de places dans l'administration des finances

11. *L'Avant-Garde de Normandie,* in *Œuvres de combat I, op. cit.,* p. 966.
12. Variante de *Scandale,* in *la Grande Peur des bien-pensants,* Le Livre de poche, 1969, p. 436.

ou même dans la presse d'information » mais voudrait les « tenir éloignés de la politique » et de « l'éducation des jeunes Français [13] ».

Cependant, l'arrivée de Hitler au pouvoir, la persécution des Juifs en Allemagne, la nouvelle vague d'antisémitisme que gonflent les puissants journaux d'extrême droite en France, la fin des années trente et la guerre qui suit vont nécessairement modifier, d'abord dans leur expression puis sur le fond, les idées de Bernanos sur la « question juive ».

Avant que n'éclate la guerre, vilipendant « la hideuse terreur antisémite [14] », il s'écrie qu'il aimerait « mieux être fouetté par le rabbin d'Alger que faire souffrir une femme ou un enfant juif [15] » ; pendant la guerre, il multiplie les accusations contre le nazisme et Vichy : « Comprenez-vous que la Victoire elle-même ne suffirait pas à effacer la tache faite à notre histoire, ne serait-ce que par la livraison des Juifs antinazis réfugiés chez nous à l'Allemagne, des républicains espagnols à Franco ? [16] » Lorsque Georges Mandel, ancien collaborateur de Clemenceau, ancien ministre de Daladier et de Reynaud, est déporté en Allemagne, Georges Bernanos écrit : « Quant à Mandel, vous vous dites peut-être que n'ayant jamais montré de goût pour les Juifs, je ne parlerai pas de celui-là ? Détrompez-vous ! C'est lui que vous haïssez le plus, vous et vos maîtres. A ce titre, il m'est mille fois plus sacré que les autres. Si vos maîtres ne nous rendent pas Mandel vivant, vous aurez à payer ce sang juif d'une manière qui étonnera l'Histoire — entendez-vous bien, chiens que vous êtes — chaque goutte de ce sang juif versé en haine de notre ancienne Victoire nous est plus précieuse que toute la pourpre d'un manteau de cardinal fasciste — est-ce que vous comprenez bien

13. Variante de *Scandale, ibid.*

14. Bulletin de la Société des Amis de Georges Bernanos, n° 47, sept.-décembre 1962.

15. *Nous autres Français,* in *Œuvres de combat I, op. cit.,* p. 735.

16. « Réflexions sur le cas de conscience français », 15 octobre 1943, in *le Chemin de la croix des âmes, op. cit.,* p. 91.

ce que je veux dire, Amiraux, Maréchaux, Excellences, Éminences et Révérences ? [17] »

Bernanos, de son lointain exil brésilien, a été infiniment sensible au drame de la communauté juive ; il n'en a nullement pris son parti comme la lecture de Drumont aurait pu l'y encourager — l'« holocauste » étant à mettre au compte d'une « justice » enfin accomplie. Dans l'hommage qu'il rend à la mémoire de Georges Torrès, le ton à l'égard des Juifs a définitivement changé :

« Les charniers refroidissent lentement, la dépouille des martyrs retourne à la terre, l'herbe avare et les ronces recouvrent le sol impur où tant de moribonds ont sué leur dernière sueur, les fours crématoires eux-mêmes s'ouvrent béants et vides sur les matins et sur les soirs, mais c'est bien loin maintenant de l'Allemagne, c'est aux rives du Jourdain que lève la semence des héros du ghetto de Varsovie [18]. »

L'évolution est évidente. Toutefois, l'éradication de ses vieilles idées n'est pas totale. « Je ne suis ni antijuif, ni antisémite... », dit-il désormais, mais un « problème » à ses yeux demeure : « Je ne suis ni antijuif, ni antisémite, mais j'ai toujours cru qu'il y a un problème juif, dont la solution importe beaucoup au monde de demain. J'ai toujours cru, je crois encore, que l'obstination — d'ailleurs admirable à bien des égards — des Juifs à ne pas se fondre totalement dans les divers milieux nationaux est un grand malheur pour tout le monde. Mais je suis aussi trop chrétien pour désirer les voir renier leurs croyances par intérêt ou même par patriotisme, et leur religion est précisément basée sur un privilège racial, concédé par Dieu à la race, à la chair et au sang juifs. En sorte que le problème est presque insoluble, mais ce serait un pas fait vers la solution future si nous consentions les

17. Article de février 1943, in *le Chemin de la croix des âmes, op. cit.*, p. 148-149.

18. « L'honneur est ce qui nous rassemble », *Français si vous saviez*, Gallimard, 1961, p. 322-327.

uns et les autres à le poser sans parti pris, au lieu de le nier [19]. »

Si Bernanos, à partir de ces années de terreur hitlérienne, tient en horreur le mot d'antisémitisme, c'est parce que celui-ci se réfère désormais à un racisme d'État contre lequel il proteste de toute son énergie. Hitler lui interdit l'antisémitisme ; Bernanos a ce mot ahurissant : Hitler « a déshonoré l'antisémitisme [20] ». Le dictateur allemand « s'est servi de l'antisémitisme, comme de l'anticommunisme, pour corrompre l'opinion européenne, la diviser, la dissocier, fournir aux peuples ses futures victimes, des thèmes de guerre civile », ce qui l'amène à déclarer : « Je n'ai jamais cru à la sincérité de l'antisémitisme hitlérien [21]. » Il récuse donc désormais ce « mot de foule », ce « mot de masse », car « le destin de pareils mots est de ruisseler, tôt ou tard, de sang innocent [22] ». Au demeurant, Bernanos n'entend nullement renier Drumont car, à ses yeux, il n'y a aucune similitude, aucune filiation, entre Drumont et Hitler.

Pourtant, ce n'est pas seulement l'abandon de certains termes de son ancien vocabulaire qui est notable dans l'évolution de Bernanos. Il n'est pas douteux que sur les origines de la « question juive », il a revu et corrigé ses premières interprétations. A preuve, ce passage tiré de l'hommage à Georges Torrès, cité plus haut, où on le voit expliquer *l'exclusion* des Juifs de la communauté chrétienne médiévale non seulement par ce qu'il appelait naguère le « racisme juif » mais par l'aveuglement de la chrétienté « sur les causes réelles de la survivance du peuple juif à travers l'Histoire, sur la fidélité à lui-même, à sa loi, à ses ancêtres, fidélité qui avait pourtant de quoi émouvoir son âme. Parce que cette fidélité n'était pas une fidélité militaire, de tradition et d'esprit militaire, elle maintenait le Juif hors d'une fraternité militaire dont n'était même pas exclu l'Infidèle. Et le Juif devait *nécessairement* [souligné par nous] s'accommoder

19. Lettre à Jean Hauser, *Correspondance,* Plon, t. 2, p. 546.
20. « Encore la question juive », *loc. cit.*
21. *Lettre aux Anglais,* Gallimard, 1946, p. 161-162.
22. « L'honneur est ce qui nous rassemble », *loc. cit.*

d'une telle exclusion, s'y installer, en tirer profit. Ainsi le malentendu n'a cessé de s'aggraver au cours des âges[23] ».

De tels propos, on le voit, ne sont certainement pas d'un disciple opiniâtre de *la France juive.* Entre 1931 et 1948, date de sa mort, il est patent que le discours bernanosien sur les Juifs a évolué. Si Bernanos continue à honorer le nom de Drumont jusqu'au bout, c'est qu'à ses yeux, dit-il, et contrairement à ceux des « imbéciles » l'œuvre de son vieux maître n'est pas réductible à l'antisémitisme. On peut dire autrement : que sous le mot désormais impossible d'antisémitisme il y avait chez Drumont une vision du monde et de l'Histoire qui reste fondamentalement celle de Bernanos[24].

Un homme de l'Ancienne France.

Aux yeux de Bernanos, le terme d'*antisémitisme* a subi un détournement de sens. Pour un lecteur attentif de Drumont, ce glissement sémantique n'est pas évident : *Mein Kampf* marche sur les talons de *la France juive.* Pourquoi Bernanos ne peut-il se résigner à accepter la continuation ? Pour une raison à la fois chronologique et affective. Il n'avait pas lu Drumont comme nous : avec un Auschwitz dans la tête. Il éprouve une dette à son égard. Dans le contexte historique et dans le milieu où Bernanos a été élevé, Drumont a été son initiateur à la révolte, non pas contre les Juifs — il nous le dit explicitement — mais contre la société contemporaine. Drumont lui a révélé l'injustice sociale, la trahison des conservateurs et l'hypocrisie des bien-pensants. Toute l'œuvre polémique de Bernanos afflue de cette lecture initiatique. De surcroît, derrière l'auteur, l'homme Drumont apparaît à Bernanos comme le représentant de cette ancienne société au nom de laquelle il se bat. La référence Drumont est

23. « L'honneur est ce qui nous rassemble », *loc. cit.*

24. Voir « Encyclique aux Français », hiver 1947, in *la Vocation spirituelle de la France,* inédits présentés et rassemblés par Jean-Loup Bernanos, 1975, p. 208.

l'assise affective de ses luttes : comment pourrait-il la renier ?

Évidemment, la lecture que fait Bernanos de Drumont est sélective. Il n'en voit ni le caractère raciste ni le délire obsessionnel. Pas une fois, l'auteur de la *Grande Peur* ne prête le moindre crédit au « mythe aryen [25] », si en vogue à la fin du XIXe siècle, si en vogue de nouveau dans les années trente. De même, il ne suit guère les explications par la « causalité diabolique [26] » dont Drumont emplit ses livres et ses articles. Bernanos reconnaît au contraire qu'il arrive à son maître de prendre l'effet pour la cause. Il ne voit pas dans les Juifs, comme lui, le principe de tout Mal, la cause de la décadence, l'entreprise de sape occulte installée dans les flancs de la chrétienté, l'obsédant complot visant à la domination du monde. Bernanos n'a cure de ces fantasmes.

Deux aspects corrélatifs de l'œuvre de Drumont l'ont enthousiasmé ; le rejet de la société capitaliste et le référentiel de l'Ancienne France.

Paraphrasant la formule de Bebel selon laquelle « l'antisémitisme est le socialisme des imbéciles », on pourrait dire aussi que l'antisémitisme a été, à la fin du XIXe siècle, le socialisme des catholiques. Catholiques sociaux et premiers démocrates-chrétiens ont mêlé dans leurs attaques la société capitaliste et la Banque juive, l'Argent et les Juifs. On sait que cette confusion n'a pas été le fait exclusif des catholiques, que maints socialistes y sont tombés. Les catholiques avaient cependant des raisons supplémentaires d'y participer. Outre la vieille tradition antijudaïque, encore vivante dans une communauté religieuse imputant aux Juifs la crucifixion de son Messie par ancêtres interposés, les catholiques étaient exclus de l'État et assiégés dans leurs institutions depuis la victoire définitive des républicains.

Les années de collège de Bernanos datent de cette époque où les catholiques les plus soucieux de la « question sociale » l'assimilent aisément à la « question juive ». *La Croix,* moniteur

25. Voir L. Poliakov, *le Mythe aryen,* Calmann-Lévy, 1971.
26. Voir L. Poliakov, *la Causalité diabolique,* Calmann-Lévy, 1981.

de l'antisémitisme catholique, pouvait alors faire écho avec sympathie à un livre de l'abbé Féret intitulé *Le capitalisme, voilà l'ennemi.* Un hebdomadaire chrétien pouvait être salué conjointement par Drumont et l'abbé Lemire en définissant ses objectifs comme la lutte simultanée contre les Juifs, les francs-maçons et les « panamites ». Un comité ouvrier catholique, constitué à Brest en 1894, pouvait proclamer dans un manifeste : « Vive la République française et chrétienne. A bas la République juive et franc-maçonnique ! [27] »

C'est chez Drumont que Bernanos apprend la protestation sociale parce que cela ne pouvait pas être pour lui chez Guesde ou chez Jaurès. Membre de la communauté catholique, il n'a pas d'indulgence pour ceux de ses coreligionnaires bien nantis, toujours prêts à s'entendre avec la bourgeoisie franc-maçonne et athée pour écraser les grévistes ou les communards. De sorte que, en 1947, au moment des grandes grèves, il pouvait dire à François Mauriac, appelant la bourgeoisie catholique à son « devoir social », que Drumont avait été dans les années 1880 un des rares à lui parler, à cette bourgeoisie, de ce devoir-là, fort oublié par l'enseignement des institutions religieuses [28]. Le Drumont affirmant le 19 mars 1898, dans *la Libre Parole :* « Les antisémites [...] sont les vrais vengeurs de la Commune » ; le Drumont dénonçant les sociétés par actions « plus collectivistes que le collectivisme lui-même [29] » ; le Drumont bravant le pouvoir de l'argent, tel est bien celui dont Bernanos s'inspire et auquel il restera fidèle.

Une fidélité qui a une autre source : Drumont ne poursuit pas la société capitaliste de ses vindictes pour rêver une utopie socialiste — ce qui serait incompatible avec l'idéal chrétien. Drumont est avant tout un « prophète de l'Ancienne France ». La critique du capitalisme chez Bernanos est en effet englobée

27. Voir Montuclard, *Conscience religieuse et démocratie,* Éd. du Seuil, 1965.
28. « Encyclique aux Français », *loc. cit.*
29. É. Drumont, *La Fin d'un monde, op. cit.,* p. 171

dans une critique plus large, celle de la société moderne. Cette société industrielle et démocratique, oublieuse des anciennes vertus et des anciens rythmes, dans laquelle le Juif est comme un poisson dans l'eau. Il y a une incompatibilité entre l'ancienne France et la prospérité juive ; il y a au contraire une équivalence entre la société moderne et la conquête juive. « Tant que la chrétienté, dit Drumont, fut fidèle à la doctrine des Pères de l'Église qui avait interdit l'usure et le prêt à intérêt, le Juif erra [30]. » L'effondrement de la doctrine chrétienne, les débuts des Temps modernes ont entraîné l'Occident dans la course au profit et, de proche en proche, dans l'édification d'une société où les laboureurs et les cordonniers ont été remplacés par des banquiers et des agents de change. La révolution industrielle qui a suivi la révolution du capital a métamorphosé le peuple en « prolétariat définitivement coupé de ses racines nationales, politiques, sociales [31] ».

Dans *la France contre les Robots,* qu'il écrit dans les dernières années de sa vie, Bernanos exprime la continuité de ses premières intuitions : « Je suis un homme de l'Ancienne France, j'ai la liberté dans le sang. Vous me direz que l'Ancienne France n'a pas été tendre pour les Juifs. Je n'approuve pas ces injustices, mais il faut les comprendre. Les Juifs ont toujours été des précurseurs. Dès le XIe siècle, ils se sont efforcés par tous les moyens de constituer, à l'intérieur de la cité chrétienne, une société capitaliste [32]. » La « question juive » est née selon lui du monde moderne. Non que le Juif ait créé ce monde-là mais il en est l'expression la plus démonstrative. La chrétienté médiévale, avec une brutalité que condamne Bernanos, a su tenir ses Juifs à leur place ; les Temps modernes ont libéré leurs énergies maintenues sous le joug pendant des siècles.

C'est sur cette équivalence Juif = Moderne que repose ce qui a constitué l'antisémitisme bernanosien. Dans sa vision, le Juif est

30. É. Drumont, *La Libre Parole,* 15 avril 1895.
31. « Édouard Drumont », conférence citée.
32. *La France contre les Robots,* Le Livre de poche, 1973, p. 228.

moins l'image séculaire de l'Usurier que le mythe polyvalent de la modernité. Ce qui n'est pas incompatible avec la représentation de plus en plus répandue qu'on se fait de l'Amérique, parangon de démesure technocratique. Ce n'est pas par hasard si, dans la seule ville de New York, tête de ce « géant au cerveau de baby », vivent trois millions de Juifs. De là résulte peut-être cette évidence pour Bernanos : « Un Français est beaucoup plus près d'un Anglais et plus capable de le comprendre qu'un Américain [33]. » *Do you understand ?*

La France contre les Robots, dénonciation du machinisme et du productivisme, déclaration de guerre à la société industrielle, reste inspirée par une vision du monde qui sous-tendait déjà l'œuvre de Drumont et qui témoigne d'une nostalgie et d'une angoisse décelables au cœur du mouvement antisémite.

La nostalgie n'est sans doute pas le mot qui eût plu à Bernanos. Utilisons-le néanmoins pour exprimer cette conviction qu'il a existé jadis un modèle de société, sinon parfaite, à tout le moins en harmonie avec la nature humaine et la conscience chrétienne. A cette société, fondée sur l'honneur et la liberté, s'est substituée la société moderne, fondée sur l'argent et l'*ubris* technologique : « L'ardente minorité juive, écrit Bernanos dans la *Grande Peur,* devint tout naturellement le noyau d'une nouvelle France qui grandit peu à peu aux dépens de l'ancienne [34]. »

Cette nostalgie d'un monde perdu est une autre manière de formuler son angoisse. Celle-ci particulièrement manifeste dans les couches moyennes de la société, menacées ou ruinées par les conséquences de la révolution industrielle. Bernanos comme Drumont, de ce point de vue, sont sociologiquement représentatifs de ce monde d'artisans et de petits commerçants, que l'usine et le grand magasin ont fait entrer dans le déclin depuis le second Empire. L'antisémitisme donne une identité à la menace obscure

33. *Le Chemin de la croix des âmes, op. cit.*, p. 476-477.
34. *La Grande Peur des bien-pensants,* in *Œuvres de combat I, op. cit.*, p.133-134.

qui pèse sur leurs existences. Ils s'y raccrochent comme le paranoïaque à son délire interprétatif.

La menace n'est pas seulement d'ordre économique — elle est spirituelle et morale. Ce que la révolution industrielle est en train de casser, ce ne sont pas seulement des anciens moyens de vivre mais une psychologie collective, une philosophie séculaire de la vie elle-même. Les Juifs apportent avec eux « une mystique nouvelle, admirablement accordée à celle du Progrès, au moderne Messianisme qui n'attend que de l'homme la révélation du dieu futur [35] ».

Dans *la Petite Peur du XX*e *siècle,* Emmanuel Mounier écrit que « l'homme européen a achevé vers l'aurore des Temps modernes une sorte de vie utérine, qu'il menait au sein d'un univers clos sur lui comme un œuf sur son germe, au cœur d'une Église qui gardait directement en tutelle ses premiers pas [36] ». La nostalgie de ce monde ancien, dont l'image protectrice est reconstruite pour les besoins de la cause, reflète l'angoisse éprouvée par l'homme moderne face à un avenir indéchiffrable. L'accélération des transformations matérielles et la perte des vieilles croyances ont créé conjointement un véritable « malaise dans la civilisation ».

Nous tenons là une des motivations les plus fortes de l'antisémitisme moderne — en tout cas tel qu'il s'exprime chez Drumont et chez ses disciples. Chez eux, l'image du Juif est liée à celle de l'errance, de l'instabilité, du changement. « Que font parmi nous ces errants ? demande Bernanos. Qu'ils se fixent ou supportent que nous imposions des lois à leur errance [37]. » Sur ces « vagabonds éternels », il a des regards de terriens menacé par des nomades. La dualité chrétien/Juif s'enchaîne sur les polarités : stable/changeant, immobilité/évolution, construction de pierre/

35. *La Grande Peur des bien-pensants,* in *Œuvres de combat I, op. cit.,* p. 329.

36. E. Mounier, *Œuvres,* Éd. du Seuil, 1962, t. 3, p. 354.

37. « A propos de l'antisémitisme de Drumont », variante de *Scandale, op. cit.*

tente de toile. Péguy avait écrit qu'il y avait un *grand vice* qui était aussi une *grande vertu secrète,* une « grande vocation » d'Israël : d'être un « peuple pour qui les plus immobilières maisons ne seront jamais que des tentes ». Or Bernanos, qui cite ce texte, oubliant délibérément « la grande vertu » ne parle que du « vice » : « Ce vice a fini par devenir celui du monde moderne. N'est-ce qu'une coïncidence [38] ? » Bernanos avait à cœur de défendre ainsi contre les agressions de la mobilité moderne les « races comme les nôtres, si étroitement liées au sol, au foyer, à la pierre de leur seuil ».

Depuis l'Antiquité, bien des auteurs, Platon en tête, ont interprété le changement comme synonyme du Mal ; l'idéal de l'immobilité rassure. Une immobilité qui se fait terre et pierre, foncière et immobilière. La technique, bancaire et industrielle, a brisé le vieux monde stable, la « société close » dont parle Karl Popper [39], celle qui pendant des millénaires a été le cadre « naturel » de l'humanité. Une société où chacun était à sa place, où chacun perpétuait l'œuvre de ses parents, où les lendemains ressemblaient aux jours passés. Cet ordre ancien est rompu. « Le passage de la société *close* à la société *ouverte,* écrit Popper, est une des plus grandes révolutions que l'humanité ait connues [40]. » La fin de la société rurale et de la famille patriarcale, le développement des villes, l'individualisation de la société, les responsabilités personnelles que les hommes les plus modestes arrachés à leur « tribu » ont dû assumer, cette formidable mutation qui commence lentement à la fin du Moyen Age et s'accélère aux XIXe et XXe siècles, c'est un « saut dans l'inconnu et dans l'incertain » (Popper).

Comme Drumont, Bernanos a certainement exprimé cette angoisse du monde moderne, qui est le fruit de son déracinement. Mais là où réside l'ambivalence de son œuvre et qui

38. « A propos de l'antisémitisme de Drumont », *loc. cit.*
39. K. Popper, *La Société ouverte et ses ennemis,* Éd. du Seuil, 1979, 2 t.
40. *Ibid.,* t. I, p. 143.

l'oppose aux réactionnaires habituels, c'est qu'à ses yeux l'Ancienne France était tout le contraire d'une « société close », celle que rêvent de reconstruire, sur de nouvelles bases, les mouvements fascistes et communistes : « Rien ne ressemble moins au totalitarisme, en effet, que notre ancien ordre français avec son accumulation presque inextricable de services et de privilèges découlant les uns des autres et s'équilibrant entre eux [41]. »

Cette idéalisation de la société préindustrielle a concouru à l'antisémitisme. Mais chez Bernanos l'antisémitisme a été l'expression erronée de valeurs *morales* (honneur et liberté) si fortement ancrées chez lui qu'elles l'ont détourné de la logique *politique* où l'antisémitisme a conduit ordinairement les antisémites, de 1933 à 1945. De là découle la situation proprement inclassable de Bernanos, ce transfuge qui n'a jamais cessé d'être fidèle à lui-même.

Au moment de la publication des *Grands Cimetières sous la lune,* André Thérive s'étonnait dans *le Temps* de l'incohérence d'un Bernanos dont *la Grande Peur des bien-pensants,* pamphlet antilibéral, antibourgeois et antidémocratique, annonçait le fascisme ; or voilà que « cet élève de Drumont deviendrait dreyfusard [42] ». En fait, à qui lit attentivement la conclusion de *la Grande Peur,* Bernanos s'impose comme l'adversaire le plus résolu de tous les totalitarismes. Ce n'est pas assez dire : toute son œuvre est tendue, dressée contre les multiples avatars de la tyrannie moderne et leur oppose, non point une stratégie (en est-il ?) mais « une certaine conception, proprement religieuse, de la personne humaine ». Ce qui nous guette, nous menace et bientôt nous exclura si nous refusons d'y entrer au pas cadencé,

41. *Le Chemin de la croix des âmes, op. cit.,* p. 419.
42. Cité par Joseph Jurt, « *Les Grands Cimetières sous la lune* devant la presse non catholique en 1938 », *Études bernanosiennes* 13 *(la Revue des Lettres modernes,* 1972, t. 2).

c'est « l'Usine universelle, l'Usine intégrale » que l'ingénieur flanqué du banquier ou du commissaire du peuple est en train de construire. Cette société sans but — « sinon celui de durer le plus longtemps possible » — aura pour terme « le total asservissement de l'individu, son écrasement ». Comme un signal d'alarme, les dernières phrases du livre retentissent : « L'air va manquer à nos poumons. L'air manque. » L'ennemi n'est donc pas à gauche ou à droite ; il est partout où la liberté de l'homme est en danger.

Il n'est pas contestable que ses références peuvent paraître aujourd'hui chimérique : dans l'image de sa chrétienté l'imagination du poète a fait sa part. Mais quand Bernanos affirme : « L'histoire de mon pays a été faite par des gens qui croyaient à la vocation surnaturelle de la France [43] », nous voilà revenus dans une réalité historique : les rédacteurs des droits de l'homme, les quarante-huitards, un bon nombre de communards et de dreyfusards [44] ne la qualifiaient pas de « surnaturelle » mais croyaient certainement dur comme fer à la « mission » de la France.

L'important, me semble-t-il, n'est point tant la référence chrétienne-médiévale que l'esprit qu'elle traduit. Le rêve d'une société perdue peut également inspirer des hommes d'ordre et des esprits libertaires. Bernanos a imaginé un archétype de Français, homme fier et libre, qui s'est incarné dans l'« homme de l'Ancien Régime ». Celui-ci « avait la conscience catholique, le cœur et le cerveau monarchistes, et le tempérament républicain [45] ». Il n'a pas inventé ce portrait-robot pour mettre les gens au pas mais pour l'opposer à l'esclave des tyrannies modernes.

De même, l'antisémitisme qui affleure dans l'œuvre de Berna-

43. *Scandale de la vérité,* in *Œuvres de combat I*, *op. cit.*, p. 581.

44. A dessein, je ne fais référence ici qu'à la tradition républicaine mais sans trahir, je crois, Bernanos qui, si peu complaisant qu'il fût envers les dreyfusards, affirmait néanmoins : « Il y a des milliers de Français qui ont été dreyfusiens, parce qu'ils croyaient à l'innocence de Dreyfus, refusaient de sacrifier un innocent à la raison d'État. De quoi je ne saurais les blâmer... » (*Nous autres Français,* in *Œuvres de combat I, op. cit.*, p. 666).

45. *Scandale...,* in *Œuvres de combat I,* p. 588.

nos n'est point central comme dans l'œuvre de son « cher vieux Drumont ». Il s'en est servi parfois, comme d'une mauvaise rhétorique ; il n'a jamais récité un « bréviaire de la haine ». Ce serait manquer à la vérité et à la justice que de laisser suggérer entre l'œuvre de Bernanos et les influences antisémitiques dont celle-ci porte les marques une commune mesure.

Conclusion

L'antisémitisme est un fait social total, irréductible à toute interprétation unicausale. Ses origines et les causes de son développement sont multiples ; il n'a pas été question ici d'en faire l'inventaire. A travers quelques cas français, il m'a paru important d'insister sur deux sortes — inégales — d'antisémitisme : celui qui exprime la nostalgie d'une *société close,* selon le concept de Popper, et celui qui se réclame de l'universel socialiste.

C'est dans la famille contre-révolutionnaire, traditionaliste, catholique que le premier s'est exprimé le plus naturellement et le plus continûment. Pour simplifier les choses, on pourrait distinguer trois étapes dans la construction idéologique de la contre-révolution ; on verra qu'à chacune d'elles, le Juif, dans son mythe, unifie les objets de la réaction.

1° La révolution politique de 1789-1793 a suscité contre elle et ses prolongements lointains une littérature qui a progressivement fait des Juifs, bénéficiaires de l'émancipation de 91, les véritables destructeurs de l'Ancien Régime. L'osmose entre les Juifs et les francs-maçons explique, aux yeux des antisémites, la suite de l'histoire républicaine : la laïcisation de la société, la séparation de l'Église et de l'État, la destruction de la famille (c'est le Juif Naquet qui fait voter le rétablissement du divorce en 1884), l'expulsion des congrégations, etc. Le « complot judéo-maçonnique » s'est appliqué avec acharnement à la destruction de la chrétienté.

2° La révolution industrielle ne s'est pas faite en France avec la brutalité qui la caractérisa en Angleterre. Toutefois, les transformations économiques, à la fois bancaires, commerciales et industrielles, qui ont marqué la période d'expansion que fut le second Empire, ont heurté les esprits mieux disposés au train antique des choses qu'à l'accélération des changements. La guerre civile dont Paris est le théâtre sanglant à l'issue de la défaite de 1871 cause un premier effroi : les « classes dangereuses » cernent les « honnêtes gens ». Dans son rapport à l'Assemblée nationale sur l'insurrection du 18 mars, le parlementaire Martial Delpit, exprimant « la grande et honnête opinion conservatrice », a dit carrément, à propos des ouvriers révolutionnaires : « Nous sommes en présence d'une nouvelle invasion de barbares. » A cause des travaux démentiels lancés par Napoléon III, Paris les a attirés : « Grâce aux chemins de fer, à la facilité des communications et à leur bon marché, Paris est devenu le rendez-vous de tous ceux qui cherchent fortune, une *Californie intérieure...* » Paris est devenu Babylone, un pandémonium de vices, de crimes et d'incrédulité, aboutissement des plus inquiétantes immigrations. Drumont consacre l'un de ses premiers livres à son *Vieux Paris,* désormais dominé par les cosmopolites et où « bientôt, nous autres, les natifs, ne serons plus que des étrangers ». Le Juif préside nécessairement, pour l'antisémite, à la révolution urbanistique. Lui, le sans-racines, l'éternel nomade, c'est dans la Ville qu'il prospère. Il est encore ici, par le truchement de la Banque et de la Bourse qu'il contrôle, le bénéficiaire opulent du changement. Les crises économiques portent les fureurs antisémitiques à leur plus grande violence : dans les dégâts du progrès, on désigne l'éternel Juif. L'idéologie contre-révolutionnaire, entée sur le rêve d'une ancienne France, dont l'harmonie repose sur un combiné des vertus rustiques et des vertus chrétiennes, oppose les valeurs terriennes de nos ancêtres aux fausses valeurs du monde moderne. Le Juif s'impose dans cette vision bucolique comme l'anti-Paysan ; celui dont la fortune repose sur le déracinement des peuples et sur la frénésie du Progrès.

3° La révolution socialiste et communiste achève la cristallisation du mythe juif. Il n'est pas seulement l'homme du Capital ; il est aussi le Subversif révolutionnaire. Non seulement il détruit la société par le haut (banquiers, hommes d'affaires, politiciens francs-maçons...) mais il en sape les fondements. Rothschild et Marx, un seul combat : la démolition de la société occidentale. La révolution bolchevique de 1917 apparaît comme un des derniers avatars du « complot juif » pour les antisémites. Le thème du « judéo-marxisme », du « judéo-bolchevisme », sera usé jusqu'à la corde dans la presse d'extrême droite au cours des années trente, quand bien même Staline avait entrepris la liquidation des communistes juifs.

Ces trois éléments d'antisémitisme se sont relayés ou additionnés. Ils furent l'expression fantasmatique de milieux en proie, économiquement et culturellement, à des menaces, tantôt précises : la République laïque, le développement industriel, l'essor du grand commerce, la montée du mouvement ouvrier ; tantôt obscures : la crainte d'un avenir incertain, privé des bornes rassurantes dont les siècles passés ont balisé la société — une famille, une Église, une corporation, une hiérarchie. Plus profondément, l'antisémitisme a exprimé l'effroi de certaines couches sociales ou de certains milieux culturels devant le changement, l'accélération des mouvements sociaux, la mobilité géographique, « la fin d'un monde », comme dit Drumont, conçu comme celui d'un temps quasiment immobile. Toute l'œuvre d'un Drumont est sous-tendue par le sentiment douloureux de ce que Durkheim a appelé l'« anomie » — cette régulière décomposition des sociétés traditionnelles. « Tant que le lis éblouissant eut ses racines dans la forte terre des traditions et des croyances, il s'éleva majestueux et poétique sous le ciel ; aujourd'hui le sol est aride et le lis, déjà flétri sous les exhalaisons impures des envahisseurs, se penche, prend les teintes jaunâtres de ce qui va mourir [1]. »

Ce goût de mort et d'entropie, ce qui reste d'extrême droite en France ne l'a pas perdu, sauf à occuper son esprit des images riantes du bon vieux temps : « Moi, disait François Brigneau, éditorialiste de *Minute,* en 1978, j'aime la France et une certaine France, une France agricole, familiale, artisanale ; je n'aime pas la France des villes [...], je suis plus près du pays des fileuses, des lavandières, des ateliers d'autrefois ; on travaillait peut-être douze heures par jour, mais on chantait dans les ateliers ; on ne chante plus. J'ai horreur des villes, j'ai horreur des cités ouvrières, j'ai horreur du mécanisme, c'est vrai [2]. »

Dès lors, l'antisémitisme aurait dû se fixer politiquement à droite, à l'extrême droite réactionnaire, antilibérale. Or l'antisémitisme a sévi aussi à gauche, particulièrement jusqu'à l'affaire Dreyfus. Sans doute faut-il remarquer d'emblée que, dans cette société de la fin du XIXe siècle (et aujourd'hui donc ?), il n'y a pas de cohérence interne dans la droite et dans la gauche — deux catégories trop réductrices pour rendre raison de la complexité des mentalités. De plus, les partis politiques n'en sont qu'à leur état embryonnaire. La crise boulangiste, entre autres, montre la confusion idéologique qui peut se mêler à la vie politique. Bien des sentiments partagés par les catholiques l'étaient aussi par des électeurs de gauche. La « causalité diabolique » ne manquait pas d'être utilisée par ceux-là mêmes qui ne croyaient pas au Diable. Drumont a été populaire dans l'électorat de gauche comme dans l'électorat de droite, à tout le moins jusqu'en 1898.

Outre les assimilations que l'on fait couramment entre les Juifs et les banquiers depuis la monarchie de Juillet, d'autres raisons ont pu nourrir dans certaines zones de la gauche l'hostilité aux Juifs. Le fait que ceux-ci, par leur tradition religieuse et juri-

1. É. Drumont, *La Fin d'un monde, op. cit.,* p. 530.
2. Cité par Harris et Sédouy, *Qui n'est pas de droite ?,* Éd. du Seuil, 1978, p. 90.

dique, renforcée par leur situation minoritaire, aient été constamment respectueux de l'État les a certainement rendus suspects, surtout dans les courants libertaires et anarchistes. Les bonnes relations qu'entretiennent les élites sociales de la communauté juive avec la monarchie de Juillet et avec le second Empire ont assurément nourri ici et là de l'animosité antijuive.

Reste une autre raison, plus durable celle-là : la contradiction, au moins apparente, existant entre le projet universaliste issu des Lumières, repris par l'idéal républicain et socialiste, et la spécificité juive ; entre l'idéal laïc et le fondement religieux de cette communauté. Un moment, la gauche et bon nombre de Juifs français ont bien cru régler le problème par l'*assimilation*. Mais elle impliquait, de la part des Juifs, le sacrifice de leur identité, l'infidélité à leurs ancêtres et à leur foi. Là gisait la source d'un malentendu qui n'a jamais pu être réellement dépassé. L'universalisme républicain socialiste rencontrait le même écueil que l'universalisme chrétien (le catholicisme) : l'irréductibilité de la conscience juive.

Deux ethnocentrismes inverses (« culturocentrismes » serait peut-être mieux dire) ont concouru à créer ou à envenimer l'antisémitisme : un ethnocentrisme singulariste et un ethnocentrisme universaliste.

Le premier est le fait des contre-révolutionnaires. Ceux-ci, comme le dit bien Joseph de Maistre, ne croient pas à l'Homme (« Il n'y a point d'*homme* dans le monde. J'ai vu dans ma vie des Français, des Italiens, des Russes... ; mais quant à l'homme, je déclare ne l'avoir rencontré de ma vie ; s'il existe c'est bien à mon insu. ») ; ils croient aux groupes humains particuliers — aux singularités nationales et religieuses. Pour ceux-là, le Juif existe ; il a ses attributs, ses traditions, sa culture propre. Certains diront : sa race. Dans ce courant, l'antisémitisme nourrit une aversion pour le monde moderne et défend une harmonie sociale perdue, dont la figure mythologique du Juif émancipé est le « dissolvant » perpétuel ; l'Autre, le non-pareil, l'ennemi acharné de la Norme, l'instigateur de la mobilité, l'errant, le destructeur. Ethnocentrisme exclusif : le Juif est voué au ghetto ou à l'exil.

Le second est le fait d'hommes de gauche. Son ethnocentrisme universaliste veut étendre à tous les peuples les bienfaits des Lumières à la française. Au nom de la Raison ou de la société sans classes, il tend à la négation du fait juif. La communauté juive, dans cette perspective progressiste, est appelée à se dissoudre dans la fraternité humaine comme les vieilles croyances et les superstitions sont destinées à s'éteindre. Ethnocentrisme inclusif, cette fois : le Juif est voué à l'assimilation ou au mépris.

Bien des Juifs, on le sait, ont choisi la voie de l'assimilation. Allant plus loin, de nombreux intellectuels juifs ont participé au rêve d'une révolution annonciatrice de la société harmonieuse et de la nouvelle humanité. Sans regret pour un passé qui les avait ordinairement maltraités, beaucoup d'entre eux ont concouru à l'utopie socialiste. Mais cette identité, qu'ils avaient sacrifiée sur l'autel de la révolution, les autres se chargèrent bien de la leur rappeler. Fût-il athée ou converti, fût-il dans le mouvement ou contre le mouvement, il redevenait Juif à son corps défendant sous l'œil de l'antisémite. Le « socialisme réel », tel qu'il s'est édifié à l'est de notre continent, s'est révélé une autre société « close », où les Juifs, aussi bien que d'autres minorités, cherchent encore leur place.

L'acceptation de l'altérité, de la pluralité, de la différence, ne va pas de soi. Quand elle existe, elle tend à hiérarchiser et à exclure. Le groupe homogène dominant impose ses normes ; il faut que les groupes marginaux les adoptent pour prix de leur existence. Seule la « société ouverte », également prémunie contre la nostalgie contre-révolutionnaire et l'utopie totalitaire, peut offrir les chances d'une véritable démocratie pluraliste, à même d'intégrer les Juifs sans les contraindre à aliéner leur être propre, leur mémoire collective, leur double solidarité (française *et* juive).

L'ère de la décolonisation nous a amenés peu à peu à en

rabattre de notre « mission civilisatrice » ; notre regard n'est plus dirigé de haut en bas ; en fait de civilisation, nous en avons découvert d'autres. Bref, nous commençons à penser l'universel à travers les différences. Souhaitons que, de leur côté, les Juifs, occupés de leur légitime différence, gardent le souci de penser celle-ci dans l'universel.

Bibliographie sommaire

Pierre Andreu, *Notre Maître, M. Sorel,* Grasset, 1953.

Hannah Arendt, *Sur l'antisémitisme,* Calmann-Lévy, coll. « Diaspora », 1973.

Jean-Pierre Azéma, *La Collaboration,* PUF, « Documents-Histoire », 1975.

Robert F. Byrnes, *Antisemitism in Modern France,* New Brunswick (New Jersey), Rutgers University Press, 1950.

Claude Digeon, *La Crise allemande de la pensée française (1870-1914),* PUF, 1959.

Simon Doubnov, *Histoire moderne du peuple juif,* Payot, 1933, 2 vol.

Yves Guchet, *Georges Valois,* Albatros, 1975.

Jules Isaac, *L'antisémitisme a-t-il des racines chrétiennes ?,* Fasquelle, 1960.

Annie Kriegel, *Les Juifs et le Monde moderne,* Éd. du Seuil, 1977.

Bernard Lazare, *L'Antisémitisme, son histoire, ses causes,* Léon Chailley, 1894.

——, *Contre l'antisémitisme. Histoire d'une polémique,* Stock, 1896.

Michaël R. Marrus, *Les Juifs de France à l'époque de l'affaire Dreyfus,* Calmann-Lévy, coll. « Diaspora », 1972.

Michaël R. Marrus, Robert O. Paxton, *Vichy et les Juifs,* Calmann-Lévy, 1981.

Jacques Petit, *Bernanos, Bloy, Claudel, Péguy : quatre écrivains catholiques face à Israël,* Calmann-Lévy, coll. « Diaspora », 1972.

Pierre Pierrard, *Juifs et catholiques français 1886-1945,* Fayard, 1970.

Léon Poliakov, *De l'antisémitisme à l'antisionisme,* Calmann-Lévy, 1969.

——, *Le Mythe aryen,* Calmann-Lévy, 1971.

——, *Histoire de l'antisémitisme,* t. III, *De Voltaire à Wagner,* Calmann-Lévy, 1977, 4 vol.

Karl Popper, *La Société ouverte et ses ennemis,* Éd. du Seuil, 1979, 2 vol.

René Rémond, *La Droite en France,* Aubier, n[lle] éd., 1982.

Jean-Paul Sartre, *Réflexions sur la question juive,* Gallimard, 1954.

Pierre Sorlin, *« La Croix » et les Juifs,* Grasset, 1967.

Zeev Sternhell, *Maurice Barrès et le nationalisme français,* Presses de la Fondation nationale des sciences politiques, 1972.

——, *La Droite révolutionnaire (1885-1914), les origines françaises du fascisme,* Éd. du Seuil, coll. « L'univers historique », 1978.

Jeannine Verdès-Leroux, *Scandale financier et antisémitisme catholique. Le krach de l'Union générale,* Éd. du Centurion, 1969.

Pierre Vidal-Naquet, *Les Juifs, la Mémoire et le Présent,* PCM/Petite Collection Maspero, 1981.

Eugen Weber, *L'Action française,* Stock, 1954.

Nelly Wilson, *Bernard Lazare. Antisemitism and the Problem of Jewish Identity in Late Nineteenth-century France,* Cambridge University Press, 1978.

Références

Hormis l'introduction et la conclusion, cet ouvrage est la reprise de plusieurs articles déjà publiés ; certains ont été complétés.

Le chapitre 1 a été publié sous le titre « L'incendie du Bazar de la Charité » dans *L'histoire,* n° 2, juin 1978.

Le chapitre 2 a été publié dans *Esprit,* mai 1971, sous le titre : « Édouard Drumont et l'antisémitisme en France avant l'affaire Dreyfus ».

Le chapitre 3, « Jeanne d'Arc et les Juifs », a paru dans *H/ Histoire,* n° 3, 1979.

Le chapitre 4, « La gauche et les Juifs », a été publié dans *L'histoire,* n° 34, mai 1981.

Le chapitre 5, « Le fascisme en France », a été publié dans *L'histoire,* n° 28, novembre 1980.

Le chapitre 6, « Les catholiques français face aux fascismes », est le chapitre d'un ouvrage collectif, *2 000 ans de christianisme,* t. 9, S.H.C. internationale, 1975.

Le chapitre 7, « Une parabole fasciste : *Gilles* de Drieu La Rochelle », a été publié dans *le Mouvement social,* n° 80, juill.-septembre 1972.

Le chapitre 8, « Le cas Bernanos », est inédit, sauf la première partie, qui a paru dans *le Monde* du 4 juin 1971, sous le titre : « Un prophète au-delà des idéologies ».

Index

Table

IMP. HÉRISSEY À ÉVREUX
DÉPÔT LÉGAL FÉVRIER 1982. N° 6088 (28915)